CONCEIVING THE CITY

Conceiving the City: London, Literature, and Art 1870–1914

NICHOLAS FREEMAN

OXFORD
UNIVERSITY PRESS

*This book has been printed digitally and produced in a standard specification
in order to ensure its continuing availability*

OXFORD
UNIVERSITY PRESS

Great Clarendon Street, Oxford OX2 6DP

Oxford University Press is a department of the University of Oxford.
It furthers the University's objective of excellence in research, scholarship,
and education by publishing worldwide in

Oxford New York

Auckland   Cape Town Dar es Salaam   Hong Kong   Karachi
Kuala Lumpur Madrid Melbourne Mexico City   Nairobi
New Delhi Shanghai   Taipei Toronto
With offices in
Argentina Austria Brazil Chile Czech Republic France Greece
Guatemala Hungary Italy Japan South Korea Poland Portugal
Singapore Switzerland Thailand Turkey Ukraine Vietnam

Oxford is a registered trade mark of Oxford University Press
in the UK and in certain other countries

Published in the United States
by Oxford University Press Inc., New York

ISBN 978-0-19-921818-9

Cover illustration: 'View Across Queen Victoria Towards St Paul's Cathedral' (1870)
© Guildhall Library, City of London

Jacket design: Grounded

Preface

This book is an investigation of the ways in which writers and artists approached the representation of London between the death of Charles Dickens in 1870 and the outbreak of the First World War. During these years, London was the most heavily populated city in the world, and one whose physical and psychological limits seemed all but impossible to demarcate. The fluid nature of the English capital alarmed some and excited others, prompting great debate about how literature and art might cope with the profound challenges of such an environment. Much recent scholarship has concentrated on 'reading' London, that is to say, on applying contemporary critical theory to a canon of literary works which seem to foreshadow the metropolitan developments and concerns of our own time. The results have been valuable and stimulating, but such studies have often underestimated the extent to which contemporary theory is anticipated by the insights of a previous century.

This book attempts to give some sense of the ways in which figures from the worlds of journalism, sociology, literature, and visual art grappled with devising a language of metropolitan representation during the *fin de siècle*. The emergence of this language was scarcely a coherent or unified project, for it took many forms and had widely varying degrees of success. Nonetheless, individuals who ostensibly have little in common and are now very differently regarded—Monet is a major modern artist, E. V. Lucas is a forgotten hack—made a determined search for a way in which they might communicate their sense of a new metropolitan realm. How could any literary or artistic work hope to do justice to the vastness of London, with its hordes of people, its noise, its fogs, its insatiable consumption of the surrounding countryside? Answering this question taxed writers from George Gissing to E. M. Forster, from Henry James to Arthur Machen, and artists from William Powell Frith to James McNeill Whistler. It produced a bewildering selection of responses.

At the heart of the search for a new language was the dominant art form of the nineteenth century: realism. Ridiculed and misrepresented by modernists, realism was actually a superbly malleable and adaptable set of procedures. In the period under discussion, it absorbed a semi-scientific materialistic naturalism, mutated into a fragmentary, evanescent impressionism that sought what Robert Browning had earlier called 'the instant made eternity', and embraced a brooding, mystically informed symbolism that delved into the deeper realities that lay beneath outward perceptions. More importantly, these differing skeins of realist art continued to intertwine, meaning that a writer such as Ford Madox

Ford could move from a discursive sociological style that drew upon Dickens and Victorian 'social explorers' such as Mayhew, to a far more 'modern' fragmentariness in the space of a few paragraphs. Artistic allegiances had yet to calcify into fixed positions, and the results of continued experiment were often fascinating, as well as far-reaching.

Conceiving the City begins by alerting the reader to some of the problems and challenges posed by London in the late nineteenth century. It then proceeds to consider some of the forms realism assumed, or some of the moulds into which it was poured, over an approximately fifty-year period. Rather than focus on individual writers or works, it attempts to read a wide variety of textual and artistic productions alongside one another. It is hoped that this will not only blur the boundaries of the canon of late-Victorian literature and art but will also show how often ideas which might now be regarded as those of Foucault or de Certeau were developed by writers who are now rarely read, let alone studied. The study is therefore less a criticism of contemporary theory than a timely recognition of its origins.

The writing of this book has incurred a great number of intellectual, practical, and social debts. I therefore thank the following institutions and individuals for their help and encouragement.

At the University of the West of England where much of this book was written, I especially thank Dr Alice Entwistle, Dr Kent Fedorowitch, Dr Bill Greenslade, Dr Ben Highmore, Professor Robin Jarvis, Dr Jenni Lewis, Professor Peter Rawlings, Dr Graham Saunders, and Dr Victoria Stewart, all of whom offered constructive suggestions and advice and answered an unreasonably high number of foolish questions. Thanks are also due to Amanda Salter and the staff of the university library, whose help was always prompt and courteous.

I began my exploration of literary London while a postgraduate student at Bristol University. Here I was fortunate enough to be supervised by Professor Timothy Webb and Dr Peter McDonald. Only now do I appreciate their struggles in reining in and directing my enthusiasm. Professor Webb in particular did much to clarify my ideas and approach, and I am forever grateful for his insight and hard work, as well as for the scholarly model he offered. I must also thank Dr Michael Bradshaw, Dr Stephen Cheeke, Marjorie Dunderdale, Janet Gliddon, Dr Stephen James, and Dr Tom Mason. My fellow postgraduates Robert Dimbleby, Richard Evans, Dr Ben Hawes, Dr Bethan Jones, and Dr Adam Rounce were astute critics as well as convivial companions: I am grateful to them in many ways.

Further afield, Professor Max Saunders of Kings College, London, Dr Sara Haslam of the Open University, and Barrie Johnson of the Ford Madox Ford Society kindly shared their knowledge of Ford's early career. Michael Bott, archivist par excellence at the University of Reading introduced me to the Alvin Langdon Coburn photographic collection and other treasures, and could not have been more generous with his time and expertise. The staff of the British Library, the Museum of London, and the University of Birmingham library tracked down a plethora of elusive works. Thanks too to Janet Walwyn of the Bodleian Library for her much appreciated efforts on my behalf. Professor Simon Eliot of London University is a mine of good sense to whose encouragement and advice I am greatly indebted. Delegates at *The City and the Sublime* (University College Cork, 2000), and the first *Literary London* conference (Goldsmiths, University of London, 2002) also offered interesting suggestions. Other valuable support has come from Paul Dignum, Jon Watson, Lisa Gledhill, Dr Tom Hibbert, and those doughty survivors of the College of Knowledge, Norma, Christopher, Emma and Jessica McCormack, Keith Ripley, and John Windsor.

Andrew McNeillie and his colleagues at OUP have proved helpful and supportive throughout. Thanks are also due to the anonymous readers who made a number of valuable criticisms and suggestions, all of which have, I am sure, greatly improved the final product. I need hardly add that any errors are my own.

Finally, this book could not have been begun, let alone completed, without the support of my family. My most profound thanks and gratitude are reserved for them.

For permission to quote from the works of Ford Madox Ford, I thank David Higham Associates. Brian Reade granted permission to quote from the writings of Arthur Symons. For permission to quote from the works of Arthur Machen, I thank A. M. Heath and Company. For permission to include *Punch*'s 'The Winter Art Exhibitions', I thank *Punch*. The reproduction of Whistler's *Nocturne in Blue and Silver—Cremorne Lights* is courtesy of the Tate Gallery, and Alvin Langdon Coburn's *On the Embankment* is courtesy of the Science and Society Picture Library. The cover picture is courtesy of the Guildhall Library, Corporation of London.

The matter of capitalization is tricky throughout (and always has been). The *Oxford Manual of Style* differentiates between 'Impressionis/m, -t, -tic' which is 'a specific artistic movement or style of music or writing' and the uncapitalized 'general tendency or style'. However, I have seen a variety of other usages, and my script changes therefore attempt to differentiate between 'Impressionist' (which I have used to refer to to the artistic movement and specific works by Monet, Degas, etc.) and 'impressionist' which has been used for work that is less easily identified as such. I haven't capitalized literary impressionism (or literary impressionists) as I think this gives the misleading implication that impressionist writers were a coherent school or grouping.

I've tried to apply a similar distinction where Symbolism is concerned in an attempt to differentiate between those writers Symons and others term 'Symbolists' (Huysmans, Maeterlinck, etc) and the more vague 'symbolist' which I've used a lot less precisely. I think this is in line with wider academic use of the term, which seems remarkably vague and contradictory.

Contents

List of Illustrations

Introduction: The Problem of London

Life in modern London . . . is stuff sufficient for the fresh imagination of a youth to build its 'palace of art' of.

Walter Pater, Marius the Epicurean (1885)

London is a city of transitions. It is a city of a million houses—and no homes; of millions upon millions of inhabitants—and no natives. . . . London is at once the oldest, the newest, the most stable, and the most fictile of all cities. It is consistent only in its inconsistency.

Edwin Pugh, The City of the World: A Book about London and the
Londoner (1912)

Very few words are needed to explain why London, a hundred years hence, will be very like it is now.

G. K. Chesterton, The Napoleon of Notting Hill (1904)

ACCUMULATING IMPRESSIONS

Edward Ponderevo, the cynical peddler of patent medicine in H. G. Wells's *Tono-Bungay* (1909), is not a man given to understatement; yet, in a revealing aside, he confesses to his nephew George that London 'takes a lot of understanding'.[1] George becomes fascinated by the city, and later in the novel muses that he could 'fill a book, I think, with a more or less imaginary account of how I came to apprehend London, how first in one aspect and then in another it grew in my mind'. He continues:

Each day my accumulating impressions were added to and qualified and brought into relationship with new ones, they fused inseparably with others that were purely personal and accidental, I find myself with a certain comprehensive perception of London, complex indeed, incurably indistinct in places and yet in some way a whole that began with my first visit and is still being mellowed and enriched.
London![2]

---

[1] H. G. Wells, *Tono-Bungay*, ed. J. Hammond (1909; London: Dent, 1994), 77.
[2] Ibid. 85.

This book is not, I hope, 'incurably indistinct', but its composition places its author in similar quandaries to those of Wells's hero. Where should one start? How can one ever be said to have reached an end? Ford Madox Ford noted in 1905 that the last thing a newcomer to the capital will ever get is 'any picture, any impression of London as a whole'.[3] Any claims of 'comprehensive perception' must, indeed, admit their incomprehension, the disorienting blur of knowledge and ignorance that Robert Graves summarizes as 'a new confusion of. . . understanding | . . . a new understanding of my confusion'.[4] G. S. Street considered London to be 'a subject for an epigram or a library', and steering between these two poles is fraught indeed.[5]

In this, as in many other respects, the fate of Henry James's unfinished 'London Town', the proposed work for which Frederick Macmillan offered James's largest ever advance of £1,000 in 1903, serves as a salutary lesson for those seeking to study the English capital. Initially granted a generous allowance of 120,000 words, James quickly realized that it would be impossible 'to treat my subject in *less* than 150,000 words'.[6] The book so short, the city so long to learn. The novelist laboured under an intolerable burden of 'accumulations', at last confessing in 1911 that he was 'so *saturated* with impressions that I can't take in new ones'.[7] 'The Londoner bites off from his town a piece large enough for his own chewing,' wrote Ford.[8] If London could choke an experienced diner such as James, how then can the urban epicure of today hope to succeed within the confines of a standard monograph? Any vision of the city must, of necessity, be a partial one.

The theoretical revolutions of recent decades have changed the way that we think about our own disciplines and their relation to other forms of knowledge. They should also have made us sceptical towards words such as 'absolute', 'complete', and 'definitive', especially where the metropolis is concerned. Deborah Parsons observes how

Increasingly, academic criticism is recognizing that cities have aggregate and multiple identities, made up of their many selves, and geographical, sociological, literary, and

---

[3] F. M. Ford, *The Soul of London: A Survey of a Modern City*, ed. A. G. Hill (1905; London: Dent, 1995), 9.

[4] R. Graves, 'In Broken Images', *Poems 1929* (London: Seizin Press, 1929).

[5] G. S. Street, 'London in General', in *A Book of Essays* (London: Archibald Constable, 1902), 3.

[6] The contract for 'London Town', dated 19 June 1903, is in the Macmillan papers in the British Library, vol. cxlvi. James revised his word limit in a letter to Macmillan dated 17 June 1903. *The Correspondence of Henry James and the House of Macmillan, 1877–1914*, ed. R. S. Moore (London: Macmillan, 1993), 205.

[7] H. James, Preface (1908) to *The Princess Casamassima*, ed. D. Brewer (1886; London: Penguin, 1987), 30; *The Diary of Arthur Christopher Benson*, ed. P. Lubbock (London: Hutchinson, 1926), 225.

[8] Ford, *The Soul of London*, 15.

art historical analysis are beginning to combine in an interdisciplinary approach to the urban landscape that needs to be studied as a feature that brings the psychological and the material into collusion, in terms of theories and aesthetics that construct modern subjectivity and modern art from material urban experience. This is to interrelate the observed with the observer, and to assess how the identity of one affects the other.[9]

Parsons is correct in so far as the emergence of 'urban studies' is concerned, but the academics of the late twentieth century were hardly the first to grasp that the study of the city would require a reassessment of the relationship between the individual and the metropolis. Richard Lehan points out how sociologists such as Max Weber, Emile Durkheim, and Georg Simmel were writing books 'that consider the city as a subject in and of itself' before the First World War: the 'relatively recent discipline' of 'urban history' is still trying to catch up.[10] Nonetheless, the privileging of social science here somewhat misrepresents the fervid discussion of the city taking place in literary and artistic circles during the second half of the nineteenth century. The recognition that a discourse of the urban would of necessity be a constantly evolving blend of ideas from a variety of sources—literature, painting, photography, philosophy, sociology, criminology, cartography—came from writers as diverse as George Sims, Henry James, and Arthur Symons, men whose combined interests include fiction, travel writing, civic history, art and dramatic criticism, the Continental avant-garde, popular melodrama, and sociology, not to mention composing ballads such as 'In the Workhouse: Christmas Eve'. Each would write on the city in ways that combined their diverse skills with years of first-hand observation of the metropolis and residence within it.

This is not to claim that the European intellectuals of the *fin de siècle* were the first to puzzle over the relationship between the city and the self, or to recognize the gap between urban representation and reality. One could note, as Cynthia Wall has done, the reconstruction of London in words and maps after the Great Fire of 1666, or, acknowledge, alongside much recent Romantic scholarship, the importance of London to Wordsworth and Shelley.[11] What was new in the late nineteenth century was a sustained, albeit haphazard, interest in developing a specialized language of urban life. This was not the political and economic critique of Marx and Engels but an attempt to articulate a condition of 'cityness' that seemed of urgent importance in an era of unprecedented metropolitan expansion. Some late-Victorian thinkers

[9] D. L. Parsons, *Streetwalking the Metropolis: Women, the City, and Modernity* (Oxford: Oxford University Press, 2000), 1.

[10] R. Lehan, *The City in Literature: An Intellectual and Cultural History* (Berkeley and Los Angeles: University of California Press, 1998), 6.

[11] C. Wall, *The Literary and Cultural Spaces of Restoration London* (Cambridge: Cambridge University Press, 1998).

have left their mark on modern theory; the innovations of others have been discarded, superseded, or simply forgotten. *Conceiving the City* is an attempt to examine how this language, here a language of London, imperial capital and, in James's words, 'multitudinous world centre', developed between the death of Charles Dickens in June 1870 and the outbreak of the First World War.

THE CITY OF THE WORLD

Malcolm Bradbury points out that 'The belief that Paris was the true capital of the Modernist arts, and London an anti-capital, was familiar enough from the 1880s onwards.'[12] As a city, however, London posed challenges very different from those of its French counterpart. First and foremost, it was far larger. The sheer scale of late-Victorian London defied belief. As Roy Porter has written:

Rising between 1800 and 1900 from just under a million inhabitants to some 4.5 million, London was the super-city *de luxe*. Driven by market forces, 'it just growed,' without central command. A patchwork of dozens of autonomous districts, unevenly governed by often unrepresentative vestries, the metropolis sprawled on . . . .

In 1800 around one in ten inhabitants of England and Wales dwelt in the metropolis, by 1900 it was a breathtaking one in five.[13]

The population of Paris, though it grew steadily throughout the nineteenth century, did not reach the one million mark until 1853. Even by the standards of an increasingly urbanized Victorian Britain, the London megalopolis was something quite new, not least because it was both a city and a potent, if ambiguous symbol. In the eyes of positivists and imperialists, London stood for British power, wealth, and ingenuity, the seat of its government, the home of its sovereign, but for others it encapsulated the vicious and depraved aspects of city life and, disturbingly, human nature. It was the literal centre of the world through the founding of the Greenwich Meridian in 1884, and the symbolic centre of it through being the heart of empire. London was 'the centre of the legal system and the learned profession, the hub of the scientific and literary world'.[14] For the proud, it was the new Athens or Augustan Rome re-born. For many others, however, it was the new Babylon, and it was this

[12] M. Bradbury, 'London 1890–1920', in M. Bradbury and J. McFarlane, eds., *Modernism: A Guide to European Literature 1890–1930* (1976; Harmondsworth: Penguin, 1991), 174. Afterwards *Modernism*.

[13] R. Porter, *London: A Social History* (1994; London: Penguin, 2000), 226, 249. He adds that by 1911, the population had risen to over seven million. See too A. Briggs, *Victorian Cities* (London: Odhams Press, 1963), 324.

[14] Briggs, *Victorian Cities*, 335.

association which impressed itself most firmly on the late-Victorian psyche. Babylonian London symbolized the worship of money and power and the ruthless extinction of Christian ideals. Rousseau had 'declared his aversion to "la nouvelle Babylone"' in *La Nouvelle Héloise* (1761) and (1762), but while he tarred all cities with the Babylonian brush, English writers concentrated on the horrors of their capital.[15] The parallel between the two great cities served as a memorable image of the capital's failings, especially for an audience raised on biblical images of the ancient world, and it was frequently drawn, most notably in 'The Maiden Tribute of Modern Babylon' (1885), W. T. Stead's sensational exposé of child prostitution.[16]

Whether it was good or evil, London represented a challenge for politicians and administrators. When Sherlock Holmes made his debut in *A Study in Scarlet* (1887), London's population was climbing towards five million and the city was sprawling outwards in all directions. A century of irresistible growth had brought with it chronic social problems and municipal chaos. By 1910, E. M. Forster's Margaret Schlegel could confess, 'I hate this continual flux of London' since it is 'an epitome of us at our worst—eternal formlessness'.[17] However prestigious its international status, London remained in many ways a medieval city, administered by 'a crazy paving of jurisdictions whose rationale lay in historical accident rather than efficiency'.[18] A system of vestries, or parishes, imbued some districts with a strong sense of individual identity, but because basic utilities, chiefly water and gas, were not under central control, the overall effect was one of randomness, division, and inequality. There were attempts to counter this—the establishing of the Metropolitan Board of Works in 1855, the Local Government Act of 1888, which led to the creation of London County Council (LCC)—but as John Richardson remarks, the net result of the latter 'was to impose on a largely unmodernized and inadequate local structure a county administration more suited to the shires'.[19] Ben

---

[15] G. R. Stange, 'The Frightened Poets', in H. J. Dyos and M. Wolff, eds., *The Victorian City: Images and Realities*, 2 vols.(London: Routledge Kegan Paul, 1973), ii. 477.

[16] See L. Nead, *Victorian Babylon: People, Streets and Images in Nineteenth Century London* (New Haven: Yale University Press, 2000). Disraeli had pronounced London 'a modern Babylon' in *Tancred* (1847), and the pairing of ancient and modern cities became increasingly familiar as the century progressed. Henry James termed London 'the murky modern Babylon' in 'London', *English Hours* (London: Heinemann, 1905), 1. For the Christian fantasist Marie Corelli, the capital was 'the restless modern Babyon' in *The Sorrows of Satan* (1895; Oxford: Oxford University Press, 1996), 172. The term was so established by 1902 that Arnold Bennett's 'fantasia on modern themes', *The Grand Babylon Hotel*, pointed out that the hotel had been named after its founder, Félix Babylon, and 'not with any reference to London's nickname'. *The Grand Babylon Hotel* (1902; London: Penguin, 1972), 16.

[17] E. M. Forster, *Howards End*, ed. O. Stallybrass (1910; London: Penguin, 1983), 184.

[18] Porter, *London: A Social History*, 181.

[19] J. Richardson, *The Annals of London* (London: Cassell, 2000), 311.

Highmore, following Michel de Certeau's recognition of the city as 'the most immoderate of human texts', classes such gestures as 'a form of moderation, a way of managing the superabundance of the city'.[20] Julian Wolfreys alerts us to the problems that this may bring. 'The city resists ontology,' he writes, 'and thus affirms its alterity, its multiplicities, its excesses, its heterogeneities.'[21] In their differing ways, Sherlock Holmes and the LCC are responses to the same anxieties about the ungovernable urban, since each attempts to address the city's lawlessness and solve its mysteries. Holmes may be individualistic, the LCC bureaucratic, but both are motivated by a determination to explain, organize, and moderate a realm proverbially disorganized and inexplicable.

Politicians and administrators grappled with medieval systems of government until 1888, and with the complexities of modern bureaucracy in the years that followed: Holmes used his powers of observation and deduction to unravel the 'most confusing' of 'all the mazes that ever were contrived'.[22] Detectives and bureaucrats were not alone in their struggle to make sense of London. It taxed the ingenuity of architects, planners, and engineers in schemes that ranged from a revolutionary drainage system and an underground railway to the clearance of 'rookeries'. It prompted public concern over the spread of crime and the efficacy of the police, especially during the Whitechapel murders of 1888. The clergy despaired at the godlessness, immorality, and poverty of its slums. The emerging Labour movement focused on its high unemployment, unhealthy working conditions, and low pay. The military authorities joined with eugenicists in expressing concern that city dwellers, and Londoners in particular, were degenerate and unfit. Alison Hennegan notes a profusion of responses to the late-Victorian capital, arguing that 'it could be tamed by being anatomized [as in Sala's *Twice Round the Clock* (1859)] . . . antiquarianized, rendered charming, quaint and safe, by histories of the many villages which together made up London's corporate being'. It could also be 'exposed by savage gazeteers' such as Andrew Mearns, or see its slums and poor 'regarded as a new land, desperately in need of benign conquest and colonization' at the hands of 'General' Booth.[23]

---

[20] M. de Certeau, *The Practice of Everyday Life* (Berkeley: University of California Press, 1984), 92; B. Highmore, *Cityscapes: Cultural Readings in the Material and Symbolic City* (Basingstoke: Palgrave Macmillan, 2005), xi.

[21] J. Wolfreys, *Writing London Volume 2: Materiality, Memory, Spectrality* (Basingstoke: Palgrave Macmillan, 2004), 4.

[22] Jefferson Hope in A. Conan Doyle, *A Study in Scarlet* (1887). *The Penguin Complete Sherlock Holmes* (London: Penguin, 1981), 78.

[23] A. Hennegan, 'Personalities and Principles: Aspects of Literature and Life in *Fin-de-Siècle* England', in M. Teich and R. Porter, eds., *Fin de Siècle and its Legacy* (Cambridge: Cambridge University Press, 1990), 196.

This study, however, is more concerned with the challenges that the city posed for writers and artists, and the ways in which they represented London and life within it. As Richard Le Gallienne recalled in 1926, 'in prose as well as in verse there was, for a time, quite a cult of London and its varied life, from costers to courtesans'.[24] This was not simply the preserve of the elevated, for London encompassed and generated every type of textual production. By 1900, London supported a publishing industry that ranged from old established firms to individual concerns issuing an unclassifiable variety of pamphlets, posters, chapbooks, and squibs. There were histories, from the most broad and general narratives catering for children and 'new' readers empowered as a result of the 1870 Education Act and its successors, to the most detailed and specific analyses of everything from particular buildings to investment opportunities. Sir Walter Besant offered both studies of individual boroughs and dramatic recreations of key moments in the city's past, recounted in a stolid prose whose popularity a younger generation of writers found inexplicable. W. J. Loftie enlivened the scholarly approach of *The Colour of London* (1907) with delicate watercolours by the Japanese artist Yoshio Markino. A. R. Hope Moncrieff derived useful income from editing *Black's Guide to London*, continually in print and updated between 1891 and 1926, while finding time to pursue spin-off projects such as his *London* (1910), which accompanied his celebratory prose with 32 colour illustrations. Social researchers, cartographers of economic distribution, mapped the city on a street by street, house by house basis, subjecting its districts to a thoroughness of examination that staggers the modern observer. There were borough guides, street guides, and the now familiar trade in recommending hotels and restaurants was well established. There were many specialist works for tourists, notably the annual Thomas Cook *Handbook*, first published in 1877. The mercantile metropolis spawned a whole subindustry of directories and yearbooks, while the city's status as the Empire's major population centre led to a slew of works such as *The Househunter's ABC for Suburban Districts around London* (1910) and ratepayers' valuation guides.

On top of these, particular places in London attracted especial attention. The Thames was endlessly celebrated as a mythic concourse, a vital economic artery of Empire and a backdrop for stirring adventures in both children's and adult fiction. It was also a perennial attraction for painters and illustrators, becoming notably significant for Whistler and the Impressionists from the

---

[24] R. Le Gallienne, *The Romantic '90s* (1926; London: Robin Clark, 1993), 122. Le Gallienne's enthusiasm for the capital was adroitly parodied by Owen Seaman in 'An Ode to Spring in the Metropolis (After R. Le G.)', which offered the deathless couplet, 'London still remains the missus | Of this Narcissus.' Owen Seaman, *The Battle of the Bays* (London: John Lane/The Bodley Head, 1896), 38.

1870s onwards. The Tower of London was another popular inspiration. An 1894 edition of Harrison Ainsworth's *The Tower of London* (1840), augmented by a series of tales by later writers and illustrated by George Cruickshank, was reprinted in 1903 and went through four more reprints in the next six years.[25] This was by no means an exceptional occurrence.

London also loomed large in memoirs and similar writings. These ranged from Clarence Rook's *The Hooligan Nights* (1899), the story of a small-time criminal which hovered between apparent confession and fictionalized spice, to *Adventures in London* (1909), the recollections of James Douglas, director of Express newspapers. Such works addressed a complex audience, part of which lay outside the city and was hungry for any information concerning it, another part of which lived within London and compared the cities of Rook and Douglas with its own experience. Following John Murray's rejection of the book that would become *The Soul of London* in December 1902, Ford's illustrator, William Hyde, sent him a revealing examination of the publishing market that gives some suggestion of the plethora of books about the capital in circulation in the early twentieth century. 'I am afraid that Murray was right. There is too much "London,"' he notes. 'I saw McWilliams which is good . . . thin but well-illustrated, there is also Besant's big work (a 30/- book) . . . there is a new magazine called "London" and there are quite six books about it, if not of this season they are very recent.'[26] A market for 'London books'—Hyde had already collaborated with Alice Meynell on *London Impressions* (1898) and would reuse some of its illustrations in Ford's *England and the English* (1907)—certainly existed in the Edwardian period, but it was becoming as overcrowded as the city itself.

The London of the *fin de siècle* was widely perceived as quite distinct from other world cities yet continuing to change, develop, and, to use relatively new Darwinian terminology, evolve, as it had always done. Historians of the capital, most famously Besant, offered readings of the past that drew on an essentialist construction of London as a city both forward-looking and prepared to revere the past.[27] This somewhat complacent view was expressed at length by Hilaire

[25] W. H. Ainsworth, *The Tower of London* (1840; London: John Dicks, 1894).

[26] Unpublished letter, William Hyde to Ford, Shere, 4 December 1902, Carl A. Koch Library, Cornell University.

[27] Recent reactions to this stance are typified by John A. Stotesbury and Susana Onega confessing that they 'sigh' in 'exasperation at [the] "essentialist" sentimentality' of 'Christopher Hibbert's concluding words in his now obsolescent study of *London: The Biography of a City* [1969].' Hibbert suggests that 'London is in essence immutable; for all its faults it remains to those who have learned to love it uniquely emotive, uniquely seductive, uniquely beautiful,' an estimation very much in keeping with the views of James, Symons, Ford, and others during the late nineteenth century. *London in Literature: Visionary Mappings of the Metropolis*, ed. Onega and Stotesbury (Heidelburg: C. Winter, 2002), 11.

Belloc, who, in his introduction to Alvin Langdon Coburn's photographic folio, *London* (1909), wrote blithely of a 'spiritual unity' that 'strikes every foreigner and possesses every native observer'.[28] The ideal writer on London, Ford maintained, 'ought to be alive to the glamour of old associations. . . . But he ought to be equally inspired with satisfaction because . . . new haunts are being formed for new people around whom will congregate new associations.'[29] If the modernist text is an amalgamation of forms and styles that disregards once neatly inscribed cultural boundaries—though when such boundaries existed is not entirely clear—then the written representation of the city reflects its own heterogeneous streets and spaces, its juxtapositions of past and present. *The Waste Land*'s jarring shifts of tone and history owe almost as much to a walk down a London street, where one might still see the architecture of five centuries jumbled into a partially legible whole, as they do to a radical literary aesthetic.

At the same time, recognition of change was accompanied by a new-found anxiety about loss. London was not 'modernized' as Haussmann's Paris was between 1853 and 1870, or redeveloped as coherently as Vienna was between 1857 and 1880, but it saw nonetheless major civil engineering projects such as the construction of the Albert, Victoria, and Chelsea Embankments (1868–74) and the building of railways.[30] 'In London, something of the order of eight hundred acres of central land was taken for railway uses in the course of the nineteenth century; an area sufficient for a fair sized town in itself,' John Kellett observes.[31] It also saw a policy of demolition of churches from 1874 as attendance dwindled.[32] Historic landmarks disappeared: Doctor's Commons was demolished in 1867, Temple Bar between December 1877 and early 1879, the Old Palace at Bromley-by-Bow in 1893, the Egyptian Hall in Piccadilly in 1905. In 1911, 17 Gough Square, where Samuel Johnson had worked on his *Dictionary*, was threatened with the same fate, only to be saved by Lord Harmsworth after a public outcry.

Those who elsewhere expressed their fondness for the capital, Arthur Machen, for instance, or Henry James, often mourned the passing of favourite buildings or streets. The latter's notes for 'London Town' are a moving record of the cost of change. In Spring Gardens in August 1907, the elderly novelist lingered 'in front of the great demolitions and temporary hoardings'

[28] H. Belloc, introduction to A. L. Coburn, *London* (London: Duckworth, 1909), 19–20.

[29] Ford, *The Soul of London*, 5.

[30] The struggles of London's planners are documented in detail in J. Winter, *London's Teeming Streets 1830–1914* (London: Routledge, 1993).

[31] J. Kellett, *The Impact of Railways on Victorian Cities* (1969), quoted in E. de Maré, *The London Doré Saw: A Victorian Evocation* (London: Allen Lane, 1973), 56.

[32] Richardson, *The Annals of London*, 298, 302.

and examined 'the old houses, few, very few, that survive, the good old brick fronts, the spoiled windows; the 2 or 3 with good 18th century doors and door-tops behind the back of the hideous new Admiralty extension'. Such encounters made it clear to him that the London he wished to write about was vanishing before his eyes.[33] Other notes record 'the ghostly sense, the disembodied presences of the old London', which are threatened by development.[34] St Swithin's Church in Cannon Street has been 'dishonoured' by modernization, while Change Alley, rebuilt in 1874, 'looks as if it were going to be "something" but is only a mere modernized desolation,' he notes on 8 October 1907.[35] Even St Bride's Church in Fleet Street, designed by Christopher Wren, has been 'mercilessly modernized'.[36] It was to counter such depredation that William Morris had founded the Society for the Protection of Ancient Buildings in 1877, supported by Thomas Carlyle, Edward Burne-Jones, and William Holman Hunt. The Ancient Monuments Protection Act followed in 1882, though this at first applied mainly to prehistoric and Roman remains. The Act was, however, revised in 1900 to encompass medieval antiquities, and further regulations were introduced in 1913 to allow the protection of individual 'listed' buildings.

Another response to London was to argue that although the city was appalling in many respects, it was a fixture of the modern world and art must therefore adapt to it: 'This is an urban age,' announced Grant Allen in 1895.[37] George Gissing was one of those who strove to make the uncongenial the basis of artistic expression. 'I dislike the immense predominance of London,' he complained. 'London is increasing in size past all reason, her evils growing simultaneously.'[38] Yet, as he told Clara Collet in 1897, 'I need London for my work, for in very truth, I can do little away from it.'[39] 'A modern city is the exact opposite of what everyone wants,' said Oscar Wilde, forcing himself to adapt to a luxurious house in Chelsea, a thriving theatre, the irresistible temptations of commercial sex, and the dinner menu of the Café Royal.[40]

Other writers, Ford Madox Ford for example, were excited by the city's dynamism, or, like Arthur Symons, intoxicated by its modernity and artifice.

[33] *The Notebooks of Henry James*, ed. F. O. Matthiessen and K. B. Murdock (Oxford: Oxford University Press, 1961), 325.

[34] James, 23 August 1907. Ibid. 326.   [35] Ibid. 327–8.

[36] 8 October 1907, 21 September 1909. Ibid. 329, 333.

[37] G. Allen, introduction to *The British Barbarians: A Hill-Top Novel* (London: John Lane, 1895), ix.

[38] Briggs, *Victorian Cities*, 368.

[39] Gissing to Clara Collet, 11 March 1897. *Victorian Writers and The City*, ed. J-P. Hulin and P. Coustillas (Lille: University of Lille, 1979), 127.

[40] Quoted by P. J. Waller in *Town, City & Nation: England 1850–1914* (Oxford: Oxford University Press, 1983), 68.

For them, London was as much an opportunity as a threat. It was not that Ford was blind to the human or environmental misery that followed in the wake of metropolitan expansion, but that he rejected the sentimental appeal of the countryside. 'It is this tyranny of the Past that is one of the main obscurers of our view of the Future,' he wrote in 1909, criticizing Ebenezer Howard's garden city movement for producing 'a spirit that is narrow and provincial' by seeking to 'withdraw the population into small knots'.[41] Symons was similarly disdainful. He praised instead the 'artificiality' of the urban landscape, adding 'I prefer town to country; and in the town we have to find for ourselves, as best we can, the *décor* which is the town equivalent of. . . fields and hills.'[42] He sought also to emulate the French poets of a previous generation, Baudelaire, Gautier, and Gérard de Nerval, men who had 'made Paris vital, a part of themselves, a form of creative literature'.[43]

Discussing London's place among 'the cities of modernism', Bradbury draws attention to its 'ambiguous reputation'. 'It is the obvious centre of English-language Modernist activity,' he writes, 'and between 1890 and 1920 it sustained and generated a vital sequence of experimental movements and phases.' However:

it is also in the record as one of the dullest and most deadening of capital cities, with no real artistic community, no true centres, no coteries, no cafés, a metropolis given to commerce and an insular middle-class life-style either indifferent or implacably hostile to the new arts. Its image lives in Modernist writing itself. Its fascination and its repulsion, its status at the centre of vivid multiple impressions and as the city of dreadful night, have entered deeply into poetry and fiction, where a cluster of unforgettable associations surrounds it.[44]

As he observes, although London may have lagged far behind Paris in its support for artistic innovation, it nonetheless attracted many of the leading creative figures of the late nineteenth and early twentieth centuries. Crucially, he notes how 'a fruitful symbiosis of the cosmopolitan and the nativist' helped to shape modernist aesthetics during this period.[45] The representation of the city was at the heart of this process. London was a testing ground for French

[41] F. M. Ford, 'The Future in London', (1909), *The Ford Madox Ford Reader*, ed. S. J. Stang (London: Paladin, 1986), 299, 302.

[42] A. Symons, 'Preface: Being a Word on Behalf of Patchouli', *Silhouettes*, 2nd edn (1896). *Collected Works: Poems I* (London: Martin Secker, 1924), 97.

[43] A. Symons, *London: A Book of Aspects* (1909), in *Cities and Sea-Coasts and Islands* (London: W. Collins, 1918), 198. Afterwards *London*.

[44] Bradbury, 'London 1890–1920', *Modernism*, 172. The Vorticists would later argue that these conditions were actually conducive to the production of 'good artists from time to time'. *Blast*, ed. Wyndham Lewis, 20 June 1914, 32.

[45] Bradbury, 'London 1890–1920', *Modernism*, 174.

artistic and, as William Greenslade has shown, social theories, but its writers and artists were certainly not simply in thrall to the Continent.[46]

Historians and literary critics such as Jonathan Schneer and Joseph McLaughlin have demonstrated some of the ways in which the imperial capital negotiated with its subjects.[47] The London of the *fin de siècle* was an international city in which everything from communism to theosophy had its adherents. Karl Baedeker pointed out that 'there were more Scotsmen in London than in Aberdeen, more Irishmen than in Dublin, more Jews than in Palestine, and more Roman Catholics than in Rome.'[48] The city was the home of Karl Marx until his death in 1883, and, in the wake of the tsarist pogroms of the 1880s, attracted a number of Eastern European political dissidents. The presence of such men gave rise to what David Glover terms 'the spectre of East End anarchism, projected as a secret conspiracy of foreign revolutionaries ready to strike at the heart of the nation'.[49] The belief shaped newspaper editorials, parliamentary legislation such as the Aliens Act (1905), and, with varying degrees of irony, a literature of terrorism and subversion that ran from *The Princess Casamassima* (1886) to *The Secret Agent* (1907) and beyond.

London was popular with artistic as well as political radicals. It saw frequent visits from French painters and poets, especially in the aftermath of the Franco-Prussian war, and attracted influential thinkers from across the Atlantic, notably J. M. Whistler, Henry James, and T. S. Eliot.[50] Leading European artists such as Fernand Khnopff wrote for the London periodical *The Studio*, and while London's audiences were not always sympathetic to new ideas, they were curious enough to attend plays by Ibsen and read, when they could, the fiction of Zola and Maupassant.[51] To denounce London as

[46] W. Greenslade, *Degeneration, Culture and the Novel* (Cambridge: Cambridge University Press, 1994), 15–31.

[47] J. Schneer, *London 1900: The Imperial Metropolis* (New Haven: Yale University Press, 1999); J. McLaughlin, *Writing the Urban Jungle: Reading Empire in London from Doyle to Eliot* (Charlottesville: University of Virginia Press, 2000).

[48] Briggs, *Victorian Cities*, 330.

[49] E. Wallace, *The Four Just Men*, ed. D. Glover (1905; Oxford: Oxford University Press, 1995), xviii.

[50] On the influence of European and American intellectuals on the perception of the city, see, for example, E. Starkie, *From Gautier to Eliot: The Influence of France on English Literature, 1851–1939* (London: Hutchinson, 1960); A. Holder, *Three Voyagers in Search of Europe: A Study of Henry James, Ezra Pound and T. S. Eliot* (Philadelphia: University of Pennsylvania Press, 1966); C. Mackworth, *English Interludes: Mallarmé, Verlaine, Paul Valéry, Valery Larbaud in England, 1860–1912* (London: Routledge Kegan Paul, 1974), and L. Gordon, *Eliot's Early Years* (Oxford: Oxford University Press, 1988). For a more wide-ranging study of reactions to Victorian Britain see R. Christiansen, *The Visitors: Culture Shock in Nineteenth-Century Britain* (London: Chatto and Windus, 2000).

[51] The impact of Continental literature and drama is discussed at greater length by Karl Beckson in *London in the 1890s: A Cultural History* (New York: W. W. Norton, 1992). For a

insufferably bourgeois and intellectually stifling is as misguided as believing that all Parisians are fascinated by and sympathetic to artistic innovation. It is as if the riots at the premieres of *Ubu Roi* (1896) or *Le Sacre du printemps* (1913) had not occurred, *Les Fleurs du Mal* and *Madame Bovary* had been welcomed with open arms in 1857, and Monet had never been misunderstood, let alone ridiculed. Did not all the important French writers and painters of the *fin de siècle* inveigh against the philistinism of their countrymen? No wonder Bradbury terms the imagined Paris of men such as Arthur Symons 'a fantasy city', and alerts us instead to the 'dialectical relationship between the two capitals'.[52]

'London is a great, slip-shod, easy-going, good-humoured magnet,' wrote Ford in one of *The Soul of London*'s many sententious moments.[53] The magnet had long attracted writers and artists from all over the world: now it pulled in the Polish Conrad and the Japanese watercolourist Markino. It also drew writers and artists from throughout the British Isles: even Dickens, London's most famous chronicler, had been born in Portsmouth. Many of those who contributed to the artistic conception of London during the *fin de siècle* had come from outside it. Somerset Maugham, for instance, was born in Paris and spoke French as his first language until the age of 10. Symons and Machen were Welsh, and the Rhymers' Club to which the former belonged had a strong Celtic component. Gissing had arrived in London via northern England and the United States, Kipling from India. Wilde was Irish; Conan Doyle and John Davidson were Scotsmen. More importantly still, London writers rarely confined themselves to the capital, regularly journeying to Europe and even beyond. James and Symons in particular travelled widely and were on friendly terms with many leading cultural figures of the day. In short, London was the site of all kinds of intellectual cross-pollination, and its leading writers and artists were keenly sensitive to developments in their respective fields.

Bradbury never resolves the paradox of the 'double' London, the city that is at once the cradle of radical art and its implacably philistine opponent. Yet the opposition is, in some senses, a false one, since the single noun actually applies to a multitude of cities uneasily coexisting in the same space. Joseph McLaughlin suggests that we should approach with caution any notion of London as a 'totalizing concept', since the notion is as misleading and damaging as that of 'the orient'. 'To generalize about London has seemed irresponsibly abstract,' he writes. 'Yet it also seems important to

concise summary of Zola's impact, see P. Keating, *The Haunted Study: A Social History of the English Novel 1875–1914* (1989; London: Fontana, 1991), 241–54. It is notable that many of the most controversial French novels of the late nineteenth century were not translated into English until much later. There was no unexpurgated version of Huysmans's *À rebours* (1884) until 1959.

[52] Bradbury, 'London 1890–1920', *Modernism*, 174.   [53] Ford, *The Soul of London*, 20.

recognize that London . . . as a totalizing construct, is an important referential category—however imprecise it may be—in the imaginative geography of Victorians and others.'[54] Rather than being a unified site, London is a chaotic agglomeration of contradictions, juxtapositions, and inconsistencies which makes generalization both inevitable and unwise. For Benjamin Disraeli, London was 'a nation, not a city', with 'a population greater than some kingdoms, and districts as different as if they were under different governments and spoke different languages'.[55] Henry James agreed. 'One has not the alternative of speaking of London as a whole,' he argued, 'for the simple reason that there is no such thing as the whole of it. It is immeasurable—embracing arms never meet. Rather it is a collection of many wholes, and of which of them is it most important to speak?'[56] When the city was so vast, writers were forced to accept the limited basis of their knowledge. '[W]hat do I know of it?', asks Disraeli's Lothair. 'I have been living here six months, and my life has been passed in a park, two or three squares, and half a dozen streets.'[57] 'One says, "He knows his London",' wrote Ford, 'yet how little more will he know of London that is actually "his".'[58] A consequence of this was the curiously atomized condition of London's citizens identified by Thomas Hardy, one which again underlines the danger of generalization. 'London appears not to *see itself*,' he noted. 'Each individual is conscious of *himself*, but nobody conscious of themselves collectively, except perhaps some poor gaper who stares around with a half-idiotic aspect. There is no consciousness here of where anything comes from or goes to—only that it is present.'[59] These Londoners do not embody the sophisticated formulations of subjectivity dear to Walter Pater. They display instead a profound lack of 'civic consciousness'.[60]

There was undoubtedly generalization throughout the period—James's essay is filled with it—and indeed essentialism about the city's 'character', but there was also a realization of London's plurality. Conan Doyle's 'The Adventure of the Six Napoleons' (1894) depicts a metropolitan environment strikingly resistant to unitary observation:

In rapid succession we passed through the fringe of fashionable London, hotel London, theatrical London, literary London, commercial London, and, finally, maritime London, till we came to a riverside city of a hundred thousand souls, where the tenement houses swelter and reek with the outcasts of Europe.[61]

54 McLaughlin, *Writing the Urban Jungle*, 196.
55 B. Disraeli, *Lothair*, ed. V. Bogdanor (1870; Oxford: Oxford University Press, 1975), 87.
56 James, 'London', *English Hours*, 30.
57 Disraeli, *Lothair*, 87.   58 Ford, *The Soul of London*, 7.
59 F. E. Hardy, *The Life of Thomas Hardy* (London: Macmillan, 1962), 206–7.
60 James, 'London', *English Hours*, 34.
61 Conan Doyle, *The Penguin Complete Sherlock Holmes*, 588.

That these successive Londons can be categorized and neatly traversed itself suggests that a process of fictionalization is at work, making apparent sense of the city's apparent randomness. A similarly organizing sensibility manifests itself in the first of G. K. Chesterton's Father Brown stories, 'The Blue Cross' (1911), when an omnibus journey acquires Dantean associations in 'passing through thirteen separate vulgar cities all just touching each other'.[62] London is 'a congregation of cities', proclaimed Hope Moncrieff.[63] Ford distinguished 'a little arbitrarily' between 'psychological London, where the London spirit is the note of life,' the 'Administrative County', and what he termed 'the London of natural causes, the assembly of houses in the basin of the lower Thames'. He also suggested that 'London begins where tree trunks commence to be black,' though he added that the glow from the city's lights could be seen as far away as Maidstone, Folkestone, and even Colchester, and that, in terms of how a London spirit shaped one's view of the world, the capital extended as far as Hastings, Brighton, and Southend-on-Sea.[64] In the 'Author's Note' to *England and the English*, he offered another vision of the capital. 'London is not the City and not Hampstead,' he wrote, 'it is a whole world of other little districts. It is Peckham; it is Tower Hamlets; it is West Ham; it is Kensington; it is Highgate; it is Greenwich; it is Richmond.'[65] E. V. Lucas pursued similar ideas. '[T]here is no one London at all,' he wrote in a popular guide to the city in 1906. 'London is a country containing many towns.'[66] The second chapter of Edwin Pugh's *The City of the World*, 'In Search of London', visits the City, the Strand, Trafalgar Square, Oxford Street, Whitechapel, and suburbia before asking:

What meaning, then, do we extract from this welter of different Londons, each representative of some characteristic phase of London life, each alike significant of some nuance of the inner spirit of London? I think that if we glean any light at all from this helter-skelter survey of the unwieldy metropolis it is only a faint sidelight upon the fact already stated: that London is no abiding city.[67]

The conception of London as a plethora of cities jostling for precedence within the same ever-expanding and unstable space anticipated Foucault's notions of the *heterotopia* and created difficulties for London's administrators as well as its authors. The municipal behemoth that was the LCC found itself in a particularly difficult position when attempting to unify districts that

---

[62] G. K. Chesterton, *The Father Brown Stories* (London: Cassell, 1929), 15–16.

[63] A. R. Hope Moncrieff, *London* (1910), reprinted as *Victorian and Edwardian London* (London: Brockhampton Press, 1999), 19.

[64] Ford, *The Soul of London*, 25–6.

[65] F. M. Ford, 'Author's Note', *England and the English: An Interpretation*, ed. S. Haslam (1907; Manchester: Carcanet, 2003), 328.

[66] E. V. Lucas, *A Wanderer in London* (1906; London: Methuen, 1913), 18.

[67] Edwin Pugh, *The City of the World* (London: Thomas Nelson, n.d. [1912]), 47.

could possess a keenly defended sense of personal identity, an idea taken to memorable extremes in the internecine strife of Chesterton's *The Napoleon of Notting Hill* (1904). Although the Local Government Act that had created the LCC had been widely applauded, it did not apply to the City, which remained largely self-determining, a London within London that operated by different rules and regulations. The impact of the London Government Act (1899) complicated matters yet further in establishing twenty-eight borough councils whose independent powers inevitably clashed with those of the older body. By now, 'London' was a textual and cartographic concept as well as an actual city, governed by by-laws, edicts, maps, and timetables that represented myriad Londons in myriad ways. From the continually shifting boundaries of electoral wards, to the 1933 map of the Underground, the LCC was forced to concede the gulf between the city it governed and the city it sought to represent. As Baedeker's *London and its Environs* (1911) pointed out, 'The name "London" is a word of indeterminate scope, and no official use of the name corresponds exactly to the huge continuous mass of streets and dwellings that now forms the great and constantly extending Metropolis.' The guide's compilers distinguished between the Administrative County of London, which included the City, the LCC, 'Greater London', and those areas under the jurisdiction of the Central Criminal Court, the Metropolitan water-area, the Main Drainage area, and the London postal district. The final quartet comprised 'four other "Londons," all differing in size and population'.[68] Even the precise sociological researches of Charles Booth had suggested that there were three Londons, a rich west, a poor east, and a 'comfortable' London somewhere in between, each of which could be divided further according to income and professional status. Of the making of Londons there was, it seemed, no end.

The multiplicity of London was far from being the only challenge confronting its chroniclers. For some, the city could only be approached with fear and loathing, or a nostalgic pastoralism. 'Forget six counties overhung with smoke,' wrote William Morris in *The Earthly Paradise* (1868–70):

> Forget the snorting steam and piston stroke,
> Forget the spreading of the hideous town;
> Think rather of the pack-horse on the down,
> And dream of London, small and white and clean,
> The clear Thames bordered by its gardens green.[69]

Richard Jefferies relished the capital's destruction in *After London: Wild England* (1885): a thriving subliterature pictured London as a victim of

---

[68] *Baedeker's Handbook for London: London and its Environs* (Leipzig: Karl Baedeker, 1911), xxx.

[69] W. Morris, 'Prologue: The Wanderers', *The Earthly Paradise* (1868–70), ll.1–6.

war or natural disaster in works such as Grant Allen's 'The Thames Valley Catastrophe' (1897) and M. P. Shiel's *The Purple Cloud* (1901). In 1907, Stephen Philips imagined London as 'a monster' that did 'Blacken and grasp and seize and wither up' until 'all this island grew one hideous town'.[70] The metropolis was a filthy and dehumanizing environment, and poor soil for sensitive plants such as Philips. Its population was rocketing, and, as it did so, the capital city 'spread' even faster than in the nightmares of its opponents. According to H. J. Dyos, the population of Camberwell increased from 7,059 in 1802 to 253,076 in 1898 as the district was inexorably swallowed by the city.[71] Wilkie Collins had observed the new housing developments of the 1840s with alarm and disgust in *Basil* (1852), where Holyoake Square, a wasteland at the northern end of Regent's Park, offers only 'Unfinished streets, unfinished crescents, unfinished shops, unfinished gardens'.[72] By *The Law and the Lady* (1875), the situation had deteriorated further, acquiring disturbing Gothic overtones perhaps informed by the appearance of James Thomson's *The City of Dreadful Night* the previous year. 'Boards and bricks were scattered about us,' recalls Collins's heroine. 'At places, gaunt scaffolding-poles rose like the branchless trees of the brick-desert.'[73] In Gissing's *The Nether World* (1889), the narrator views the growth of Crouch End with a mixture of horror and resignation:

Look at a map of greater London, a map on which the town proper shows as a dark, irregularly rounded patch against the whiteness of suburban districts, and just on the northern limit of the vast network of streets you will distinguish the name of Crouch End. Another decade, and the dark patch will have spread further.[74]

Gissing is at once precise cartographer and visionary pessimist: the dark stain that represents Crouch End is a moral judgement and a portent, a bloodstain on the body politic, as much as a literal observation. Five years later, he apostrophized London as 'devourer of rural limits', mourning its

---

[70] S. Phillips, 'A Nightmare' from *Poems* (1907), in C. Logue, ed., *London in Verse* (London: Penguin, 1984), 80.

[71] H. J. Dyos, *Victorian Suburb* (Leicester: Leicester University Press, 1961), 19.

[72] W. Collins, *Basil*, ed. D. Goldman (1852; Oxford: Oxford University Press, 1990), 32.

[73] W. Collins, *The Law and the Lady*, ed. D. Skilton (1875; London: Penguin, 1998), 189. Compare section IV of *The City of Dreadful Night* with its repeated line, 'As I came through the desert thus it was.' *The Penguin Book of Victorian Verse*, ed. D. Karlin (London: Penguin, 1997), 557–60. Walter Hartright in *The Woman in White* (1859–60) is similarly scathing about Welmingham, the 'English country town' that inspires his outburst, 'The deserts of Arabia are innocent of our civilised desolation; the ruins of Palestine are incapable of our modern gloom!' *The Woman in White*, ed. J. Sutherland (1860; Oxford: Oxford University Press, 1996), 493. Thomas Pynchon was still stressing the parallel in 1963, remarking that 'The city is only the desert in disguise.' *V* (1963; New York: Vintage, 1985), 83.

[74] G. Gissing, *The Nether World*, ed. S. Gill (1889; Oxford: Oxford University Press, 1992), 364.

'hideous encroachment upon the old estate' and the felling of ancient elms that accompanied it.[75] His friend John Davidson noted how 'the whetted fangs of change | Daily devour the old demesne' in his 'A Northern Suburb' (1896), yet showed sympathy for the inhabitants of the 'draughty cupboards' who live there.[76] In the final pages of *Howards End*, suburbia manifests itself as a 'red rust' that creeps ever closer.[77] Looking back from 1912, Edwin Pugh struck an elegiac note:

Now, where thirty years ago these blossoms blew wild and lent their perfume to the sweet melodious air, there are prim discreet suburbs, geometrically divided up into terraces and avenues, and densely populated with the families of black-coated clerks; suburbs already falling here and there into a state of premature decline and afflicted with that last taint of shabby-gentility which is the first sure sign in any neighbourhood of ultimate ruin and degradation.[78]

More positive images of suburbia emerged in the Grossmiths' *Diary of a Nobody* (1892) and Arnold Bennett's *A Man from the North* (1898), where Mr Aked insists that 'the suburbs *are* London', a thesis he plans to defend in his proposed book, *The Psychology of the Suburbs*.[79] The city's colonizing of the countryside inspired nonetheless widespread alarm and denunciation: Hampstead Heath had required an Act of Parliament to save it from development in 1871. Much of the rural land around London was less fortunate. Kate Flint, following Dinah Birch, notes Ruskin's splenetic description of Camberwell's Croxted Lane in *Fiction, Fair and Foul* (1880–1), and quotes George Egerton's attack on 'jerry-built' housing in 'Wedlock' (1894).[80] By 1924, Arthur Machen was even prepared to liken urban expansion to the depredations of the First World War. The erosion of London's green space was, he wrote, 'more awful in a way, perhaps, than the German invasion of France'.[81]

The topographical definition of London, its rapid and unceasing expansion, and its bewildering multiple identities all posed difficult obstacles for the London writer. However, for novelists in particular, there was another problem: inheritance.

---

[75] G. Gissing, *In the Year of Jubilee*, ed. P. Delany (1894; London: Dent, 1994), 183–4.

[76] J. Davidson, *The Poems of John Davidson*, ed. A. Turnbull, 2 vols. (Edinburgh: Scottish Academic Press, 1973), i. 109.

[77] Forster, *Howards End*, 329.   [78] Pugh, *The City of the World*, 12.

[79] E. A. Bennett, *A Man from the North* (London: John Lane/The Bodley Head, 1898), 106.

[80] G. and W. Grossmith, *The Diary of a Nobody*, ed. Kate Flint (1892; Oxford: Oxford University Press, 1995), xvi–xvii; D. Birch, 'A Life in Writing: Ruskin and the Uses of Suburbia', in J. B. Bullen, ed., *Writing and Victorianism* (London: Longman, 1997), 234–49. For a detailed consideration of late Victorian suburbia, see L. Hapgood, *Margins of Desire: The Suburbs in Fiction and Culture 1880–1925* (Manchester: Manchester University Press, 2005).

[81] A. Machen, *The London Adventure or The Art of Wandering* (1924; London: Village Press, 1974), 43.

PASSING THE BATON

There are two important reasons why the period discussed in this book begins with the death of Dickens. The pragmatic one is that Dickens's construction of a highly personalized London has been widely studied elsewhere and need not be recapitulated in detail.[82] The second, and more important reason, is that the death of Dickens presented prose writers with a far-reaching choice. Writing in a culture in which Dickens's works overshadowed their own, and in which competition for a widening readership was ever more intense, would they decide to inhabit a 'Dickensian' London, or would they instead seek new ways of representing the capital in fiction?[83]

'I suppose myself to know this rather large city as well as anyone in it,' Dickens announced, a boast he made good in over thirty years' worth of fiction and journalism.[84] When he died in the summer of 1870, national grief was overwhelming. Victorian Britain had, it seemed, lost its greatest and most entertaining chronicler, a writer who was 'emphatically the novelist of the age' while yet being so much a part of everyday life that *The Times* could regard his death as a 'personal bereavement' for millions.[85] Dickens was a unique literary phenomenon, but this did not mean that he was irreplaceable. Almost before he was buried, critics, reviewers, and publishers began scrabbling around for a new novelistic 'laureate'. A diverse group of writers, from Anthony Trollope and George Eliot in the 1870s to Thomas Hardy to George Meredith and finally, Rudyard Kipling, was celebrated both critically and commercially, but

---

[82] See, in particular, A. Welsh, *The City of Dickens* (Oxford: Clarendon Press, 1971); P. Collins, 'Dickens and London', in Dyos and Wolff, eds., *The Victorian City: Images and Realities*, ii. 537–57, and his later 'Dickens and the City', in W. Sharpe and L. Wallock, eds., *Visions of the Modern City* (Baltimore: Johns Hopkins University Press, 1987), 101–21; R. Williams, *The Country and the City* (London: Chatto and Windus, 1973); F. S. Schwarzbach, *Dickens and the City* (London: Athlone, 1979); P. Ackroyd, *Dickens* (London: Sinclair Stevenson, 1990).

[83] R. L. Patten provides some remarkable statistics in 'The Sales of Dickens's Works'. Perhaps the most striking is the fate of the Charles Dickens edition, which began publication in 1867. By Dickens's death, nearly 30,000 sets of this had been sold, comprising over half a million copies, and by 1882, 4,239,000 volumes had been sold in England alone (*Dickens: The Critical Heritage*, ed. P. Collins (London: Routledge Kegan Paul, 1971), 602). Competition for readers is demonstrated by the continual rise in the number of novels published from 1880 onwards. In 1880, there were 380 new novels, in 1891 there were 896, while in 1895 there were 1,315. N. Cross, *The Common Writer: Life in Nineteenth Century Grub Street* (Cambridge: Cambridge University Press, 1985), 206, quoting V. K. Daniels, *New Grub Street: 1890–1896*, PhD thesis, University of Sussex, 1966, 243.

[84] Quoted by Collins, 'Dickens and London', 546.

[85] Unsigned article, 'The Death of Mister Charles Dickens', *Daily News*, 10 June 1870, 5; *The Times*, unsigned leader, 10 June 1870, 9. For further tributes in similar vein, see *Dickens: The Critical Heritage*, 502–41.

without ever having quite the same reputation, or, perhaps more importantly, the same national function. Dickens's role as a commentator on the British (or rather the English) character and mores was an extraordinary one, and one which affected all levels of mid-Victorian society.

London was a, perhaps *the*, central component of Dickens's imagination, and a key element of his success. All his most popular novels had utilized London settings. Only *Hard Times* (1854) does not feature London scenes, and even *The Mystery of Edwin Drood* (1870), which seemed to signal a change of emphasis in being set in a fictional cathedral city, makes London's opium dens a seemingly important element of its plot. Dickens had chronicled the growth and development of Victorian London as both a novelist and a journalist, detailing the sights and sounds of his obsessive explorations in *Sketches by Boz* (1836–7), *The Uncommercial Traveller* (1860, enlarged 1865 and 1875), and elsewhere. His London is a bizarre and grotesque world in which warm-hearted human relationships live cheek by jowl with evil and depravity: nine deaths and a planned judicial execution in *Bleak House* (1852–3) considerably upset John Ruskin. Both in his writing and in its accompanying illustrations, Dickens created a powerfully mythic locale, one to which visitors almost inevitably compared the actual city, rather than vice versa.

In drawing attention to the ways in which Dickens's version of London supplanted the actual city in the public (and, in some ways, historical) imagination, Burton Pike remarks that 'Dickens's London and London, England, are located in two different countries.'[86] As early as the 1830s, Philip Collins reports, 'people were "doing" Oliver Twist's London,' signalling the imposition of fictional associations onto topographical realities.[87] By the beginning of the twentieth century, the Dickens industry had reached such a height that even Gissing's 1898 critical study of the novelist had been augmented by F. G. Kitton's sketches of Dickensian locales. Gissing would later write that 'In time I came to see London with my own eyes, but how much better when I saw it with those of Dickens!'[88] In 1904, Francis Miltoun published *Dickens' London*, a work that mapped the identifiable realities of the capital against the fictions of the novelist. Miltoun used photographs of actual London sites to give geographical legitimacy to Dickensian settings, anticipating the ways in which Henry James and Alvin Coburn would experiment with placing the real at the service of the fictional in their series of photogravure frontispieces to James's New York edition. Arthur Compton Rickett's *The*

---

[86] B. Pike, *The Image of the City in Modern Literature* (Princeton: Princeton University Press, 1981), 13.

[87] Collins, 'Dickens and the City', in *Visions of the Modern City*, 118.

[88] G. Gissing, 'Dickens in Memory' (1901), in *The Immortal Dickens* (London: Palmer, 1925), 10.

London Life of Yesterday (1909) is still more comfortable with the idea of historicizing Dickens, devoting a chapter to the 1830s' London of Dickens and Francis Place, and tacitly suggesting that this literary incarnation of the capital is more 'real' than the city itself. Immigrants as diverse as Henry James, Theodore Dreiser, Joseph Conrad, and the narrator of V. S. Naipaul's *The Enigma of Arrival* (1987) all found London disappointing after being reared on the Dickensian simulacrum, while Edgar Allan Poe's 'The Man of the Crowd' (1840) betrays an obvious debt to the urban descriptions of *Sketches by Boz*.[89]

Dickens's conception of London had established its hold on the British imagination during the 1830s, and few of those who sought to depict the capital in subsequent writings could completely avoid entering into some sort of creative negotiation with his achievement. His fiction repeatedly configured the city as a massive web of intricate interconnection, offering, in *Bleak House*, a vast social panorama of guilty aristocrats, stricken crossing-sweepers, self-serving philanthropists, murderous French maids, profiteers, and policemen. Metropolitan survival in many respects depends upon the links and connections that the individual can forge, but Dickens invariably accentuated their strength in the interests of narrative cohesion and reinforcement.

'Dickensian' London was a fictional construction that its creator was free to alter in terms of the internal logic of his creative practices, rather than surrender to slavish notation of metropolitan development. This meant that it was never bound to the limitations of quotidian reality. Dickens had responded to the city's alteration and growth in his lifetime, turning a satirical eye on suburbia in the Veneerings of *Our Mutual Friend* (1864–5) and Wemmick's literal belief that an Englishman's home is his castle in *Great Expectations* (1860–1). However, he was just as likely to avoid other aspects of the capital, not wishing to alienate his family readership. The type of subject matter he and his readers deemed unsavoury would form key components of the naturalist London of Gissing, Maugham, and Arthur Morrison during the 1880s and 1890s.

By the time Dickens began work on *Edwin Drood* in August 1869, his London was older than a number of the British Empire's newly founded cities. It was established and coherent enough to function on its own terms,

[89] See, for example, James's 'London' and 'George du Maurier' from *Partial Portraits* (1883); Dreiser's remark, 'I am one of those who have been raised on Dickens and Thackeray and Lamb, but I must confess that I found little to corroborate the world of vague impressions I had formed' (*A Traveller at Forty* (1913; New York: Century, 1920), 141); Conrad, 'Poland Revisited' (1914); Naipaul, 'The London I knew or imaginatively possessed was the London I had got from Dickens. It was Dickens—and his illustrators—who gave me the illusion of knowing the city' (*The Enigma of Arrival: A Novel in Five Sections* (London: Penguin, 1987), 122) For Dickens and Poe, see Highmore, *Cityscapes*, 36–8.

and consequently able to combine elements as diverse as impeccably detailed realism and romanticized moral fable. Add to this a flair for comedy and characterization, and a enduring commitment to social justice, and it seemed that Dickens had exhausted, at least for others, the possibilities of approaching the capital in the way that he did. To appropriate Dickensian urban styles seemed as foolhardy as Eliot's abortive adoption of the heroic couplet in drafting *The Waste Land*: Dickens, like Pope, was simply unsurpassable on his own terms. Certain aspects of Dickens could be imitated to good effect—there is a lot of Dickensian comedy in *The Diary of a Nobody*, for example—but no other writer could offer the same overall blend of ingredients or exert such a hypnotic hold over his audience.

Any novelist attempting to set their fiction within the bounds of the English capital faced the overwhelming challenge of breaking from the Dickensian model, or from his mode of characterization.[90] From the relationship between Miss Pynsent and the young Hyacinth Robinson in James's *The Princess Casamassima* (1886), to the darkly ironic rewriting of *Great Expectations* in *The Nether World*, from the child criminals of Arthur Morrison to Wells's Alfred Polly hacking through the linguistic undergrowth, Dickens continued to affect the way in which London and its citizens were represented in fiction. Even those who claimed to reject Dickensian methods could scarcely help acquiring a familiarity with Dickens's work, though their attitudes towards it reflected three decades of debate concerning his reputation and status. In *London: A Book of Aspects* (1909), Arthur Symons invoked the pre-Victorian London of Charles Lamb, embraced the modernity of Baudelaire, Monet, and Degas, and pondered a synaesthetic new art of city writing. Nonetheless, as a resident of Fountain Court, he could not escape the fact that Dickens had been there first, using the small fountain as the site of John Westlock's wooing of Ruth Pinch in *Martin Chuzzlewit* (1844). Symons praises the peaceful isolation of the place, and quotes Paul Verlaine's poem on it, but eventually acknowledges that 'Dickens of course has written about the fountain,' his 'of course' suggesting both impatient dismissal and grudging acceptance of the inevitable.[91] Dickens had even influenced contemporary sociology. It is hard to read Henry Mayhew's interviews with the London poor without being reminded of Dickens, even if the patterns of influence were far from one way.

Poets and painters did not have to contend with the same overpowering single influence as novelists, though illustrators certainly felt the weight of Cruickshank and Phiz, and Lionel Lambourne cites Henry Wilson's account

---

[90] I am not, of course, suggesting that Dickens wrote to a formula, only that his novels display certain recurring features, notably their presentation of elaborately interconnected narratives.
[91] Symons, *London*, 189.

of a 'well-known artist' dancing for joy at news of Ruskin's death in 1900.[92] As E. D. H. Johnson and Robert Stange point out, there were Victorian poems and paintings which dealt with London in the first half of the Victorian era, but they emerge as interesting isolated examples rather than a coherent grouping or dialogue.[93] This is not to suggest that London disappeared from British art and literature after the Romantics, only to point out that the Victorians were perhaps more preoccupied with building cities than with painting or poeticizing them.

Nonetheless, by the late-Victorian era, artists too had to choose between maintaining the status quo or pursuing innovation in subject matter and technique. Important painters, Frederic Leighton, for example, or Edward Burne-Jones, sought inspiration from myth or an idealized Middle Ages, but others recognized the opportunities offered by the modern city. In the mid-nineteenth century, William Powell Frith's 'successful formula' led to a series of hugely popular tableaux of scenes from contemporary life from George Elgar Hicks, John Ritchie, William Maw Egley, and, a little later and a little higher up the social scale, James Tissot.[94] Such pictures can appear posed and static to modern eyes, but they were influential in revealing the possibilities of urban subject matter. However, while these scenes depicted the inhabitants of the city, there was little of the boldness encouraged by F. G. Stephens, who, as early as 1850, incited painters 'to go out into life' and exploit the aesthetic potential of:

the poetry of the things about us; our railways, factories, mines, roaring cities, steam vessels, and the endless novelties and wonders produced every day; which if they were found only in the *Thousand and One Nights*, or in any poem classical or romantic, would be gloried over without end.[95]

Stephens's rallying did not fall entirely on deaf ears, but the 'roaring city' was only slowly absorbed into Victorian art. Even then, London was often primarily a backdrop to the human interest of Richard Redgrave's 'social realism', the later social criticism of Luke Fildes, sentimental genre painting, reworked 'progress' pictures such as Augustus Egg's *Past and Present* (1858),

[92] L. Lambourne, *Victorian Painting* (London: Phaidon, 1999), 487.

[93] Stange, 'The Frightened Poets'; E. D. H. Johnson, 'Victorian Artists and the Urban Milieu', in Dyos and Wolff, eds., *The Victorian City: Images and Realities*, ii. 449–75. See also Donald J. Gray, 'Views and Sketches of London in the 19th Century', in I. B. Nadal and F. S. Schwarzbach, eds.,*Victorian Artists and the City: A Collection of Critical Essays* (New York: Pergamon, 1980), 43–58.

[94] Lambourne, *Victorian Painting*, 269.

[95] 'Laura Savage' [F. G. Stephens], 'Modern Giants', *The Germ*, 4, 30 April 1850. Quoted by E. D. H. Johnson, *Painting of the British Social Scene from Hogarth to Sickert* (London: Weidenfeld and Nicolson, 1986), 217.

and landscapes with a human interest, Ford Madox Brown's *An English Autumn Afternoon* (1852–5), for example. London's factories had been left behind by those of the industrial north earlier in the century, yet, as Briggs reminds us, '[s]ome trades prospered . . . Soap, food, drink and bricks were obvious examples'.[96] The works that produced them, however, lay outside the parameters of art, at least until Impressionist and Whistlerian pictures began to transfigure the city's industry.

According to Robert Stange, there was little about the modern city in the writing of canonical, high Victorian poets such as Tennyson, Browning, Arnold, and Swinburne.[97] The modern city is largely absent from Tennyson's poetry, and when it does appear it is often either brutal and frightening as in *Maud* (1855) and 'Locksley Hall Sixty Years After' (1886), or swiftly abandoned for the imaginative vistas of the medieval world, as in 'Godiva' (1842). Browning, who seems so assured in his presentation of an urbanized Renaissance, often avoids describing the Victorian conurbation, though he does occasionally evoke contemporary urban types, such as the fake spiritualist and his followers in 'Mister Sludge, "The Medium"' (1864). Elizabeth Barrett Browning's *Aurora Leigh* (1856) offers a number of what Stange terms 'almost luminous' glimpses of modern London, notably the account of a London fog from Book III. 'I saw | . . . the great tawny weltering fog | Involve the passive city,' Barrett Browning wrote, adding that 'Your city poets see such things | Not despicable.'[98] However, the verse novel was never likely to play a major role in the future representation of London, especially when its author's health precluded metropolitan residence. The artistic radicals of the 1860s such as Swinburne, D. G. Rossetti, and William Morris, also preferred to forsake their own time for a largely imaginary past, except in occasional pieces such as Rossetti's 'Jenny' (1870). Even a late work such as Morris's *News from Nowhere* (1890) owes more to his conception of the Middle Ages than to contemporary circumstances.

William Thesing cites few poetic engagements with the modern metropolis between the 1820s and the late-Victorian period, beyond the efforts of popular balladeers and writers of light verse such as Thomas Hood, though he makes a somewhat quixotic case for the importance of Frederick Locker Lampson.[99] More recently, Daniel Karlin has claimed that the city 'becomes of central importance in Victorian poetry', in arguing that 'Only Emily Brontë, of the major poets of the period, goes against the urban grain,' but this remains

---

[96] Briggs, *Victorian Cities*, 323.

[97] Stange, 'The Frightened Poets', 475–88. He makes an exception of Arnold's 'A Summer Night' (1852).

[98] Stange, 'The Frightened Poets', 484; E. Barrett Browning, *Aurora Leigh*, III, 179–80, 186–7.

[99] W. B. Thesing, *The London Muse: Victorian Poetic Responses to the City* (Athens: University of Georgia Press, 1982).

debatable, at least during the first half of Victoria's reign, and scarcely applicable to Swinburne.[100] It is only with the publication of James Thomson's work, most notably *The City of Dreadful Night*, that the modern metropolis, rather than its individual speakers, Augusta Webster's *A Castaway* (1870), for example, becomes a genuinely important subject for poetry. Indeed, only in the 1890s does Le Gallienne's 'cult of London' become fully evident.

London certainly represented exciting new territory for the poets of the late nineteenth and early twentieth centuries. The adoption of urban subject matter represented both a break with the past and a rather self-conscious proclamation of modern allegiances. Reviewing W. E. Henley's *London Voluntaries and Other Verses* in August 1892, Symons insisted that to devote poetic attention to the conurbation was 'something revolutionary' and a commitment to 'what is surely a somewhat new art, the art of modernity in verse'. The review continues:

In the *London Voluntaries*, for instance, what a sense of the poetry of cities, that rarer than pastoral poetry, the romance of what lies beneath our eyes, in the humanity of streets, if we had but the vision and point of view. Here, at last, is a poet who can so enlarge the limits of his verse to take in London. And I think that might be the test of poetry which professes to be modern: its capacity for dealing with London, with what one sees or might see there, indoors or out.[101]

Symons's enthusiasm for 'the poetry of cities' was an important element of his most successful collections, *Silhouettes* (1892) and *London Nights* (1895), and his poetic ambition as a whole. He mourned the lack of 'a Walt Whitman for London', a poet who knows 'no distinction between what is called the work of nature and what is the work of men' and creates, as a consequence, 'a vital poetry of cities'.[102] As a poet, critic, and theorist from the late 1880s until his breakdown in 1908, Symons was at the forefront of attempts to make the city 'a form of creative literature', exploring impressionism, symbolism, and decadence in an effort to produce an elusive synthesis of experience and expression.

Despite Symons's bold proselytizing for Whitman, it was novelists who properly realized the potential of the modern city in the period 1870–1914. By the time the First World War broke out, all of Stephens's ingredients would be established in fiction that ranged from Sherlock Holmes's awesome mastery of Bradshaw's railway timetable to D. H. Lawrence's depiction of the lives of mining communities and the 'endless novelties and wonders' of H. G. Wells's

[100] Introduction, *The Penguin Book of Victorian Verse*, ed. D. Karlin (London: Penguin, 1997), xl.

[101] Symons, 'Mr Henley's Poetry'. Originally printed in the *Fortnightly Review* (August 1892), and reprinted with additions in Symons, *Studies in Two Literatures* (London: Leonard Smithers, 1897), 186–203.

[102] Symons, *London*, 199.

scientific romances. What was only dimly emerging was art that dwelt with the experience of city life rather than using the city as a backdrop for melodrama, romance, intrigue, or, in the fiction of Elizabeth Gaskell, for example, a blend of these and political agitation. It was London's shift from setting to character in its own right that underlay one avenue of fictional exploration from *Bleak House* to *Mrs Dalloway* (1925). However, such developments placed enormous pressure on the dominant art form of the nineteenth century: realism. As the century progressed, realism became an overheated alloy, buckling and twisting into shapes that had never before been imagined.

BEING REALISTIC

During the period 1870–1914, reactions to London can be divided into five broad categories. The first two, wholesale delight and disgust, are traditional responses to the urban, and will be considered only incidentally. The other three are more significant, since they are attempts to interpret and represent the city in artistic media rather than being primarily emotional reactions. As one would expect, they are not the only ways of classifying responses to the city; indeed, in the manner of Paul Wheelwright's taxonomy of the archetypal symbol, they are 'permissive, not prescriptive'.[103] Such epistemological uncertainties reveal both what Alan Robinson has called 'the ineluctable subjectivity of all constructions of "London" ', and some of the ways by which writers and artists of the late nineteenth century used the vocabulary available to them.[104] Rather than map a late-twentieth-century discourse of urban theory onto the past, I have tried where possible to show how Victorian writers and artists attempted to conceive of a city for which earlier languages were no longer adequate, and develop their own discourses in line with contemporary artistic and, to a lesser extent, scientific innovation.

What I have termed 'empiricist' London was founded on a positivist belief that the city could be mapped and eventually understood by processes of painstaking investigation and analysis. This approach motivated both sociological enquiry and certain types of realist fiction, but its underlying assumptions became increasingly untenable as the city continued to expand, although the detective stories of Conan Doyle resisted this trend in some respects. 'Impressionist' London was less ambitious in conceding that, if the

---

[103] P. Wheelwright, 'The Archetypal Symbol', in J. Strelka, ed., *Perspectives in Literary Symbolism* (University Park: Pennsylvania State University Press, 1968), 214.
[104] A. Robinson, *Imagining London, 1770–1900* (Basingstoke: Macmillan, 2004), 249.

city could be known, then it could be so only fleetingly, and from a wholly subjective position. It was, however, more ambitious, or at least more 'modern' in its techniques, in that innovations in visual art took priority over those of literature, particularly in topographic writing. Finally, 'symbolist' London offered a more mystical response. In it, the metropolis was either one of William Blake's 'portions of Eternity too great for the eye of Man', or a series of secret patterns discernible only to the initiate, and sometimes not even then, for the neophyte might recognize patterns but not what might be meant by them. Such an approach rejected empiricist assumptions. 'I hate rationalism,' wrote Arthur Machen, 'since, when it is called in, in a little difficulty or perplexity, its advices and explanations are always so stupid, so wide of the mark, so absolutely futile.'[105] For him, writing on London became the composition of 'a mystical treatise', which approached the city as a site of mystery, not simply in the vulgar sense of an unsolved enigma, but as a sacred ritual.[106] However, it did so by encoding such meanings in writing that seemed, to the unsuspecting eye, realist in style, one reason for symbolism's present-day invisibility, as I will explain later.

What connects empiricist, impressionist, and symbolist renderings of London is their underlying belief in the use of realist techniques, even if they disagree with the assumptions that realism, in its most basic form, makes about mimesis. Realism can be more or less detailed, more or less concerned with the relationship between external realities and inner 'truths', but it remained a vital intellectual resource for the London writers of the *fin de siècle*. This is not to suggest that the final decades of the nineteenth century represented realism's 'last stand', but to posit that the evolution of different realist strategies was an enormously important aspect of the literature of the period, and of the imaginative conception of the modern city. Empiricism, impressionism, and symbolism should not be thought of as mutually exclusive categories—most of the writers examined in this study experimented with a mixture of them through their careers. They were instead sets of procedures, discourses, or techniques that allowed writers and artists to begin to answer a question later posed by Burton Pike: 'How does one make printed statements, ink on paper, into "London"... aside from the associations evoked' by the name itself?[107]

Linda Dowling has noted how, in disguising or denying its relationship with late-nineteenth-century art, modernism encouraged belief in 'the parthenogenesis of the *avant garde* disavowing its past in order to regenerate itself

---

[105] A. Machen, *Things Near and Far* (London: Martin Secker, 1923), 145.
[106] A. Machen, *Far Off Things* (London: Martin Secker, 1923), 61.
[107] Pike, *The Image of the City in Modern Literature*, 10–11.

and gain creative space'.[108] In an effort to make 'modernism newer, fathering themselves', modernist manifestos caricatured, discarded, and simply ignored late-Victorian art, subjecting it to patronizing critiques from which it took decades to recover. Realism was systematically misrepresented despite being no more a monolithic cultural form than modernist movements themselves, with a caricature of it insisting on its concern with exteriority and claiming that it was insufficiently subtle or penetrating to represent the speed and complexities of modern life. Virginia Woolf's 'Mr Bennett and Mrs Brown' (1924) has proved especially influential in trivializing its concern with fact and surface detail. 'The tools of one generation are useless for the next,' Woolf announced, for it suited her artistic purposes to make a seemingly clean break with the past, and her class prejudices to ridicule Arnold Bennett.[109]

Academic criticism has often endorsed Woolf's judgement, just as it has sided with Henry James in his arguments with first Walter Besant and then H. G. Wells, and English realism has suffered the consequences. As Peter Keating remarks:

> Modernist fiction has associated itself so completely with fractured time, with relativity, with the epiphany which claims to encapsulate the very essence of life, that the realistic novel dealing in a fairly uncomplicated way with present social conditions now has little chance of being regarded as literature at all.

Such fiction has often been consigned to the lesser categories of 'social history' or 'documentary', and, despite some recent suggestions of reappraisal, still receives far less critical attention than canonical modernist writing.[110] Yet for all that it has been regarded as static and unitary, late-nineteenth-century realism, rather than simply 'the realist novel', was highly self-conscious and anxious about its limitations, possibilities, and future, notably in the portrayal of the city. Considering the late-Victorian cultural legacy in 1913, Holbrook Jackson noted that 'although the forward movement in pictorial art absolved itself from all charges of literariness, its very existence was part of the trend of modern ideas which was affecting all the arts. In literature the tendency was called Realism, in the graphic arts it was called Impressionism.'[111]

Acknowledging the link between the two movements—impressionism was regularly paired with literary naturalism during the 1880s and 1890s—Jackson

---

[108] Linda C. Dowling, *Aestheticism and Decadence: A Selective Annotated Bibliography* (1977), quoted by Ian Fletcher and Malcolm Bradbury in the Preface to their edited collection, *Decadence and the 1890s* (London: Arnold, 1979), 7.

[109] V. Woolf, *Collected Essays*, ed. L. Woolf (London: Hogarth Press, 1966), i. 331.

[110] P. Keating, *The Haunted Study: A Social History of the English Novel 1875–1914* (1989; London: Fontana, 1991), 285.

[111] H. Jackson, *The 1890s: A Review of Art and Ideas at the Close of the Nineteenth Century* (1913; Harmondsworth: Pelican, 1950), 276.

prefers to term both 'the search for reality', but I would add the important qualification that reality was itself a disputed term. For Gissing, attention to physical and sensuous detail was an essential component of establishing a believable setting for fiction, though he shared the suspicions of French writers and artists such as Courbet and Champfleury regarding the term 'realism'. For impressionists, reality lay in transient sensation and subjective perception, whereas for symbolists, it was transcendent and eternal.

Modernist intellectuals may have dismissed it as a nineteenth-century phenomenon, but realism was an explicitly modern form of writing and its later offshoot, naturalism, even more so. It had the credentials modernists elsewhere admired, in that it emerged from France, defined itself against previous literary movements while slyly incorporating or ironizing elements from them, melodrama for instance, that helped its case, and met an at-first distinctly muted commercial response. The debates in the French press of the 1850s were not quite those that were stirred up by *Blast* in 1914, but realism had at once alarmed conservatives and offered radicals an exciting vision of creative possibilities. It took as its subject matter everyday events, and its 'hero' the ordinary man, often displaying an almost scientific respect for exact documentation and 'getting the facts right'.[112] Its focus on the material conditions of existence, from Balzac to Zola and his followers, demanded careful observation and linguistic exactitude: Balzac famously expended nine adjectives on a dilapidated chair in *Le Père Goriot* (1834–5). Dickens may have given free rein to sentimentality, fancy, and the workings of Providence, opposing a dulling emphasis on fact in *Hard Times*, but he obeyed nonetheless many of realism's informal precepts.

By the late nineteenth century, however, urban realism faced a number of serious challenges, or rather, was confronted by a number of alternative readings of the city that threw into relief the artistic fashioning of its material. As Lynne Hapgood notes, these emerged from areas as diverse as Christian evangelism, secularism, Marxist and Fabian socialism, and positivism, a list to which might be added various forms of 'journalese', mysticism, municipal practicality, and avant-garde aesthetics.[113] Realist art, which had once seemed relatively dispassionate and objective in its portrayal of 'reality', now found itself questioned on technical, political, and philosophical grounds.

These questions took several forms. The burgeoning popularity and professionalism of empiricist sociology on both sides of the Channel left naturalist

---

[112] J. A. Cuddon, 'Realism', *The Penguin Dictionary of Literary Terms and Literary Theory* (London: Penguin, 1998), 731.

[113] L. Hapgood, 'Urban Utopias: Socialism, Religion and the City, 1880 to 1900', in S. Ledger and S. McCracken, eds.,*Cultural Politics at the Fin de Siècle* (Cambridge: Cambridge University Press, 1995), 185.

'studies' of the urban environment risk seeming amateurish. Sociologists and anthropologists had 'no interest in weakening the force of their findings by wrapping them up in the distracting packaging of art', and the publication of Émile Durkheim's *Règles de la méthode sociologique* in 1895 was, in many respects, a crucial blow to naturalist pretensions to objectivity.[114] In the hands of such theorists, sociology was becoming increasingly sophisticated in its attempts to analyse and explain the condition of urban existence. In Europe, works such as Gustave Le Bon's *Psychologie des foules* (1895) and Georg Simmel's 'Die Grosstädte und das Geistesleben' ('The Metropolis and Mental Life', 1900) pondered 'the attempt of the individual to maintain the independence and individuality of his existence against the sovereign powers of society'.[115] British social investigation was drawn less to theorizing than to empirical research. Interviews with individuals only gradually coalesced into grander hypotheses about the city, although the appearance of an English translation of *Das Kapital* in 1886 raised awareness of the Marxist terminology that could underpin both.[116] Its most notable achievement in the period from 1870 to 1914 was Charles Booth's massive survey of poverty, *Life and Labour of the People in London* (1889–1902), a seventeen-volume study that brought to bear unprecedented levels of statistical detail and personal testimony. The new science viewed its subject matter from a seemingly objective, analytical perspective that endeavoured to reveal, rather than dramatize, urban living. It offered an alternative reading of the conurbation, one which, while it did not suggest fiction was necessarily 'wrong', exposed in ever more insistent detail the liberties taken by novelists in constructing their versions of 'reality'.

The increasingly visible presence of sociology insisted on its own objectivity, a claim it supported with pages of seemingly neutral maps and statistics. That later critics have found these to be subtly tainted by the outlook of their compilers is less important than their possible implications for fiction at the time. However, it is too simplistic to suggest a neat division between 'objective' social science and 'subjective' literature in Britain, since their respective rhetorical strategies had interbred to the bewilderment of the most dedicated genealogist. By the 1880s, Hapgood comments, 'there was a general sense that the thinking about social issues had overtaken the public discourse available

---

[114] F. W. J. Hemmings, ed., *The Age of Realism* (London: Penguin, 1974), 362.

[115] G. Simmel, 'The Metropolis and Mental Life', trans. E. Shills, in P. Kasinitz, ed., *Metropolis: Centre and Symbol of Our Times* (London: Macmillan, 1995), 30.

[116] As Victor Neuberg points out in his edition, because Mayhew's notebooks have been lost, 'we know little or nothing about his methods of work,' though he undoubtedly conducted many interviews with London's poor. H. Mayhew, *London Labour and the London Poor* (1865; London: Penguin, 1985), xx.

to articulate it.'[117] What this created, she argues, was the 'unintended irony' of sociological language straining after objectivity yet falling back on literary devices. The anecdotal reporting of Keating's 'social explorer' was particularly prone to mixing apparent sociological objectivity with literary flourishes, and 'human interest' journalism was similarly culpable. The rhetorically charged pamphlet *The Bitter Cry of Outcast London* (1883) called itself 'a plain recital of plain facts': it was nothing of the kind.[118] Jack London's *The People of the Abyss* (1903), while nominally derived from its author's personal observation of city life, is especially addicted to figurative effects, to the extent that the reader is never able to forget that its detail is being transfigured by a markedly literary individual consciousness.

Another notable alternative to 'realism' was philosophically inflected literature and criticism that focused on the artist's openly subjective perception of their environment. During the 1870s, literature and visual art began to experiment with openly impressionistic responses to the world, which are, as Jesse Matz has noted, 'personal but universal—subjective, but not therefore wholly idiosyncratic' and fall 'somewhere between analytic scrutiny and imaginative invention'.[119] The work of Walter Pater, notably his self-suppressed conclusion to *Studies in the History of the Renaissance* (1873), was particularly influential in propounding ideas of the individual's unique perceptions and their personal expression. Pater's essay on Coleridge (1866) had argued for the primacy of the 'relative' rather than 'absolute' spirit, remarking that 'To the modern spirit nothing is, or can be rightly known, except relatively and under conditions.'[120] This association of modernity with relativity would be a cornerstone of his philosophy, and would, in the eyes of Pater's followers, help to undermine and historically distance realist pretensions to objectivity. What Graham Hough memorably terms an 'atomised and solipsistic epistemology' of 'radical scepticism' was one that many young writers and artists found extremely stimulating during the late nineteenth century.[121]

Paterian relativity opposed Oscar Wilde's 'careless habits of accuracy', in encouraging, wittingly or otherwise, a fascination with subjective perceptions of truth, the '*vraie vérité*' derived from 'those more liberal and durable impressions' that 'lie beyond, and must supplement, the narrower range

[117] Hapgood, 'Urban Utopias: Socialism, Religion and the City', 184.

[118] P. Keating, ed., *Into Unknown England 1866–1913: Selections from the Social Explorers* (Glasgow: Fontana, 1976), 93.

[119] J. Matz, *Literary Impressionism and Modernist Aesthetics* (Cambridge: Cambridge University Press, 2001), 16.

[120] W. Pater, 'Coleridge's Writings', in his *Essays on Literature and Art*, ed. J. Uglow (London: Dent, 1973), 2.

[121] G. Hough, *The Last Romantics* (1948; London: Duckworth, 1979), 140.

of... strictly ascertained facts'.[122] Pater's expression of the subjective nature of existence proved especially potent for English writers, articulated as it was through a combination of influential journals, the publishing might of Macmillan, and a mildly notorious lectureship at Brasenose College. His suspicions of objectivity, suspicions shared by a number of other *fin de siècle* intellectuals, extended to the increasingly scientific discipline of history. Faced with 'a multitude of facts', Pater argued in 'Style' (1889), historians were forced into selection, and through selection, revelation of 'something that comes not of a world without but of a vision within'.[123] Much the same might be said of sociological surveys, in that even their driest data had been subjected to individual and hence subjective framing and interpretation.

Pater was less concerned with establishing detail than with subtle responses to it. He sought to affirm the artist's presentation of 'his peculiar sense of fact' and collapse imaginative fiction and non-fictional prose into one another in an aesthetic that, as Peter Rawlings notes, 'depends on erasing lines, not drawing them'.[124] In the 'persuasive writer', Pater suggested, there is 'an expression no longer of fact but of his sense of it, his peculiar intuition of a world'.[125] This description seems as well suited to Dickens as it does to a Paterian aesthete, but realism did not draw such explicit attention to its 'peculiar intuition', except by the obvious means of first person or intrusive narrators. Indeed, Hubert Crackanthorpe, often regarded as a naturalist writer whose work 'retains a certain feeling of having been translated from French originals' openly allied Paterian epistemology with contemporary realist fiction.[126] 'We are each of us conscious, not of the whole world, but of our own world; not of naked reality, but of that aspect of reality which our peculiar temperament enables us to appropriate,' he argued, words that inescapably recall 'Style' and the conclusion of *The Renaissance*.[127]

Pater was too cautious to dismiss facts completely, much as he suggested that knowledge was provisional and truth subjective, but younger writers had far fewer inhibitions. When Conan Doyle drew attention to historical inaccuracies in Max Beerbohm's 'Dandies and Dandies', Beerbohm retorted,

[122] O. Wilde, *The Decay of Lying* (1889), *Complete Works* (London: HarperCollins 1994), 1073–4; W. Pater, *The Renaissance: Studies in Art and Poetry*, ed. A. Philips, 4th edn (1893; Oxford: Oxford University Press, 1986), 179.

[123] Pater, *Essays on Literature and Art*, 70.

[124] P. Rawlings, 'Pater, Wilde, and James: "The Reader's Share of the Task",' *Studies in English Language and Literature* (Kyushu University), 48, February 1998, 48.

[125] Pater, *Essays on Literature and Art*, 71.

[126] P. J. Keating, ed., *Working Class Stories of the 1890s* (London: Routledge, 1971), x.

[127] H. Crackanthorpe, 'Reticence in Literature: Some Roundabout Remarks' (1894), in N. Denny, ed., *The Yellow Book: A Selection* (London: The Bodley Head, 1948), 96.

'Facts are easier than style.'[128] In *The Decay of Lying*, Vivian awaits the day on which 'Facts will be regarded as discreditable,' while elsewhere Wilde announced that 'When a truth becomes a fact it loses all its intellectual value,' iconoclasm he even managed to espouse at the Old Bailey.[129] Those who found themselves at odds with the statistical approach to the city employed by the LCC, *Life and Labour of the People in London*, or a British empirical tradition that encouraged, in Charles Kingsley's words, 'a greater respect for facts', regarded the domain of the factual with particular scepticism.[130] Their London had neither respect nor need for maps and columns of figures. Israel Zangwill may have subtitled his novel *Children of the Ghetto* (1892) 'a study of a peculiar people', but he had only limited sympathy for anthropological methods or Zola's concern with 'human documents', arguing that objectivity was impossible in the terms of individual perception. 'Life is in the eye of the observer,' he insisted, '*in human life there are no facts.*'[131] Ford announced that *The Soul of London* would be 'anything rather than encyclopaedic, topographical, or archaeological'.[132] Henry James told Edmund Gosse that 'London Town' would be 'a romantical-psychological-pictorial-social' book about the city: tellingly, he struggled with accounts of the metropolis that were anchored in a less persuasive historical methodology.[133] More sensitive than most to the follies of presumed objectivity, James was magisterial in proclaiming 'the fatal futility of Fact' in the preface to *The Spoils of Poynton* (1908).[134]

Other writers had similar qualms. 'Facts are difficult of digestion, and should be taken diluted, at infrequent intervals. They suit few constitutions when taken whole,' quipped Arthur Symons.[135] He prefaced his revised edition of *London Nights* (1897) with a critic-baiting espousal of subjectivity, in which he maintained that none of his poems was 'a record of actual fact', being instead the 'sincere attempt to render a particular mood which has once been mine'.[136] In Chesterton's *The Club of Queer Trades* (1905), Rupert Grant is invariably led astray by his 'cold and clear reasoning' but saved by the intuitive insights of poetry, while his brother Basil coolly maintains that facts 'obscure the

---

[128] M. Beerbohm, 'Dr Conan Doyle's Latest Case', *Saturday Review*, 2 January 1897, 16.

[129] Wilde, *Complete Works*, 1090, 1242.

[130] C. Kingsley, *Sanitary and Social Lectures and Essays* (1880) in Beckson, *London in the 1890s*, 293.

[131] I. Zangwill, 'The Realistic Novel', from *Without Prejudice* (1896), cited in his *Children of the Ghetto: A Study of a Peculiar People*, ed. M.-J. Rochelson (Detroit: Wayne State University Press, 1998), 42.

[132] Ford, *The Soul of London*, 3.   [133] James, *The Notebooks of Henry James*, 325.

[134] James, 'Preface' to *The Spoils of Poynton* (1908; New York: Augustus M. Kelley, 1976), vii.

[135] A. Symons, 'Fact in Literature', in *Studies in Prose and Verse* (London: Dent, 1904), 3.

[136] A. Symons, *London Nights* (1895; London: Leonard Smithers, 1897), i.

truth'.[137] Only by entertaining the irrational and unsubstantiated, he suggests, can one hope to make sense of modern London. 'Do you really admit,' cries Basil in 'a kind of despair', 'are you still so sunk in superstitions, so clinging to dim and prehistoric altars, that you believe in facts? Do you not trust an immediate impression?'[138] '[A] fact *qua* fact has no existence in art at all' was the blunt opinion of Arthur Machen.[139] Ford Madox Ford went further still, first embracing not 'accuracy' but 'suggestiveness', and later professing 'a profound contempt' for facts. He was even prepared to claim that 'dwelling on facts leads at best to death'. His was part of a wider scepticism regarding 'objective reality' and the failings of what he later termed 'our terrific, untidy, indifferent empirical age'.[140] At last Symons, moving from impressionism to symbolism, concluded that although realism had wrought 'miracles in the exact representation of everything that visibly existed, exactly as it existed', the time had come for a more visionary art. '[T]he world has starved its soul long enough in the contemplation and the re-arrangement of material things,' he wrote in 1899. It was now 'the turn of the soul'.[141]

Such were the theoretical, technical, and conceptual problems facing the London writer in the final decades of the nineteenth century. The city seemed to be out of control, growing rapidly in all directions and continually generating new versions of itself. Within it, life moved at an ever faster pace and spoke what Forster termed 'the language of hurry'.[142] London was impossible to imagine as *in toto* other than on the level of abstraction or generalization. The exhaustion of earlier literary and artistic techniques was becoming ever more manifest to the radically minded, even if some of their practitioners remained popular with the public.

What was to be done?

---

[137] G. K. Chesterton, 'The Eccentric Seclusion of the Old Lady' and 'The Tremendous Adventures of Major Brown', in *The Club of Queer Trades* (1905; London: Penguin, 1986), 103, 18.

[138] G. K. Chesterton, 'The Painful Fall of a Great Reputation', in ibid. 33.

[139] A. Machen, *Hieroglyphics: A Note upon Ecstasy in Literature* (1902; London: Unicorn Press, 1960), 85.

[140] F. M. Ford, *The Cinque Ports* (Edinburgh and London: William Blackwood, 1900), vi; *Ancient Lights and Certain New Reflections* (London: Chapman and Hall, 1911), xv–xvi; 'Nice People' (1903), in M. Saunders, *Ford Madox Ford: A Dual Life*, i. 67; *Joseph Conrad: A Personal Remembrance* (1924), in *The Ford Madox Ford Reader*, 221.

[141] A. Symons, *The Symbolist Movement in Literature* (1899; London: Constable, 1908), 5–6.

[142] Forster, *Howards End*, 116.

1

'Inclusion and Confusion': Empiricist London

DARLING: I do not know where Whitechapel is.
MUIR: Beyond Aldgate, my lord.
Judge Charles Darling at the trial of Stinie Morrison, 6 March 1911

The purpose of this chapter is show how two very different forms of realist writing engaged with the London that was becoming the regular haunt of social explorers, journalists, and evangelical campaigners. 'Slum novels' and the detective fiction of Arthur Conan Doyle would approach their task in markedly differing ways, but both represented means of invigorating the subject matter and techniques of realist art. They were sustained by a fundamentally positive belief that London could be understood, represented, and communicated if only the correct methods could be discovered and employed, but their faith in such an enterprise was often challenged by the unsavoury details of city life. Henry James was uncomfortable with those things 'we may have to apologise for . . . uglinesses, the "rookeries", the brutalities, the night-aspect of many of the streets, the gin-shops and the hour when they are cleared out before closing', recognizing that his personal artistic practice, not to mention the squeamishness of libraries and publishers, could produce only a partial portrait.[1] Twenty years later, the narrator of *Howards End* disdained such material altogether with his feline aside, 'We are not concerned with the very poor. They are unthinkable, and only to be approached by the statistician or the poet.'[2] Forster could offer such comment because the previous three decades had seen intense debate about the parameters of realist fiction. It was through Gissing's work, claimed C. F. G. Masterman in 1904, that 'London first became articulate', yet Gissing himself was increasingly unconvinced by such directions of the

---

[1] H. James, 'London' (1888), in *English Hours* (London: Heinemann, 1905), 30.
[2] E. M. Forster, *Howards End*, ed. O. Stallybrass (1910; London: Penguin, 1983), 58.

realist project.[3] 'Our "realist" . . . takes it for granted that the truth can be got at, and that it is his plain duty to set it down without compromise,' he observed sardonically in 1898, voicing sentiments he could no longer share.[4] 'Our realist' was not alone. Sociologists, evangelists, journalists, and civic reformers all made a knowable London an article of faith, and the basis of their endeavours.

FACT VERSUS FICTION

As the nineteenth century drew to a close, scientific methodology's concern with precise evidence, alongside writing that openly embraced the subjective, the impressionist, and even, on occasion, the mystical, confronted realist art in very different ways. The most detailed realist writing looked somehow sketchy and incomplete in the face of Charles Booth's ambitious scheme to ascertain the distribution of London's wealth. This had grown from an individual impression about levels of poverty to a sophisticated taxonomy involving a team of researchers who visited thousands of homes and businesses to interview their occupants. *East London*, the first volume of the monumental survey, *Life and Labour of the People in London*, represented three years of work by Booth and his colleagues. Their methods were laborious and complex. An area was assessed according to official documentary sources such as the 1881 census, the reports of School Board visitors, Poor Law statistics, and police lists of registered lodging houses. This information was then logged against Booth's eight-part scale of class and income which ran from Class A, the poorest of the poor, to H, the comfortable middle classes. These classes were colour coded, with black being used for A and yellow for H, allowing for maps of poverty to be drawn up from the statistical evidence gathered from the official data.[5] Finally, Booth compiled a list of the thirty-nine known occupations in the East End. This allowed him to match occupation to income with a precision no previous investigation had ever attempted, let alone matched. It was only after this statistical mapping was complete that Booth's researchers

---

[3] P. Coustillas, 'Gissing's Variations on Urban and Rural Life', in J.-P. Hulin and P. Coustillas, eds., *Victorian Writers and the City* (Lille: University of Lille, 1979), 115.

[4] G. Gissing, *Charles Dickens: A Critical Study* (1898; London: Gresham, 1903), 82.

[5] As Booth ventured into more prosperous areas of the city, he revised his initial scheme until it ran from '*Black*: Lowest class. Vicious, semi-criminal' to '*Gold*: Upper-middle and Upper classes. Wealthy'. Franco Moretti remarks that this colour code is 'either quite naïve or very very ironic' (*Atlas of the European Novel 1800–1900* (London: Verso, 1998), 77).

carried out more personal investigation, producing the accounts of domestic life that revealed the distress and want at the heart of the Empire. Booth was determined that inevitably personal responses should be supported by accurate documentary evidence.

East London appeared in April 1889, the same month as George Gissing's *The Nether World*. There are marked similarities between the accounts of researchers and the novel's descriptive detail, but while Gissing purported to be objective, he rarely masked his prejudices and never sought to evolve a theoretical framework for his observations. For all the sociological interest of his work, he was above all 'a conscious, frequently self-conscious, artist rather than a social reformer', and his work was founded upon personal perceptions instead of the mass of analytical detail sifted by Booth and his team.[6] However, Booth also failed to find a truly 'objective' language for his accounts of poverty, falling back on terms such as 'loafers' and 'scroungers' that, while in widespread popular use, hardly suggested critical neutrality. His treatment of London's Jewish community was also less than objective, as David Englander has shown.[7]

In 1889, Gissing was in an awkward aesthetic predicament. His fiction was rooted in the minute observation of its milieu, about which he wrote with obvious authority, yet he could not hope to match the accumulated detail of Booth's survey. Besides, an internalized cultural hierarchy compelled him to assert the superiority of the artist. The novelist might not have reached the heights of the classical poet, but he was far nearer the summit of Parnassus than the sociologist or, worse still, the journalist: Gissing rejected an offer of writing for the *Pall Mall Gazette* on the grounds that he considered journalism degrading. His version of realist art was squeezed between an avant-garde attracted to various modes of impressionist and symbolist response to the city, the empirically focused analysis of social science, and a populist press which, in catering for a growing readership brought about by successive educational reforms since 1870, favoured the bluntly everyday or extravagantly sensational. Detailed and observant as Gissing's writing may have been, there was much that it did not, even could not, say, and its silences were beginning to become deafening.

Newspapers played a major role in publicizing the horrors of deprived areas, and competition for readers prompted particularly lurid reporting. Amy Levy's 'Ballade of a Special Edition' (1889) pictures the newsvendor as

[6] P. J. Keating, *The Working Classes in Victorian Fiction* (London: Routledge and Kegan Paul, 1971), 94.
[7] D. Englander, 'Booth's Jews: The Presentations of Jews and Judaism in *Life and Labour of the People in London*', *Victorian Studies*, 32(4) (summer 1989), 551–71.

a 'Fiend' and 'Bird of ill omen', the 'friend' of 'slaughter, theft, and suicide'.[8] 'In newspaperland,' Edgar Wallace cynically observed, 'a dull lie is seldom detected, but an interesting exaggeration drives an unimaginative rival to hysterical denunciations.'[9] London's press responded to the Jack the Ripper panic of autumn 1888 with grotesque depictions of Whitechapel and its residents that overwhelmed any efforts to uncover everyday realities. They may have been motivated by values very different from those of evangelical reformers, but journalists and novelists made a similar equation between social deprivation and hell itself, with Margaret Oliphant showing the infernal regions as horribly reminiscent of modern London in her allegory 'The Land of Darkness' (1887). Gissing meanwhile designated East London 'a city of the damned' in the tellingly titled *Nether World*, allowing Mad Jack, a homeless eccentric, to tell the citizens of Clerkenwell that 'this place to which you are confined is Hell!'[10] In Arthur Morrison's *A Child of the Jago* (1896), the elderly Mr Beveridge remarks that 'there can be no hell after this', a comment that draws the droll reply, 'that's a comfort, Mr Beveridge, any'ow'.[11] The coverage of the Ripper murders by all sections of London's press insisted upon a similarly bleak view of Whitechapel as a vile waste land where drunken, homeless whores met fates all the more hideous for being seemingly inevitable.[12] One famous letter to the press, purportedly written by the murderer, was headed 'From hell'.[13] The coverage of the Ripper murders, Judith Walkowitz notes, was 'not intended to elicit human sympathy for the people of Whitechapel as much as to promote "an argument from geography" about the territorially based nature of the crime.'[14]

[8] A. Levy, *The Complete Novels and Selected Writings of Amy Levy 1861–1889*, ed. M. New (Gainesville: University Press of Florida, 1993), 387–8. The poem first appeared in *The Star* on 5 March 1888 and was collected in Levy's *A London Plane-Tree and Other Verse* the following year.

[9] E. Wallace, *The Four Just Men*, ed. D. Glover (1905; Oxford: Oxford University Press, 1995), 24.

[10] M. Oliphant, 'The Land of Darkness', *Blackwood's Edinburgh Magazine*, January 1887; G. Gissing, *The Nether World*, ed. S. Gill (1889; Oxford: Oxford University Press, 1992), 164, 345.

[11] A. Morrison, *A Child of the Jago*, ed. P. Miles (1896; London: Dent, 1996), 12. All future references are to this edition, which reprints earlier prefaces and reviews.

[12] See the collection of news and inquest reports in S. P. Evans and K. Skinner, *The Ultimate Jack the Ripper Sourcebook: An Illustrated Encyclopedia* (London: Robinson, 2000) and the discussion of Whitechapel in J. R. Walkowitz's *City of Dreadful Delight: Narratives of Sexual Danger in Late Victorian London* (London: Virago, 1992), 193–5. The diverse nature of crime in Whitechapel is well documented by W. J. Fishman in *East End 1888: A Year in a London Borough among the Labouring Poor* (London: Duckworth, 1988), 177–229. Blanchard Jerrold noted how, when visiting Whitechapel in the early 1870s, 'demands for gin assailed us on all sides' (*London: A Pilgrimage* (1872; New York: Dover, 1970), 149). The government eventually responded to widespread drunkenness in urban areas with the largely ineffectual Habitual Inebriates Act of 1898.

[13] P. Sugden, *The Complete History of Jack the Ripper* (London: Robinson, 2002), 263–77.

[14] Walkowitz, *City of Dreadful Delight*, 195.

Dickens had seen no contradiction in being at once a novelist and a writer for the press but a later generation of artists found the rapid expansion of London's media deeply disturbing. 'We review and report and invent: | In drivel our virtue is spent,' moans Brian in John Davidson's *Fleet Street Eclogues* (1894).[15] The denunciation of journalism is usually seen as a defining feature of the avant-garde, but it is frequently evident in less exalted late-Victorian writers. In a discussion of Gissing's horror of modern culture, John Carey draws attention to the parody of *Tit-Bits* in *New Grub Street* (1891) and the death of the 'incurable newspaper addict' John Pether in *Workers in the Dawn* (1880). The latter is killed in a fire after piles of papers on his bed catch alight, and Carey notes that 'The dangers of inflammatory journalism could scarcely be more graphically illustrated.'[16] While critics have seen the dislike of journalism as one aspect of a wider fear of democracy and the challenge to 'high' culture posed by increasingly widespread literacy, late-Victorian realists were keen to define themselves against it for another important reason. By the late 1880s, journalism and realist fiction were fighting over the same subject matter, and although H. G. Wells could later tell Henry James that he would rather be regarded as a journalist than an artist, he made his comments from a position of wealth and established reputation. Besides, he had shown an ability to write fiction of many different styles and had been a successful literary journalist: Gissing had not. Journalism was therefore denounced because novelists wanted the freedom to use 'real life' as the raw material of art without foregrounding the gulf between lived experience and its artistic transmutation.

A neat opposition of 'objective' journalism and 'subjective' art proved problematic. Gissing retained a lingering respect for *The Times* as a newspaper of record, writing to it to report the Reverend A. Osborne Jay's unacknowledged borrowings from *The Nether World* in *Life in Darkest London* (1891).[17] He could not extend this respect to the local London press, however, which he found replete with inconsistency, emotive language, and uncongenial political bias. During the late 1880s, radical newspapers had shown themselves willing to provoke the establishment not simply over the Ripper affair, which was, in any case, a free-for-all where criticism of the police was concerned, but also over demonstrations by the unemployed, strikes, and matters of sexual hypocrisy such as Stead's 'Maiden Tribute' and the Cleveland Street scandal

---

[15] J. Davidson, 'New Year's Day', *The Poems of John Davidson*, ed. Andrew Turnbull, 2 vols. (Edinburgh: Scottish Academic Press, 1973), i. 194.

[16] J. Carey, *The Intellectuals and the Masses* (London: Faber, 1992), 105.

[17] Gissing wrote to *The Times* protesting that Jay had not acknowledged his work: the letter appeared on 9 September 1893 headed 'Borrowed Feathers'. Jay apologized, blaming an error by his printer. Although Gissing initially found this a lame excuse, the printer admitted his mistake in *The Times* on 13 September, and Gissing mellowed towards the priest.

of 1889–90. It was not that Gissing was opposed to the exposure of vice and corruption; more that he scarcely welcomed ill-written reminders of London's deceptions and brutality.

Nothing in late-Victorian fiction went into quite the detail of the London press in reporting what were persistently termed 'outrages'. Naturalism certainly chronicled some vicious fights, notably in Morrison's 'Lizerunt' (1894) and the ferocious battle between Liza and Mrs Blakeston in Maugham's *Liza of Lambeth* (1897), but it could not rival press reports where explicit revelation was concerned. The murder of Emma Smith, a prostitute who is sometimes seen as the Ripper's first victim, was widely reported in April 1888. The deployment of euphemism in describing Smith as 'an unfortunate', and the occlusion of meaning resulting from medical terminology demonstrates that even the press recognized limits, but cannot disguise that a Sunday newspaper, *Lloyd's Weekly News*, was prepared to offer an account such as this:

Dr Hellier described the internal injuries which had been caused, and which must have been inflicted by a blunt instrument. It had even penetrated the peritoneum, producing peritonitis, which was undoubtedly the course of death, in his opinion . . . . He was in no doubt that death was caused by the injuries to the perineum, the abdomen, and the peritoneum. Great force must have been used.[18]

A century later, the post-mortem has become a standard conduit for the revelation of bodily detail in popular entertainment, but during the 1880s and 1890s, its novelty thrilled and horrified the reading public, or at least that section of it with access to medical dictionaries. Although some of the most explicit material was confined to *The Lancet*, reports such as that of Emma Smith's murder were a highly visible indication of the limitations of English fiction, which simply could not offer a comparable level of exactitude, even if it had wished to do so. H. G. Wells's *Tono-Bungay* (1909) gives a vivid evocation of the 'smudgily illustrated sheets' in which:

vilely drawn pictures brought home to the dullest intelligence an interminable succession of squalid crimes, women murdered and put into boxes, buried under floors, old men bludgeoned at midnight by robbers, people thrust suddenly out of trains, happy lovers shot, vitrioled and so forth by rivals.[19]

Such material was not confined to the pink pages of the *Illustrated Police News*, and neither did it stop at 'vilely drawn pictures', for the language of its reports was equally horrifying. As Dallas Liddle points out, when Charles Reade responded to a negative review from *The Times* in 1871, claiming that 'the journal has been the preceptor, and the main source of my works'

---

[18] 'Horrible Murder in Whitechapel', *Lloyd's Weekly News*, Sunday, 8 April 1888, 1.
[19] H. G. Wells, *Tono-Bungay*, ed. John Hammond (1909; London: Dent, 1994), 37.

for some eighteen years, the newspaper responded by signalling a difference between journalism and sensational literature. A newspaper contained facts that a mother might forbid her daughter to read, but it did not contain '*fictions like Mr Reade's*'.[20] Gissing was a very different novelist from Reade—there had, after all, been many changes in fictional fashion between 1871 and the late 1880s—but his work nevertheless contained elements found in the 'smudgily illustrated sheets'. *The Nether World* offered a shocking account of a vitriol attack, but Gissing had no wish to meet the rudimentary needs of the 'dullest intelligence'. Inevitably, he struggled to dress his appalling material in terms that would appeal to educated liberal bourgeois readers only too aware of the detail he excluded from his novels.

To write fiction about the poor quarters of London at this time was therefore to consciously compete with a variety of other discourses, and any distinction between fact and fiction was a very uncertain one. Hubert Crackanthorpe made such rivalry explicit in his dismissal of 'the serious minded spinster, bitten by some sociological theory' who sought to use the novel as a medium for social improvement. For Crackanthorpe, fiction was a creative rather than purely mimetic art that 'endeavours to produce, through the adaptation of a restricted number of natural facts, an harmonious and satisfactory whole'. Literature was consequently distinguished by 'ultimate suggestiveness' rather than by explanation or description: it was always 'subjective', he insisted, because 'a work of art can never be more than a corner of Nature, seen through the temperament of a single man.'[21] Reactions against the realist art of Bastien-Lepage took a similar form, with Walter Sickert maintaining in 1891 that great art was 'not a catalogue of facts' or 'the sterile idea of the instantaneous camera', 'but the result of the observation of these facts on an individual temperament'.[22]

Crackanthorpe's essay raised further questions about the limits of representation, and debated the relationship between a writer's commitment to what its author called 'the jealous worship of truth' and his or her equal commitment to imagination.[23] These issues continued to attract critical comment long after his death, with Ford Madox Ford arguing that 'facts so beset us that the gatherer of facts is relatively of very little value'. What was needed, in the face of the 'complexities of modern life', was 'to be brought really into contact with

[20] *The Times*, 31 August 1871, 4. D. Liddle, 'Anatomy of a "Nine Days" Wonder: Sensational Journalism in the Decade of the Sensation Novel', in A. Maunder and G. Moore, eds., *Victorian Crime, Madness and Sensation* (Aldershot: Ashgate, 2004), 90.

[21] H. Crackanthorpe, 'Reticence in Literature' (1894), in N. Denny, ed., *The Yellow Book: A Selection* (London: The Bodley Head, 1949), 103, 95–6.

[22] W. Sickert, 'Modern Realism in Painting', in *Sickert: Paintings*, ed. W. Baron and R. Shone (London: Royal Academy, 1992), 90.

[23] Crackanthorpe, 'Reticence in Literature', 103, 95.

our fellow men', a need that makes the artist evermore important.[24] Gissing too, though briefly entertaining notions of the novel as a vehicle for reformist campaigns, always elevated the role of the novelist above those of the journalist or sociologist, and would never have ranked himself as a mere 'gatherer of facts'. For him, 'the business of art [was] to select, to dispose—under penalties if the result be falsification'.[25] George Moore made a similar point in 1892 when criticizing the painting of Stanhope Forbes. 'Realism, that is to say, the desire to compete with nature, to be nature, is the disease from which art has suffered most in the last twenty years,' he wrote.[26] That same year, Crackanthorpe was the editor of the short-lived *Albemarle Review*, in which the painter Charles Furse maintained that 'it is not the painter's business to record what he sees, but to suggest what he feels'.[27] Clearly, innovative writers and artists were uneasy with mimetic responses to the world; yet, where realist fiction was concerned, such techniques seemed unavoidable.

The relationship between fiction, sociology, and journalism was especially fraught, and saw furious debate in the literary press. Wilde's *The Critic as Artist* (1890) praised the 'odd journalistic realism' of Kipling's short stories—whether 'journalistic' applies to style, content, or both is uncertain—but Edward Garnett censured parts of Somerset Maugham's proposed 'A Lambeth Idyll' for being simply 'clever reporting'.[28] 'The disparity which separates literature from the reporter's transcript is ineradicable,' Crackanthorpe observed in an essay at pains to differentiate between the two.[29] It was widely alleged that what was increasingly termed 'slum fiction' was plagiarized from evangelical or other sources; that it exaggerated the horrors of working-class life; and that it was remorselessly pessimistic and one-sided.[30] In other words, fiction that encouraged its readers to believe in its objectivity was often either little more than fantasy, or violated the canons of art in extending its interest in the

---

[24] F. M. Ford, *The Critical Attitude* (London: Duckworth, 1911), 66.

[25] Gissing, *Charles Dickens: A Critical Study*, 82–3.

[26] G. Moore, 'The Royal Academy Exhibition', *Fortnightly Review* (June 1892), reworked as 'Our Academicians', in his *Modern Painting* (London: Walter Scott, 1893), 116–17.

[27] *Impressionists in England: The Critical Reception*, ed. K. Flint (London: Routledge, 1984), 112.

[28] O. Wilde, *The Critic as Artist* from *Intentions* (1891), in *Complete Works* (London: HarperCollins, 1994), 1151. The dialogue was first published in two parts as 'The True Function and Value of Criticism', in *The Nineteenth Century*, July and September 1890. Edward Garnett's reader's report for T. Fisher Unwin on 'A Lambeth Idyll', eventually published as *Liza of Lambeth*, in A. Curtis and J. Whitehead, eds., *W. Somerset Maugham: The Critical Heritage* (London: Routledge and Kegan Paul, 1987), 22.

[29] Crackanthorpe, 'Reticence in Literature', 96.

[30] For fuller treatment of this topic, see for example Keating's introduction to Arthur Morrison, *A Child of the Jago* (1896; London: Panther, 1971) and *The Haunted Study: A Social History of the English Novel 1875–1914* (1989; London: Fontana, 1991), esp. 285–329. Peter Miles reprints many of the key documents in the arguments surrounding Morrison's work in his edition of *A Child of the Jago*, 216–52.

unpalatable. '[R]ealism, pursued for its own sake, sinks into incurable nasti-
ness,' remarked the *Academy* when reviewing *Liza of Lambeth* in September
1897.[31] 'The materials for sensational stories lie plentifully in every book of
our notes,' Charles Booth maintained, 'but even if I had the skill to use my
material in this way—that gift of the imagination which is often called "realistic"—I should not wish to use it here.'[32] It seems that Booth regarded realist
fiction and sensationalism as one and the same, although he was prepared to
make an exception of Gissing's *Demos* (1886).[33] The same novel would form
the cornerstone of Mrs Humphry Ward's research for the East End sections
of *Robert Elsmere* (1888), further complicating the relationship between the
authority of the factual and the dramatic appeal of the invented.

By the late 1880s, realist and naturalist writers, terms late-Victorian critics
often used interchangeably, were increasingly aware of the presence of other
modes of depicting the city. To revisit an earlier Darwinian parallel, they faced
various keen competitors, and thus had to adapt to a milieu very different
from that known by an earlier generation of realists. The days when, as Gissing
said of Dickens, one could write 'at enormous length, & with profusion of
detail; . . . tell everything, . . . leave nothing to chance' were drawing to an end,
assuming they had ever existed.[34]

DEALING WITH DICKENS (AND ZOLA)

Those writers whose careers overlapped with that of Dickens, and those who
followed him, had to contend with both London and Dickens's image of it.
The versions of Paris recorded or imagined—the two words become almost
synonymous—by Balzac and Zola added to their difficulties. The French
novelists revealed their city on an epic scale and showed, through the use
of the interconnected chronicle, the complexity of its human relations as
well as its accelerating development and change. Zola applied Balzac's detailed
observation of everyday life to evermore frank subject matter, from alcoholism
in *L'Assommoir* (1877) to the minutiae of sex and commerce in *Nana* (1880).
He had also mapped Paris with remarkable accuracy, making his settings an

[31] Unsigned review, *Academy* LII, 11 September 1897, 65–6 in *Maugham: The Critical Heritage*, 23.

[32] C. Booth, *Life and Labour of the People in London, Volume I: East London* (London: Williams and Norgate, 1889), 6.

[33] Ibid. 157.

[34] Gissing to Algernon Gissing, 1895, in S. J. James, *Unsettled Accounts: Money and Narrative in the Novels of George Gissing* (London: Anthem, 2003), 50.

integral aspect of his storytelling. Perhaps most startlingly of all, he allied the novelist with the scientist, reformulating the artistic purpose of fiction and, through his gleeful deployment of versions of Darwinian theory, undermining traditional notions of human relationships. Naturalism was, Zola suggested, an insistently modern philosophy beside which older conventions were utterly inadequate for depicting contemporary life.

By working on the epic scale of the chronicle, Balzac and Zola patch-worked together versions of Paris too complex and detailed for a single novel. Dickens had preferred discrete texts to the sequence, but by setting virtually all his fiction in London, he created a 'shadow' city that offered an alternative version of it from the 1780s to the 1860s. It would be too simplistic to describe Gissing's London as Dickens's rewritten by a naturalist, but there was certainly a sense by which the two methods collided in his work. Dickens embodied techniques that Gissing could not entirely prevent himself from inheriting, but Zola offered ideas and theories with which he was keen to experiment. The writers who followed Gissing into the slums during the 1890s inherited from him a mixture of Dickensian plotting and characterization, and a naturalist's understanding of social processes and the relationship between character and environment, though Gissing's pessimism remained uniquely his own, informed by bitter experience and an immersion in classical philosophy. Any process of influence was, of course, far less schematic than this may suggest, not least because of the many debates about the proper role and content of fiction that raged during the final decades of the nineteenth century.

Dickens had been dead for ten years when Gissing published his first novel, *Workers in the Dawn*, but his influence was still strongly felt where the imaginative accommodation of London was concerned. As late as 1888, Henry James was prepared to concede that 'the London of Dickens' is 'still recoverable, still exhaling its queerness', though only in those few days before Christmas when many have left the capital.[35] James was relatively comfortable with the Dickensian legacy since his own fiction was generally distinct from that of the earlier writer, but English authors born between the late 1850s and 1880 were unsure whether to bury or to praise him. Gissing's admiration for his work jostled with an awareness of his limitations and shifts in literary fashion and readership. In Robert Blatchford's *A Bohemian Girl* (1899), 'good old Charlie' is seen as a relic of bygone days: veteran actor Horatio Harkness has, as his dying wish, that *Pickwick* be read to him in his final moments.[36]

---

[35] This was true, at least to a certain extent, since Dickens's son, Charles, had been publishing an annual gazetteer since the late 1870s. See C. Dickens (Jr.), *Dickens's Dictionary of London, 1888: An Unconventional Handbook* (London: Macmillan, 1888); James, 'London', *English Hours*, 33.

[36] R. Blatchford, *A Bohemian Girl and McGinnis* (London: Clarion Newspaper Company, 1899), 160.

'So great a change has come over the theory and practice of fiction in the England of our times that we must needs treat of Dickens as, in many respects, antiquated,' wrote Gissing in 1898, pondering his relationship to the older writer as well as the development of 'new' fiction.[37] Gissing admitted his enjoyment of aspects of Dickens elsewhere in his study, but could not indulge his predecessor's 'humouring', or allow objectivity to be sacrificed to moral purpose. 'He had to make his Cheap-Jack presentable, to disguise anything repellent,' Gissing wrote, arguing that Dickens's idealism led him into 'misrepresentation of social facts'. Dickens had 'a moral purpose', he concluded, 'the one thing above all others scornfully forbidden in our schools of rigid "naturalism"'.[38] Gissing himself had long since abandoned 'rigid naturalism' but he may have had in mind *Liza of Lambeth*'s determined refusal to entertain Dickensian consolations. Moralizing was going out of fashion very quickly where 'progressive' novelists were concerned.

Dickens's major novels had been written at a time when sociology was a relatively new addition to the English lexicon—the *OED* gives a first citation from 1843—and typified by the individualistic, anecdotal, almost 'Dickensian' approach of Henry Mayhew. Gissing, by contrast, was writing alongside a very different breed of investigative journalists, evangelical urban reformers and professional researchers, and his fiction from *Workers in the Dawn* to *The Nether World* nine years later took account of their methods in charting a world of deprivation and despair. The result was an odd fusion of the old and new, since, as Simon James notes, it was in these novels that 'engagement with Dickensian forms of narrative is most strongly felt'.[39] Attitudinally, however, Gissing and the earlier novelist were poles apart. Rather than peddling escapism or the panacea of Providence, Gissing's work insisted that it be read in the context of factual, or quasi-factual, investigations of urban poverty while yet remaining distinct from them in a separate sphere of Art.

Some of these explorations, the penny pamphlet *The Bitter Cry of Outcast London* (1883), for instance, and W. T. Stead's 'The Maiden Tribute of Modern Babylon', had been unafraid to yoke sensationalism to moral outrage. Indeed, both sought in their different ways to incite controversy as the catalyst for social change. More muted offerings had a similarly shocking impact on the reading public. A survey of working-class districts by the Marxist Social Democratic Foundation, serialized in the *Pall Mall Gazette* in 1885, focused attention on the lot of the urban poor, offering the claim that a quarter of Londoners lived in abject poverty and prompting Charles Booth's survey of the city.

---

[37] Gissing, *Charles Dickens*, 63. See too his essay 'Dickens in Memory' (1901). The relationship between Gissing and Dickens is considered at length by J. Goode in *George Gissing: Ideology and Fiction* (London: Vision Press, 1978), 13–40, and S. J. James in *Unsettled Accounts*, 36–62.
[38] Gissing, *Charles Dickens*, 86, 83.   [39] James, *Unsettled Accounts*, 38.

Dickens's humanist optimism and his reluctance to endorse the systematic were far removed from research of this kind, let alone its stark conclusions.[40]

Politically progressive novelists could not ignore the unpleasant aspects of the metropolis, or, crucially, the means by which they were perceived. Gissing would turn a wry eye to questions of social theory in *Our Friend the Charlatan* (1901), but he did not show the same ironic detachment in the 1880s. Dyce Lashmar's suave appropriation of Jean Izoulet's *La Cité moderne* is very different from Gissing's stark diary entry of 1 March 1888, written after the discovery of his estranged wife's body in a Lambeth lodging house. His description of the room suggests the sociological inquiry of one of Booth's home visits:

> It was the first floor back; so small that the bed left little room to move . . . On the door hung a poor miserable dress and a worn out ulster; under the bed was a pair of boots. Linen she had none; the very covering of the bed had gone save one sheet and one blanket. I found a number of pawn tickets, showing that she had pledged these things during last summer,—when it was warm, poor creature! . . .
>
> I drew out the drawers. In one I found a little bit of butter and a crust of bread, most pitiful sight my eyes ever looked upon. There was no other food anywhere.

After a pathetic inventory of the dead woman's possessions, Gissing vows 'Henceforth, I never cease to bear testimony against the accursed social order that brings about things of this kind.'[41] In 1884, he had told his brother that 'I can get savage over social iniquities but . . . my rage at once takes the direction of planning revenge in artistic work.'[42] The 'testimony' or 'revenge' of art was, it seems, more instructive than the methods of sociological analysis. Gissing was knowledgeable about sociology: less than three weeks after viewing his wife's body, he was reading Arnold White's *Problems of a Great City* (1886, rev. 1887). He was, however, sceptical as to its benefits. *Our Friend the Charlatan* pointedly avoids London settings, implying the ways in which its theories are perhaps fatally divorced from their sphere of application. Political solutions to social problems are equally unlikely, since Lashmar is never able to put 'his' ideas into practice, and he finishes the novel trapped in an unsatisfactory marriage, his ambitions of a parliamentary career in ruins.

Gissing's plotting could sometimes slide into melodrama, as for instance when Arthur Golding hurls himself over Niagara Falls at the conclusion of *Workers in the Dawn*, but his fiction was founded on the conscientious and

---

[40] For further discussion of this material, see G. Stedman Jones, *Outcast London* (Oxford: Oxford University Press, 1971), especially ch. 16.

[41] *London and the Life of Literature in Late Victorian England: The Diary of George Gissing*, ed. Coustillas (Hassocks: Harvester Press, 1978), 22–3.

[42] Gissing to Algernon Gissing, 12 June 1884, in *Letters of George Gissing to Members of his Family*, collected and arranged by Algernon and Ellen Gissing (London: Constable, 1927), 138.

unblinking observation of his surroundings. Even his detractors concede that 'what distinguishes his writing is reporting of individual miseries that broad statements about the masses gloss over'.[43] It was inevitable that a melding of this observation with extreme pessimism would make his relations with Dickens, and with the city that formed his subject matter, problematic. As Keating observes, 'The genuineness of [Dickens's] sympathy for the poor and his genius as a humorist were never doubted. What made many late-Victorian writers uneasy about him was his apparent lack of artistic seriousness, especially on the question of realism.'[44] 'Dickens' art was emotionally inclusive,' observes Philip Collins. 'He had a go at everything (often in a single novel).'[45] Dickens's humour and faith in Providence seemed, to Gissing in particular, especially dangerous misrepresentations of the world, and his treatment of unpleasant topics such as prostitution, domestic violence, and alcoholism were too often influenced by his obedience to prevailing standards of taste. The areas of the city, plots, and types that he had not colonized would be eagerly investigated as the century drew to its close.

'A RESTRICTED NUMBER OF NATURAL FACTS': LONDON UNDER THE MICROSCOPE

According to Alan Robinson, 'the salient feature of Victorian London was *mobility*'. Consumer culture brought with it 'unprecedented possibilities of social mobility', a 'seasonally and cyclically fluctuating labour market' and 'unceasing physical mobility', with vast numbers of migrants converging on the capital as the century progressed.[46] A crucial way by which realism responded to the increased pace and fragmentation of city life was to ignore it, or rather, to accept limits upon representation imposed by political, economic, or social circumstances as much as by the imagination of the individual writer. It was the struggle between these pressures and the demands of narrative that Conrad recalled in his 'Author's Note' (1920) to *The Secret Agent* (1907), when noting how Mrs Verloc's story 'had to be disengaged from its obscurity in that immense town'.[47] As middle-class London, or

---

[43] Carey, *The Intellectuals and the Masses*, 115.

[44] P.J. Keating, ed., *Working Class Stories of the 1890s* (London: Routledge and Kegan Paul, 1971), x.

[45] P. Collins, 'Dickens and the City', in W. Sharpe and L. Wallock, eds., *Visions of the Modern City* (Baltimore: Johns Hopkins University Press, 1987), 114.

[46] A. Robinson, *Imagining London, 1770–1900* (Basingstoke: Palgrave, 2004), 45.

[47] J. Conrad, *The Secret Agent: A Simple Tale*, ed. John Lyon (1907; Oxford: Oxford University Press, 2004), 231.

even the upper sections of working-class London became increasingly mobile, and as the metropolis became 'compartmentalized into functionally and socially specialized districts', naturalism in particular homed in on closed environments that denied the possibility of such movement, or at least restricted it as much as possible.[48]

Pondering the unstoppable spread of the city in 1870, Henry Wheatley had remarked that 'a complete account of its history is more than one man can successfully grapple with . . . it is only by dividing it into parts, and describing each part separately in detail, that justice can be done to the subject as a whole.'[49] Naturalism has been criticized for its pessimistic response to urban deprivation, and the tacit acceptance that the poor have no hope beyond stoical endurance of their misery. In many respects, however, naturalism's subject matter was an inevitable consequence of its means of narrative organization. To focus on a single street or district was a literary strategy, allowing the metropolis to be managed and controlled by the novelist even though such management and control of the actual city was impossible. Since the streets most easily 'enclosed' were those of poorer districts, the life within them became the primary ingredient of the fiction they inspired. Frederick Rolfe's *Hadrian VII* (1904), for example, opens with an extraordinarily detailed account of George Rose's shabby London room, down to the description of each of the pictures he has pinned to 'a large sheet of brown packing paper' tacked to the wall above the fireplace.[50] Only in a room he rarely leaves, the description implies, can Rose properly exert his influence on his surroundings. It is telling that, when the struggling author and failed priest finally becomes Pope, the novel moves to the Vatican for further descriptions of ritual and decoration within a strictly confined space. Rose's influence of course extends far beyond the papal chambers, yet the novel's technique remains that of the cataloguing naturalist, a determined attempt to fix and limit a mutable reality for the purposes of analysis.

Pessimism was therefore both an aesthetic and a political position, in that it recognized how novelistic horizons had contracted from the ambitious social panoramas of *Bleak House* (1852–3) and *The Way We Live Now* (1874–5) to the single microscope slide that is Rose's bed-sitting room. In her 1954 study, *The American City Novel*, Blanche Gelfant proposed a helpful framework for categorizing such changes in urban fiction. Her oldest form, the 'portrait' novel, revealed the city through the activities of a single protagonist. This was succeeded by the 'synoptic' novel, which emphasized the city's own character and the myriad experiences it contained, and what she termed the 'ecological'

[48] Robinson, *Imagining London*, 47.
[49] H. B. Wheatley, *Round about Piccadilly and Pall Mall* (London: Smith, Elder, 1870), ix–x.
[50] F. Rolfe, *Hadrian VII* (1904; London: Picador, 1987), 14.

novel, which focused on 'one small spatial unit such as the neighbourhood or city block and explore[d] in detail the manner of life identified with this place'.[51] As Burton Pike points out, each type provides 'the necessary reduction and simplification by subtly imposing a preliminary ordering on the reader's perception of the word-city', the inevitably metaphorical literary construction that serves as the unrepresentable urban world in novels and poetry.[52] However, where London was concerned, such 'reduction' was far subtler than Gelfant's taxonomy implies. The distinction between portrait and synoptic works is difficult to apply to *Moll Flanders* (1722), let alone *Our Mutual Friend* (1864–5), while the ecological was often embedded within the synoptic, as in the descriptions of Bleeding Heart Yard in *Little Dorrit* (1855–7), a work itself readable in some ways as a portrait novel concerned with the (mis)adventures of Arthur Clennam.

Nonetheless, the idea that a detailed study of an area might offer a solution to the challenge of writing about the modern city is one that appealed strongly to those writers aware of the growing disparity between conventions of fixed narrative perspective and the restless and unstable world that constituted their subject matter. Pondering New York, Henry James was alarmed by the narrative challenge posed by the skyscraper's blurring of story and storey, telling Joseph Pennell, 'difficult, yes; no, impossible; each forty stories, each story forty windows, each window forty people, each person forty tales—my God! Maddening!'[53] London was not yet so lofty, but was even more densely populated. In Arthur Machen's *The Three Impostors* (1895), Edgar Russell, a 'realist and obscure struggler' in the manner of Gissing's Harold Biffen, plans his own version of Balzac's *Comédie Humaine* and Zola's chronicle of the Rougon-Macquart family:

It dawned on me that I would write the history of a street. Every house should form a volume. I fixed upon the street, I saw each house, and read as clearly as in letters the physiology and psychology of each... And yet it was, at the same time, a symbol, a *via dolorosa*, of hopes cherished and disappointed, of years of monotonous existence without content or discontent, of tragedies and obscure sorrows... These were my fancies; but when pen touched paper they shrivelled and vanished away.[54]

Machen's parody is a gentle one. He too had lived a reclusive and penurious existence, tormented by his literary ambitions and aware always of the

[51] B. Gelfant, *The American City Novel* (Norman: University of Oklahoma Press, 1954), 11.

[52] B. Pike, *The Image of the City in Modern Literature* (Princeton: Princeton University Press, 1981), 10.

[53] J. Pennell, 'Adventures of an Illustrator II: In London with Henry James', *The Century Magazine* (February 1922), 549.

[54] A. Machen, *The Three Impostors or The Transmutations*, ed. David Trotter (1895; London: Dent, 1995), 103, 107.

achievements of Dickens and Balzac: the incomprehensible novel produced by Lucian Taylor in *The Hill of Dreams* (1907) owes much to Balzac's 'Le Chef-d'oeuvre inconnu' (1831, 1847). In *The Three Impostors*, Russell is unable to start work on his sequence because he is morbidly sensitive about the limitations of his abilities, but also because there is too great a gulf between them and his models. Until Bennett and Galsworthy began to chronicle the events of the Five Towns and the Forsytes, the Rougon-Macquart novels offered a panorama and ambition no English novelist could match. Trollope's work had become increasingly unfashionable during the 1870s, and Hardy, who was in any case associated with the rural rather than the urban and industrial, would publish his last novel, *Jude the Obscure*, in 1895. Indeed, in the year that Hardy had abandoned novels and Machen had published *The Three Impostors*, Edwin Pugh's *A Street in Suburbia* had been a collection of vignettes rather than anything of Russell's proposed scope. Even Mr Aked's bold recognition of fictional possibility had come to nothing in Arnold Bennett's *A Man from the North* (1898). 'There is more character within a hundred yards of this chair than a hundred Balzacs could analyse in a hundred years,' Aked announces:

How many houses are there in Carteret Street? Say eighty. Eighty theatres of love, hate, greed, tyranny, endeavour; eighty separate dramas always unfolding, intertwining, ending, beginning,—and every drama a tragedy. No comedies, and especially no farces![55]

Aked's vision of narrative plenitude seems almost an anticipation of modern soap opera, but it is one he cannot realize. Zola's composite chronicles were practised instead by Charles Booth and Walter Besant, not in fiction but in studies of individual boroughs and, in Besant's case, dramatic recreations of key moments of London's past. In 1894, he had begun a 'Great Survey' of London, but, as if to illustrate the truth of Wheatley's observation, it remained unfinished at his death in 1901. It is somehow fitting that Besant's life, 1836–1901, should parallel Victoria's reign almost exactly, since one version of Victorianism, typified by a positivist response to the material world, died with him. His failure to complete the survey suggests the seeming impossibility of an individual ever again offering a single, all-encompassing vision of the metropolis.

At the centre of the argument concerning the factual basis of realist art was London's 'East End', a term which had acquired widespread currency by the early 1880s. As a seemingly self-contained metropolis within London, it possessed obvious appeal for writers seeking ways to avoid tackling the city as

[55] E. A. Bennett, *A Man from the North* (London: John Lane / The Bodley Head, 1898), 102–3.

a whole. 'There is no need to say in the East End of what,' wrote Morrison in 1891, for 'The East End is a vast city, as famous in its way as any the hand of man has made.'[56] Long a source of anxiety to politicians and social reformers, the East End was now home to approximately 900,000 people, many of whom were classed as the 'residuum', the 'recalcitrant hard-core of urban unemployed, usually seen as unemployable, feckless, violent and incurably criminal'.[57] This was the 'moral sewage' of *Our Mutual Friend* or Tennyson's 'Locksley Hall Sixty Years After' (1886), where 'City children soak and blacken soul and sense in city slime,' and where 'among the glooming alleys Progress halts on palsied feet | Crime and hunger cast our maidens by the thousand on the street.'[58] 'Invention about 1880 of the term "East End" was rapidly taken up by the new halfpenny press, and in the pulpit and the music hall,' noted *The Nineteenth Century*. The term was, it maintained, a 'concentrated reminder to the public conscience that nothing to be found in the East End should be tolerated in a Christian country'.[59]

The East End was an object of disgust and fascination to those who lived beyond its borders. Commentators were inclined to treat it as a homogenous social unit, even though Booth's research would reveal considerable variations in income and moral attitudes. The evangelist 'General' William Booth depicted it as a realm of heathen savagery where the city's waste products festered in a monstrous cesspool. 'Darkest England, like Darkest Africa, reeks with malaria,' he claimed, 'The foul and fetid breath of our slums is almost as poisonous as that of the African swamp.'[60] 'All the anxieties about the city in general then became attached to the East End in particular,' Peter Ackroyd writes, discussing the aftermath of the Ripper murders, 'as if in some peculiar sense, it had become a microcosm of London's own dark life.'[61]

With such a reputation, the East End attracted a profusion of researchers, reformers, and reporters. By the late 1880s, pamphlets and the press were

---

[56] A. Morrison, 'A Street' (1891), *Tales of Mean Streets* (1894; Woodbridge: Boydell Press, 1983), 19.

[57] W. Greenslade, *Degeneration, Culture and the Novel 1880–1940* (Cambridge: Cambridge University Press, 1994), 48. The *OED* suggests the term was first used by John Bright in 1867. Booth's *East London* recorded a total population of 908,959, of whom only 1.2% could be adjudged to belong to the residuum. Walter Besant, however, glibly put the overall population at 'Two millions of people, or thereabouts' in *All Sorts and Conditions of Men* (1882; Oxford: Oxford University Press, 1997), 28.

[58] C. Dickens, *Our Mutual Friend*, ed. A. Poole (1865; London: Penguin, 1997), 30; Alfred, Lord Tennyson, *A Selected Edition*, ed. C. Ricks (London: Longman, 1989), 649.

[59] *The Nineteenth Century* 24 (1888), 262, in Fishman, *East End 1888*, 1.

[60] W. Booth, Preface to *In Darkest London and the Way Out* (London: International Headquarters of the Salvation Army, 1890).

[61] P. Ackroyd, *London: The Biography* (London: Chatto and Windus, 2000), 678.

revealing its horrors in graphic detail, and what Philip Larkin would later call 'bridal London' could no longer 'bow the other way'.[62] Social explorers, evangelical campaigners, sociologists, and artistic and photographic records such as Gustave Doré's images of 'London Charity', John Thomson's *Street Life in London* (1877), and Luke Fildes's *Applicants for Admission to a Casual Ward* (1874) had dramatized such material and also made it 'the done thing among the liberal intelligentsia to inspect the poor'.[63] Less charitably inclined tourists and sensation seekers preferred to reduce poverty to a spectator sport. 'It used to be the fashion for visitors to London', wrote Robert Machray in 1902, 'to form a party to make a tour of the East End on Saturday evening.'[64] Blanchard Jerrold headed for Whitechapel in the early 1870s dressed in 'rough clothes' and accompanied by a policeman and 'two or three companions who will not flinch even before the humours and horrors of [Limehouse's] Tiger Bay'.[65] Arthur Symons and his friend Frank Willard 'used to wander about London every night in the East End, and about the Docks, and in all the more squalid parts of the city'.[66] West End observed East End with 'the inevitable blend of prurience, fear, conscience, breast-beating and voyeuristic slumming'.[67] It also appealed to novelists, perhaps because it was one area of Victorian London to which Dickens had not devoted substantial attention.[68] 'I expect you to take me into the slums—into very bad places,' the Princess tells Hyacinth Robinson in *The Princess Casamassima*, her face 'lighted up' by 'the idea of misery'. The Princess considers such places to be 'real London', but while the textual slum insistently proclaimed its roots in real-life counterparts, only the most naïve reader would have expected realist fiction to offer anything beyond an approximation of actual locations and behaviour.[69]

The literary representation of the East End was first studied in the context of the literary representation of the working class, the impact of naturalism, and the relationship of literature to late-Victorian socialism and civic reform. More recent criticism, from William Greenslade's *Degeneration, Culture and the Novel* (1994) to Angelique Richardson's *Love and Eugenics*

[62] P. Larkin, 'Deceptions', *The Less Deceived* (London: The Marvell Press, 1955).
[63] Jerrold and Doré, *London: A Pilgrimage*. See especially 179–91, and Doré's oil painting, 'An East End Poor House' (*c.* 1870). R. Porter, *London: A Social History* (1994; London: Penguin, 2000), 334.
[64] R. Machray, *The Night Side of London* (London: John Macqueen, 1902), 45.
[65] Jerrold and Doré, *London: A Pilgrimage*, 142.
[66] A. Symons, *London: A Book of Aspects* (1909) in *Cities and Sea-Coasts and Islands* (London: W. Collins, 1918), 189.
[67] Porter, *London: A Social History*, 334.
[68] See Keating, *The Working Classes in Victorian Fiction*, 121–2.
[69] H. James, *The Princess Casamassima*, ed. D. Brewer (1886; London: Penguin, 1987), 253, 201, 411.

in the Late Nineteenth Century (2003), has investigated the proliferation of discourses of degeneration and eugenics, or, like Joseph McLaughlin in *Writing the Urban Jungle* (2000), explored how the polarization of East End and West End, together with images of the jungle and the savage, reveals late-Victorian concerns with reverse colonization.[70] Influential feminist readings of the city by Judith Walkinowitz and Deborah Nord have shown how middle-class women in particular became 'social actors' in *fin de siècle* London, engaging in aspects of metropolitan life that would have been unthinkable, or at least unrecordable, earlier in the century. Novelists who set fiction in deprived areas of the city are now invariably studied in the light of these ideas, or subsumed within general discussions of late-Victorian literature.

I argue instead that by choosing to work within a deliberately restricted geographical area, writers such as Gissing, Morrison, and Maugham were not simply applying sociological methods to post-Dickensian city novels or reflecting contemporary political anxiety. They were also seeking means by which realism could pursue its aim of minute delineation of the external world at a time when that world was increasingly chaotic and unmanageable and when realism's own position as its chronicler was notably uncertain. Their work was therefore both radical, in that it attempted to infuse English fiction with startling ideas from France and the new science of sociology, and conservative, in that it deployed the circumscribed horizons of the seemingly self-contained slum as a metaphor for its own fictional practice. Besides, there was no reason why observations made about the part should not occasionally stand for the whole. 'This street... is hundreds of miles long,' observed Morrison in 1894, terming the East End a place of 'sordid uniformity'. 'The city is, for the most part, an endless series of replicas,—similar streets, similar people: crowded existence, drifting through the choked and narrow ways,' wrote Gissing ten years later.[71] Even here, however, Dickensian echoes can be heard, since the blank monotony of London recalls the unchanging industrial housing of Coketown, where streets and days are indistinguishable from one another.[72]

---

[70] See, for instance, J. L. Kijinski, 'Ethnography in the East End: Native Customs and Colonial Solutions in *A Child of the Jago*', *English Literature in Transition 1880–1920*, 37(4) (1994), 490–501; C. Bloom, 'West is East: Nayland Smith's Sinophobia and Sax Rohmer's Bank Balance', in his *Cult Fiction: Popular Reading and Pulp Theory* (Basingstoke: Macmillan, 1996), 178–91.

[71] Morrison, *Tales of Mean Streets*, 28; Coustillas, 'Gissing's Variations on Urban and Rural Life', *Victorian Writers and the City*, 139. Gissing is commenting on G. W. Steevens's *Glimpses of Three Nations* (1901), 'a book swarming with figures and statistics' that, he says, passes before his eyes 'like a tale of little meaning'.

[72] Dickens, *Hard Times*, ed. Kate Flint (1854; London: Penguin, 1995), 28.

SLUMMING IT

Even before some of the most notable (or infamous) slum fiction appeared, Wilde was already critical of 'the prison-house of realism' and 'that great and daily increasing school of novelists for whom the sun always rises in the East-End', writers 'who find life crude and leave it raw'.[73] Israel Zangwill's *The Big Bow Mystery* (1891) challenged the assumptions of those writers, telling readers of '*The Pell-Mell Press*', obviously the *Pall Mall Gazette*:

You seem to have imbibed the idea that the East-end is a kind of Golgotha, and this despite that the books out of which you probably got it are carefully labelled 'Fiction'. Lamb says somewhere that we think of the 'Dark Ages' as literally without sunlight, and so I fancy people like you, dear, think of the East-end as a mixture of mire, misery, and murder.[74]

Despite this rebuttal, the alliterative trinity lodged deep in the popular consciousness, supplanting the realities of East End life with a persistent emphasis on squalor and violence. Critics tended to ignore the careful label of fiction in judging novels by their presumed fidelity to actual conditions. This response prompted questions about the sources of their own knowledge of social deprivation and demonstrated the accuracy of Wilde's gibe, 'The nineteenth century dislike of Realism is the rage of Caliban seeing his own face in a glass.'[75] H. D. Traill's 'The New Realism', which appeared in the *Fortnightly Review* in January 1897, went so far as to accuse Arthur Morrison of distorting the East End to such an extent that his characters were no more 'realistic' than Swift's Houyhnhnms. The *Spectator* had made a similar observation in reviewing *Tales of Mean Streets* in March 1895. 'By all means let us abate the evils of London life,' it had argued, 'but do not let us delude ourselves into imagining that half London is inhabited by a race of Yahoos.'[76] It seemed that London's literary critics were as concerned with the accurate representation of the East End as reformers were with its salvation.

As Wilde had suggested, slum fiction was invariably associated with the East End, but its specificity was economic rather than purely topographic. Writers explored both sides of the Thames and ventured south-west into

---

[73] Wilde, *The Decay of Lying: An Observation*, in *Complete Works*, 1081, 1074–5.

[74] I. Zangwill, *The Big Bow Mystery* in *Three Victorian Detective Novels*, ed. E. F. Bleiler (New York: Dover, 1978), 231.

[75] Wilde, Preface to *The Picture of Dorian Gray*, in *Complete Works*, 17.

[76] 'Tales of Mean Streets', *Spectator*, 74 (9 March 1895), 329, in Morrison, *A Child of the Jago*, 219. Bill the Yahoo, 'a hooligan grown into manhood', later received sustained consideration as the archetypal Cockney in E. Pugh's *The City of the World* (London: Thomas Nelson, 1912), 51–64.

Wandsworth, and south into Lambeth and Camberwell. Gissing's fiction of the 1880s delineates the deprivation of Lambeth, Hoxton, and Islington as well as Clerkenwell. In *How the Poor Live*, George Sims roved around the city from Drury Lane to the East End and beyond. Jack London perhaps overstated the case in *The People of the Abyss* (1903) when remarking that 'Nowhere in the streets of London may one escape the sight of abject poverty, . . . five minutes' walk from almost any point will bring one to a slum,' but even Wilde's sumptuously furnished house in Tite Street, Chelsea, overlooked a far less privileged world.[77] Besides, in the 1840s, Friedrich Engels had observed how 'Close to the splendid houses of the rich' might be found 'the lurking place of the bitterest poverty', rookeries such as St Giles that was 'surrounded by broad, splendid avenues in which the gay world of London idles about'.[78] One hesitates to generalize too much about a coherent 'school' or even movement, since Gissing considered *A Child of the Jago* to be 'poor stuff', Crackanthorpe found himself classed as a decadent, and Edwin Pugh and W. Pett Ridge openly admitted their admiration for Dickens. Nonetheless, novelists such as Gissing during the 1880s and Morrison during the 1890s were undoubtedly interested in the conditions of life in areas that could be detached from the wider city and studied in detail.

Such a method was familiar from French naturalist fiction, the 'troughs of Zolaism' denounced in 'Locksley Hall Sixty Years After', with Moretti noting that 'Zola's Paris novels are mostly confined to very small spaces whose boundaries are crossed only on special occasions . . . or else, at the risk of one's life.'[79] English slum novelists were consequently drawn to districts where the populace rarely ventured beyond its immediate surroundings. Zangwill's *Children of the Ghetto*, which focused on Jewish life in the East End, is a memorable example of this process, in that it at once 'reveals' its world to those outside it while yet subjecting it to geographical and social enclosure. It did, however, differ from the work of Gissing and Morrison in that it was much discussed by London's Jewish immigrants, the very people whose lives its author had dramatized. It is unlikely that many in Clerkenwell's slums expended time or money on *The Nether World*, even if they were able.

Ana Parejo Vadillo has shown how often-neglected women poets such as Rosamund Marriott Watson embraced the opportunities which public transport offered for travel, social intercourse, and artistic stimulus, but it is important to remember that such writers were only a tiny minority of London's

[77] J. London, *The People of the Abyss* (1903; London: Thomas Nelson, n.d.), 18; P. Jullian, *Oscar Wilde* (London: Constable, 1969), 145–6.

[78] F. Engels, *The Condition of the Working Class in England* (1845; Harmondsworth: Penguin, 1987), 71.

[79] Moretti, *Atlas of the European Novel*, 90.

citizens and not over-estimate their influence or their abilities.[80] In deprived environments, poverty restricted urban mobility, or else doomed the walker to a circling of the city that was often as desperate and repetitive as that of the prisoners Gustave Doré drew in Newgate Yard.[81] A Stepney School Board inspector told Beatrice Webb that casual labourers rarely migrated from the district, but in regularly changing their lodgings, 'they are like the circle of the suicides in Dante's *Inferno*; they go round and round within a certain area'.[82] The 'slum saviours' of Margaret Harkness's *In Darkest London* (1889) patrol a familiar beat, visiting the sick, the needy, and the destitute. In *The Nether World*, the depressed John Hewett spends hours wandering the West End at night, perhaps, as the narrator suggests, seeking 'food for his antagonism in observing the characteristics of the world in which he was a stranger' and reversing the usual trend of rich contemplating poor.[83] Walking was a pleasant pastime for those, like Henry James, who chose a leisurely stroll in order to savour 'the ripe round fruit of perambulation', but the roles of *flâneur* and commuter were mutually exclusive. 'I walked a great deal,' James remarks of his life in the 1880s, 'for exercise, for amusement, for acquisition'.[84] Such promenading is a far cry from Kipling's 'The Record of Badalia Herodsfoot' (1890), where the heroine, abandoned by her husband, initially survives by taking in washing, childminding, and 'an occasional sale of flowers'. As Kipling points out, 'This latter trade is one that needs capital, and takes the vendor very far westward' in trekking from 'Gunnison Street, E.' to the Burlington Arcade.[85] Arthur Symons could mourn the death of the *flâneur* in an increasingly mechanized city, but he never lost the crucial element of choice in his movements: if he was late for dinner, he could always catch a hansom. Such luxuries are impossible for those at the bottom of the social pyramid.

The lack of capital and the slow pace of travel on foot forced an intimate connection between the home and the workplace, since one had to be within easy reach of the other if omnibus, cab, or train was prohibitively expensive. *The Bitter Cry of Outcast London* offers a memorable formulation of this idea. 'These wretched people must live somewhere. They must live near the centres where their work lies.' They are unable to afford transport, 'and how, with their poor emaciated, starved bodies, can they be expected—in addition to working twelve hours or more . . . —to walk three or four miles each way to take and

---

[80] A. P. Vadillo, *Women Poets and Urban Aestheticism: Passengers of Modernity* (Basingstoke: Palgrave Macmillan, 2005).

[81] 'Newgate—Exercise Yard', Jerrold and Doré, *London: A Pilgrimage*, illustration to 136.

[82] B. Webb, *Autobiography* (London: Longmans Green, 1926), 299.

[83] Gissing, *The Nether World*, 209.

[84] James, Preface (1909) to *The Princess Casamassima*, 33.

[85] R. Kipling, 'The Record of Badalia Herodsfoot', in *Many Inventions* (1893; London: Macmillan, 1928), 296. The story first appeared in *Harper's Weekly*, 15 and 22 November 1890.

fetch?'[86] Walking freed even the moderately well off, but the poor had either to stay put or accept rootless roaming and the perils of the streets. John Davidson's pose as the 'random itinerant' was founded on being paid by the *Glasgow Herald* for reports of his chance discoveries as he roamed city and suburb, and Symons spent hours seeking out 'impreshuns and sensashuns' as a basis for travel essays and poetry.[87] The hopeless wanderers observed by Jack London as he walked from Commercial Street to the docks via Spitalfields and Whitechapel had no such prospects, and usually far more pressing domestic responsibilities.

Characters in the early fiction of Gissing or the stories of Morrison invariably travel on foot, mapping out a city within the city, trudging through the filth in ruined shoes. In such a world, any use of modern transport is a notable event. It is often associated with revelry and carnival in escapades such as the train ride to the Crystal Palace in *The Nether World*, or the horse-bus outing to Chingford in *Liza of Lambeth*. In Morrison's 'To Bow Bridge' (1894), Saturday night drinkers head west to take advantage of longer licensing hours since 'the week's work is over', 'swarming' onto trams and often getting a free ride when the conductor is overwhelmed by passengers on busy stretches of the route.[88]

Usually, however, modern transport spells danger rather than delight for the impoverished Londoner. Edward Lear, elderly and virtually blind, 'walk[ed] daily in this mucilaginous metropolis . . . horribly exasperated by the quantity of respirators or refrigerators or percolators or perambulators or whatever those vehicles are called that bump your legs with babies' heads'. Lear was also menaced by 'distressing Bycicles [*sic*]' and found that 'the noise and confusion so bewilder me that I have little knowledge of my personal identity left'.[89] Jack London noted how he had to be 'more lively in avoiding vehicles' when disguised as an unemployed stoker, since 'my life had cheapened in direct ratio with my clothes'.[90] Francis Thompson had similar experiences on London's streets as a penniless opium addict, and it is less melodramatic convenience or the wages of sin than grim likelihood that see Bob Hewett hit by a cart at the end of *The Nether World*.[91] The pedestrian economy of impoverished London is dramatically revealed in the finale of George Egerton's 'Gone Under' (1894),

---

[86] Keating, ed., *Into Unknown England*, 105.

[87] J. Davidson, *A Random Itinerary* (London: Elkin Matthews and John Lane, 1894). See too his later poem 'The Aristocrat of the Road' from *Fleet Street and Other Poems* (1909). Symons's sensation-seeking was reported by 'Josiah Flynt' [Frank Willard] in *My Life* (1908). R. Lhombreaud, *Arthur Symons: A Literary Biography* (London: Unicorn Press, 1963), 81.

[88] Morrison, *Tales of Mean Streets*, 59. Even here, 'from nearer parts they walk, or do their best to walk'.

[89] Edward Lear to Chichester Fortescue, 19 May 1880. V. Noakes, *Edward Lear* (1968; London: Ariel Books, 1985), 237.

[90] London, *The People of the Abyss*, 26–7.

[91] See too *Punch*'s cartoon, 'A "Colinderies" Puzzle: Saturday—To find your right 'bus and cross the road safely?', 10 July 1886, 23.

when Edith Grey, dissipated and ill, flees through Soho and loses one of her satin shoes, a final token of her once more successful life. Journalists covering the Ripper murders specialized in deductive, if moralistic, interpretations of detail through their fascination with the pathetic possessions of murder victims, reading a life of dereliction into a few dirty handkerchiefs, brass rings, and clay pipes, as Gissing had done at the bedside of his dead wife. The narrator of 'Gone Under' is equally skilled in these arts, interpreting the abandoned shoe as 'a mute epitome of a tragedy of want' while the doomed Edith disappears into the rainy darkness.[92]

The 'ecological' descriptions of enclosed environments often suggested those found in sociological research, but there was also impatience with specific detail as naturalism recognized its limitations. As we have seen, there was tension between the detailing of Gissing's wife's possessions and the wider sociopolitical context of her ruin, and a similar parallel can be drawn between fictional accounts of individual dwellings and their relation to the wider city. *Workers in the Dawn* opens with the narrator providing a guided tour of Whitecross Street north of 'the dim and quiet regions of Barbican', a self-conscious introduction to a probably unfamiliar world.[93] Although later novels are slightly subtler in their scene setting, Gissing's fiction of the 1880s rarely misses an opportunity to make readers confront areas of the city that they either do not know or would prefer to forget.

In *The Nether World*, Sidney Kirkwood lives in Tysoe Street, Clerkenwell. Gissing's situating of his room is precise, but spiced with generalization and asides:

It is a short street, which, like so many in London, begins reputably and degenerates in its latter half. The cleaner end leads into Wilmington Square, which consists of decently depressing houses, occupied in the main, as the lower windows and front-doors indicate, by watchmakers, working jewellers, and craftsmen of allied pursuits. The open space, grateful in this neighbourhood, is laid out as a garden, with trees, beds, and walks.[94]

The narrator's tone is confident and judgmental, and the close observation of houses and their inhabitants gives the unwelcome suggestion, as so often in slum fiction and social exploration literature, of a visit to the zoo. Walter Besant expressed his delight at the East End's 'wonderful collection of human creatures': Wilmington Square even has names on its cages in the form of inscribed brass plates on the doors.[95] The use of detail provides an apparently

[92] G. Egerton, *Discords* (London: John Lane, 1894), 113–14.
[93] Gissing, *Workers in the Dawn*, ed. P. Coustillas (1880; Hassocks: Harvester, 1985), 3.
[94] Gissing, *The Nether World*, 50.
[95] W. Besant, *The Autobiography of Sir Walter Besant* (London: Hutchinson, 1902), 244.

authentic basis for subsequent analysis, but the narrator, like the shabby genteel Gissing himself, is keen to stress his separateness from any squalor or even dignified labour. What William Morris might have applauded as a community of craftsmen is tainted with notions of the 'decently depressing', perhaps showing how Gissing's regard for Morris had ebbed since the portrayal of Westlake in *Demos*.

However, Gissing at least considers Tysoe Street worthy of description as well as assessment. Later in the novel, Pennyloaf Candy returns to her home in Shooter's Gardens, running 'into the jaws of that black horror with the indifference of habit'. The narrator is first icily sarcastic, labelling the place 'a picturesque locality which demolition and rebuilding have of late transformed'. He then moved on to 'a blind offshoot' of the Gardens known as 'The Court'. By 1889, Gissing's study of social degradation had made him increasingly sensitive to seemingly minute divisions of status and respectability within the working class. The subdivision of the Gardens is just one means by which Gissing refines social classification and in order to stress how notions of hierarchy endure even at the apparent bottom of the social heap.[96] The Court receives impatient and despairing dismissal:

Needless to burden description with further detail; the slum was like any other slum; filth, rottenness, evil odours, possessed these dens of superfluous mankind and made them gruesome to the peering imagination. The inhabitants felt nothing of the sort; a room in Shooter's Gardens was the only kind of home that most of them knew or desired.[97]

Gissing's account of The Court is ripe with prejudice and distancing devices which sit awkwardly with the bleak compassion displayed elsewhere in the novel. Adjectives are evocative but imprecise, as Gissing finds himself adjudicating unsuccessfully between the claims of fidelity to detail and his own recoiling from the scene. Denying his description the anchoring specificity usually considered essential to realist writing, Gissing forces his reader either to plunder their own experience, or to take refuge in the textual slums recorded or conjured by his contemporaries.

The 'peering imagination' is of particular interest here, since it seemingly includes both the novelist's faculty of invention and the notion of 'reproductive' imagination, which according to the *OED* forms 'images or concepts of external objects not present to the senses' and delineates their relation to 'each other or to the subject'. At the same time, the phrase

---

[96] See, for instance, David Trotter's discussion of the preparation and consumption of food in the novel in *Cooking with Mud: The Idea of Mess in Nineteenth-Century Art and Fiction* (Oxford: Oxford University Press, 2000), 249–57.

[97] Gissing, *The Nether World*, 74.

licenses the invasion of individual lives by the probing eye of the explorer. Henry James would formulate similar ideas as the 'penetrating imagination', although writing at two decades' remove from Gissing, he was careful to claim no knowledge beyond the superficial, and sought only to convey 'our not knowing, . . . society's not knowing, but only guessing and suspecting and trying to ignore' anything 'beneath the vast smug surface'.[98] In some respects, the 'peering imagination' is a practical demonstration of the arguments Crackanthorpe would advance in *The Yellow Book* five years later, but his essay presumes a conscious, Flaubertian control over the writer's material. For all the determination with which Gissing distances himself from Clerkenwell, his knowledge of it puts him in such close proximity that the lines between observation, recollection, and invention are no longer precise. Perhaps the categories themselves are of only limited use or meaning, something Gissing may have felt in moving from the 'ecological' *Nether World* to more complex 'synoptic' techniques in later fiction. The relationship between character and environment remains of crucial importance, but as characters become increasingly mobile, first in the capital and then, in novels such as *The Whirlpool* (1897), on the European mainland, 'the meaning of London is to be found not only in specific landscapes, but in a condition of contemporary life, shaped by forces which drove forward nation and empire.'[99]

Arthur Morrison managed to defend the authentic nature of his knowledge while yet decrying realist art and concealing his class origins. His 'Jago' was certainly vivid enough to alarm reviewers, but for all that Morrison may have been indebted to lived experience rather than his notebook, he nonetheless made crucial alterations to his material. In his treatment of it, the Jago was as much a fictional space as it was the genuine 'Shoreditch parish of 8,000 people, with a death rate four times that of the rest of London' and 'a record of criminality which none could surpass or even equal'.[100] Hardy's Wessex novels had demonstrated how the slight misalignment of reality and imaginative construction permitted the novelist to be 'realistic' while allowing artistic invention to be untrammelled by actuality. Morrison boldly transplanted this technique to East London, making the Old Nichol, the notoriously criminal quarter of Bethnal Green, a world in which fictional structures had their basis in personal experience. In the General Preface to the *Wessex Edition* of his novels (1912), Hardy pondered the thankless labour involved in authenticating minor details, insisting that he had corrected 'tricks of memory' and resisted the temptation to exaggerate in preserving 'a fairly true

[98] James, Preface to *The Princess Casamassima*, 48.
[99] W. Greenslade, introduction to G. Gissing, *The Whirlpool* (1897; London: Dent, 1997), xvii.
[100] The Revd. A. Osborne Jay, *A Story of Shoreditch* (1896), 5, in Fishman, *East End 1888*, 7.

record of a vanishing life'. Morrison was equally aware of the need for accuracy and equally unwilling to be hidebound by it. 'Fairly true' was, in essence, more true than the narrow detail of sociological surveys. Like Hardy, he prefaced his novel with a map of his fictive terrain, with 'Honey Lane', for example, being a version of Bethnal Green's 'Mead Street' that took from it those elements most suited to fiction without being its direct transcription.[101] He also exploited an element of historical distance, in that he referred to an area in the process of demolition as Gissing had done in *The Nether World*. It seemed that realism was prepared to employ temporal as well as geographical limits to its delineation, while also denying comparisons between the textual and the real that would have exposed the novel's compromises. In setting fiction in a world that no longer existed, something Dickens had done in novels from *Barnaby Rudge* (1841) to *Great Expectations* (1860–1), Morrison was able to evade the question of whether it had ever truly existed in the first place.

Whether those unfamiliar with East London were aware of the subtleties of the shift from the Old Nichol to a fictionalized Jago is a moot point, since Morrison made none of Hardy's more obvious gestures towards the invented nature of his material.[102] Provincial readers in particular may have seen the novel's 'realism' as far less problematic than the capital's reviewers, especially when Morrison was seemingly at pains to reproduce language and customs so carefully, allowing for inevitable toning-down of language and sexual behaviour. Alternatively, Zangwill's careful label of fiction may have encouraged the Jago to be read in the context of earlier imaginative renderings of the metropolis. The obvious influence of Dickens's Fagin lingered in Morrison's fence, Aaron Weech, a similar corrupter of youth who speaks 'amiably to boys, looking sharply into their eyes'.[103] Through such connections, the crooks' real-life counterparts become less significant than the textual relationship between *A Child of the Jago* and *Oliver Twist* (1837–9), a point noted by several contemporary reviewers of the book. This allows Morrison to inhabit the Dickensian version of London familiar to his readers while at the same time protesting his own integrity and profiting from the increased frankness permissible in fiction of the 1890s.

As Keating notes, 'It was Morrison more than any other author who had picked up the new sociological objectivity and applied it to fiction,' adopting a

[101] T. Harper Smith mapped the Jago onto the Old Nichol and revealed the telling gap between the two in 'Re-Readings 2: The Jago', *East London Papers*, 2(1) (1959), 39–47.

[102] Hardy was as much indebted to personal experience and newspaper reports as any slum novelist, but his settings were often more obviously historical than Morrison's, who would not write fiction of this type until *Cunning Murrell* (1900), set during the years of the Crimean War. For Hardy's use of newspaper and documentary material, see *Thomas Hardy's 'Facts' Notebook*, ed. W. Greenslade (Aldershot: Ashgate, 2004).

[103] Morrison, *A Child of the Jago*, 37.

viewpoint at once 'distanced and familiar' and 'a descriptive method that might have come straight from Booth's notebooks'.[104] Morrison and his supporters responded to charges of exaggeration by protesting their accurate and detailed knowledge of the area, with Morrison telling the *Spectator* that he never needed 'the help of a note-book' since his knowledge was derived from lived experience rather than mere observation.[105] Besides, as Henry James had argued in rebuking Besant, where note-taking was concerned, the writer 'cannot possibly take too many, he cannot possibly take enough'.[106] Yet, although Morrison insisted on the accuracy of his material, he denied that he was a realist. In the detailed preface to the third edition of *A Child of the Jago* in 1897, the novelist maintained that the term 'realism' was nothing more than the label of 'the schoolmen and the sophisters'. 'Realist', Morrison wrote, was a term used 'with no unanimity of intent, and with a loose, inapprehensive application': he, by contrast, was a 'man with the courage of his own vision' who 'interprets what he sees in fresh terms, and gives to things a new reality and an immediate presence'.[107] Such words echoed Gissing's wish 'that the words realism and realist might never again be used' since where novelists were concerned 'they never had a satisfactory meaning and are now become mere slang'.[108]

The Old Nichol was popularly known as the Jago, but by blurring the distinction between an actual place and his rendering of it, Morrison once again showed how naturalist fiction was a set of literary techniques rather than an uncomplicated mimetic response to external reality. Such observations are critical commonplaces nowadays, but they are important in showing how self-aware 'realists' could be during the 1890s. Tellingly, in defending his position, Morrison drew explicit parallels with art rather than literature, arguing that should one's work last twenty years, it becomes 'a classic' and transcends other categorizations. For Morrison, realism is as much temporally as generically or technically determined. 'Constable was called a realist; so was Corot. Who calls these painters realists now?', he asked, before extending his argument to Japanese art.[109] The latter was a particular interest of Morrison's, and one on

---

[104] Keating, *The Haunted Study*, 307.

[105] Somerset Maugham, by contrast, kept detailed notebooks while writing *Liza of Lambeth*. See his 1896 recording of 'Cockney', *A Writer's Notebook* (London: Heinemann, 1949), 16.

[106] H. James, 'The Art of Fiction', in *The House of Fiction: Essays on the Novel*, ed. Leon Edel (London: Rupert Hart-Davis, 1957), 33. James would later maintain that note-taking was 'the ineluctable consequence of one's greatest inward energy: to take them was as natural as to look, to think, to feel, to recognise, to remember, as to perform any act of understanding'. Preface to *The Princess Casamassima*, 47. This rather suggests that it is the use that Besant makes of his notes to which James objects.

[107] Morrison, *A Child of the Jago*, 3–4. Preface to the third edn, February 1897.

[108] Gissing, 'The Place of Realism in Fiction', *The Humanitarian* 7 (July 1895), in J. and C. Korg, eds., *George Gissing on Fiction* (London: Enitharmon Press, 1978), 82.

[109] Morrison, *A Child of the Jago*, 3–4.

which he became an acknowledged authority. However, to use it as a touchstone in a preface to a novel was to venture into Whistlerian or aesthetic territory, and to identify, by implication, with the subjectivity of such views. Here, as in Crackanthorpe's deployment of Pater, a naturalist writer forges unexpected allegiances, and engages in practices replete with contradiction. The result is work at once 'authentic' and 'imaginative', 'realist' yet anti-realist. Surely aware of the irreconcilable nature of these competing claims, Morrison increasingly moved away from the type of fiction that had made him briefly notorious, and had largely abandoned literature by the outbreak of the First World War.

Morrison's preface was both a proclamation of observational authenticity of his knowledge and a defence of the right of his imagination to deal with such knowledge as it saw fit. Its conclusions were something of a cleft stick for the realist writer, since 'imaginative' realism seemed a contradiction in terms, but realism without imagination was all but unreadable. In *New Grub Street*, Harold Biffen's magnum opus, 'Mr. Bailey, Grocer', seeks 'absolute realism in the sphere of the ignobly decent', portraying in minute detail 'something unutterably tedious', but his determinedly objective and muted novel meets with public indifference and critical ridicule.[110] Not wishing to produce a 'Mr. Bailey', Morrison pursued a similar argument to Crackanthorpe, arguing for the novelist's autonomy in the treatment of his subject, but neither writer wholly succeeded in balancing the seemingly competing pressures of art and life. *The Nether World* demonstrated the problem all too clearly in combining a novelistic response to an actual setting and forcing the reader to respond to a skewed perception of the city by denying them any alternative to it. 'What terrible barracks, those Farringdon Road Buildings!', Gissing wrote. 'Pass by at night, and strain imagination to picture the weltering mass of human weariness, of bestiality, of unmerited dolour, of hopeless hope, of crushed surrender, tumbled together within those forbidding walls.'[111] One wonders how many of the novel's readers took him at his word, or could argue the contrary from the basis of their own observation.

As Zangwill and others pointed out, poverty did not always equal depravity and barbarism, although countering this view could lead to equal misrepresentation of deprived areas. Walter Besant's *All Sorts and Conditions of Men* (1882) was tellingly subtitled 'An Impossible Story', though it did lead eventually to the establishment of the People's Palace.[112] His later novel, *Children of Gibeon* (1886), offered a sympathetic, if occasionally melodramatic account

---

[110] Gissing, *New Grub Street*, ed. J. Goode (Oxford: Oxford University Press, 1993), 144–5.

[111] Gissing, *The Nether World*, 274.

[112] The tangled story of the Palace, a project that involved Morrison as well as Besant, is unravelled by D. E. B. Weiner's essay, 'The People's Palace: An Image for East London

of Hoxton: the parish doctor of Harkness's *In Darkest London* is firmly critical of Besant's 'pretty stories about the East End'.[113] Tellingly, both his novels appeared before the Ripper's crimes plunged popular understandings of the East End into the darkness once more. Zangwill's own fiction, such as *Children of the Ghetto*, displayed a Biffen-like concern with the 'ignoble decency' of Stepney's working-class Jews, while Harkness's novels invigorated their realism with socialist politics and sympathetic portrayals of practical evangelical work. Even Booth's *East London* was keen to distinguish between the industrious and resourceful urban poor who suffered through no clear fault of their own, and those delinquents who 'degrade whatever they touch' and are 'perhaps incapable of improvement'.[114]

Despite the diversity of responses to East End life during the 1880s and 1890s, the image of destitution and violence was easily the most influential on readers with little first-hand knowledge of districts such as Whitechapel. Stereotypical assumptions about origin and behaviour abounded in London's media. 'A shabby man from Paddington, St Marylebone or Battersea might pass muster as one of the respectable poor,' noted *The Nineteenth Century*. 'But the same man coming from Bethnal Green, Shadwell or Wapping was an "East Ender",' whose appearance encouraged polite society to reach for 'bug powder' and lock up its spoons.[115] In Conrad's *The Nigger of the 'Narcissus'*, Donkin is memorably labelled 'East End trash', while in Stevenson and Osbourne's *The Ebb-Tide* (1894), Huish is 'Whitechapel carrion'.[116] As William Fishman has shown, the content of journalistic narratives undoubtedly played a substantial role in conditioning responses to the poorer quarters of the city at the end of the nineteenth century.[117] I would add to this that their form also had considerable implications for its fiction. The journalist's report, seemingly self-contained and ultimately disposable, has clear affinities with the detective's 'case' and the sociologist's 'case study'. Each implies a narrative derived from objective factual observation, a systematic process of inquiry, and, in some respects, a clear connection between cause and effect. This is not to say that a policeman's

in the 1880s', in D. Feldman and G. Stedman Jones, eds., *Metropolis London: Histories and Representations since 1800* (London: Routledge, 1989), 40–55.

[113] M. Harkness, *In Darkest London* (Cambridge: Black Apollo Press, 2003), 154. First published as *Captain Lobe: A Story of the Salvation Army* by 'John Law' (London: Hodder and Stoughton, 1889).

[114] *Charles Booth's London*, ed. A. Fried and R. Elman (1969; Harmondsworth: Pelican, 1971), 56.

[115] *The Nineteenth Century*, 24 (1888), 262, in Fishman, *East End 1888*, 1.

[116] J. Conrad, *The Nigger of the 'Narcissus'* (1897; Harmondsworth: Penguin, 1977), 47. R. L. Stevenson and L. Osbourne, *The Ebb-Tide*, ed. D. Daiches (1894; London: Dent, 1993), 113.

[117] Fishman, *East End 1888*, 1–24.

search for a motive is akin to Booth's survey of want, but to suggest that both promise resolution or explanation from purportedly analytical methods. In the popular imagination, each 'covers' a story to its finish, implying the possibility of its seamless closure. 'There are eight million stories in the naked city,' concluded the 1948 film *The Naked City* in what could be an updating of *A Man from the North.* 'This has been one of them.'[118]

In the London of the late 1880s, however, the comforting fiction that stories had neat conclusions seemed increasingly untenable, at least among literary radicals. Obedience to it smacked of custom and compromise rather than objectivity, although it could reap impressive commercial rewards. Newspaper reports may have appeared self-contained, but their genuine contents sprawled outside the neat rules of type and column and defied the most determined editor. A major criminal investigation may have been granted sustained attention, but less absorbing events received only transient coverage. The sociologist could document the forlorn details of individual existence at a particular moment, yet such details were ultimately secondary to grander schemes. Social science, like Nature, was careless of the single life, and the files of the Metropolitan Police were filled with unsolved cases long before the failure to capture Jack the Ripper brought with it sustained criticism and humiliation.

TELLING TALES

In such a context, fiction's traditional endings of death and marriage seemed the anachronistic bondage of the lending library ridiculed by the treatment of Miss Prism's novel in *The Importance of Being Earnest* (1895), but rebellion against such orthodoxy was commercially risky. Even those such as George Moore and Thomas Hardy, who made trenchant objections to what amounted to library censorship, were primarily concerned with its implications for subject matter rather than novelistic form. Gissing, however, did go a little further in declaring in 1895 that his mode of realism represented 'nothing more than artistic sincerity in the portrayal of contemporary life'. His stance refused to countenance the popular view that 'disagreeable facts must always be kept out of sight, the human nature must be systematically flattered, that the book must have a "plot", that the story must end on a cheerful note'.[119] Although

---

[118] *The Naked City* (d. Marvin Wald, Albert Maltz, Universal, 1948). As Leslie Halliwell notes, 'The narrator's last words became a cliché' (*Halliwell's Film Guide*, ed. J. Walker (London: HarperCollins, 2001), 569).
[119] Gissing, 'The Place of Realism in Fiction', 84.

the frank subject matter of naturalist fiction attracted criticism, its formal properties seem equally contentious, since the concern with an apparently totalizing and objective 'realism' invariably throws into relief the means by which fictional narratives are shaped. 'Novels have ceased to revolve around a plot,' says Harkness's narrator in *In Darkest London*, yet such developments did not meet with commercial endorsement, for, as Gissing observed, 'Nothing [is] so abhorred by the multitude as a lack of finality in stories, a vagueness of conclusion which gives them the trouble of forming surmises.'[120] 'Experience is never limited and never complete,' wrote Henry James in 'The Art of Fiction' (1884).[121] Though their fiction was very different, Gissing and James shared a distaste for neat contrivance at the expense of artistic truth.

In crude terms, the events on either side of a fictional excerpt, the world before the story begins, and the continuation of events after its formal closure, presented a particular problem for naturalists. Their response was to seek to cordon off districts, streets, houses, and even lives in order to study them in detail. Naturalism's fascination with the workings of the laboratory meant that it frequently operated within a confined space, conducting its experiments with volatile human elements in such locales as the house or shop. This central premise underlay fiction as diverse as *Thérèse Raquin* (1867) and *À rebours* (1884), finishing with the conclusion of the experiment: the deaths of Thérèse and Laurent, and Des Esseintes's return to Parisian society. However, when such experiments were conducted within a community, such as Morrison's Jago or Vere Street in *Liza of Lambeth*, they were much harder to control or demarcate. Their conclusions could only be obvious if predetermined by either moral or formal considerations, one reason why both books end in the death of their protagonists even though they were single-volume novels written after the collapse of Mudie's. Newspapers could defer or avoid ending their stories, but few publishers would gamble on fiction that played by such rules, although some short stories, Morrison's 'To Bow Bridge' for example, exploited the possibility of the inconclusive 'sketch', itself a journalistic tradition derived from ideas of atmosphere and 'local colour'. The result was a tying off of loose ends which, while it was an established tradition in nineteenth-century fiction, looked especially artificial in the context of a quasi-objective naturalist text.

However detailed and accurate its observation of London's poor, fiction was still forced to compromise by concluding in conventional ways. Gissing would challenge this in novels such as *New Grub Street*, which offered endings that were structurally rather than emotionally satisfying, and he applauded the death of the three-decker system, but in the 1880s he continued to shuffle

---

[120] Harkness, *In Darkest London,* 105; Gissing, *Charles Dickens,* 93.
[121] James, 'The Art of Fiction', 31.

an increasingly dog-eared pack. The final page of *The Nether World* lapses into rhetoric in its final pondering of Sidney and Jane bringing 'some comfort to hearts less courageous than their own':

Where they abode it was not all dark. Sorrow certainly awaited them, perchance defeat in even the humble aims which they had set themselves; but at least their lives would remain a protest against those brute forces of society which fill with wreck the abysses of the nether world.[122]

Here Gissing offers a fusion of sonorous archaism and unfocused social criticism, tradition dictating that he offer the expected plagal cadence rather than the provocative dissonance heard elsewhere in the novel. However, even this is not a neat resolution of the characters' emotional struggles, for, as Simon James persuasively argues, Gissing, unlike Dickens, will not allow the creation of 'a narrative (en)closure perfect enough to exclude an outside world' of Darwinian struggle.[123]

Finally, and crucially, naturalism was limited by what it did not, and indeed, could not, say. In a discussion of *The Bitter Cry of Outcast London*, Carol Bernstein argues that even in a non-fictional text, language 'can only be a form of displacement', frequently drifting from the details of observation to metaphor, allegory, and other figurative effects.[124] This approach, founded on a post-structuralist recognition of the fundamental inadequacy of language as an instrument of representation, is, however, homogenizing, since, should one accept its premises, all texts are ultimately displacements of reality. The insight is hardly specific to an evangelical pamphlet or late-Victorian realist anxieties about the representation of the city. Judith Walkowitz's influential *City of Dreadful Delight* adopts a different approach in citing Rosemary Jackson's discussion of fantasy when considering how the Ripper killings and their coverage in the press oddly resemble the 'literature of the fantastic'. Their incorporation of 'the narrative themes and motifs of modern fantasy—social inversion, morbid psychological states, acts of violation and transgression, and a descent into the social underworld' meant that the whole affair 'gave utterance to "all that is not said, all that is unsayable through realism"'.[125]

I argue instead that realist fiction, at least that which appeared following accounts of the Ripper killings, *had* proved itself capable of incorporating all

---

[122] Gissing, *The Nether World*, 392.   [123] James, *Unsettled Accounts*, 41.

[124] C. L. Bernstein, *The Celebration of Scandal: Toward the Sublime in Victorian Urban Fiction* (University Park: Pennsylvania State University Press, 1991), 19.

[125] Walkowitz, *City of Dreadful Delight*, 196, quoting R. Jackson, *Fantasy: The Literature of Subversion* (London: Methuen, 1981), 26. Jackson uses 'realistic forms' rather than a monolithic 'realism', but the point remains.

of these ingredients, since most of them can be found in *The Nether World*, for example. Realism was outflanked here not so much by fantasy, which had always represented an alternative or complement to it, as ironically, by the resolutely quotidian. The detail reported by sociologists and journalists of everything from the living conditions of the Lambeth poor to the violence inflicted on the female body by the Whitechapel murderer created a realm that was less fantastic than hideously 'real'. It provided material that could not be depicted in fiction and it supported its arguments with statistical data and a plethora of eyewitness accounts that no realist text could match without capsizing its narrative. David Trotter has argued that naturalism became 'notorious' for its use of 'surgical' and 'pornographic' detail, but even here it could not compete with contemporary discourses and took refuge in other forms of disclosure.[126] The result was that what realist art could not say was being said elsewhere, and being read by a greater number of readers than would have been likely forty or fifty years earlier. When Jane Findlater criticized *Liza of Lambeth* on the grounds that '[w]e are spared nothing: the reek of the streets; the effluvia of unwashed humanity', she was only partially correct.[127] Even Maugham left some gaps, and readers may well have been surprised by Liza's coy admission, towards the end of the novel, that 'I think I'm in the family way.'[128]

So, on the one hand, naturalist fictions sought to bring to bear modern scientific techniques on a world that had been largely ignored by novelists since the 'Newgate novel' controversy of the late 1830s. They lined up alongside sociology, journalism, and parliamentary and municipal investigation in portraying an environment unfamiliar to many in the provinces and wider world and which many more prosperous Londoners preferred either to ignore or to pity from a safe distance. Each of these various forms insisted on its accuracy. In their preface to *Street Life in London*, John Thomson and Adolphe Smith had acknowledged that some might accuse them of 'either underrating or exaggerating' the material that they examined, a criticism they hoped to pre-empt by using 'the precision of photography' as part of their depiction of the poor. It was, they maintained, 'testimony' of 'unquestionable accuracy'.[129] Booth had also invoked photographic parallels, attempting, he claimed, 'to produce an instantaneous picture, fixing the facts on my negative as they appear at a given moment' but asking 'the imagination of my readers [to] add the movement, the constant changes, the whirl and turmoil of life'.[130] The

---

[126] Trotter, *Cooking With Mud*, 232.   [127] J. Findlater in *A Child of the Jago*, 243.

[128] W. S. Maugham, *Liza of Lambeth* (1897; London: Pan, 1978), 103.

[129] J. Thomson and A. Smith, *Street Life in London* (London: Sampson Low, Marston, Searle and Rivington, 1877), 1.

[130] Booth, *East London*, 26.

idea that the researcher articulated a factual skeleton which the reader clothed with imaginative flesh asked readers to treat sociology as if it were fiction, and stressed the interaction between empirically verifiable reality and subjective responses to it. Smith and Thomson naively asserted the unimpeachable objectivity of photography's negotiated moments; Booth used the notion of photographic development and the collaboration of author and reader to produce an interpretative composite. In their differing ways, each had claimed a verifiable and objective representation of the external world, one which realist fiction, notably by Morrison and, indeed, Clarence Rook, whose *The Hooligan Nights* (1899) purported to be 'neither a novel, nor in any sense a work of imagination', also attempted to sustain.[131]

On the other hand, however, the limitations of realism were becoming evermore apparent, both in the narrative conventions preferred by libraries, publishers, and, indeed, readers, and in relation to the bustling, dynamic, and complexly fragmented city it sought to chronicle. Even detail itself, so crucial to the realist enterprise, was, while shocking to readers and reviewers, far less graphic than the illustrated stories of murder and rapine that filled the *Illustrated Police News,* or the accounts of life among the poor found in the pages of Charles and William Booth. Life is 'all inclusion and confusion', wrote Henry James, whereas art is 'all discrimination and selection'.[132] By 1891, Ibsen was using the set of *Hedda Gabler* as a means of attacking the suffocating claustrophobia of bourgeois life, but less exalted playwrights regarded staging primarily as a means of establishing a recognizable facsimile of the exterior world. Inclusiveness encouraged the astonishingly cluttered stage of George Sims's play *The Lights O' London* (1881), where, in what was 'considered the last word in realism', the Borough Market in Southwark was re-enacted on stage.[133] For all that James proposed a neat distinction between art and life, others sought to narrow the gap between the two while yet realizing that however detailed one's set, much remained unsaid or unsayable.

What might be termed 'empiricist' London was therefore a highly contested textual arena, in which realism and naturalism were as much concerned with 'fact' and objectivity as any more obviously 'modern' art. Whichever way realism approached the representation of the city, it was hemmed in by limitations. How then did it deal with the most visible obstacle to verisimilitude, Londoners themselves?

---

[131] C. Rook, *The Hooligan Nights* (1899; Oxford: Oxford University Press, 1979), xxi.

[132] H. James, Preface to *The Spoils of Poynton* (1908; New York: Augustus M. Kelley, 1976), v.

[133] M. R. Booth, Introduction to *The Lights O' London and other Victorian Plays* (Oxford: Oxford University Press, 1995), xxiii.

'O WOT 'ORRID LANGWIDGE': TALKING
TO THE COCKNEYS

As George Bernard Shaw's *Pygmalion* (1914) demonstrates, London's varying accents carry all manner of political significance. Just as Sherlock Holmes can distinguish the typeface of any British newspaper, so Shaw's Higgins, the Professor of Phonetics, can pronounce 130 'distinct vowel sounds', mapping the city, even the country as a whole, by its enunciation.[134] 'The speech of the folk stimulates observations,' wrote W. Pett Ridge in 1923, 'it provides a clue that would otherwise be absent; it furnishes a welcome riot of individuality.'[135] In the best traditions of social investigation, Higgins is an indefatigable collector and keen to embrace the possibilities of new technology. He records examples of different accents on a wax cylinder phonograph and collects speech from individual streets, rather as Charles Booth had made the individual dwelling the basis of his surveys. The play's preface displays Shaw's political position and his idiosyncratic interest in the language of the day, arguing that 'West End shop assistants and domestic servants are bi-lingual'.[136] It is the notion of 'bi-lingualism' that is so important for the naturalist depiction of Londoners.

Gareth Stedman Jones has alerted us to the ways in which the late nineteenth century began the fabrication of an enduring tradition and stereotype of the 'cockney'. It is one that assumes an indivisible association between cockneys and 'low-life slang or cant', and that 'an equation can be made between this speech and a putative cluster of attitudes'. Theatrical, music hall, journalistic, and literary discourses that fed in turn from earlier writings by Pierce Egan, Dickens, Mayhew, and E. J. Milliken, whose 'Arry appeared in *Punch* between 1877 and 1897, coalesced at last in the coster songs of Albert Chevalier and other performers.[137] The music hall represented an intersection of 'polite, bohemian and popular culture' in which acts fashioned an all-purpose 'cockney' from several distinct strains of accent, dialect, and behaviour.[138] This cockney was also quite different from the language and character of genuine members

---

[134] G. B. Shaw, *Pygmalion: A Romance in Five Acts* (1914; London: Penguin, 1983), 34.

[135] W. Pett Ridge, *A Story Teller: Forty Years in London* (London: Hodder and Stoughton, 1923), 78.

[136] Shaw, 'Preface: A Professor of Phonetics', *Pygmalion*, 9.

[137] G. Stedman Jones, 'The "Cockney" and the Nation, 1780–1988', in Feldman and Stedman Jones, eds., *Metropolis London: Histories and Representations since 1800*, 280, 278; P. Marks, 'Tipping Mr. Punch "the Haffable Wink": E. J. Milliken's Cockney Verse Letters', in J. A. Wagner-Lawlor, ed., *The Victorian Comic Spirit: New Perspectives* (Aldershot: Ashgate, 1999), 67–90.

[138] Stedman Jones, 'The "Cockney" and the Nation, 1780–1988', 300.

of London's working class, whose engagement with the stereotype was both selective and critical. Music hall songs, and their wider influence on literature, mapped the fictive onto the real in ways akin to those in which Morrison treated the Old Nichol. It is also notable that while Shaw's experience of West End consumerism had suggested that some members of the London working class could switch from dialect to a version of standard English, the same ability is rarely shown in fiction. Instead, the bi-lingualism emerges in the differing languages of characters and narrators, with the working-class characters marooned on an island of glottal stops and slang. In 1890, the seventy-fifth edition of that repository of popular knowledge and prejudice, *Enquire Within Upon Everything*, went so far as to assume that many Londoners would 'desire to correct the defects of their utterance' and prescribed a series of verbal exercises, along with a taxonomy of common cockney mannerisms culled from the 'very able schoolmaster . . . the loquacious Mr. *Punch*'.[139]

However misleading the literary image of the slum-dwelling cockney may have been, writers from Dickens to Pett Ridge and Edwin Pugh were prepared to use versions of it in order to allow dialect speakers to express a full range of human emotion. Rather than simply replaying in modern guise the division of class and genre typified in Elizabethan drama by the division of blank verse and prose, some late-Victorian literature challenged the association of cockney with low comedy or crime in granting dignity to the underprivileged dialect speaker. Other writers, however, insisted on a neat divide between the middle class and their presumed inferiors. The working-class roughs of E. W. Hornung's 'Gentlemen and Players' from *The Amateur Cracksman* (1899) and H. G. Wells's 'The Hammerpond Park Burglary' (1894), for example, are clearly demarcated as comic characters, even if, in Wells's story, their criminal intrigue is ultimately successful.

Hornung's A. J. Raffles is distinguished not only by his Oxford education, his criminal daring, and his skill on the cricket field, but also by his ability to conceal his class status through alterations of voice and appearance. Discarding his favoured Sullivan cigarettes for rough shag and his silk hat for the rags of 'a dilapidated tramp', Raffles boasts that, in order to protect himself from blackmail when dealing with fences, 'I drive all my bargains in the tongue and raiment of Shoreditch.'[140] His ability to shed or acquire the trappings of class in order to enter other social realms, the basis of *Pygmalion*, is also a favoured tactic of the social explorer, dating back to James Greenwood's *A Night in a Workhouse* (1866). In *The Picture of Dorian Gray* (1891), Dorian

[139] Anon., *Enquire Within Upon Everything 1890* (1890; Moretonhampstead: Old House Books, 2003), 66–7.

[140] E. W. Hornung, 'A Costume Piece', from *The Amateur Cracksman* (1899). *The Collected Raffles* (London: Dent, 1985), 27, 29.

frequents 'a little ill-famed tavern near the Docks', employing both an alias and a disguise, and later visits an opium den 'dressed commonly', though he makes no attempt to disguise his speech.[141] These double lives show how, in the space of thirty years, the techniques of the social investigator had become assimilated by popular entertainment. From *The People of the Abyss* to George Orwell's *Down and Out in Paris and London* (1933), to the work of female investigators documented by Deborah Nord and the more general consideration of the woman's relationship with the city articulated by Elizabeth Wilson, the problematic freedoms of disguise have received sustained critical analysis which will not be reprised here.[142] My focus is instead on the ways in which naturalism used bi-lingualism in the representation of London's poorer quarters, and the problematic implications of this procedure.

The 1890s saw several influential advocates of what Ezra Pound later dismissed as 'cawkney woices'.[143] As Stedman Jones suggests, music hall entertainers such as Chevalier had a significant effect on the representation of London life. Arthur Symons likened his 'uncompromising realism' to 'one of Mr Zola's "human documents"', while the *Morning Leader* saw him as akin to Kipling in that he took 'the common clay of Whitechapel' and fashioned it 'into real works of art'.[144] As these comments suggest, the performer was read in terms of literary models rather than social realities. It is difficult to imagine that Chevalier's act could be regarded as 'uncompromising', if only because of its extraordinary popularity. The relationship between the 'art' of the halls and the wider world is further complicated by fictional characters performing actual music hall songs: the references to 'Knocked 'em in the Old Kent Road' in *Liza of Lambeth*, for example, or the 'happy harlot' who hums 'Ta-ra-ra-boom-de-ay' in Davidson's 'A Ballad of the Exodus from Houndsditch' (1894).[145] Music hall stereotypes may also have influenced some of those who wrote to the press and police purporting to be Jack the Ripper, in that certain turns of phrase and humour imbued the murderer with an exuberantly cockney persona. This swaggered into middle-class homes

---

[141] Wilde, *The Picture of Dorian Gray*, in *Complete Works*, 98, 133.

[142] D. E. Nord, *Walking the Victorian Streets: Women, Representation and the City* (London: Cornell University Press, 1995), 207–36; E. Wilson, *The Sphinx in the City: Urban Life, the Control of Disorder, and Women* (London: Virago, 1991).

[143] Pound used the expression in a critical account of T. S. Eliot's *Murder in the Cathedral* in January 1936. P. Ackroyd, *T. S. Eliot* (London: Abacus, 1985), 119. For a detailed discussion of the debates surrounding the evolution and recording of cockney dialect(s), see Keating, *The Working Classes in Victorian Fiction*, 246–68.

[144] A. Chevalier, *A Record by Himself* (1895) in Stedman Jones, 'The "Cockney" and the Nation', 296–7.

[145] J. Davidson, 'A Ballad of the Exodus from Houndsditch', in *The Poems of John Davidson*, i. 74.

via newspaper coverage, causing all the shock and alarm of Eliza Doolittle's perfectly enunciated 'Not bloody likely'.[146]

More significant where literature was concerned was Rudyard Kipling, who had pioneered short slum fiction in 'The Record of Badalia Herodsfoot' and, even more influentially, was prepared to introduce London dialects into serious poetry. 'Mr Kipling is a genius who drops his aspirates,' drawls Gilbert in *The Critic as Artist*, pondering the immense success of *Plain Tales from the Hills* (1888) and the poems later collected in *Barrack Room Ballads* (1892).[147] These put Milliken's 'Arry into khaki, offering the 'cunning demotic populism' recognized by Isobel Armstrong.[148] As she suggests, Kipling's celebration of the 'resilience of the common soldier in colonial service' was very different from the political critique articulated in similar vernacular and rhythm by John Davidson's 'Thirty Bob a Week' (1894). Neither writer ventures into the slums in his verse, though Davidson's harassed 'Suburbean' clerk is well aware how he treads a 'string across a gulf' with millstones about his neck.[149]

Yet despite Kipling's huge commercial success, the poet with the keenest interest in London speech during the 1890s was possibly W. E. Henley. Henley was an avid collector of slang, compiling a vast dictionary of it with J. S. Farmer, and wrote a series of sonnets, *London Types* (1898), that act as a poetic field guide to London's citizens. However, while Kipling attempted to let his soldiers to speak in apparently unmediated ways, allowing for the euphemistic substitution of taboo adjectives, Henley instead used a technique familiar from slum fiction, in that the working-class speaker's words were embedded within a larger frame of comment and judgement. Slang terms were italicized, contrasting typographically as well as accentually with the standard English that surrounded them, a mixing of registers that led one review to remark that 'When slang intrudes into serious poetry, the result is lamentable.'[150] The most notable example is the sixth poem of the sequence, ''Liza', which begins:

> 'Liza's *old man*'s perhaps a little *shady*,
> 'Liza's *old woman*'s prone to *booze* and cringe;
> But 'Liza deems herself *a perfect lady*,
> And proves it in her feathers and her fringe.[151]

---

[146] C. Bloom, ' "The Ripper Writing": A Cream of a Nightmare Dream', in *Cult Fiction: Popular Reading and Cult Theory*, 162; Shaw, *Pygmalion*, 78.

[147] Wilde, *The Critic As Artist*, in *Complete Works*, 1151.

[148] I. Armstrong, *Victorian Poetry: Poetry, Poetics and Politics* (London: Routledge, 1993), 481.

[149] J. Davidson, 'Thirty Bob a Week' from *Ballads and Songs* (1894), *The Poems of John Davidson*, i. 65.

[150] 'Recent Verse', *The Athenaeum*, 21 December 1901, 838.

[151] W. E. Henley, *Poems* (London: Macmillan, 1926), 210.

By using the sonnet as the medium for a case study, Henley manages to demarcate a precise subject for his description. Naturalist fiction had marked out the district, the street, even the single house, but Henley focuses entirely on the individual, though he does perhaps suggest that since she is a 'type', there are plenty more where she came from. The sonnet offers as well an ironic, and demotic, reconsideration of the earlier Pre-Raphaelite vogue for poems on paintings. 'Liza might well have painted by Rossetti in the same way he painted Fanny Cornforth, silencing her 'vulgar' linguistic mannerisms and transforming her instead into the brooding siren of paintings such as *The Blue Bower* (1865), but Henley refuses to romanticize his model. There remains though a strong suggestion that she is drawn not from life but from the pages of Morrison and Somerset Maugham, whose Liza also delights in sensational hats, eye-catching dresses, and 'an enormous fringe, puffed-out and curled and frizzed'.[152]

Henley's sonnet is an audacious experiment that, like the city from which it originates, combines contemporary fashion with enduring tradition. It may disdain aureate diction and fanciful imagery, but it remains a lingering remnant of courtly love poetry in the patronizing recounting of the relationship between 'Liza and her 'bloke' and in a fascination with its subject that is all the more marked for being veiled by class and linguistic distance. The incorporation of Liza's vernacular expressions gives the poem the vitality Henley prized, but because the sonnet is a portrait rather than a monologue, it never allows access to 'Liza's consciousness, preferring convenient categorization to more sympathetic engagement. As William Thesing points out, 'The excitement of Henley's street figures . . . derives in part from the vigour of their own words, but they have little to say.'[153] While James's Millicent Henning is 'a daughter of London . . . the muse of cockneyism', Henley's 'Liza is pinned and mounted like a dead butterfly.[154] The splitting of the poem's linguistic registers also implies unbridgeable social division, and it is as well that 'Liza and her boyfriend seem happy within the circumscribed world of their class, since the poem denies them the opportunity of anything beyond it.

Gissing was markedly sensitive to equations of class and geography, particularly where he himself was concerned. In Chapter 12 of *The Nether World*, 'Io Saturnalia!', he draws arch parallels between the Roman festival and a day trip to the 'Crystal Paliss'. The technique wryly questions notions of human progress, but its classicism is less an ironic distancing mechanism than a desperate plea to the educated reader not to include him among the revellers

[152] Maugham, *Liza of Lambeth*, 8.

[153] W. B. Thesing, *The London Muse: Victorian Poetic Responses to the City* (Athens: University of Georgia Press, 1982), 187.

[154] James, *The Princess Casamassima*, 93.

despite his detailed knowledge of them. By the same token, it is unlikely that Eliza Doolittle knows the legend of Pygmalion and Galatea, allowing Shaw to signal his own distance from those that he describes. A similar device is employed in Chapter 5 of *Liza of Lambeth*, where Maugham's laborious use of pastoral convention leads to 'The Idyll of Corydon and Phyllis'. Liza and Tom share a glass of beer, an everyday recreation Maugham renders as 'Gallantry ordered that the faithful swain and the amorous shepherdess should drink out of one and the same pot.'[155] Each writer uses high culture as a buffer between himself and his presumed inferiors, flaunting his observational skills while at the same time refusing to be seen as associated with those he describes. In his discussion of Baudelaire's translation of Poe's 'The Man of the Crowd', Walter Benjamin observes that the French poet's fascination with crowds was founded upon a fundamentally ambivalent relationship. 'If he succumbed to the force by which he was drawn to them and, as a *flâneur*, was made one of them,' Benjamin writes, 'he was nonetheless unable to rid himself of a sense of their essentially inhuman make-up. He becomes their accomplice even as he dissociates himself from them. He becomes deeply involved with them, only to relegate them to oblivion with a single glance of contempt'.[156] For Gissing and Maugham, the studied allusion, the elitist reference, or the disdainful aside becomes the written equivalent of this 'glance of contempt'. However, while Baudelaire 'cautiously admits' to the ambivalence of his relationship to the crowd in poems such as 'Le Crépuscule du soir', the English writers must demonstrate their distance from those they describe. 'Keep apart, keep apart, and preserve one's soul alive,' Gissing wrote in 1885, after learning that William Morris had been arrested for assault at a political demonstration. As Phil Cohen has argued in a slightly different context, such moments suggest the growing difficulty faced by writers who attempted to preserve a dualistic division between the self and the city. The observer could no longer remain distinct from the phenomena he sought to observe, though he could struggle against absorption by erecting a bulwark of personal or intellectual references.[157]

Other writers used these cultural and linguistic divides as the basis for more sympathetic depictions of working-class life. In Richard Whiteing's *No. 5 John Street* (1899), the narrator ponders by 'how little' a dying girl is separated from her social betters: 'the Cockney aspirate, the Cockney vowel, a tendency to eat jam with a knife'.[158] Peter Keating notes how Kipling's determination 'to learn

[155] Maugham, *Liza of Lambeth*, 34.

[156] W. Benjamin, 'On Some Motifs in Baudelaire', *Illuminations*, trans. H. Zohn (London: Fontana, 1992), 168.

[157] P. Cohen, 'Dual Cities, Third Spaces and the Urban Uncanny', in G. Bridge and S. Watson, eds., *A Companion to the City* (Oxford: Blackwell, 2003), 316–30.

[158] R. Whiteing, *No. 5 John Street* (London: Grant Richards, 1899), 291.

how to speak for the inarticulate working man . . . without imposing upon him attitudes and values alien to his natural [*sic*] way of his life' influenced later writers in encouraging them to reject upper and middle-class characters and deploy 'elaborate phonetics' to 'capture the actual sound of London working-class voices'.[159] The result is an inevitable opening up of fault-lines of class and language, a process that is put to widely varied uses.

In 'The Record of Badalia Herodsfoot', the contrast between Badalia's cockney speech and the more refined tones of the Reverend Eustace Hanna makes a telling point about the unbridgeable social chasm that prevents Badalia's longings for the clergyman from ever achieving their object. Morrison exploits this divide for satirical effect in *A Child of the Jago*, when his omniscient narrator employs his most ponderous polysyllables in ridiculing the 'radiant abstractions' of the 'East End Mission and Pansophical Institute', a caricature of Toynbee Hall.[160] In Hubert Crackanthorpe's story 'Dissolving View' (1893), the unsettling effects of linguistic division expose the hypocrisy of the wealthy Vivian Marston, who sits in his luxurious flat on a foul November evening 'complacently pitying' the 'wretches' outside. Marston has received a letter from his erstwhile mistress, a chorus-girl named Kit Gilston, announcing that she is dangerously ill and that he is the father of her child, and he goes to pay her off, only to find that both she and the baby are dead. After a moment's pause, he returns home to a hearty breakfast, pleased to conclude a sordid chapter of his life. A month later, he marries his rich fiancée.

Kit's pathetic letter to Marston prompts a display of his financial muscle, in that he plans to give her 'a large sum of money, the loss of which he would not feel' so that she will leave London. What Marston sees as 'mis-spelt scrawlings' on 'cheap, shiny half-sheets of note-paper' reveals a distance even greater than that between Badalia and Hanna, although the letter displays only Kit's limited education, not her speaking voice:

Dear Viv,
      i am very ill the Dr says i shall get better but it is not true. i have got a little boy he was born last tusday you are his farther so you will see to him when I am ded will you not dear Viv . . . . Viv dear for the sake of old times com and see me gest once it is not a grand place were i am but I do long to see your dear face again.[161]

The events of the story are familiar ones in some respects, with Viv's wretched epistle an updating of the letter from Mrs Loveit to Dorimant in Etherege's London comedy *The Man of Mode* (1676). However, while Etherege

---

[159] Keating, ed., *Working Class Stories of the 1890s*, xi.

[160] Morrison, *A Child of the Jago*, 19.

[161] I. Fletcher, ed., *British Poetry and Prose 1870–1905* (Oxford: Oxford University Press, 1987), 391.

expected his audience to side with the charismatic young rake, Crackanthorpe's allegiances seem quite the reverse. When he goes to Kit's lodgings, Marston hears from the landlady a tale of woe that leaves him notably unmoved:

'The baby died along with 'er, . . . She didn't leave a blessed sixpence behind 'er. Two week an a arf rent she owed me, besides 'er food, all sorts of delictasses I used to git for 'er.' Then with a change of tone, perhaps desirous of a gossip, perhaps struck by Vivian's prosperous appearance, 'Jest wait a minute. I'll come up and tell yer all about it.'[162]

Here, the 'change of tone' from 'delictasses' to 'desirous of a gossip' reinforces Marston's distance from the scene and fundamental lack of sympathy for it. Any straightforward critique of class is, however, compromised by the greed and loquacity of the woman, who shows no more loyalty towards Kit than Marston has done. 'Dissolving View' illustrates social hierarchy through the speech of its characters: its narrator seems to adopt Marston's tones for ironic effect. A reading that confines itself to individual characters will dismiss Marston as a callous hypocrite, but a more generalized consideration of the story as a class parable may have disconcerted bourgeois readers of the 1890s, keen to separate Marston's behaviour from their own attitudes towards the poor.

Any late-Victorian fiction with realist pretensions had to grasp the nettle of demotic speech, and accept that the language of the slums in particular could be far from pleasant to middle-class ears. *The Bitter Cry of Outcast London* remarked that 'we have been compelled to tone down everything, and wholly omit what most needs to be known, or the eyes and ears of our readers would have been sufficiently outraged,' the result of which was a 'qualified narration'.[163] Describing the prostitutes of Piccadilly Circus in 1902, Robert Machray wrote:

You look into their faces, and there is a story in every face, if you could but read it. And such stories! Ah, if the stones on which they tread could speak! They can hardly be beautiful stories; they might well be terrible.[164]

Speaking to the women and discovering their stories is not, it seems, possible for a commentator of this type. He offers instead an appeal to interpretation that combines traditional notions of the female as unreadable Other alongside the implication that their stories cannot be told, or rather, that they cannot be read by those who bought *The Night Side of London*. Of course, versions of these stories could be and were read by coroners, journalists, and newspaper readers, and the legal process itself occasionally shone a spotlight on prostitutes' lives,

---

[162] Ibid. 394.   [163] Keating, ed., *Into Unknown England*, 93.
[164] Machray, *The Night Side of London*, 19.

notably in the testimonies of Lou Harvey, Eliza Masters, and Elizabeth May during the trial of the poisoner Thomas Neill Cream in 1892.[165]

The necessarily sexually explicit conversation of prostitutes represented one frontier for Victorian fiction. Swearing represented another. It disgusted Gissing, who termed it 'that vituperative vernacular of the nether world, which has never yet been exhibited by typography and presumably never will be'.[166] Francis Thompson found that London's homeless had 'almost lost the faculty of human speech' and either 'howl and growl like animals' or 'use a tongue which is itself a cancerous disintegration of speech'.[167] Walter Besant saw the behaviour of working-class youths as a cause for particular concern, observing in a *Contemporary Review* essay of 1886 that their conversation 'grows continually viler, until Zola himself would be ashamed to reproduce the talk of these young people'.[168] Despite these concerns, no writer with an interest in 'authenticity' could ignore such utterances. In the early pages of *Liza of Lambeth*, Maugham insists on several occasions that 'it is not possible always to give the exact unexpurgated words . . . the reader is therefore entreated with his thoughts to piece out the necessary imperfections of the dialogue.'[169] Here there is not only the familiar distinction between decorous standard English and Liza's raucous cockney, but also an open recognition of the limitations of the realist project.

Keating has noted how these tactics alerted the reader to a compromise that meant that 'the eyes and ears of the public are not desecrated, and the authors' realism not entirely sacrificed'.[170] I maintain that the reader becomes implicated in the uttering of taboo language, in that these evasions both imply and erase the missing words, magnifying their presence by drawing attention to what is not said, and giving naturalist fiction a means of subverting, albeit temporarily, the linguistic order. Maugham's aims in this respect are quite explicit, and Margaret Harkness's recurrent references to 'the universal adjective' in *In Darkest London* have a similar effect. In *A Child of the Jago*, Kiddo Cook mocks delicate sensibilities and popular stereotypes of foul-mouthed slum dwellers when rebuking his companion's ''orrid lagwidge' in implying that cockney itself is an offence.[171] Shaw would later exploit linguistic

---

[165] A. McLaren, *A Prescription for Murder: The Victorian Serial Killings of Dr. Thomas Neill Cream* (Chicago: University of Chicago Press, 1993), 49–62.

[166] Gissing, *The Nether World*, 158.

[167] Thompson's notebook quoted by John Walsh, *Strange Harp, Strange Symphony: The Life of Francis Thompson* (London: W. H. Allen, 1968), 48.

[168] Besant quoted in Allison Pease, *Modernism, Mass Culture, and the Aesthetics of Obscenity* (Cambridge: Cambridge University Press, 2000), 48.

[169] Maugham, *Liza of Lambeth*, 10.

[170] Keating, *The Working Classes in Victorian Fiction*, 249.

[171] Morrison, *A Child of the Jago*, 12.

propriety for similarly comic effect in *Pygmalion* when, after Eliza has initiated a brief vogue for the use of 'bloody' among her social betters, Mrs Eynsford Hill worries that she will 'never be able to bring myself to use that word'. 'It's not compulsory, you know,' Pickering tells her, 'Youll get on quite well without it.'[172] All these writers are very much aware of the complex social dynamics involving what can be said, where it can be said, and by what means it can be recorded: the laughter of their audience is an act of complicity when exposing the artificiality of stage and novelistic dialogue.

Sometimes, however, gestures towards unrecordable language exposed both literary conventions and the barbarities of their subject matter. At the end of *The Nether World*, Ned Higgs and others squabble over whom has the right to puff a discarded cigar stub:

'I 'ollered fag-end after Snuffy Bill!'
'You're a _____ liar! I did!'
'You! You're a _____ _____ _____ ! I'll _____ your _____ in arf a _____ second!'
Then came the sound of a scuffle, the thud of blows, the wild-beast bellowing of infuriate noises.[173]

Here Gissing again seeks to distinguish between his knowledge of street rituals and his sympathy for them, offering a precisely punctuated report complete with the bestial imagery familiar from elsewhere in the novel. That Higgs and his fellows should be driven to such linguistic extremes over so trivial an incident shows them as irrevocably degenerate and their world as vicious as the hell of Oliphant's 'The Land of Darkness'. However, Gissing has left the reader in little doubt as to the foulness of the nether world in the previous pages, and this final flourish seems an admission of how anything other than 'partial narration' or 'necessary imperfection' is possible in realist fiction of this type. It is little wonder that Henry James counselled that such elements be omitted from literature altogether.

Late-Victorian realist writing was a profoundly compromised art where the rendering of London was concerned. It had contracted in scope, studying ever-smaller settings in ever-greater detail, while at the same time recognizing its limitations in terms of the frankness of its subject matter and the conventions of narrative development and closure. It could, however, still produce animated representations of its milieu, and its technique of careful observation of the everyday remained the basis of much urban writing in the years leading up to the First World War. Empiricist London refused to disappear, and its underlying assumptions are the basis of this study's most conspicuous example of popular success, the Sherlock Holmes stories of Arthur Conan Doyle.

[172] Shaw, *Pygmalion*, 80.   [173] Gissing, *The Nether World*, 338–9.

THE EXACT KNOWLEDGE OF SHERLOCK HOLMES

Social investigators focused on poverty and deprivation, studying people, their clothes, possessions, and homes, should they have had them, in line with ideological or systematic preconceptions. Booth's survey of the London poor divided the city on the basis of income in order to determine an individual household's social position and degree of 'respectability' on economic grounds. Much could be read from small details, as in the case of the couple who are forced to sell a bedstead and burn old boots for fuel in Booth's second volume (1891).[174] Newspapers' fascination with the possessions of murder victims was echoed in the precise inventories taken by arresting officers. In Thomas Holmes's *Pictures and Problems from the London Police Courts* (1900), Kate Henessey, a twenty-four-year-old 'Irish girl of the slum, a mother at fifteen', has been arrested for drink-related offences well over a hundred times, and now has:

men's boots . . . , no hat or bonnet, no jacket or mantle; her arms are bare; her dress, what there is of it, is short; her forehead is low, her broad face is cut and bruised, her eyes are inflamed, and her hair hangs loosely down.[175]

In such readings, the woman is described entirely in negative terms, defined through what she lacks or by how she falls short of respectable norms. We might be reading a passage of Gissing, or indeed an anthropologist's description of a 'specimen', instead of the memoirs of a police court missionary. Even Gothic fiction occasionally fell back on these devices, using them to establish a 'realist' setting which could then be violated to extraordinary effect. Here one might cite Richard Marsh's *The Beetle* (1897), where Robert Holt, refused admission to Hammersmith workhouse, reflects on the ease of his social descent, offering the type of case history familiar from the research of Charles Booth and his contemporaries.[176]

Analysis based upon the reading of external detail underpins an extraordinary range of late-nineteenth-century cultural production from the criminal taxonomies of Lombroso to Mrs Humphry's *Manners for Men* (1897). A proliferation of guides and etiquette books clearly indicates a growing need to find ways of endorsing judging by appearances, since the pace of life and the chaotic aggregations of major cities militated against sustained analysis. It also

---

[174] *Charles Booth's London*, ed. Fried and Elman, 154.

[175] T. Holmes, *Pictures and Problems from the London Police Courts* (London: Thomas Nelson, n.d.), 37.

[176] R. Marsh, *The Beetle* (1897) in *The Penguin Book of Victorian Villainies*, sel. H. and G. Greene (London: Penguin, 1984), 455.

suggests an anxiety about the relation between appearance and reality: if one has the correct analytical system and attends to its methods, the correct conclusions can be reached. 'Every detail points to something, certainly; but generally to the wrong thing,' remarks Chesterton's Basil Grant.[177] Pondering metropolitan life in his essay, 'London', Henry James identified the problem with typical acuity. '[T]he eyes', he writes, are 'solicited at any moment by a thousand different objects.' Reflecting further in the preface to the New York edition of *The Princess Casamassima*, James expressed this as 'a mystic solicitation, the urgent appeal, on the part of everything, to be interpreted, and, so far as may be, reproduced'.[178] The individual who could answer these urgent appeals would be, for James, a certain sophisticated Anglo-American novelist of the early twentieth century, but for the public at large, it would be the detective. '[N]ature is a chaos of unconscious forces, a city is a chaos of conscious ones,' wrote Chesterton. '[T]here is no stone in the street and no brick in the wall that is not actually a deliberate symbol—a message from some man, as if it were a telegram or a post card.'[179] James's 'In the Cage' (1898) had depicted a telegraphist whose 'eye for types amounted nevertheless to genius,' and who possessed 'an instinct of observation and detection', but the most accomplished reader of telegrams and postcards was the eccentric Baker Street sleuth, Sherlock Holmes.[180]

'I should like just to remember the order of the houses here,' Holmes tells Dr Watson in 'The Red Headed League' (1892). 'It is a hobby of mine to have an exact knowledge of London. There is Mortimer's, the tobacconist, the little newspaper shop, the Coburg branch of the City and Suburban Bank, the Vegetarian Restaurant, and McFarlane's carriage-building depot.'[181] By matching the order of the buildings on Saxe Coburg Square with those on the arterial road behind it, Holmes is able to show how 'the line of fine shops and stately business premises' parallels the 'faded and stagnant' square that lies on its other side. It transpires that the bank backs on to a pawnbroker's shop, and that criminals are tunnelling through the cellar walls of the one in order to loot the bullion vault of the other. Holmes sets a trap for the thieves, who are caught red-handed, and the story closes with whiskies and soda at 221b Baker Street. 'You reasoned it out beautifully,' says an awed Watson, 'It is so long a chain, and yet every link rings true.'[182]

---

[177] G. K. Chesterton, 'The Painful Fall of a Great Reputation', *The Club of Queer Trades* (1905; London: Penguin, 1986), 18.
[178] James, *English Hours*, 9; Preface to *The Princess Casamassima*, 33.
[179] G. K. Chesterton, 'A Defence of Detective Stories', in *The Defendant* (London: Johnson, 1902), 160.
[180] H. James, 'In the Cage' (1898; London: Hesperus, 2002), 18.
[181] A. Conan Doyle, *The Penguin Complete Sherlock Holmes* (London: Penguin, 1981), 185.
[182] Ibid. 190.

On one level, Holmes's claim to have an 'exact knowledge of London' is a typically blithe assertion of his superiority to ordinary mortals, a party piece that astonishes and delights his dogged amanuensis and army of devoted readers. On another, however, his hobby constitutes a singularly beguiling and comforting fantasy. In a later story, 'The Empty House' (1905), Watson is impressed by Holmes's 'extraordinary knowledge' of 'the byways of London' during a march 'through a network of mews and stables, the very existence of which I had never known'.[183] This is the 'knowledge' of later taxi-drivers, an ability to remember complex routes and shortcuts based on observation, memory, and practice, and which, while impressive, is far from unique. An 'exact knowledge' of the sprawling, unruly, and atomized metropolis is quite another thing, however, and inconceivable long before 1892.

'The Red Headed League' nonetheless suggests that by memorizing the order of houses on the city's streets, a chain can be forged between apparently discrete events. Its links are both literal, in that the bank and the pawnbroker share a common interior wall, and symbolic in their representation of London's tangled finances, the uncomfortable pairing of need and security. Britain's royal house lends its name to a microcosm of its empire, complete with the startling juxtaposition and uncomfortable proximity of rich and poor. What seems to be a random assemblage of shops and businesses is actually coherent after all, or at least, can be made to seem so through close observation and inspired deduction. Holmes's ability to map the city's surface onto its depths harmonizes and makes coherent two seemingly separate spheres. Subversive, literally 'underground' energies are thwarted, and order is restored.

Holmes solves the case and brings the villainous John Clay to justice, but the story raises intriguing questions about Doyle's configuration of the late Victorian city. The detective understands the link between the pawnshop and the bank, a bricks-and-mortar metaphor for the connection of other narratives. However, although he is famously well informed about felony and intrigue, devouring newspapers and keeping detailed records of crime, he seems to know nothing of the Red Headed League, despite its advertisement having caused an almighty traffic jam in nearby Oxford Street some days before the story opens. Holmes's lack of knowledge may merely be an authorial contrivance on the part of Watson, who enters in the middle of Jabez Wilson's account of his experiences, and thus requires a recapitulation of events. It may, though, suggest that a wider point is being made about 'exact knowledge', its possibility and, most importantly, its extent.

[183] Ibid. 489.

Doyle's confidence was certainly a marked contrast to the scepticism of more 'progressive' writers, as Edmund Gosse and Max Beerbohm suggested in their joint sonnet, 'To Henry James' (1908):

> Your fine eyes, blurred like arc-lamps in a mist,
> Immensely glare, yet glimmerings intervene,
> So that your May-Be and Might-Have-Been
> Leave us still plunging for your general gist.
> How different from Sir Arthur Conan Doyle,
> As clear as water and as smooth as oil . . . [184]

At first sight, Doyle's creation seems far removed from the concerns of slum fiction or sociology. Holmes is wealthy, well connected, and extremely mobile, both geographically and, since he is a master of disguise, socially. Slum dwellers 'booze and cringe', but Holmes relaxes with fine tobacco—he is an authority on different types of ash—music, and, in the early stories at least, his infamous 'seven percent solution' of cocaine. Doyle's contemporaries grappled with the representation of 'outcast London', but Holmes virtually ignored it, sealing vice within 'narrow and defined areas'.[185] As Moretti points out, only one Holmes short story has an East End setting, 'The Man with the Twisted Lip' (1892), and even here the detective ventures into the slums and opium dens of a highly stylized Whitechapel in search of an errant suburban businessman, Neville St Clair.[186] Where realist fiction agonized over the relationship between fact and imagination, or struggled to differentiate itself from newspaper reportage, Holmes has complete faith in analytical intelligence, using newspapers as a resource, and, via their personal columns, a vital means of communication.

However, the difference between the Holmes stories and realist fiction is not as great as it initially seems. In some respects, Doyle is the opposite of Morrison, just as Morrison's determinedly dull Martin Hewitt is the opposite of the flamboyant Holmes, but the opposition is based on the different ends of their methods rather than the methods themselves. Both study an area or incident in detail; both vaunt the accuracy of their knowledge and observations. Doyle, however, remains optimistic in the face of the metropolitan world, rather than compromised by limitations of perspective or language. In fact, he turns these limitations to his advantage to offer a comforting illusion of Holmesian omnipotence that conceals the exceptionally selective nature of

---

[184] M. Beerbohm and E. Gosse, 'To Henry James', *Max in Verse*, ed. J. G. Riewald (London: Heinemann, 1964), 19. The two men wrote alternate lines of the poem—this quotation begins with one of Beerbohm's.

[185] C. Watson, *Snobbery with Violence: English Crime Stories and their Audience* (1971; London: Eyre and Spottiswode, 1987), 24.

[186] Moretti, *Atlas of the European Novel, 1800–1900*, 134. *A Study in Scarlet* and *The Sign of Four* did, however, see Holmes in action in Lambeth and Camberwell.

the detective's response to the English capital and, indeed, Holmes's inability to act as any form of criminal deterrent. Thus, when Watson boasts that Holmes lies 'in the very centre of five millions of people, with his filaments stretched out and running through them, responsive to every little rumour or suspicion of unsolved crime', he equates his friend with universal Providence when Holmes is, in truth, far less committed to justice than the good doctor supposes.[187]

In 'The Adventure of the Red Circle' (1917) Holmes remarks that London is 'surely the most valuable hunting ground that was ever given to a student of the unusual', but his own favoured territory is the West End and the suburbs.[188] 'Fictional crime in the London of wealth; real crime, in the London of poverty,' Moretti concludes.[189] Holmes has no interest in the squalid villainies committed in the Jago, or by the young tearaways of The Hooligan Nights, still less does he wish to ponder the horrors revealed daily in the East London Advertiser. Whatever the human cost of these robberies, rapes, and murders, they hold no intellectual appeal for the detective, and are too close to actual city life to appeal to his readers. For all that Holmes seems to be able to achieve the totalizing vision of the metropolis increasingly abandoned by realist fiction, his version of London remains markedly circumscribed by class, geography, and mental piquancy.

Instead, Holmesian authority is built upon limitation and enclosure: the solving of the individual case, usually in a matter of hours or a few days, and with few thoughts of the consequences. Simon Joyce, for instance, asks how Neville St Clair will be able to maintain his affluent family life once Holmes exposes his activities as a professional beggar, though perhaps it is only just that the consequences of crime fall upon the criminal rather than the detective.[190] Although Holmes is seen in West and suburban London rather than in the East End, and is famously mobile in cab and train, he remains confined in the sense that he pursues one self-enclosed narrative to its conclusion, rather than giving a genuine suggestion of the city as a complex web. Narrative form is his crucial limitation. Slum fiction had continued to contract in scope and length, from the sprawling condition-of-England novel, Workers in the Dawn, to the brief sketches of Tales of Mean Streets and the brisk novella Liza of Lambeth. Similarly, detective fiction had contracted from the textual profusion of Wilkie Collins's The Moonstone (1868) to the short story tailored to magazine publication. It was here that Holmes was most

---

[187] A. Conan Doyle, 'The Resident Patient' (1894), Complete Sherlock Holmes, 423. Conan Doyle reprises this passage in 'The Adventure of the Cardboard Box' (1917).

[188] Ibid. 904.   [189] Moretti, Atlas of the European Novel, 136.

[190] S. Joyce, Capital Offenses: Geographies of Class and Crime in Victorian London (Charlottesville: University of Virginia Press, 2003), 149.

successful: the novellas tend to lose their focus when he is absent; yet unless he is absent they cannot hope to generate suspense or mystery. The individual case or 'adventure' exploits its limitations, with Doyle paring away the types of detail that would impede narrative momentum, one reason why his criminals invariably confess upon exposure rather than seeing what a skilled barrister might do to Holmes, or, more particularly, Watson, in the witness box.[191]

Similarly, the restrictive length of the short story removes the need for lengthy description of scene or atmosphere, since time and again, Watson is able to conjure these with a brief reference to the weather or the time of day. It is Holmes's especial skill to pounce on the crucial, pertinent detail, most famously the dog that does not bark in 'Silver Blaze' (1894), and it is his creator's ability to slice away extraneous material that allows him to do this. Watson's medical background establishes his direct, scientific view of the world, even if he remains an incorrigible romancer in the eyes of the detective. Rather than exposing limitations and admit 'partial narration', Doyle embraces them and makes them a central pillar of his fiction. Holmes is capable of 'exact knowledge', but only once its object has been refined to its essentials.

In 'A Case of Identity' (1892), Holmes offers a cunning analysis of the relationship between his improbable adventures and the life of the city:

'Life is infinitely stranger than anything which the mind of man could invent. We would not dare to conceive the things which are really mere commonplaces of existence. If we could fly out of that window hand in hand, hover over this great city, gently remove the roofs, and peep in at the queer things which are going on, the strange coincidences, the plannings, the cross-purposes, the wonderful chains of events, working through generations, and leading to the most *outré* results, it would make all fiction with its conventionalities and foreseen conclusions most stale and unprofitable.'[192]

Gissing's 'peering imagination' had spied on the poor in the interest of dramatizing, if not necessarily ameliorating, their plight. Holmes's 'peeping', by contrast, is used to support the venerable contention that truth is stranger than fiction. 'One should always be a little improbable,' Wilde counselled in 1894.[193] Doyle, it seems, took him at his word, using fiction to insist that life is more bizarre and surprising than literature could ever be, while at the same time serving up a sequence of extraordinary criminal intrigues. The Holmes stories are consequently able to place realist techniques at the service

---

[191] In 'The Adventure of the Copper Beeches' (1892), Holmes reveals that he has appeared in many 'sensational trials', but that Watson has preferred to recount cases 'which have given room for those faculties of deduction and of logical synthesis which I have made my special province' (*Complete Sherlock Holmes*, 316–17).

[192] Ibid. 190–1.

[193] Wilde, 'Phrases and Philosophies for the Use of the Young' (1894), *Complete Works*, 1245.

of fantasy, so that, for all Holmes's 'exact knowledge', the stories are never imprisoned by objectivity.

STORIES WITHOUT ENDS

In *The Soul of London*, Ford Madox Ford recounts a curious though familiar urban experience. His train into the city has stopped for some unexplained reason, and he gazes out of the window in an attempt to make sense of his surroundings:

I looked down upon the black and tiny yards that were like cells in an electric battery. In one, three children were waving their hands and turning up white faces to the train; in the next, white clothes were drying. A little further on a woman ran suddenly out of a door; she had on a white apron and her sleeves were tucked up. A man followed her hastily, he had red hair, and in his hand a long stick. We moved on, and I have not the least idea whether he were going to thrash her, or whether together they were going to beat a carpet. At any rate, the evening papers reported no murder in Southwark.

Incidents even so definite as these are more or less the exception, but the constant succession of much smaller happenings that one sees, and that one never sees completed, gives to looking out of train windows a touch of pathos and dissatisfaction. It is akin to the sentiment ingrained in humanity of liking the story to have an end.[194]

At such moments, Ford identifies a crucial challenge for London writers, and indeed, for 'modern' artists in general. It was one that literary realism had often been forced to shirk because of the conventions of novelistic closure, even after the collapse of the three-volume system. The generation of writers to whom Ford belonged felt leisurely triple-deckers were unable to capture the dynamic energies of city life, hence, in some ways, their enthusiasm for the single-volume novel, the novella, and the short story.

As Ford recognized, not only does London life move quickly, it often refuses to allow its observer a stable vantage point from which to study or narrate it: the train moves on before events resolve themselves, and he can only speculate as to how they might have been concluded. In a complex Dickens serial such as *Little Dorrit*, readers must trust that the narrative will eventually connect its disparate ingredients into a harmonious whole, with the story and the city ultimately 'making sense' by making explicit their disguised or buried communality. This resolution of order offered the hope that the city was both explicable and meaningful rather than an existential void. Raymond Williams

---

[194] F. M. Ford, *The Soul of London: A Survey of a Modern City*, ed. A. G. Hill (1905; London: Dent, 1995), 42–3.

notes of Dickens that relationships between characters may seem 'unknown and unacknowledged' but ultimately become 'the necessary recognitions and avowals of any human society'.[195] Detective fiction would place these 'recognitions and avowals' at the centre of its ideological project, sewing up tears in the social fabric so neatly that the reader could easily be forgiven the comforting thought that the world was a logical and orderly one.

The world Ford saw from his railway carriage was neither of these things. His experience has much in common with the type of eyewitness statement that initiates a Holmes investigation, filled as it is with details that seem as though they must be significant if only they could be interpreted correctly. However, whereas Holmes might deduce the involvement of the Red Headed League, Ford's response to the scene remains speculative and inconclusive. The deliberate frustration of expectation, the admission of the limits of his own knowledge, provide the incident with 'pathos and dissatisfaction' and signal immediately one reason for the different commercial fortunes of Ford and Conan Doyle. Holmes made his creator a rich man through meeting the human need for 'the story to have an end', specifically, a happy ending of sorts. Indeed, Doyle's stories courted his readers in the very ways Gissing had thought unconscionable in 1895. Ford by contrast asked instead awkward and often unanswerable questions concerning the perception of the metropolis, questions that exposed the imaginative concessions Doyle made to his readers' sensibilities.

The Soul of London managed to steer a course between the objective detail of sociology and the obligations of realist closure by classing itself as a subjective 'survey of a great city'. Clearly, Ford was well aware of the competing claims of realism, journalism, and sociology where the portrayal of London was concerned. His book offers a stylish fusion of modes, from an account of a matchbox maker that would not have surprised Mayhew, let alone Charles Booth, to personal evocations of high-speed travel in cars and trains, to topographic word painting. It represents, as Alan Hill has noted, a clear indication of 'how literary concerns and priorities were changing in the new century', but it did not render realism obsolete or bring about the collapse of the Sherlock Holmes industry.[196] Instead, it showed how the portrayal of London was becoming evermore contested as radical new art forms came to prominence, and how 'traditional' realism was forced to adapt as it faced successive challenges.

Ford's impressionist response to London, hastily scribbled as a series of essays in the autumn and winter of 1902, professed itself sceptical where facts

[195] R. Williams, *The Country and the City* (1973; London: Paladin, 1975), 190–1.
[196] Ford, *The Soul of London*, xix.

were concerned, yet was quite prepared to offer the detailed description chiefly associated with first realist fiction and latterly with sociological case studies. Ford denounced newspapers for killing the art of conversation, but hoped the *Daily Telegraph* or the *London Magazine* would be interested in serializing his book. Finally, he sought to reveal the 'modern city' while accepting his publisher's imposition of a determinedly old-fashioned title. Clearly, the contradictions that troubled critically aware practitioners of realism such as Gissing and Morrison had not disappeared in the new century, and neither were they confined to more established modes of writing. Realism had once promised much, only to see its limitations and constraints become increasingly obvious and constricting. However, as Ford and a number of other writers would discover, impressionist responses to the English capital were to be just as problematic.

2

Shadows and Fog: Impressionist London

Shall I give way,
Copying the impression of the memory,
Though things remembered idly do seem
The work of Fancy?

> William Wordsworth, *The Prelude*, Book VII: Residence in London
> (1805)

'I suppose London is a tremendous place to collect impressions, but a refuge like this, in the country, must be much better for working them up. Does he get many of his impressions in London, do you think?'

> Henry James, 'The Author of *Beltraffio*' (1884)

'THE ALMOST AWFUL CLARITY OF HENRY JAMES'

Max Beerbohm's caricature, 'London in November, and Mr Henry James in London' (*c*.1907) shows the venerable novelist in what amounts almost to silhouette. A tangram swathed in dark grey fog, James has been reduced to his external trappings: a drooping top hat, a black overcoat, a furled umbrella. He might be a businessman, a commuter trying in vain to conjure a hansom from the monochrome wastes about him. Nothing else is visible as James squints through the murk at the hand he holds before his face. Beerbohm's caption reads:

. . . It was, therefore, not without something of a shock that he, in this to him so very congenial atmosphere, now perceived that a vision of the hand which he had, at a venture, held up within an inch or so of his eyes was, with an almost awful clarity being adumbrated . . .

As in his other parodies of James, such as 'The Mote in the Middle Distance' (1912), Beerbohm's skill in imitating the novelist's labyrinthine style moves beyond caricature into the affectionate pastiche Linda Dowling terms his 'accommodative spirit': James was, after all, his friend and a writer he much admired.[1] As a caricaturist, however, Beerbohm also saw his subjects through a distorting lens that magnified their especial traits and absurdities. The image of the elderly James, portly and preoccupied in the fog, offers a comic counterpoint to the famous first page of *Bleak House*, where London sinks again beneath 'implacable November weather' and 'it would not be wonderful to meet a Megalosaurus, forty feet long or so, waddling like an elephantine lizard up Holborn Hill'.[2] The effect is humorous, but as is so often the case with Beerbohm's pictures, it is also a critical comment, an identification and implicit analysis of a recurrent trait or problem. Beerbohm suggests James's ironic affection towards the 'very congenial' capital, his tolerance of its meteorological quirks, and, crucially, his attempts to convey the experience of life within 'the dreadful, delightful city'.[3]

By the time of Beerbohm's drawing, James had been writing about London for thirty years, and was desultorily committed to the major book on the capital he had tentatively yet grandly entitled 'London Town'. He had, however, made no substantial progress beyond a few initial jottings and the purchase of some volumes of the city's history by W. J. Loftie, Edgar Sheppard, and Walter Besant, to which he gave only cursory attention.[4] The project, he told Ford Madox Ford in April 1904, when Ford was revising *The Soul of London*, was 'relegated to a dim futurity', and, although James tinkered with it until 1909, he made little meaningful headway.[5] To see James as almost at one with the fog is therefore to remark upon his close identification with London and its overwhelming imaginative stimulus, but to suggest as well the difficulties of this relationship. 'There is nothing in the world quite like a London fog,' wrote Arthur Symons, 'You breathe black foulness and it enters into you and contaminates you.'[6] Towards the end of his life, James found himself absorbed into and subtly poisoned by the same 'thick brown [November] fog' that settles on Maida Vale in 'In the Cage' (1898), and acts as a 'postponement' of questions and interpretation. A combination of *The Princess Casamassima*'s 'eternal dirty intellectual fog' and the same novel's 'permeating London' had overwhelmed

---

[1] L. Dowling, *Language and Decadence in the Victorian Fin de Siècle* (New Haven: Yale University Press, 1986), 179.

[2] C. Dickens, *Bleak House*, ed. N. Bradbury (1853; London: Penguin, 1996), 13.

[3] H. James, 'London' (1888), in *English Hours* (London: Heinemann, 1905), 8.

[4] John L. Kimmey notes that while there are fourteen volumes by Sir Walter Besant in the James Library at the University of Virginia, none of them are marked, and many pages are uncut. 'The "London Book" ', *Henry James Review*, 1 (1979), 68.

[5] James to Ford, 14 April 1904, in M. Saunders, *Ford Madox Ford: A Dual Life*, Vol. i: *The World before the War* (Oxford: Oxford University Press, 1996), 165.

[6] A. Symons, *London: A Book of Aspects* (1909), in *Cities and Sea-Coasts and Islands* (London: W. Collins, 1918), 212. Henceforth *London*.

him.[7] James's extraordinary intellectual precision is far beyond that of the anonymous telegraphist, or that of Conrad's Assistant Commissioner in *The Secret Agent* (1907), a figure similarly 'suffocated by the blackness of a wet London night, which is composed of soot and drops of water'.[8] Nonetheless, the fog, literal, linguistic, symbolic, and psychological, makes him equally unable to communicate his experiences or explain their meaning.

Fog was a potent symbol of what James called his 'incurable cockneyship', and, as Beerbohm's drawing implies, his almost impenetrable late manner.[9] He was fascinated by 'London partic'lars', noting how the city seemed to have 'its own system of weather and its own optical laws' amid an atmosphere that 'magnifies distances and minimises details', and 'makes everything brown, rich, dim, vague'.[10] Dickens invested fog with symbolic properties; later 'realist' writers had used it for practical demonstrations of the difficulties of urban life or else, in a version of the antipathetic fallacy, to suggest the environment's malign incompatibility with human wishes. *Punch*'s versifier detailed 'The muck and mud that still our movements clog', while Conrad made the same point more sonorously in describing 'the enormity of cold, black, wet, muddy, inhospitable accumulation of bricks, slates, and stones, things in themselves unlovely and unfriendly to man'.[11] In the detective fiction of Arthur Conan Doyle or Richard Harding Davis, fog underlay or encouraged the city's criminal associations, with Sherlock Holmes speculating as to how the 'thief or murderer could roam London' 'as the tiger does the jungle', since figures are but 'dimly seen, then blend once more into the cloud bank'.[12] For Morley Roberts, the fog was even the agent of the capital's destruction in his exuberantly apocalyptic tale 'The Fog', printed in *The Strand* in October 1908. All of these writers placed fog at the service of grander designs, but James's London essays recognized its centrality to the character of the metropolis itself, responding enthusiastically to its transformations of the cityscape and the ways in which it might be perceived by the individual.

Radical artists such as Whistler and Monet were exploring similar possibilities during the 1870s. Such figures moved away from the particularization

---

[7] H. James, 'In the Cage' (1898; London: Hesperus, 2002), 97–8; *The Princess Casamassima*, ed. D. Brewer (1886; London: Penguin, 1987), 281, 480.

[8] J. Conrad, *The Secret Agent: A Simple Tale*, ed. John Lyon (1907; Oxford: Oxford University Press, 2004), 110.

[9] James to Frederick Macmillan, 20 September 1880, *The Correspondence of Henry James and the House of Macmillan, 1877–1914*, ed. R. S. Moore (London: Macmillan, 1993), 53.

[10] James, 'London', *English Hours*, 16.

[11] 'A Rondel of the Fog', *Punch* (4 December 1886), 273; Conrad, *The Secret Agent*, 42.

[12] A. Conan Doyle, 'The Adventure of the Bruce-Partington Plans', *His Last Bow* (1917), *Penguin Complete Sherlock Holmes* (London: Penguin, 1981), 913; R. Harding Davis, *In The Fog* (New York: R. H. Russel, 1901).

of realist art and conventional topographic painting, concerning themselves
with atmospheric evocation. James's immersion, in all senses, in London's fog
was therefore something he shared with its most famous visual chroniclers,
impressionist painters, even though he initially had little obvious sympathy for their art. Discussing Paul Durand-Ruel's Impressionist exhibition in
May 1876, James contrasted the 'laborious' attention to detail he found in
the Pre-Raphaelites with the 'generalizations of expression' typical of contemporary French art. 'The Englishmen, in a word, were pedants, and the
Frenchmen are cynics,' he concluded, dismissing Impressionist painting as
'incompatible . . . with the existence of first-rate talent'.[13]

He was equally unimpressed by Whistler, at least during the late 1870s, but
his contemporaneous descriptions of London suggest that he was rather more
sympathetic towards impressionism in practice than he was when reviewing
exhibitions. His 1877 essay 'London at Midsummer', an account of 'the
little voyage from Westminster Bridge to Greenwich', offers a memorable
description of the fog's effects on the perception of the metropolis:

Few European cities have a finer river than the Thames, but none certainly has
expended more ingenuity in producing an ugly river-front. For miles and miles you
see nothing but the sooty backs of warehouses, or perhaps they are the sooty fronts:
in buildings so very expressionless it is impossible to distinguish. They stand massed
together on the banks of the wide, turbid stream, which is fortunately of too opaque
a quality to reflect the dismal image. A damp-looking, dirty blackness is the universal
tone. The river is almost black, and is covered with black barges; above the black
housetops, from among the far-stretching docks and basins, rises a dusky wilderness
of masts. The little puffing steamer is dingy and gritty—it belches a sable cloud that
keeps you company as you go. In this carboniferous shower your companions, who
belong chiefly, indeed, to the less brilliant classes, assume an harmonious grayness; and
the whole picture, glazed over with the glutinous London mist, becomes a masterly
composition.[14]

The reiterated blackness of this scene is a less obviously symbolic version
of the fogged and muddied panorama that opens *Bleak House*. Also lurking
within the description are Robert Browning's evocative lines, 'There's where
we painters call our harmony! | A common greyness silvers everything,— | All
in a twilight, you and I alike'.[15] Whether or not James saw himself as the
'the faultless painter', the veiled allusion to 'Andrea del Sarto', and perhaps,
through its concern with harmony and greyness, to the work of Whistler, is
an entirely appropriate one. Although James goes on to consider the scene

    [13] H. James, 'Parisian Festivity', *New York Tribune* (13 May 1876), 2.
    [14] H. James, *Portraits of Places* (London: Macmillan, 1883), 219–20. The essay first appeared
in *Lippincott's Magazine* in November 1877, and was lightly revised for *English Hours* in 1905.
    [15] R. Browning, 'Andrea del Sarto (called 'The Faultless Painter')', *Men and Women* (1855).

in an 'intellectual light', the description itself is insistently preoccupied with visual detail, demonstrating how sight is so often the dominant sense in impressionist epistemology and that, as Holbrook Jackson observed, 'thought must take second place to vision'.[16] Despite the profusion of noises and smells James must have observed, the journey is eerily silent, something seen rather than felt. Accounts of London by Dickens, and, even more so, by Gissing, repeatedly emphasized the city's aromas and the tidal roar of its 'flaring and clamorous' streets where 'the odours of burning naphtha and fried fish were pungent on the wind'.[17] To judge from *The Princess Casamassima*, the Thames is equally noisy and smelly, with Hyacinth Robinson observing the 'grinding, puffing, smoking, splashing activity of the turbid flood', but in his own trip down river, James concentrates on the tonal limitations of the scene, its blacks and sables, silvers and greys.[18]

To practise impressionist writing, Arthur Symons maintained, '[t]he first thing is to see, and with an eye which sees all . . . and then to write, from a selecting memory.'[19] This seems both an application of Whistler's 'memory method' to literature and a partial explanation for the insistently visual quality of James's description. It is not that James was consciously following Whistler's instructions, or that he expresses so insistently as Conrad 'the power of the written word . . . to make you *see*' but that keen observation, rather than complete reliance on note-taking, lay at the heart of his evocation of the river.[20] Indeed, despite the low esteem in which he held Whistler's work during the 1870s, his essay is strongly suggestive of Whistler's representation of the Thames, down to the 'harmonious grayness' of James's unindividuated fellow passengers who are the familiar compositional devices of a Whistler painting. It is hardly coincidental that the essay appeared only a few months after the opening of the Grosvenor Gallery in May 1877, where the American's pictures attracted such attention.

Patricia Crick points out in her notes to *The Princess Casamassima* that Londoners burned eight million tons of coal in 1882, but there are additional sources for 'the feeling and smell of the carboniferous London damp' that Hyacinth Robinson so savours in the novel.[21] One of the most significant contributors to metropolitan pollution was the Battersea firm Morgan's

[16] H. Jackson, *The Eighteen Nineties: A Review of Art and Ideas at the Close of the Nineteenth Century* (1913; Harmondsworth: Pelican, 1950), 277.

[17] G. Gissing, *Thyrza* (1887; London: Eveleigh Nash and Grayson, 1927), 111.

[18] James, *The Princess Casamassima*, 439.

[19] A. Symons, 'Impressionistic Writing' (1893), in D. Stanford, ed., *Critics of the 'Nineties* (London: John Baker, 1970), 116.

[20] J. Conrad, Preface to *The Nigger of the 'Narcissus'* (1897; Harmondsworth: Penguin, 1977), 13.

[21] James, *The Princess Casamassima*, 595, 106.

Plumbago Crucible Company, one of the world's leading crucible makers. Morgan's imported and burned vast quantities of Ceylonese graphite, encouraging suggestive links between the pollution that prevented, or at least changed, art and the materials used for writing and drawing.[22] Joseph Pennell, who illustrated 'London at Midsummer' with suitably murky charcoal drawings, and who also prepared illustrations for 'London Town', later noted that charcoal was 'made for London effects'.[23] London, carbon, fog, and James himself merged into 'harmonious grayness', an amalgamation Beerbohm's caricature actively encourages. A resonant adjective but also the name of a geological period, 'carboniferous' reinforces the historical layers underlying the city's present, something to which James would be keenly sensitive in making notes on London's churches in 1907.

A *Punch* cartoon from December 1886, 'The Winter Art Exhibitions', shows a fog-bound art gallery where critics peer at art they can barely see.[24] Whistlerian painting is, it seems, only too successful at representing the murky darkness. 'Where, if not from the Impressionists, do we get those wonderful brown fogs that come creeping down our streets, blurring the gas-lamps and changing the houses into monstrous shadows?', asked Wilde in *The Decay of Lying* (1891). 'The extraordinary change that has taken place in the climate of London during the last ten years is entirely due to a particular school of Art,' his Vivian maintains. 'At present, people see fogs, not because there are fogs, but because poets and painters have taught them the mysterious loveliness of such effects.'[25] John House identifies the modern consciousness behind the apparently flippant paradox:

Wilde was making a critical point, that we can only understand what we see through frameworks of expectation and classification: the earlier English view of London saw a scene as the sum of its details, of the parts that made it up, whereas an aesthete of the 'effect' could treat London's fogs as something worthy of being seen in themselves, and not just an impediment to seeing the objects that lay behind them.[26]

As Wilde suggests, the shift in certain quarters to the appreciation, rather than the denunciation, of London's atmosphere coincided with, and was in some respects attributable to, the experiments of Impressionist painters. Such

---

[22] R. Spencer, 'The Aesthetics of Change: London as Seen by James McNeill Whistler', in M. Warner et al., *The Image of London* (London: Trefoil/Barbican Art Gallery, 1987), 60–1.

[23] E. R. Pennell, *The Life and Letters of Joseph Pennell* (London: Ernest Benn, 1930), ii. 26. The 'London Town' illustrations were eventually used in Sydney Dark's *London* (London: Macmillan, 1926).

[24] 'The Winter Art Exhibition,' *Punch* (4 December 1886), 274.

[25] O. Wilde, *The Decay of Lying* (1889; revised version, *Intentions*, 1891), *Complete Works* (London: HarperCollins, 1994), 1086.

[26] J. House, 'London in the Art of Monet and Pissarro', in M. Warner et al., *The Image of London*, 86.

THE WINTER ART EXHIBITIONS

Opened last week, to the delight of all. Our Art-Critic, who sends Mr. Punch the above, has not sent any Notes or Sketches !

Figure 2.1. 'The Winter Art Exhibitions', *Punch*, 4 December 1886.

a vision of London was by no means universally endorsed: both Whistler and Monet were initially ridiculed, and many of Wilde's readers, familiar with his taste for comic inversions, overlooked the radical import of his ideas.

However, during the period from the late 1880s to the early 1900s, impressionism represented a strikingly new way of seeing the metropolis. This chapter will examine some impressionist-inflected responses to London, concentrating in particular on two distinct approaches. The first is a vogue for the impressionist 'word-painting' of London scenes, a fashion particularly associated with the work of Whistler. The second is the attempt to use impressionism to capture the speed and dynamism of the modern city. The subject matter of impressionist writing was therefore polarized between the static, slow moving, or lethargic, and the hustle and bustle that was increasingly the dominant note of metropolitan life. It was also divided between the old and the new, with the former being especially inspired by the Thames, and the latter by human inventions and the artificially induced rhythms of the commercial world.

Literary impressionism had first appeared as a critical coinage in an article on Alphonse Daudet by Ferdinand Brunétière in 1879, although, as had been the case with artistic impressionism five years earlier, the term was not intended to flatter.[27] Despite such inauspicious beginnings, its utility was quickly recognized. 'The impressionist school is strong,' Thomas Hardy noted in December 1886, 'It is even more suggestive in the direction of literature than in that of art.' Hardy was attracted by the notion that 'what you carry away with you from a scene is the true feature to grasp,' a licensing of subjectivity which helped him in his creative negotiations with realism in the wake of George Eliot, and which would later see him term *Jude the Obscure* (1895) 'simply an endeavour to give shape and coherence to a series of seemings, or personal impressions'.[28]

The version of impressionism that became increasingly popular in English writing before the First World War was an idiosyncratic hybrid of several diverse strains including Whistler, French Impressionist painting, particularly that of Monet and Degas, and Walter Pater's relativism. Also significant were the aural experiments of Paul Verlaine, who offered, for Arthur Symons, 'a twilight art, full of reticence' that 'suggests' and 'gives impressions, with a subtle avoidance of any too definite or precise effect of line or colour'.[29] The blending of art and literature that his comments implied was a notable trait in what Jesse Matz terms a climate of 'mimetic crisis'.[30] Holbrook Jackson supplies memorable examples from Whistler, who applied musical terms to his paintings, W. E. Henley, Wilde, Beardsley, and others, but 'the transposition of words from one set of ideas to another' was by no means confined to the progressive sympathies of aesthetes.[31] Similar effects also appeared in journalistic writing. Commenting on Yoshio Markino's watercolour illustrations to W. J. Loftie's *The Colour of London* (1907), for instance, the *Daily Telegraph* remarked that they revealed the 'infinite poetry of the colour of our glittering metropolis', while for *The Graphic*, each painting was a 'pictorial poem'.[32]

By the early twentieth century, distinctions between art forms were increasingly imprecise, Symons remarking that his poetry was an attempt to 'paint

[27] J. van Gunsteren, *Katherine Mansfield and Literary Impressionism* (Amsterdam: Rodoipi, 1990), 38, 193. 'L'impression dans le Roman', in *Revue des deux Mondes* (15 November 1879). The article was partially reworked for Brunétière's *Le Roman Naturaliste* (1883).
[28] T. Hardy, *The Life and Works of Thomas Hardy*, ed. M. Millgate (London: Macmillan, 1984), 191; Preface (August 1895) to *Jude the Obscure*, ed. P. Ingham (1895; Oxford: Oxford University Press, 1985), xxxv–xxxvi.
[29] A. Symons, 'Paul Verlaine,' *Black and White*, 1 (20 June 1891), 649.
[30] J. Matz, *Literary Impressionism and Modernist Aesthetics* (Cambridge: Cambridge University Press, 2001), 47.
[31] Jackson, *The Eighteen Nineties*, 142.   [32] Chatto and Windus Catalogue, Autumn 1907.

in music, perhaps'.[33] Creative synaesthesia of this type was quite distinct from realism's struggle to define itself against journalism and sociology, in that it combined literature with equally exalted cultural forms: music, painting, and philosophy. A blending of Pater, Whistler, and Monet signalled a self-conscious commitment to art, and indeed, to an equally foregrounded 'modern' spirit. Matz hails impressionism's 'positive power to undefine' in its '[l]umping together empirical psychology and aestheticism, confusing the difference between thoughts and feelings, [and] erasing the line between superficial appearances and deep knowledge'.[34] With Impressionist painting in particular absorbed into the mainstream cultural vocabulary of the twenty-first century, it is easy to overlook the radical potential it offered a hundred years earlier.

PATERNAL PROMPTING

Walter Pater's artistic sympathies lay with earlier painters, as shown by his memorable evocation of *La Gioconda*. His influence on subsequent impressionist writing derived less from his art criticism than from his formulation of consciousness, particularly as expressed in the conclusion to *Studies in the History of the Renaissance* (1873). Horrified by the excesses of aestheticism and *carpe diem* that it had been taken to sanction, Pater deleted these pages from the second edition of 1877, but this only served to magnify their transgressive potential. By restoring them to the third edition of 1888, albeit with slightly modified wording, Pater stirred the smouldering gem-like flame back into vivid life, since his initial ideas could now be read in the context of impressionist and Whistlerian art's espousal of the subjective.

As we have seen, Pater's work encouraged scepticism towards fact, and queried the pseudo-objectivity of historians. It also offered a rhapsodic evocation of a world of 'impressions, unstable, flickering, inconsistent, which burn and are extinguished with our consciousness of them'.[35] At the heart of this world lay 'that strange perpetual, weaving and unweaving of ourselves', the basis of Pater's formulation of subjectivity. Experience became 'reduced to a group of impressions . . . ringed round . . . by that thick wall of personality . . . which we can only conjecture to be without'. The combination of life as 'infinitely divisible' impressions, each 'being a single moment, gone while we try to

---

[33] Symons, *London*, 199.   [34] Matz, *Literary Impressionism*, 17.
[35] W. Pater, *The Renaissance: Studies in Art and Poetry*, ed. Adam Phillips, 4th edn (1893; Oxford: Oxford University Press, 1986), 151.

apprehend it' and experience as a 'flood of external objects' that threatens to overwhelm but which is quickly transformed through 'reflexion' into 'a group of impressions . . . in the mind of the observer' proved a beguiling one, not least because it represented a philosophically defensible rationale for positioning the self at the centre of life. It offered the means for sustaining individual identity in the face of the metropolitan world's crushing indifference towards it, as well as signalling the crucial importance of art in perceiving the external world. 'Reflexion', the process by which external stimuli were interpreted and recreated as art, aimed at the merging of 'matter and form' in line with his famous contention, 'All art constantly aspires towards the condition of music.'

Quite what this art might look or read like was unclear, unless by implication it was Pater's own. Christopher Ricks delights in pointing out both Pater's frequent inaccuracies and refashioning of quotations and observes that 'Style' 'quotes not one single instance of that consummated style which it invokes', confining itself to quotations about style, all of which are translated from French or German sources.[36] However, those less censorious towards what Ricks terms Pater's 'unions of audacity and evasion', or indeed, those inspired by them to reject empirical exactitude, found his credo a liberating one, stressing as it did an individual and subjective viewpoint as the basis of art and criticism.

Pater's model of personality addressed the conflict between the individual and his environment in ways that anticipate, in certain respects, later sociological formulations. However, there were crucial differences between a philosophically inclined aesthete and a sociologist, albeit one who was himself a philosopher. Georg Simmel's 'The Metropolis and Mental Life' (1900) perceived city life rather than existence in general as being founded upon 'the rapid telescoping of changing images, pronounced differences within what is grasped at a single glance, and the unexpectedness of violent stimuli'.[37] Simmel argued that the figure he designated as 'the metropolitan type' adapted to its environment in particular ways, creating 'a protective organ for itself against the profound disruption with which the fluctuations and the discontinuities of the external milieu threaten it'. 'Instead of reacting emotionally, the metropolitan type reacts primarily in a rational manner,' he maintained, 'thus creating

[36] C. Ricks, 'Walter Pater, Matthew Arnold and Misquotation', in his *The Force of Poetry* (Oxford: Clarendon Press, 1984), 405.

[37] G. Simmel, 'The Metropolis and Mental Life', in *Metropolis: Centre and Symbol of Our Times*, ed. P. Kasinitz (London: Macmillan, 1995), 31. Reprinted from G. Simmel, *On Individuality and Social Forms*, ed. Donald Levine (Chicago: University of Chicago Press, 1971), trans. E. Shills. Originally published as 'Die Grosstadte und das Geistesleben', in *Die Grosstadt*, ed. T. Petermann (Dresden, 1903).

a mental predominance through the intensification of consciousness, which is in turn caused by it.' For Simmel, 'intensification of consciousness' acted as a safety device, allowing what he termed the 'metropolitan type' to cope with the diverse imaginative stimuli, Pater's 'flood of external objects', to which it was subjected. However, while Simmel's experienced urbanite shunted the stimuli into a cerebral siding where it could not derail the more urgent mental processes of everyday needs, becoming blasé in the process, Pater encouraged the intellectual's celebration of the unique and fleeting moment. 'The reaction of the metropolitan person to those events is moved to a sphere of mental activity which is least sensitive and which is furthest removed from the depths of the personality,' Simmel concluded. It was a recipe for survival rather than the production of art. Pater would instead insist on moving individual reaction to the 'sphere of mental activity' that is *most* sensitive, a stance not without its dangers, as Arthur Symons would discover in the course of his catastrophic mental collapse in Italy in 1908.

Christopher Butler has characterized Simmel's essay as a mode of 'defensive intellectualism' by which the 'metropolitan type' could 'preserve an interior life of introspection against the overwhelming and machine-like activities of city life'.[38] 'How much more self-conscious one is in a big city!', complained the defensively intellectual and sexually 'nervous' T. S. Eliot in December 1914. 'One walks about the street with one's desires, and one's refinement rises up like a wall whenever opportunity arises.'[39] Simmel located such anxieties firmly within the metropolitan realm rather than in Pater's more general modern condition, but his concerns were similar in some respects. The crucial difference between them was the inspirational effect of Pater's recognition of the creative possibilities of individual existence. For Pater and his enthusiastic followers, every impression was 'the impression of the individual in his isolation', with 'each mind keeping as a solitary prisoner its own dream of a world'. The ceaseless flow of impressions took place within the ceaseless flow of time itself, a flux in which 'impressions, images, sensations' were 'infinitely divisible . . . a tremulous wisp constantly re-forming itself on the stream'. In the face of this, 'analysis leaves off', and only individual personality remains. One must therefore be 'for ever . . . courting new impressions' rather than 'acquiescing in a facile orthodoxy', or engaging in philosophical speculation that is unnecessarily 'abstract' or 'conventional'. '[W]e shall hardly have time to make theories about the things we see and touch,' Pater argues, preferring

[38] C. Butler, *Early Modernism: Literature, Music and Painting in Europe 1900–1916* (Oxford: Clarendon Press, 1994), 134.

[39] T. S. Eliot to Conrad Aiken, 31 December 1914, *The Letters of T. S. Eliot, Volume I: 1898–1922*, ed. V. Eliot (London: Faber, 1988), 74–5.

the mesmeric cadences of his prose to further analysis of the considerations he describes.[40]

These ideas, crystallized in the final pages of *The Renaissance*, influenced writers on London in several ways. First, through their dismissal of 'theory' and 'orthodoxy', they detached contemporary arguments about impressionism from their apparent roots in Hume and Berkeley, and provided them with freshness and contemporary appeal. Pater himself sought to synthesize 'two strains in philosophy which seemed so ruinously incompatible in the nineteenth century: German idealism and British Empiricism', but few of those who followed him immersed themselves in either.[41] Reading Pater offered instead an intellectual short cut for writers such as Symons who were eager to apply impressionism to urban life, rather than to philosophical inquiry, especially if it could be used to advertise a self-consciously 'modern' outlook. Wilde's critical essays, which imbued vulgarized Pater with epigrammatic elan to initiate 'a widely practised game of intellectual frivolity', in time came to offer another short cut, especially once Pater's humourless verbosity fell from favour after the First World War.[42]

Second, Pater's ideas encouraged writers to focus on the intensity of brief sensations rather than prolonged evocation or analysis. The fondness for lyric poetry and short stories during the 1890s can hardly be attributed to Pater alone, but a 'delight in momentariness' was undoubtedly part of a wider concern with the possibilities of impressionism, as well as a reaction against the triple-decker novel.[43]

Third, Pater's writing placed the individual perceiving consciousness at the centre of perception, detaching it from social or political circumstances and, though this was surely not his intention, licensing a species of egoism that would flourish in Fleet Street and beyond for years to come. The impact of *The Renaissance* was reinforced by that of *Marius the Epicurean* (1885), the subtitle of which, 'His Sensations and Ideas', also encouraged a fascination with the workings of individual perception, or, less charitably, a preoccupation with the self. 'This voracious egoism of the soul is curiously affrighting,' noted the *Athenaeum* in 1903, criticizing Symons's 'cerebral voluptuousness' and rejection of 'exteriority' in favour of 'super-consciousness of life'.[44] Pater's writing encouraged his followers to dwell on their own responses to external stimuli, prompting a peculiarly precious variety of self-absorption and attracting both criticism and parody. In James's 'The Author of *Beltraffio*' (1884), Mark Ambient, in some ways a composite of Pater and

[40] Pater, *The Renaissance*, 152–3.   [41] Matz, *Literary Impressionism*, 57.
[42] Jackson, *The Eighteen Nineties*, 145.
[43] R. Graves, 'Sick Love', *Poems 1929* (London: Seizin Press, 1929).
[44] 'Arthur Symons, *Cities*', *The Athenæum* (14 November 1903), 642.

John Addington Symonds, is an avid collector of impressions, a trait that leads to the 'malign inquiry' that serves as this chapter's epigraph.[45] Indeed, although he identified as 'that highest kind of inspiration, the inspiration of the moment', James resisted Pater's influence throughout his career, since his aestheticism posed what Jonathan Freedman terms 'a complex and multifaceted problem' that offered the dual temptations of 'a detached but monitoring scopophilia or a self-indulgent dissoluteness'.[46] Ford Madox Ford's zestful application of Paterian subjectivity to matters of autobiography has seen his reputation permanently tarnished, while Symons's poetic accounts of his amorous escapades showed little interest in the impressions and sensations of his various partners. If *Punch*'s resident parodist, Owen Seaman, could consider John Davidson a 'seedy sex impressionist' for 'The Ballad of a Nun' (1894), one can imagine how the magazine's readers reacted to the self-congratulatory eroticism of 'Leves Amores', 'White Heliotrope', and, notoriously, 'Stella Maris'.[47] Clearly, by this stage of his career, Symons had forgotten something of the 'somewhat chill asceticism, a restraint sometimes almost painful' he had recognized in reviewing Pater's *Imaginary Portraits* in 1887.[48]

Finally, in stressing that the basis of criticism is 'knowing one's own impression as it really is' rather than seeing 'the object as in itself it really is' as Matthew Arnold had maintained, Pater encouraged the use of 'the object', be it a painting, a poem, or even a city, as a starting point for solipsistic reverie. Facts were secondary, even irrelevant. In the dedication to *Cities* (1903), Symons admitted to fearing the production of 'a kind of subjective diary, in which the city should be an excuse for my own sensations'.[49] The remark suggests that although he was conscious of the perils of this approach, he was not always able to resist indulging his imaginative appetites. *The Renaissance* had maintained that 'Each art, . . . having its own peculiar and incommunicable sensuous charm, has its own special mode of reaching the imagination, its own special responsibilities to its material.' The aesthetic critic's aim was to 'define these limitations' and to help identify the characteristic feature of a work of art, 'pictorial charm', for instance, or 'poetical quality'.[50] Such terminology and practice had marked appeal for impressionist writers on London. The city's 'peculiar charm' had been mythologized since the days of Samuel Johnson, if not before, but only at the end of the nineteenth century was London

---

[45] H. James, 'The Author of *Beltraffio*', *Complete Stories 1874–1884* (New York: Library of America, 1999), 875.

[46] James, 'London,' *English Hours*, 36; J. Freedman, *Professions of Taste: Henry James, British Aestheticism and Commodity Culture* (Stanford: Stanford University Press, 1990), 143.

[47] O. Seaman, 'A Ballad of a Bun' in *The Battle of the Bays* (London: John Lane/The Bodley Head, 1896), 24.

[48] K. Beckson, *Arthur Symons: A Life* (Oxford: Clarendon Press, 1987), 39.

[49] A. Symons, *Cities* (London: J. M. Dent, 1903), 6.   [50] Pater, *The Renaissance*, 83.

transformed into an artistic image of itself so that the aesthete could applaud his own taste in recognizing its allure. This stance conveyed how a sensitive reader of Pater might feel when looking at a Whistler nocturne, but it did not necessarily correspond to the experience of city life, nor did it always attempt to.

Pater's insistence that an art object's distinguishing qualities were 'incommunicable' encouraged writers to believe in the superiority of their perceptions in recognizing these very attributes and attempting to make them manifest to the less enlightened. Oscar Wilde took such an approach to a pitch of perfection, but less humorous writers followed close behind in exalting beauty, and, more importantly, their ability to recognize and judge it for the benefit of others. Travel essays in particular demanded the persona of a connoisseur whose judgement and experience were impeccable; someone who could convey the essence of the place visited while foregrounding their reactions to it. Acting as what amounted to a foreign correspondent for his American readers, although he also essayed the role of London's adopted son, Henry James was 'a supine, archly self-conscious critic revelling in the guise of a leisured dilettante whose trade is levity and irony'.[51] Daniel Ronserra in Symons's 'An Autumn City' (1905) is a fictional version of such figures, and indeed Symons himself, dwelling on 'of the influence of places, of the image a place makes in the consciousness, of all it might do in the formation of a beautiful or uncomely disposition'.[52] Although Ronserra is at home in Arles rather than London, such formulations have obvious relevance for the artistic rendering of the English capital.

Pater was far from being the only intellectual to advocate a relativistic response to the world. As Stephen Kern has shown, the work of Nietzsche, William James, Albert Einstein, and Henri Bergson would all prove influential during the late nineteenth and early twentieth centuries. Indeed, although there were important differences between Pater's and Bergson's thought, the writings of the two men effectively bookend the evolution of artistic impressionism in Britain. Both stressed the importance of intuition, 'the kind of intellectual sympathy by which one places oneself within an object in order to coincide with what is unique in it', and distinguished between 'relative' and 'absolute' knowledge.[53] Similarly, each was sceptical towards rationalist, materialist explanations of existence, for, as Bergson remarked, 'Intellect is characterised by a natural inability to comprehend life.'[54] 'Einstein

---

[51] H. James, *Essays on Art and Drama*, ed. P. Rawlings (Aldershot: Scolar Press, 1996), 1.

[52] A. Symons, *Spiritual Adventures* (London: Archibald Constable, 1905), 177.

[53] H. Bergson, *An Introduction to Metaphysics* (1903), in S. Kern, *The Culture of Time and Space 1880–1918* (Cambridge, MA: Harvard University Press, 1983), 25.

[54] H. Bergson, *Creative Evolution*, trans. A. Mitchell (1911; London: Macmillan, 1960), 174.

considered time in relation to space [but] Bergson considered it in relation to thought,' observes Derek Jarrett, developing a notion of 'conceptual thought' which explored how, although time was continuous, human beings habitually considered it as divided into separate moments. Such thinking was, Jarrett adds, 'bound to distort reality' since, as Bergson concluded, 'In vain we force the living into this or that one of our moulds. All the moulds crack.'[55]

Remarks of this kind would surely have baffled many late-Victorian realists whose fiction dwelt on causality and sociopolitical responsibilities, though they may have struck a painful chord with Symons. Adopting a Paterian, or later, a Bergsonian, stance excused writers from explaining or even too closely analysing their everyday surroundings, since what was important was the personal response to them. Bergson's image of the inner self, 'a continuous flux, a succession of states, each of which announces that which follows and contains that which precedes it,' is suggestively Paterian, recalling *The Renaissance*'s 'perpetual, weaving and unweaving of ourselves'.[56] The effect was to restate the importance of an invariably apolitical subjectivity that embraced mystery rather than explanation: it is hard to imagine Holmes and Watson, or many of their admirers, sanctioning such views.

As this abbreviated consideration of radical thought hopefully suggests, the 'factual', the 'verifiable', and the 'objective' were often contested and distrusted categories within certain areas of *fin de siècle* culture: even Ruskin had been prepared to concede that there might be 'a truth of impression as well as form'.[57] Under the auspices of Pater and those who followed him, the explicit distrust of objectivity became an increasingly important aspect of the late-Victorian and Edwardian representation of the urban environment.

FLOATING LIKE A BUTTERFLY: WHISTLER

Pater was a quietly subversive figure whose only concessions to display were his prose style and a fondness for lemon kid-gloves. Whistler by contrast was a high-profile spokesman for the avant-garde who, particularly after his 1878 libel battle with Ruskin, represented the public face of Impressionism in Britain, at least as far as many late-Victorian art critics and *Punch* were concerned. Ruskin had once championed Turner, but Impressionist (or at

[55] D. Jarrett, *The Sleep of Reason: Fantasy and Reality from the Victorian Age to the First World War* (London: Weidenfeld and Nicolson, 1988), 179, citing *Creative Evolution*, x, 322–3.

[56] Bergson, *An Introduction to Metaphysics*, in Kern, *The Culture of Time and Space*, 25.

[57] J. Ruskin, 'Of Ideas of Truth', *Modern Painters I* (1843), in *The Complete Works of John Ruskin*, ed. E. T. Cook and A. Wedderburn, 39 vols. (London: George Allen, 1903–12), iii. 104.

least Whistlerian) art was quite another matter, being 'Cockney impudence', 'imposture', and 'ill-educated conceit' that flung 'a pot of paint in the public's face'.[58] Whistler fought back with a melange of Gautier, Baudelaire, the Flaubertian dismissal of bourgeois taste, and the young Swinburne's belief that 'Art is at her peril if she tries to do good.'[59] These ideas were the familiar currency of Anglo-French progressive thought, but were still capable of surprising those who did not dwell within its charmed circle. Besides, the originality of such contentions was ultimately secondary, for it was the manner in which Whistler presented them, and indeed himself, that inspired radicals to follow a doctrine of 'art for the artist's sake'.[60]

Whistler's skills as a performer, in court and in his *Ten O' Clock Lecture* (1885), allied with witty letters to the press reprinted in *The Gentle Art of Making Enemies* (1890), kept his name before the public. The result was that the painter remained a touchstone of artistic innovation during the following decade, with his ideas becoming increasingly appealing among those sympathetic to artistic experiment. In 1894, Hume Nisbet's 'The Phantom Model or A Wapping Romance' caricatured Whistler's acolytes as those 'youthful luminaries' who hold the Royal Academy in contempt, belong to 'the advanced school of Impressionists, and allow, with reservations, that Jimmy Whitetuft has genius'.[61] 'In the fifteen or twenty years that have elapsed since the trial Whistler v. Ruskin was heard,' wrote Frank Harris three years later, 'the position of Mr Whistler in the English world has completely changed. Then he was regarded as a mountebank and self-advertising trifler; today he is respected.'[62] Even Henry James, who had at first dismissed Whistler's painting as having 'no relation to life', and whose application of Whistlerian techniques was hitherto unannounced, was prepared to hail his work as 'one of the finest of all distillations of the artistic intelligence' by 1897.[63]

Whistler's flair for publicity, and his dramatic confrontation with the shibboleths of Victorian art, was far removed from the retiring Claude Monet, whose visits to the English capital caused less of a stir. There were also key artistic differences between 'Whistlerian' and 'Impressionist' art, though

[58] J. Ruskin, *Fors Clavigera* (2 July 1877), in J. M. Whistler, *The Gentle Art of Making Enemies* (London: Heinemann, 1890), 1.

[59] G. Lafourcade, *La Jeunesse de Swinburne, 1837–1867* (Paris: 1928), i. 211.

[60] R. McMullen, *Victorian Outsider: A Biography of J. A. M. Whistler* (London: Macmillan, 1973), 233.

[61] H. Nisbet, 'The Phantom Model or A Wapping Romance', *The Haunted Station* (1894), in H. Lamb, ed., *Gaslit Nightmares* (London: Futura, 1988), 37.

[62] F. Harris, 'Why drag in—Pennell?' *Saturday Review* (10 April 1897), 371.

[63] H. James, 'London', *Harper's Weekly*, 41 (26 June 1897), in James, *Essays on Art and Drama*, 4.

Impressionism itself was so poorly defined and understood in late-nineteenth-century Britain that any generalization would be deeply misleading.[64] Whistler had no interest in impressionist brushwork effects, rarely experimented with the rendering of sunlight, and in place of the daring impasto favoured by Monet, often 'thinned' paint 'to the consistency of a juice that let the canvas or the panel show through'.[65] In a reversal of their personalities, Monet's paintings flaunted their brilliant colours while Whistler's essayed subtler tonal contrasts in their visual austerity and insinuation, brevity, outline, and suggestiveness. Such an approach is typified by the *Nocturne: Blue and Silver—Cremorne Lights* (1872). Symons's Peter Waydelin remarks that 'Whistler sees nothing but the fine shades, which unite into a picture in an almost bodiless way, as Verlaine writes songs almost literally "without words".'[66] This characterization of Whistler's art, and its parallels with the poetry of Verlaine, frequently recurred between 1890 and 1910, especially in Symons's essays.

As Alan Bowness points out, Whistler and Monet had established 'close ties' by the mid-1880s, with Monet spending a fortnight in London with Whistler in the summer of 1887, and the art associated with these painters and their followers does have important similarities.[67] Like Verlaine's poetry, it sought to 'create imprecision by precise means'.[68] It was not bound to topographical realities or mimetic accuracy, and, like Pater, rejected dogmatic adherence to tradition or theory. 'Do not define too closely the outline of things,' counselled Monet's fellow Impressionist Camille Pissarro. 'Don't proceed according to rules and principles.'[69] At the Ruskin trial, Whistler's *Nocturne: Blue and Gold—Old Battersea Bridge* (1872–3) was mocked for perceived failures of verisimilitude, a charge the artist refuted in claiming that 'My whole scheme was only to bring about a certain harmony of colour.'[70] The *Nocturne in Black and Gold: The Falling Rocket* (1875), which Ruskin's lawyer brought out on its side to laughter from the jury, was, he said, no more than 'an artistic arrangement'.[71] Symons would later praise what Whistler can make

---

[64] The term was initially a derogatory term coined by the journalist Louis Leroy in damning the first exhibition by the heterogeneous *La Société anonyme des artistes, peintres, sculpteurs, etc.* in April 1874. '*Dilettantes* and culture-mongers in their hosts belaud impressionism as an aesthetic revolution; but very few seem to know what they really mean by the term,' noted the *Quarterly Review* ('Fathers of Literary Impressionism in England', *Quarterly Review*, 369 (January 1897), 173).

[65] McMullen, *Victorian Outsider*, 216.

[66] A. Symons, 'The Death of Peter Waydelin', *Spiritual Adventures*, 150–1.

[67] A. Bowness, *The Impressionists in London* (London: Arts Council, 1973), 35

[68] P. Verlaine, *Selected Poems*, trans. Martin Sorrell (Oxford: Oxford University Press, 1999), xxiv.

[69] P. Stowell, *Literary Impressionism: James and Chekhov* (Athens: University of Georgia Press, 1980), 46–7.

[70] Whistler, *The Gentle Art of Making Enemies*, 8.   [71] Ibid. 3.

Figure 2.2 James McNeill Whistler, *Nocturne: Blue and Silver—Cremorne Lights* (1872)

'out of "Brock's Benefit:" in place of fireworks and vulgarity you have a harmony . . . and a work of art,' but in the 1870s, Whistler's defence of his picture struck many as a sophistical smokescreen for poor technique.[72] The conservatively inclined could not accept what Whistler openly admitted, 'I did not intend it to be a "correct" portrait of the bridge.'[73] These highly subjective responses to his surroundings, combined with a refusal to direct the viewer's interpretation, 'As to what the picture represents, that depends upon who looks at it,' violated the artist's traditional relationship with his audience, not to mention the canons of good taste and common sense.

Impressionist painters were similarly unconcerned by painting's traditional obligation to record: as Eric Shanes notes, Monet invariably omitted Cleopatra's Needle from his paintings of the Thames because 'its verticality would have cut most of his compositions in two'.[74] In 1905, Whistler's disciple and biographer Joseph Pennell fell foul of *The Athenaeum* when illustrating James's *English Hours*. 'The pretty vignette above the preface represents a scene at Westminster which has no existence; Turner himself never took a greater liberty with the facts,' wrote the piqued reviewer, neatly encapsulating the distinction between aesthetic appeal and topographic accuracy.[75]

Impressionism refused to be constrained by what it regarded as the pedantic niceties of the literal, both in terms of accurate depictions of external realities and in its treatment of detail. As James suggested, Whistler's work was a 'distillation' of its subject matter, and 'not an impression but an expression'.[76] For Symons, his paintings went 'clean through outward things to their essence'.[77] Roy McMullen has argued that Whistler's experiments with 'an art based on elimination' were risky, in that such an art 'could not evolve' and was seemingly bound to degenerate into repetition.[78] Initially, however, his rejection of detail was enormously liberating. Whistler's use of outline and shadow offered 'a more fluid and less didactic reality', and thus seemed one means of evading the impasse of realism, where insufficient detail led to an unconvincing milieu but where too much caused narrative to grind

[72] A. Symons, 'Modernity in Verse', *Studies in Two Literature* (London: Leonard Smithers, 1897), 192.

[73] Whistler, *The Gentle Art of Making Enemies*, 8.

[74] E. Shanes, *Impressionist London* (London: Abbeville, 1994), 134–5.

[75] 'Henry James, *English Hours*', *The Athenaeum* (28 October 1905), 578. Pennell's illustrations date from the original publication of 'London' in 1888.

[76] John L. Sweeney, ed., *The Painter's Eye: Notes and Essays on the Pictorial Arts by Henry James* (Cambridge, MA: Harvard University Press, 1956), 165.

[77] A. Symons, 'The Painting of the Nineteenth Century,' *Studies in Seven Arts* (London: Constable, 1906), 29.

[78] McMullen, *Victorian Outsider*, 216.

to a halt in a morass of linguistic clutter.[79] Whistler's refining away of inessentials allowed him, Symons argued, 'to dispense with that amplification, that reiterance' in which a lesser artist would indulge.[80] James had initially dismissed Impressionism on the grounds that it was somehow too close to life to qualify as art, with Impressionist painters being 'absolute foes to arrangement, embellishment, selection', but Whistler's pictures proved an intriguing demonstration of the possibilities of atmosphere as opposed to detail.[81] Like Pater, and indeed, James himself, Whistler found facts, or the notion of verifiable objective reality, to be the enemy of the creative imagination, and he sought instead to hint rather than to state. The implied viewer of Whistler's canvases, like the implied reader of James's fiction, needs to be acutely aware of the power of suggestion, as well as sympathetic to panoramas of irresolution.

Whistler and the Impressionists had very little interest in historical subjects, although Whistler certainly mourned the 'old Chelsea' destroyed by the creation of the Chelsea Embankment from 1871, and preferred old buildings to, for instance, the new development of the Cadogan Estate. Impressionist art was instead concerned with the momentary and transient, rather than with rumination on the past: 'We live in the flicker,' says Conrad's Marlow.[82] A concentration on the present, or the ways by which the past was assimilated into the present through the architectural and civic juxtaposition of the two, was a key component of Impressionism's modernity and its appeal for writers and artists etiolated by Victorian tradition. Impressionism was similarly uninterested in matters of politics or morality, except when arguing for art's exemption from such discussions. As Roger Lhombreaud remarks of Symons, 'The fate of humanity, current problems and social or political events in no way held his interest: his unconcern about them was complete.'[83] This marked an important distinction from much realist art, which was, whatever its political affiliation, keenly aware of the day-to-day management of the metropolis.

The modern city offered remarkable raw material for Impressionist artists, but it was often the creations of humanity, rather than human beings themselves, that caught their eye. 'God made the country, and man made the town,' Cowper had written in *The Task* (1785), and throughout the poorer districts of London, evangelists and reformers grappled with the consequences of such division of labour. In Whistler, however, the world of

---

[79] Stowell, *Literary Impressionism*, 9.
[80] Symons, 'Impressionistic Writing' (1893), in *Critics of the 'Nineties*, 117.
[81] Sweeney, ed., *The Painter's Eye*, 115.
[82] J. Conrad, *Heart of Darkness*, ed. R. Hampson (1902; London: Penguin, 1995), 19.
[83] R. Lhombreaud, *Arthur Symons: A Critical Biography* (London: Unicorn Press, 1963), 229.

human creation was freed from moral connotations, as if, as Wilde would argue, 'An ethical sympathy in an artist is an unpardonable mannerism of style.'[84] After early pictures such as *Wapping* (1860–1) Whistler stripped London scenes of anecdotalism and moral comment and focused instead on their formal qualities. Following his lead, impressionist poetry was 'sensuous, intuitive, immediate, and amoral', and caused offence even when these qualities were not specifically announced.[85] Lionel Johnson, fundamentally opposed to this concentration on surface realities rather than deeper truths, denounced Symons's verse for replacing intellectual achievement with what he termed 'Parisian impressionism'. This he summed up, according to W. B. Yeats, as 'a London fog, the blurred tawny lamplight, the red omnibus, the dreary train, the depressing mud, the glaring gin-shop, the slatternly shivering women, three dextrous stanzas telling you that and nothing more', but it is unlikely that Symons would have seen this as an entirely negative formulation.[86] Far from being a rebuke, Johnson's stripped down critique reads as an instructive example for the aspiring impressionist writer.

In an 1898 consideration of Impressionism, Ford Madox Ford observed that 'London might be set upon paper manless; but it is better otherwise.'[87] Impressionist painters did not seem to share his views. Discussing Impressionist landscapes in 1897, the *Quarterly Review* noted that for Monet, 'man has practically no existence. If human beings appear at all in his pictures, they merely figure as patches upon the sky.'[88] Whistler's London was similarly uninhabited; its denizens reduced to the occasional compositional props in whose company Henry James sailed from Westminster Bridge to Greenwich. Whistler did paint street scenes, but he had little enthusiasm for their inhabitants, and preferred to concentrate on portraying a river far removed from the commercial artery of a thriving metropolis. George Moore claimed that Whistler painted 'the difficult populous city night', but his nocturnes rarely addressed its human face, preferring the 'the night of tall bridges and vast water rained through with lights red and grey . . . a vast blue and golden caravanry'.[89]

The systematic depopulation of London would be extremely significant for both artists who followed Whistler and impressionist writers. Katharine

---

[84] Wilde, Preface to *The Picture of Dorian Gray* (1891), in *Complete Works*, 17.

[85] J. B. Townsend, *John Davidson: Poet of Armageddon* (New Haven: Yale University Press, 1961), 233.

[86] W. B. Yeats, 'The Tragic Generation', in *Autobiographies* (London: Macmillan, 1955), 378.

[87] F. M. Ford, 'William Hyde: An Illustrator of London', *The Artist* (January 1898), 6.

[88] 'Modern French Art', *Quarterly Review*, 370 (April 1897), 378.

[89] E. Warner and G. Hough, eds., *Strangeness and Beauty: An Anthology of Aesthetic Criticism 1840–1910*, (Cambridge: Cambridge University Press, 1983), ii. 119. Moore's comments are taken from articles of 1891 and 1892, later reworked as the Whistler essay of his *Modern Painting* (1893).

Bradley and Edith Cooper, better known as Michael Field, recorded in their journal how fog was 'a glower of yellow' which swamped everything but 'the immediate pavement before one & the sudden passing faces—their flesh-tints strangely emphatic for a moment & then dim with disappearance'.[90] Arthur Machen's *The Three Impostors* (1895) observed the effects of gaslamps at dusk, a combination that meant 'casual passers-by rather flickered and hovered in the play of lights than stood out substantial things'.[91] Stephen Crane's 'London Impressions', a regular feature of the *Saturday Review* during 1897, depicted 'a great sea of night in which were swimming little gas fishes' and in which Londoners were conspicuous by their absence.[92] In *London: A Book of Aspects*, Symons maintained that the conditions of the nocturnal city mean that 'people are no longer distinguishable as persons, but are a nimble flock of shadows.'[93] Walter Sickert, once a pupil of Whistler, announced his intention of painting the 'magic and poetry' of the 'four mile radius', but largely confined his vision to interior spaces in paintings such as *The Gallery of the Old Bedford* (1895).[94] A music hall crowd, however boisterous, was at least enclosed, both temporally and spatially, and thus presented a more easily managed subject than the confusion of Piccadilly Circus. This recognition was shared by a number of the poems in Symons's *Silhouettes* (1892) and *London Nights* (1895), where concentration on the individual performer or generalized responses to the audience replaced detailed description. John Davidson's *In a Music Hall and Other Poems* (1891) gives monologues to six Glasgow 'artists', but its account of the music hall itself goes no further than classing it as 'rancid and hot'.[95] Although painters of other schools were more willing to accept its challenges, London is invariably uninhabited or unindividuated in impressionist art. Only in pictures of interiors could its citizens be properly acknowledged, as Sickert's later work, from *Ennui* (*c*.1914) to society portraiture, implicitly recognized.[96]

---

[90] Michael Field, journal entry, 28 February 1891. Cooper and Bradley also visited and enjoyed Whistler's 1892 London exhibition. A. P. Vadillo, 'Immaterial Poetics: A. Mary F. Robinson and the Fin-de-Siècle Poem', in J. Bristow, ed., *The Fin-de-Siècle Poem: English Literary Culture and the 1890s* (Athens: University of Ohio Press, 2005), 231.

[91] A. Machen, *The Three Impostors or The Transmutations*, ed. David Trotter (1895; London: Dent, 1995), 7.

[92] S. Crane, 'London Impressions', *Saturday Review* (14 August 1897), 158.

[93] Symons, *London*, 209.

[94] Sickert's preface to 'A Collection of Paintings by London Impressionists', Groupil Gallery, London, 1889, in *Sickert Paintings*, ed. W. Baron and R. Shone (London: Royal Academy, 1992), 58–9. Whistler had produced a watercolour *Nocturne in Grey and Gold—Piccadilly* in *c*.1884, though it makes little attempt to depict Londoners as 'substantial things'.

[95] J. Davidson, 'Prologue' to 'In a Music Hall', in *Poems of John Davidson*, ed. A. Turnbull, 2 vols. (Edinburgh: Scottish Academic Press, 1973), i. 22.

[96] There may also have been commercial reasons for Sickert's move into portraiture, since his music hall paintings proved difficult to sell during the 1890s and early 1900s. For some of the technical difficulties involved in painting in darkened music halls, see M. Sturgis, *Walter Sickert:*

Whistler painted London views repeatedly during the 1870s and 1880s, offering a vision of the city that in some ways supplanted the material conditions that had inspired it. Writers reinforced the importance of his version of the metropolis through continual references to his work. Wilde had initially responded to the *Nocturne in Black and Gold* as 'a simple-minded realist', claiming that the painting was 'worth looking at for about as long as one looks at a real rocket, that is, for something less than a quarter of a minute'.[97] His poem 'Impression du Matin' (1881), however, suggests his growing interest in the possibilities of Whistlerian effects. 'The Thames nocturne of blue and gold | Changed to a Harmony in grey,' it begins, employing familiarity with Whistler's paintings as shorthand for lengthier description and implying, long before *The Decay of Lying*, that nature imitates art. It could not, however, entirely abandon Victorian moralism in its closing depiction of the 'one pale woman all alone' who 'Loitered beneath the gas lamps' flare, | With lips of flame and heart of stone'. Ten years later, W. E. Henley's 'To James McNeill Whistler' (1892) pleased the painter to the extent that he allowed one of his nocturnes to be used as an illustration when its author reprinted it in *A London Garland* (1895) as 'Nocturn'.[98] By the early twentieth century, Whistlerian allusion had become almost commonplace, perhaps because a generation that had identified with Whistler as part of a wider rejection of Victorian convention was itself being challenged by increasingly radical Fauvist and Post-Impressionist art. In this context, Whistler represented a paradoxically nostalgic modernity, with the works that had enraged Ruskin becoming oddly comforting in the face of fresh innovations. E. V. Lucas credited Whistler with the discovery of fog's 'beautifying properties' in 1906.[99] By 1909, Symons was claiming that 'Whistler has created the Thames, for most people,' and four years later, Holbrook Jackson concluded that 'It was Whistler who taught the modern world how to appreciate the beauty and wizardry of cities.'[100]

The impact of French painting on London writers of the 1880s and 1890s was a little less marked, probably because it lacked an English-speaking advocate of Whistler's charisma, or a dramatic focus such as the Ruskin

A Life (London: HarperCollins, 2005), 147–61. See too D. P. Corbett, 'Seeing into modernity: Walter Sickert's Music-Hall Scenes, c.1887–1907', in D. P. Corbett and L. Perry, eds., *English Art 1860–1914: Modern Artists and Identity* (2000; New Brunswick: Rutgers University Press, 2001), 150–67.

[97] R. Ellmann, *Oscar Wilde* (London: Hamish Hamilton, 1987), 77.
[98] Henley's anthology is discussed in more detail by L. K. Hughes in 'A Woman on the Wilde Side: Masks, Perversity, and Print Culture in Poems by "Graham R. Tomson"/Rosamund Marriott Watson', in Bristow, ed., *The Fin-de-Siècle Poem*, 101–30.
[99] E. V. Lucas, *A Wanderer in London* (1906; London: Methuen, 1913), 22.
[100] Symons, *London*, 187; Jackson, *The Eighteen Nineties*, 106.

libel trial. Monet and Pissarro's contributions to the Royal Academy's 1871 spring exhibition had all been rejected, and, as Kate Flint observes, the new French art received little critical attention in Britain until Frederick Wedmore's 'The Impressionists' appeared in the *Fortnightly Review* in January 1883.[101] However, the public did gradually become familiar with Impressionist art, to the extent that although Durand-Ruel failed to sell any pictures at his grand London exhibition of 1905, he did attract many visitors and some sympathetic reviews. One assumes that when Lucas claimed that 'Words are useless' when surveying Piccadilly in spring, for the 'indescribable scene of streaming colour and gentle vivacity . . . needs Monet or Pissarro,' at least some of his audience appreciated the implications.[102]

IMPRESSIONIST CITYSCAPES

Symons may have attempted to use poetry 'to paint in music', but the blurring of art forms during the *fin de siècle*, Matz's 'mimetic crisis', led to some obvious practical difficulties. Poetry and prose could be intermingled to profitable effect, with Edward Thomas noting 'the apparent destruction of the boundaries between poetry and prose, and between verse and prose' in 1899. '[N]ot only do most writers use verse and prose,' he wrote, 'but they treat also in both styles the same subjects.'[103] Pater and Verlaine were prepared to countenance reproducible affinities between music and the written or spoken word, while W. B. Yeats and Florence Farr conducted the practical experiments recorded in Yeats's essay, 'Speaking to the Psaltery' (1902). The gulf between word and image, however, remains insurmountable, despite the ingenious attempts of critics to see, for example, Symons's use of single colour adjectives

---

[101] K. Flint, ed., *Impressionists in England: The Critical Reception* (London: Routledge, 1984), 46.

[102] Lucas, *A Wanderer in London*, 103.

[103] E. Thomas, unsigned article, 'The Frontiers of English Prose', *Literature* (23 September 1899), in *The Collected Poems of Edward Thomas*, ed. R. G. Thomas (Oxford: Clarendon Press, 1978), xv–xvi. Critical approval of this tendency was far from unanimous. The *Saturday Review* saw 'prose-poetry' as a 'meaningless phrase', being 'in actual truth much as if an art critic should say that a landscape is pervaded by a tint of exquisite scarlet-ultramarine' (4 February 1899, 150). Indeed, many remained unconvinced by the blurring of generic boundaries. In *Howards End*, Margaret Schlegel comments sourly on her sister's 'ingenious' translation of 'tunes into the language of painting, and pictures into the language of music'. Although this was Arthur Symons's ultimate ambition, Margaret is unimpressed. '[I]t's all rubbish, radically false,' she says. 'If Monet's really Debussy, and Debussy's really Monet, neither gentleman is worth his salt.' (E. M. Forster, *Howards End*, ed. O. Stallybrass (1910; London: Penguin, 1983), 52.)

as equivalent to an artist's brush-strokes.[104] As James argued in 'The Art of Fiction' (1884), fiction and painting maintained an analogous rather than a permeable relationship. 'Their inspiration is the same, their process (allowing for the quality of the vehicle), is the same,' he wrote, 'They may learn from each other, they may explain and sustain each other.' However, they could not *be* each other, whatever their similarities in attempting to 'represent life'.[105]

The rise of Impressionist painting was especially problematic for writers seeking a fusion of art and literature, since Impressionist preoccupations with the effects of sunlight inevitably lose their sparkle when transferred to the printed page. Joseph Conrad suggested that the pursuit of perfection of expression could allow 'the light of magic suggestiveness . . . to play for an evanescent instant over the commonplace surface of words', but the linguistic counterpart to shimmering paintings was difficult to achieve.[106] What remains is a similar concern with the effect of impressions and sensations upon individual perception and the challenge of their representation and transmission.

An important consequence of this has been a critical concentration on the evolution of psychological impressionism concerned with the representation of consciousness.[107] As Peter Stowell argues in his still-influential study:

Literary impressionists were interested in the impalpable surfaces of sensory data that attack consciousness. This transliteration [from artistic to literary impressionism] meant that their subjects were not the water, snow, blossoms, clouds, sailboats, crowds, steam, speed, and mist of the painters. Instead, the writers found equally ephemeral subjects: love, jealousy, growing up and growing old, daydreams, sleeplessness, modern warfare, and the myriad emotions and intrigues of changing human relationships.[108]

The city is conspicuously absent from this somewhat idiosyncratic list, for here, clouds, mist, steam, and speed, not to mention fog, did indeed loom large for impressionist writers. In writing about London, the 'transliteration'

[104] R. L. Peters, 'Whistler and the English Poets of the 1890s', *Modern Language Quarterly*, 18 (1957), 251–61. For a more sophisticated and convincing exploration of this idea, see A. Robinson, *Poetry, Painting and Ideas 1885–1914* (Basingstoke: Macmillan, 1985), 40–57.

[105] H. James, *The House of Fiction*, ed. L. Edel (London: Rupert Hart-Davis, 1957), 25.

[106] Conrad, Preface to *The Nigger of the 'Narcissus'*, 12.

[107] See, for example, M. E. Kronegger, *Literary Impressionism* (New Haven: College and University Press, 1973); I. Watt, *Conrad in the Nineteenth Century* (Berkeley: University of California Press, 1979); J. Nagel, *Stephen Crane and Literary Impressionism* (University Park: Penn State University Press, 1980); Stowell, *Literary Impressionism: James and Chekhov* (1980); P. Armstrong, *The Challenge of Bewilderment: Understanding and Representation in James, Conrad, and Ford* (Ithaca: Cornell University Press, 1988); Gunsteren, *Katherine Mansfield and Literary Impressionism* (1990); T. K. Bender, *Literary Impressionism in Jean Rhys, Ford Madox Ford, Joseph Conrad, and Charlotte Brontë* (New York: Garland, 1998); Matz, *Literary Impressionism and Modernist Aesthetics* (2001).

[108] Stowell, *Literary Impressionism*, 49.

from visual to literary impressionism produced a quite different mode of impressionist prose. Rather than taking techniques from artistic impressionism and attempting to 'transliterate' them into prose or poetry, many writers enshrined the painterly at the centre of their perception of the city, changing it from a city to a picture of a city, the 'masterly composition' of 'London at Midsummer'. Constable had remarked that Turner 'seems to paint with tinted steam', and Symons employed similar language to describe the late-Victorian city. 'English mist is always at work like a subtle painter, and London is a vast canvas prepared for the mist to work on,' he wrote. 'When the mist collaborates with night and rain, the masterpiece is created.'[109] Writers who entertained such ideas devoted themselves to describing what Impressionist art had already pictured, or replacing the city of their individual vision with a generally impressionist London that owed more to art than to lived experience. This was not *ekphrasis* in its usual sense, since, while it conjured a version of reality in the mind of the reader, it did it not simply through intense pictorial description of an object in itself but through reference to a previous artistic rendering of that object or scene. At the same time, it deployed a mixture of Pater and factitious essentialism about the city itself to excuse any reluctance to analyse its material. 'The spirit of the great city is not analytic, and, as they come up, subjects rarely receive at its hands a treatment drearily earnest or tastelessly thorough,' James suggested.[110]

Impressionism, Symons argued in 'The Decadent Movement in Literature' (1893), sought 'not general truth merely, but *la vérité vrai*, the very essence of truth' and brought with it 'a revolt from the ready-made of language, from the bondage of traditional form'. It was, he maintained, 'a new style, an entire new creative psychology'.[111] Unfortunately, this 'new creative psychology' was by no means easily attained, and impressionist responses to London often replaced personal perspectives with deferential references to French art. This could seem naïve, as in 'The Author of *Beltraffio*', where the unworldly narrator remarks that many English things struck him as 'reproductions of something that existed primarily in art or literature'. 'It was not the picture, the poem, the fictive page, that seemed to me a copy,' he continues, 'these things were the originals, and the life of happy and distinguished people was fashioned in their image.'[112] In an earlier story, 'A Passionate Pilgrim' (1871), James employs a narrator who comes to England for six weeks after exploring France and Italy. Sitting in the 'coffee-room of the Red Lion', east of Temple Bar, the narrator remarks that the room, 'like so many other places and things I was destined

[109] Symons, *London*, 162.   [110] James, 'London', *English Hours*, 9.
[111] Symons, 'The Decadent Movement in Literature', in *Critics of the 'Nineties*, 111.
[112] James, 'The Author of *Beltraffio*', in *Complete Stories 1874–1884*, 868.

to see in England, seemed to have been waiting for long years, with just that sturdy sufferance of time written on its visage, for me to come and gaze, ravished but unamazed'. The speaker is 'unamazed' because he, like James, has already created what he will see through his prior exposure to fictional representation of the capital, 'in books, in visions, in dreams, in Dickens, in Smollett, and Boswell'.[113] Distinguished rather than happy, Symons drew his inspirations from visual art, trying 'to do in verse something of what Degas had done in painting', in the ballet poems in *Silhouettes* and *London Nights*, and pronouncing a recent visit to the ballet 'a Degas, in short'.[114]

Impressionist photography was frequently explicit in its homage to painting, with the night views of Paul Martin and the work of 'pictorialist' photographers such as James Sinclair and A. H. Blake notably indebted to painterly forebears, though ironically, Degas in particular often painted from photographs.[115] Ford Madox Ford deployed painterly language in envisioning a London 'brought into composition by mists . . . or a bright and stippled foreground'.[116] Even journalistic and popular writing was occasionally inclined to employ reference to Impressionism in lieu of practising impressionism of its own, as Lucas demonstrates. If Pre-Raphaelite art had often been explicitly literary in its inspiration, a new generation of writers was placing the visual at the service of the written, taking Impressionist art as the basis of its views of the city, rather than viewing the city in itself.

Tom Gibbons comments that Symons 'equates impressionism not with vagueness but with unprecedented accuracy and immediacy of communication', but however keenly it conveyed mood or sensation, literary impressionism suffered by comparison with visual art when describing the city.[117] The major reason for this was the sheer originality of Impressionist painting, the radical innovations of which shocked its viewers even while, at the Ruskin trial at least, seeming to amuse them. Writers had attempted to depict the workings of consciousness long before Impressionist art appeared: the *Quarterly Review* cited the examples of Donne, Sterne, and Keats in 1897. However, the Impressionist eye and the smoke- and fog-shrouded modern

[113] H. James, 'A Passionate Pilgrim', in *Complete Stories, 1864–1874* (New York: Library of America, 1999), 543. He also comments on the resemblance of English life to the images of it in Johnson, Austen, Tennyson, Fanny Burney, and the paintings of Gainsborough.

[114] Symons, *London*, 205, 208.

[115] There are plentiful examples in R. Flukinger et al., *Paul Martin: Victorian Photographer* (Austin: University of Texas Press, 1977); M. F. Harker, *The Linked Ring* (London: Heinemann, 1979); M. Seaborne, *Photographers' London 1839–1994* (London: Museum of London, 1995).

[116] F. M. Ford, *The Soul of London: A Survey of a Modern City*, ed. A. G. Hill (1905; London: Dent, 1995), 9.

[117] T. Gibbons, *Rooms in the Darwin Hotel: Studies in English Literary Criticism and Ideas 1880–1920* (Nedlands: University of Western Australia Press, 1973), 75.

industrial city combined to produce something quite new, and, for a short period, literature struggled to compete.

The result was the emergence of what the *Quarterly* termed 'pseudo-impressionism', a mode that, having rejected the factual under the auspices of Pater and Whistler, offered instead 'vague mistiness substituted for realities'. There was an appreciable difference, the journal insisted, between this 'vague mistiness' and a critical engagement with the external world that was based upon 'reflections and refractions' and 'recalling and renewing', but such phrasing itself seemed suggestive of Pater and implied that boundaries between the new art and its forebears were less clear than might have been hoped.[118] Subsequent criticism and theorization of literary impressionism has tended to agree, favouring the complex evocation of consciousness in James, Proust, and Thomas Mann, for instance, over writing that is consciously imitative of visual art. However, in the context of the representation of London, the latter is of considerable importance, since it was, in some respects, the written equivalent of landscape painting. Thus, while Matz is right to query any straightforward correlation between what writers and poets 'saw in galleries and studios' and what they attempted in prose and poetry, his focus on the novel rather than topographic writing means that he neglects acts of explicit homage.[119] Also, there is a marked difference between the tentative accommodations of the new art during the 1890s and a sophisticated re-examination of them a century later. The point is not that literary impressionism succeeded in producing a written version of Whistler or Monet's paintings, assuming that this could ever exist, but that writers saw such a goal as worthy of pursuit, at least when describing particular aspects of the English capital.

Symons and others were strongly sympathetic to Impressionist (or Whistlerian) art, and their versions of London proclaimed their allegiances with the French avant-garde and their opposition to empirically derived native tradition. By adopting this stance, they produced an extremely stylized image of the capital that made no attempt to disguise its artificiality, and which, following Pater, rejected analysis in favour of recording rather than explaining the experience of urban life. In his 1886 study of Browning, Symons had argued that rather than merely duplicating the external world, a description should indicate a character's emotional state. Perhaps alluding to Washington Allston's idea of the 'objective correlative', he maintained that 'The picture calls up the mood,' but for many writing on London, the picture became a lazy reference to approved aesthetic authorities that supersedes

---

[118] 'Fathers of Literary Impressionism in England', 173.
[119] Matz, *Literary Impressionism*, 46–7.

rather than encapsulates direct experience.[120] Like the narrator of 'The Author of *Beltraffio*', certain writers measured their cultural literacy in terms of an ability to recognize experience through artistic sources, rather than within the experiences themselves. Hence the young James apparently saw London as a series of John Leech drawings, the claustrophobia of Piccadilly in terms of Tennyson's *Maud*, and his potential fate within the city as being akin to that of John Harmon in Dickens's *Our Mutual Friend*.[121] Similarly, Whistler's versions of the Thames so impressed themselves upon the consciousness of his contemporaries that they refracted the river through the renderings of it in his paintings and prose. London became a series of texts and inter-texts, within which life, or perception at any rate, imitated art. As House suggests, by creating a new framework of expectation and classification, Impressionism gave young writers a new vocabulary and set of references through which they could express themselves and, crucially, signal their differences from those they regarded as their stuffily Victorian forebears. By pursuing this idea, writers created their own version of the city, and determined the ways in which it should be understood by their readers. Lawrence Markert points out that Symons and James typically entered cities at dusk, a time when light and atmosphere produced 'an accomplished artistic whole well suited to a mind dominated by literary impressionism'.[122]

The idea that literary or artistic representations colonize or even oust 'real' places from the reader's imagination is by no means a new one. G. K. Chesterton observed that 'Dickens did not stamp these places [Holborn, Charing Cross] on his mind: he stamped his mind on these places.'[123] Donald Olsen makes a similar point, suggesting that Dickens imposed 'his brilliant but perverse vision of London on the consciousness both of his contemporaries and of posterity'.[124] Chesterton's formulation suggests another type of impressionism, the one James employed when defining a novel as 'a direct impression of life' in 'The Art of Fiction'. The process by which literature or painting 'stamp their mind on these places' is notably distinct from the prose description of a Monet cityscape.[125] The former approach would be the basis of *Bleak House* and *The Portrait of a Lady*, the latter frequently produced only uninspired pastiche

---

[120] A. Symons, *An Introduction to the Study of Browning* (London: Cassell, 1886), 24.

[121] H. James, 'George du Maurier', in *Partial Portraits* (London: Macmillan, 1888), 339; 'London', *English Hours*, 8.

[122] L. W. Markert, *Arthur Symons: Critic of the Seven Arts* (Ann Arbor: University of Michigan Press, 1988), 69.

[123] G. K. Chesterton, *Dickens* (1906), in P. Jukes, *A Shout in the Street: The Modern City* (London: Faber, 1990), 21.

[124] D. Olsen, 'Introduction: Victorian London', in D. Owen, *The Government of Victorian London, 1855–1889* (Cambridge, MA: Harvard University Press, 1982), 10–12.

[125] James, *The House of Fiction*, 29.

or journalistic convenience. Despite this, however, the vogue for perceiving one's environment in terms of art, or, more recently, cinema, has endured. Writers could not properly imitate Whistler's paintings, since they could not transfer his effects from one medium to another, but they could describe them, or respond to London views as if those views were actually of Whistlerian manufacture. Descriptions of the city consequently acquired their own limited vocabulary or lexical palette, slowly transforming those areas of London given artistic sanction by the painter's art.

IMITATING WHISTLER

Whistler is now regarded almost exclusively as a painter, but in the late nineteenth and early twentieth centuries, he influenced the portrayal of London with pen as well as brush. His celebration of the urban was another importance difference between the 'new' art and the principles of Ruskin, who denounced the metropolis with histrionic abandon. In a lecture on architecture, Ruskin poured scorn on 'our cities, built in black air which, by its accumulated foulness, first renders all ornament invisible in distance, then chokes its interstices with soot' and which are, as a consequence, 'mere crowded masses of stone'.[126] Whistler, however, saw the situation very differently.

The loftily poetic evocation of the misty Thames in *The Ten O' Clock Lecture* was widely regarded as a beautiful prose poem, and frequently imitated, especially by those who had already imbibed Verlaine's gospel of imprecision in 'Art poétique' (1874):

> Il faut aussi que tu n'ailles point
> Choisir tes mots sans quelque méprise:
> Rien de plus cher que la chanson grise
> Où l'Indécis au Précis se joint.[127]

This literary version of soft-focus recurred in Whistler's response to the avowedly commercial watercourse, which is as much a description of one of his own paintings as it is an evocation of London:

---

[126] J. Ruskin, 'The Study of Architecture in Schools', in *The Complete Works of John Ruskin*, ed. Cook and Wedderburn, xix. 24.

[127] P. Verlaine, *Jadis et Naguère* (1884). Symons rendered this as: 'Choose your words, but think not whether | Each to other of old belong: | What so dear as the dim grey song | Where clear and vague are joined together?' *Knave of Hearts* (1913) in *The Collected Works of Arthur Symons*, iii: *Poems* (London: Martin Secker, 1924), 126.

And when the evening mist clothes the riverside with poetry, as with a veil, and the poor buildings lose themselves in the dim sky, and the tall chimneys become campanili, and the whole city hangs in the heavens, and fairy-land is before us . . . Nature, who, for once, has sung in tune, sings her exquisite song to the artist alone.[128]

Whistler's elitist stance has received trenchant criticism from Graham Hough, who dismisses such writing as akin to that of the 'amateurs and dilettanti whom [Whistler] most despised'. Hough perceives an aesthetic contradiction that allowed the artist to be 'the apostle of the contemporary, of form and colour for their own sakes' yet claim to enjoy warehouses and chimneys because of their resemblance to Italianate bell-towers. The painter's insistence that such visions are unique to the possessor of heightened perceptions is, Hough suggests, both commonplace and patronizing, but, as he points out, such passages were instrumental in winning Whistler admiration 'for what he would certainly have considered all the wrong reasons'.[129] The 'poetic' description of the Thames was now no longer the provenance of the hackneyed scribbler, and Whistlerian terminology was regularly appropriated by writers who were susceptible to the pull of fashion rather than sharing Whistler's aesthetic aims. Max Beerbohm's absurd poetaster Enoch Soames mixes Whistler with the diabolism of Baudelaire in his 'Nocturne', a description of an evening stroll through London with Satan.[130] Whistler's influential proselytizing for what was popularly understood as Impressionism lent such writing dignity and, perhaps more crucially, the same sense of modernity young writers discerned in Walter Pater.

As John House discovered, such descriptive set-pieces derive from the resolutely elitist Gautier and his essay 'Une Journée à Londres' (1842), a sketch which anticipated, and perhaps inspired, Whistler's later flourish:

A forest of colossal chimneys, in the form of towers, columns, pylons and obelisks, give the horizon an Egyptian look . . . Industry, on this gigantic scale, almost attains poetry, poetry in which nature counts for nothing . . .

This smoke, spread over everything, blurs harsh angles, veils the meanness of buildings, enlarges views, gives mystery and vagueness to the most positive objects. In the smoke, a factory chimney becomes an obelisk, a warehouse of poor design takes on the airs of a Babylonian terrace, a grim row of columns changes into the porticoes of Palmyra. The symmetrical barrenness of civilisation and the vulgarity of the forms it adopts all become softened or disappear, thanks to this kindly veil.[131]

---

128 Whistler, *The Gentle Art of Making Enemies*, 144.
129 G. Hough, *The Last Romantics* (1949; London: Duckworth, 1979), 186.
130 M. Beerbohm, 'Enoch Soames' (1912), from *Seven Men and Two Others* (1919; Harmondsworth: Penguin, 1954), 18–19.
131 J. House, 'The Impressionist Vision of London', in I. B. Nadel and F. S. Schwarzbach, eds., *Victorian Artists and the City* (New York: Pergamon Press, 1980), 84. Gautier's essay first

Whistler substitutes Venice for Gautier's orientalism, perhaps because by the 1880s, Babylon was a standard reference point for the moral condemnation of the metropolis. His description of the effects of fog and smoke on the industrial landscape are notably similar, however, as is the sense that the artist, 'the creator' rather than the recorder 'of beautiful things', is the agent of its transformation.[132] The verbs of House's translation frequently recur in impressionist writing, blurring, veiling, and softening the city's 'most positive objects'.

Whistler's evocation of the river insisted on the primacy of the artist's vision, but ironically, it did so through other art forms. The poetry that 'clothes the riverside' had yet to be written in English: when it was, it claimed derivation from the painter, reference to whom became the means of validating similar responses to the Thames. Some cited Whistler by name, others by unmistakable allusion to his words or preferred terminology of nocturnes, harmonies, and arrangements. Just as reading Pater spared his intellectual disciples immersion in works they would probably have found antipathetic or tedious, so the citation of Whistler allowed some of those who came after him to dignify their perceptions of the city without having to undertake his arduous aesthetic education.[133] E. V. Lucas's *A Wanderer in London*, for instance, claimed Whistlerian precedent for maintaining that fog transformed the capital into one of 'romance' and quoted the painter's description of the Thames in support of such observations.[134] Lucas also reprised 'this morsel of Whistlerian beauty' elsewhere in his writing on London.[135] Yoshio Markino quickly absorbed Whistlerian vocabulary and attitudes. 'Perhaps the real colours of some buildings in London might be rather crude,' he wrote, 'But this crude colour is so fascinating in the mists.' His eye drawn to the 'ugly colour' of a neighbouring house, Markino noted that 'now the winter fogs cover it . . . the harmony of its colour is most wonderful.'[136] Arthur Ransome's *Bohemia in London* (1907) implied that Whistlerian description was a model for aspiring writers and painters:

Often the dawn was in the sky before I left the coffee-stall and crossed the river, and then the pale grey mist with the faint lights in it, and the mysterious ghosts of chimneys

appeared in *Revue des Deux Mondes* (15 April 1842), and was reprinted in *Zigzags* (1845) and *Caprices et Zigzags* (1852).

[132] Wilde, Preface to *The Picture of Dorian Gray*, in *Complete Works*, 17.

[133] For Pater's reading during the 1850s and 1860s, see B. A. Inman, 'The Intellectual Context of Pater's "Conclusion"', in P. Dodd, ed., *Walter Pater: An Imaginative Sense of Fact* (London: Frank Cass, 1981), 12–30.

[134] Lucas, *A Wanderer in London*, 22.

[135] E. V. Lucas, 'Disappearing London', in *Loiterer's Harvest: A Book of Essays* (London: Methuen, 1913), 11.

[136] Y. Markino, *A Japanese Artist in London* (London: Chatto and Windus, 1911), 189.

and bridges, looming far away, seemed the most beautiful thing in life, one of those promises that are fairer than reality. It was easy to be a poet, gazing into that dream that hung over the river; easy to be a painter, with that delicate picture in my eyes.[137]

That Ransome does not mention Whistler in the course of this evocation is significant in itself, since it demonstrates how his depiction of the Thames had percolated into the consciousness of the writers and artists, and indeed their readers, who followed him. 'The Surrey side [of the Thames] is dark with tall, vague buildings rising out of the mud on which a little water crawls: is it the water that moves or the shadows?', wrote Symons in *London: A Book of Aspects*, noting 'the impossible fairy peep-show of the Embankment' and the 'fairy-palaces' made by lights on the river. Barges and steamers are no longer industrial vessels but 'solid patches' in what Symons called in *London Nights* 'colour studies'. 'The buildings on the Embankment rise up, walls of soft greyness with squares of lighted windows,' he observes. 'They tremble in the mist, their shapes flicker; it seems as if a breath would blow out their lights and leave them bodiless husks in the wind.' Aestheticizing his environment without thought of its material implications, Symons even delights in the 'reddish smoke' from one of the chimneys, a doubtless noxious emission that 'floats and twists like a flag'.[138] Coburn, whom Symons originally wished to illustrate *London*, called the description of the Thames a 'gem of prose, . . . a passage Whistler would have revelled in'.[139] His own pictures, such as 'Paddington Canal' and 'Wapping' from *London* (1909), consciously imitated Whistler's work. Even the photographer's clothes admitted Whistler's influence, with Coburn adopting a markedly Whistlerian silk hat when working on his London scenes. Another stylish aesthete, E. W. Hornung's Raffles, also appreciates the winter sun 'struggling through the haze' and admires 'the infirm silhouettes of Abbey and Houses in flat grey against a golden mist'. He murmurs of Whistler, and discards his cigarette 'because the smoke would curl between him and the picture'.[140]

Symons made no secret of his fondness for Whistler, although, as Gibbons notes, he did accuse him of triviality in 1900.[141] A more unexpected Whistlerian

[137] A. Ransome, *Bohemia in London* (1907; Oxford: Oxford University Press, 1984), 18.

[138] Symons, *London*, 163, 210.

[139] A. L. Coburn, *Men of Mark* (London: Duckworth, 1913), 20–1. Coburn and Symons were unable to find a publisher for their illustrated book, and it now exists only as its component parts. In 1914, Coburn's friend Edmund D. Brooks did print a pair of copies of the complete version, but he did not publish these commercially and Symons never saw one. Coburn's is now in the library of Reading University.

[140] E. W. Hornung, 'The Raffles Relics', from *A Thief in the Night* (1905). *The Collected Raffles* (London: Dent, 1985), 412.

[141] A. Symons, 'The Art of Watts', *The Fortnightly Review*, 68 n.s. (August 1900); Gibbons, *Rooms in the Darwin Hotel*, 91.

homage appeared in Clarence Rook's *The Hooligan Nights* (1899), an otherwise journalistic account of the behaviour of a South London teenage criminal. In chapter 15, Rook loiters one night in the vicinity of Cleopatra's Needle, waiting to hear his villain's latest misadventures:

It was a clear night, with a full moon shining and turning the Thames into a fairy river spanned by bridges of gossamer. Have you ever seen Charing Cross railway bridge by moonlight? . . . Why do people not go out in parties to lean over the parapet of the Embankment and watch the Thames by moonlight?

. . . this evening it was fairyland. The tide was at the full, and the moonlight transfigured the sordid details of the Surrey side. Fairyland . . . , as you leaned over the parapet and watched the silver path of the moon upon the river break into ten million diamonds as the tug crossed it.[142]

This reminder of Rook's 'poetic credentials' is part of an ill-judged moment of social criticism in which London's beauties are contrasted with the unpleasant realities that accompany them.[143] Whistler is here reduced to mere journalistic scene-setting, and the elevated register is abandoned as soon as Young Alf arrives.

Each of these rhapsodies replaced the living metropolis with an aestheticized variant of it that 'transfigured' its 'sordid details' into self-conscious 'art'. Thomas Hardy was already sceptical about such approaches in 1892, noting how 'those marvellous sunset effects' so characteristic of late afternoon were actually comprised of 'kitchen coal-smoke and human and animal exhalations'.[144] Even Symons accepted in a rare moment of political reflection that 'Those sordid splendours of smoke and dirt which may be so fine as aspects, mean something which we can only express by the English word squalor; they mean the dishumanising of innumerable people.'[145] Other writers also resisted the pull of transformative impressionism. Grant Allen's sarcastic essay 'Beautiful London' (1893) ridiculed comparisons between London and Venice. 'How every true Englishman's heart must swell with pride of world-wide empire,' Allen writes, 'as he contrasts in memory the way up from Greenwich to the Tower with the way up from the Lido to the Doges' palace!'[146] In H. G. Wells's *Tono-Bungay* (1909), the sceptical young scientist George Ponderevo has a moment of anti-Whistlerian epiphany as his train enters London. 'I got an effect of tall warehouses, of

---

[142] C. Rook, *The Hooligan Nights: Being the Life and Opinions of a Young and Impertinent Criminal recounted by Himself and Set Forth by Clarence Rook* (1899; Oxford: Oxford University Press, 1979), 113–14.

[143] Ibid., p. xi.

[144] T. Hardy, *The Pursuit of the Well-Beloved and The Well Beloved*, ed. P. Ingham (London: Penguin, 1997), 139.

[145] Symons, *London*, 214.

[146] G. Allen, 'Beautiful London', *Fortnightly Review* (July 1893), 44.

grey water, barge crowded, of broad banks, of indescribable mud.'[147] Like
Lionel Johnson, Wells critiques impressionism through its own discourse, the
apparently unmediated moments of vision that, as Pater says, 'burn and are
extinguished with our consciousness of them'. Aesthetes from Whistler to
Symons had condescended to middle class tastes in proclaiming the new art,
but by 1909, it seemed, impressionist responses to London were becoming
standardized, and so commonplace, that they could even be vouchsafed to
scientists.

Robin Spencer suggests that Whistler's transformation of the industrial
riverside into campanili appealed to his patrons, the industrialists whose
eagerness to embrace 'the march of civilisation' made them wilfully blind to
its human and environmental cost.[148] However, the turning of the industrial
chimney into the Italianate bell tower was more than the cynical caprice of the
painter's increasingly astute marketing. Some might now regard Whistler's
aestheticizing of the Thames's filthy waterfront as environmentally irresponsible, but it was part of a wider concern with artistic vision that refused
to be trammelled or circumscribed by urban actualities. Dickens had done
much the same in his fabulous rendering of Coketown in *Hard Times* (1854),
or the horrible suburb in chapter 45 of *The Old Curiosity Shop* (1840–1),
but where his 'interminable serpents of smoke' and pistons 'like the head
of an elephant in a state of melancholy madness' had been employed to
denounce industrialization and celebrate the power of the imagination to
resist utilitarianism, Whistler seemed to have no aims beyond demonstrating his own painterly virtuosity.[149] Faced with an increasingly commercial,
industrial, and polluted metropolis, Whistler turned away from the quasi-
objectivity of realist painting. He espoused instead techniques that allowed
the artist to place the city at his mercy, whereas in truth the artist was
firmly at the mercy of it, dependent upon it for both subject matter and
livelihood.

Many writers appropriated Whistler's versions of the Thames in order
to demonstrate their modern sympathies and, as Whistler's place in the
pantheon of nineteenth-century artists became increasingly secure, to raise
their artistic status by association. By 1904, Saki's Reginald had even termed
London the 'City of Dreadful Nocturnes', perhaps thinking of poems such
as Victor Plarr's 'A Nocturne at Greenwich' (1896).[150] It is notable, however, that it was a 'New Woman' writer, George Egerton, who was perhaps

---

[147] H. G. Wells, *Tono-Bungay*, ed. J. Hammond (1909; London: Dent, 1994), 73.
[148] Spencer, 'The Aesthetics of Change', 61.
[149] C. Dickens, *Hard Times*, ed. K. Flint (1854; London: Penguin, 1995), 28.
[150] Saki, 'Reginald's Peace Poem', from *Reginald* (1904), *The Complete Saki* (London: Penguin,
1982), 15. Plarr's poem appeared in *In the Dorian Mode* (1896).

the first to place Whistlerian connotations at a more critical or ironic distance in deploying them for her own purposes. She used Whistlerian terminology on several occasions in the tellingly entitled *Symphonies* (1897), most strikingly in 'A Nocturne'. Rather than use the description as a demonstration of her 'poetic credentials' or a 'word painting', however, Egerton places these perceptions at the service of psychological investigation. Such a development suggests in ways in which the primarily visual impressionism of Whistler's imitators could be linked to the more sophisticated experiments with consciousness taking place in James's *The Spoils of Poynton* and *What Maisie Knew*, and Conrad's *The Nigger of the 'Narcissus'* (1897).

'A Nocturne' is narrated by an Irish aesthete, who surrounds himself with the trappings of the aesthetic movement in collecting fine books and wearing 'an old Jap kimono'.[151] One night, he is gazing from his window onto the Embankment, when he notices a woman gazing into the river. Concerned that she is contemplating suicide, rather than, as Rook would later have it, admiring the moon's reflection, he invites her into his rooms, where she displays cultivated taste and confesses her literary ambitions. The narrator promises to help her place some of her work, and, half-starved and exhausted, she falls asleep by the fire. The following morning, she leaves. All that remains of her is the ash of her cigarette, which the narrator tips into a matchbox as a furtive, symbolic treasure. When he sees her again, she seems set for limited journalistic success.

The story's use of Whistler is quite different from that made of him elsewhere. Here, Whistlerian language and perception are employed to emphasize the gulf between the rhetoric of artistic fashion and mature human sympathy. Cocooned in his rooms, the narrator, a well-travelled urban connoisseur a little reminiscent of Symons, has his books and a devoted servant, but his understanding of women is at best superficial. His description of the Thames is therefore a means of unwitting revelation, as well as a demonstration of his imaginative allegiance:

I have rather nice diggings. . . . They are on the embankment, just within sight of Cleopatra's Needle. I like the anachronism of a monument; it has a certain fascination for me. I can see it at night, if I lean out of my window, outlined above the light-flecked river sacred to our sewer goddess that runs so sullenly under its canopy of foggy blue.

To me the embankment has beauties unsurpassed in any city in Europe. The opaque blotches of the plane-trees' foliage, the glistening water, the dotted lines of golden light, the great blocks of buildings rearing to the clouds like shadow monuments, the benches laden with flotsam and jetsam.[152]

151 G. Egerton, *Symphonies* (London: John Lane, 1897), 97.   152 Ibid. 90.

'A Nocturne' is in some respects a parable about the relationship between the aestheticized version of London and its social realities, daringly articulated through the very language that, in the hands of others, disdains those elements of city life deemed incompatible with art. The narrator's use of 'flotsam and jetsam' is a glib legitimation of metropolitan inequality, implying that the homeless are merely a piquant enhancement of the scenery and destitution a natural and inevitable corollary of the capital's excretory processes. As Raphael Samuel points out, by 1897, the year of Victoria's diamond jubilee, the Embankment had become a traditional refuge for tramps, its 'brilliant lights only serving to enhance the darkness'.[153] Egerton's narrator intervenes to save one stricken individual, but though he derives a smug satisfaction from offering help to the woman, he remains blithely unconscious of the fate of many others. Egerton's story demonstrates the ways in which Whistlerian description could be imbued with a political charge, rather than the laissez-faire aestheticism associated with many of its male proponents. However, conservative critics tended to see its effects as merely modish, with *Punch* rewriting the nursery rhyme 'Jack and Jill' as 'Nocturne in Black-and-Blue', beginning 'The subtle colour-harmony was fading from the Western sky.'[154]

Whistler's pictures of the Thames were equally inspirational for word-painters, though their influence is harder to trace in its movement from one medium to another. Again, however, certain writers employ the Whistlerian as a badge of rank that proclaims artistic modernity and refined tastes. It should be said, however, that too showy an allegiance with Whistler could have unfortunate effects. Wilde's 'Symphony in Yellow' (1889), with its Whistlerian title and colour scheme, is a striking example of the flamboyance that occasionally accompanied this position. An omnibus crawls across Blackfriars bridge 'like a yellow butterfly', a doubly Whistlerian reference, the Thames is 'a rod of rippled jade', and St Paul's 'a bubble' that 'loomed' over the city.[155] Wilde strips the cathedral of its religious significance, making it a feature of the skyline rather than the symbol of how 'Religion towers | Above this sordid, restless life of ours' that it had been for James Thomson.[156] In *The Critic as Artist*, Wilde had maintained that the aim of criticism was 'to see the object as in itself it really is not,' and that, for the critic, 'the work of art is simply a suggestion for a new work of his own, that need not necessarily bear

[153] R. Samuel, 'Comers and Goers', in H. J. Dyos and M. Wolff, eds., *The Victorian City: Images and Realities*, 2 vols. (London: Routledge and Kegan Paul, 1973), i. 146.

[154] 'Nocturne in Black-and-Blue', *Punch* (13 November 1897), 221.

[155] Wilde, 'Symphony in Yellow' (1889), in *Complete Works*, 872.

[156] J. Thomson, 'The Approach to St. Paul's' (1855), *Poems and Some Letters of James Thomson*, ed. A. Ridler (Carbondale: Southern Illinois University Press, 1963), 5.

any obvious resemblance to the thing it criticises.'[157] 'Symphony in Yellow' demonstrated the consequences of applying these views to the city, for here, the poet becomes a critic of the metropolitan vista, and imposes on it his own artistic ingenuity. The result is that imaginative flourishes are all too obviously interspersed between the perception of the object and its record, rather in the manner of the contrived conceits of lesser metaphysical poetry. The insistence on comparisons makes the end product seem decorative rather than spontaneous, and as such, it is the precise opposite of Whistler's own method.

Henley's 'To James McNeill Whistler' by contrast attempts to evoke the Thames without describing Whistler's own paintings of it:

> Under a stagnant sky
> Gloom out of gloom uncoiling into gloom,
> The River, jaded and forlorn,
> Welters and wanders wearily—wretchedly—on;
> Yet in and out among the ribs
> Of the old skeleton bridge, as in the piles
> Of some dead lake-built city, full of skulls,
> Worm-worn, rat-riddled, mouldy with memories,
> Lingers to babble to a broken tune
> (Once, O, the unvoiced music of my heart!)
> So melancholy a soliloquy
> It sounds as it might tell
> The secret of the unending grief-in-grain
> The terror of Time and Change and Death,
> That wastes this floating, transitory world.[158]

John Sweetman suggests that these lines refer to Whistler's *Nocturne: Blue and Gold—Old Battersea Bridge* and that they represent 'Baudelairean sentiments', but they seem more reminiscent of Thomson's *The City of Dreadful Night* (1874/1880) and the vile marshes of Richard Jefferies's *After London* (1885).[159] The poem's rough blank verse gives it the lack of finish Burne-Jones noted of Whistler's paintings, but the rhetorical posturing and laboured asides, '(River, O River of Journeys, River of Dreams!)', are more typical of Henley's tub-thumping than the painter's subtlety. Henley is more suggestive of Whistler in his reference to the 'floating, transitory world', a gloss on *Ukiyo*, which signals a connection between poet and painter through their shared interest in painting of this kind. The leading school of Japanese art from the seventeenth

---

[157] Wilde, *The Critic as Artist*, in *Complete Works*, 1128.

[158] W. E. Henley, *Poems* (London: Macmillan, 1926), 135.

[159] J. Sweetman, *The Artist and the Bridge 1700–1920* (Aldershot: Ashgate, 1999), 153; R. Jefferies, *After London, or Wild England* (1885; Oxford: Oxford University Press, 1980), 36–8.

to the nineteenth century, *Ukiyo* conveys 'a feeling for the minute and transitory detail of the world, and for things felt by intuition rather than seen through the eyes', a definition that has much in common with late-nineteenth-century conceptions of impressionism and indeed, in its concern with the limitations of visual perception, Symbolism.[160] The poem is, though, neither an example of *Japonisme* nor genuinely Whistlerian, since Henley soon lapses back into abstractions, with the poem's closing lines, a pondering of 'these poor Might-Have-Beens', performed much more effectively by D. G. Rossetti in 'A Superscription' (1869). There is nothing here of the 'light, atmosphere, distance and mystery' Sadakichi Hartmann felt Whistler had brought to Japanese methods of composition.[161]

Henley's *London Voluntaries* (1892) had been praised by Symons for their 'revolutionary' attention to the city and the 'modernity in verse' that they represented. 'Here, at last,' Symons wrote, 'is a poet who can so enlarge the limits of his verse to take in London' and thus pass the 'test of poetry which professes to be modern', the 'capacity' for dealing with the English metropolis.[162] Symons saw Henley as embodying the same spirit as Whistler and Verlaine, but it is not easy to endorse his judgement, not least because the review never properly considers the form that 'modern' poetry will take. Subject matter is, it seems, all, unless one assumes that the Paterian Symons has taken matter and form as inextricable. *London Voluntaries* is not consistently impressionist in manner, and is marred by frequently unimaginative rhyming and erratic scansion. The second Voluntary, 'Andante con moto', describes the Thames by night and gives a sense of the poems' unfulfilled promise:

> A sense of space and water, and thereby
> A lamplit bridge ouching the troubled sky,
> And look, O, look! a tangle of silver gleams
> And dusky lights . . .
> What miracle is happening in the air,
> Charging the very texture of the gray
> With something luminous and rare? [163]

Resonant neologism jostles with a colour scheme of grey and silver and gold in a description that suggests the atmosphere of Whistler's pictures and the application of Verlaine's 'Pas la Coleur, rien que la nuance'.[164] Unfortunately, these suggestions of what impressionism might be able to achieve in depicting nocturnal London are undermined by insistent gesturing,

---

[160] P. Redgrove, *The Black Goddess and the Sixth Sense* (1987; London: Paladin, 1989), 42.
[161] S. Hartmann, *The Whistler Book* (Boston: L. C. Page, 1910), 67.
[162] Symons, 'Modernity in Verse', *Studies in Two Literatures*, 188.
[163] Henley, 'Andante con Moto', *Poems*, 194.
[164] 'Colour, away! Come to me, shade!' 'Art poétique', Symons, *Collected Works*, iii: *Poems*, 126.

a tendency towards moralizing, and uncertain indulgence in fantastic imagery. This last trait is combined with archaic diction to produce such inept coinages as 'A rakehell cat—how furtive and acold!' and the transformation of barges into 'goblin floats, | Black, hag-steered, fraught with devilry and dream!'[165] Henley's impressionism had been far more effective in the short poems he had written in Edinburgh during the 1870s, particularly the unrhymed sequence, *In Hospital* (1875). Here he had shown that by disdaining affected diction and concentrating on evoking moments of intensely realized experience, he could achieve strikingly original effects. Each 'Voluntary', however, sprawled over several pages, diluting its impact through flaccid structure and a fondness for laboured whimsy.

Pater claimed that 'a sudden light transfigures a trivial thing', and in the third of his *London Voluntaries*, Henley follows suit in noting how the sunlight 'transfigures' the city, bestowing a 'luminous transiency of grace' and transforming the noise of trains to 'the speech | Of lazy seas on a lotus-haunted beach.'[166] Nine years later, however, in 'For England's Sake', the image of 'a golden fog' had taken a disturbing political turn, suggesting a Britain complacently at peace, 'mellowing, dozing, rotting down | Into a rich deliquium of decay', as in the 'atmosphere of powdered old gold' in Conrad's *The Secret Agent*.[167] These images of yellow fog, lotus lands, and complacency would reappear in 'Prufrock' (1917), offering one of the most memorable images of the early-twentieth-century city. Ironically, Henley's most effective impressionist response to London occurs not in his own work but in a parody of him by Owen Seaman. Here, describing the Thames beside Parliament, Seaman/Henley anticipates the depiction of the river in 'The Fire Sermon' of *The Waste Land* (1922):

> With swirl of oozy ebb the River goes
> Bedridden, bargee-blasphemous,
> Lipping the terraced stones
> Outworn with commerce of tea and cakes
> And jaunty legislators' junketings.[168]

The Seaman/Henley composite offers surprising adjectives which, while purportedly comic and inappropriate—the tortuous pun of a 'bedridden' river—are no more ridiculous than the audacious juxtapositions of Eliot's early poetry, and far more vivid than the studied conceits of 'Symphony in Yellow'. What had seemed ludicrous to an artistic conservative in the early

---

[165] Henley, *Poems*, 195.   [166] Pater, *The Renaissance*, 113.
[167] Henley, *Poems*, 196–7, 240; Conrad, *The Secret Agent*, 9.
[168] O. Seaman, *Borrowed Plumes* (1902; London: Constable, 1916), 130.

1890s was, by 1917, the launching pad for the radical new poetry of the interwar era.

IMITATING MONET

Monet had initially found it difficult to respond to the artistic challenge posed by the English weather, managing only six paintings in eight months during his first visit to the capital in 1870–1. His later paintings of the Thames and Parliament, however, begun on a balcony of the Savoy Hotel in the winter of 1899, completed from memory in his studio, and first exhibited between 1902 and 1904, are now regarded as some of the defining images of *fin de siècle* London. Rarely has air pollution received such extravagant artistic homage. Buildings loom through fogs of violet, yellow, and green, a testimony not only to Monet's chromatic vision and artistic daring, but also to the extraordinary atmospheric conditions of the early-twentieth-century capital.

For Dickens in *Our Mutual Friend*, fogs were 'dark yellow, and . . . brown, and then browner, and then browner, until at the heart of the City . . . it was rusty black'.[169] Monet, however, rendered fogs as a psychedelic mirage. 'Their brilliantly unreal colours are completely unlike the filthy greys of London fogs,' Virginia Spate remarks, 'yet they are intensely revealing of the effects which inspired them,' while for John House they are 'improvisations which took London's atmospherics as their starting point' rather than being 'direct notations of observed effects'.[170] Paintings such as the series of views of Parliament in sun and fog (1903) and the startling *Leicester Square, Londres, la nuit* (c.1918) undoubtedly offer a remarkable re-imagining of the metropolis. In them, Monet offers a quite literal blurring of the distinctions between observation, memory, and fancy that had interested Wordsworth in the London sections of *The Prelude* a century earlier. He stripped the fog of any symbolic significance, with his fog-shrouded Parliament an aesthetic effect rather than an implied criticism of its workings. Finally, he was highly selective in the types of fog he chose to paint. 'The fog in London assumes all sorts of colours,' he wrote in 1901. '[T]here are black, brown, yellow, green, purple fogs, and the interest in painting is to get the objects as seen through all these fogs.' However, though he could list the colours in a letter, they were by no means easy to put onto canvas. 'It's hard to have a beautiful image to paint

---

[169] C. Dickens, *Our Mutual Friend*, ed. A. Poole (1865; London: Penguin, 1997), 417.
[170] V. Spate, *Claude Monet: The Colour of Time* (London: Thames and Hudson, 1992), 250; House, 'London in the Art of Monet and Pissarro', in *The Image of London*, 88.

and to have suddenly in front of you a layer of darkness of an unnameable colour,' he complained. 'Alas, the fog persists, from dark brown it has become olive green, but always as dark and impenetrable.'[171]

Monet's version of the city's fog was only one of many literary and artistic responses to what James had identified as the city's 'optical laws', but all of them had to adjudicate between the claims of shimmering prismatic fog, which made for spectacular visions, and the more 'Dickensian' black or brown fog that was best used symbolically since its visual qualities were minimal. If, as Yeats's father suggested, the young poets of the period were 'the Hamlets of our age', then it was only right that they should inhabit a London that was a 'pestilent congregation of metropolitan vapours'.[172] While it was responsible for a monochrome wilderness in the winter months, or even, as James discovered at Greenwich, the summer ones, the fog could also offer extraordinarily vivid colours, especially at sunset. It might be argued that Monet was responding to the same stimuli as many London writers, but, as with the depiction of the Thames, it is often hard to read impressionist writing without superimposing the painter's work upon it, even when it is not explicitly invoked. It is as if Impressionist art conditioned the eyes of those sympathetic to its strategies, just as Wilde had suggested.

In March 1899, a semi-serious dialogue in *The Artist* presented a painter rhapsodizing about a London sunset:

There's nothing to be seen like it ever—in any town in Europe. They say it's due to the smoke and it may be; but just look at it. Look at the purple and crimson, the scarlet and gold . . . And see how it all dies back and dies back, until with just the tiniest fleck of pink it sinks into the palest green.[173]

Symons responded to fog and sunsets with similar enthusiasm, evoking the sky above Marble Arch in terms that suggest personal experience has been laced with Monet's prismatic largesse. 'I remember hearing Claude Monet say, at the time when he came over to the Savoy Hotel, year by year, to paint Waterloo Bridge from its windows,' he wrote, 'that he could not understand why any English painter ever left London.' Such comments must have licensed his own response to Monet's subject matter. '[Y]ou may see conflagrations of jewels,' he wrote, 'a sky of burning lavender, tossed abroad like a crumpled cloak, with broad bands of dull purple and smoky pink, slashed with bright gold and decked with grey streamers.' All this was perceived 'through a veil of

---

[171] G. Seiberling, *Monet in London* (Atlanta: High Museum of Art, 1988), 61–2.

[172] W. B. Yeats, *The Oxford Book of Modern Verse, 1892–1935* (Oxford: Clarendon Press, 1936), x; R. Blatchford, *A Bohemian Girl and McGinnis* (London: Clarion Newspaper Co., 1899), 109

[173] Vox, 'Talks by Three, V.–On the Victoria Embankment', *The Artist* (March 1899), 166.

moving mist, which darkens downwards to a solid block, coloured like lead'. Elsewhere, fog and gas-light 'collaborate' in 'the supreme London decoration', twin impresarios managing Beauty's debut.[174] 'The smoke ascends | In a rosy-and-golden haze,' noted Henley, 'The spires | Shine, and are changed.'[175]

Other writers were equally keen to experiment with fog effects. John Davidson's 'London, W.' from 'November' (1905) describes how a sunset 'welling like a crimson fount | Underneath the Marble Arch, o'erbrimm'd | All the smoky west,' while the 'darkling sky' was 'lit with faded light of lavender'.[176] In 'The Thames Embankment' (1908), sunshine on the river's mudbanks becomes 'A thing extravagantly beautiful: | The glistening, close-grained canvas of the mud | Like hammered copper shone,' with Davidson insisting on the painterly connotations of his images.[177] *The Testament of a Prime Minister* (1904) mixes the vivid colours of impressionist description with industrial processes in depicting the polluted River Lea as 'Enamelled filthily in many hues— | Purple and faded crimson, pallid gold | And swarthy soot in wrinkled creases.'[178] Davidson's impressionism was inspired less by French painters or Whistlerian abstractions than by Turner, who, he believed, 'often painted with torches instead of pencils, or if he used pencils they were of asbestos and dipped in wells of crimson fire and gold.'[179] However, although the model is different, the principle remains the same: a writer with progressive artistic sympathies again transcribes a scene from visual art as much as from personal observation. '[I]n London,' wrote Symons, 'it is the atmosphere that makes the picture, an atmosphere like Turner, revealing every form through the ecstasy of its colour.'[180] The young Henry James made a similar observation, telling Grace Norton that a letter that offered a 'picture of your London fog-world was really Turneresque.'[181] The profusion of accounts of fog worried Wilde's Vivian. 'Now, it must be admitted, fogs are carried to excess,' he quipped. 'They have become the mere mannerism of a clique, and the exaggerated realism of their method gives dull people bronchitis. Where the cultured catch an effect, the uncultured catch cold.'[182]

Julian Wolfreys has observed that 'fog not only obscures the city, *it becomes it*', in the process 'phantomizing' the metropolis through 'the very language

---

[174] Symons, *London*, 187, 164, 211.   [175] Henley, 'I. M. Margaritae Sororis', *Poems*, 105.
[176] J. Davidson, 'November' from *Holiday and Other Poems* (1905) in *The Poems of John Davidson*, i. 167.
[177] J. Davidson, 'The Thames Embankment' from *Fleet Street and Other Poems* (1909), in ibid. 179.
[178] J. Davidson, *The Testament of a Prime Minister*, in *The Poems of John Davidson*, ii. 355.
[179] Townsend, *John Davidson: Poet of Armageddon*, 236–7.   [180] Symons, *London*, 164.
[181] James to Norton, Rome, 5 March 1873. *The Letters of Henry James, Volume I, 1843–1875*, ed. L. Edel (Cambridge, MA: Harvard University Press, 1974), 349.
[182] Wilde, 'The Decay of Lying', in *Complete Works*, 1086.

that articulates it' and making it 'neither material nor immaterial . . . neither wholly there nor wholly not there'.[183] One should, however, distinguish between fog at street level and the spectacular displays in the skies above. Veiling and disguising the city's realities in 'the muffle and smother of . . . fallen clouds', the fog oppressed and menaced London's citizens, yet continued to inspire its artists.[184] In January 1897, a *Punch* cartoon depicted a Frenchman on his first visit to London. '[N]ow I understan' vot you mean ven you say ze Sun nevaire set in your dominion,' he says, '*It does not rise!*'[185] Monet was kinder. 'It is the fog which gives London its marvellous breadth,' he wrote in 1920, recalling how 'its regular, massive blocks become grandiose in this mysterious cloak.' 'Above all, what I love is the fog,' he remembered, wondering 'How could the English painters of the 19th century paint houses brick by brick? These people painted bricks that they didn't see, that they couldn't see.'[186]

Monet might have asked the same questions about realist writers, since Gissing had pronounced 'fogs and mists' to be 'Terrible enemies of mine' that 'destroy my power of work and make my whole nature *limp*'.[187] Dick Helder in Kipling's *The Light that Failed* (1891) blames atmospheric conditions for what he regards as the dismal state of English painting. '[T]hey don't know any better,' he remarks of his rivals, before pointing to a 'yellow fog' and asking 'What can you expect from creatures born and bred in this light?' He later concedes, though, that 'there is something in impressionism, after all'.[188] 'Poor blind idiots,' Monet remarked in a dismissal of traditional realism, 'They want to see everything clearly, even through a fog!'[189] Henry James remarked on how 'the smoke and fog and the weather in general' caused 'a confusion, a complication'.[190] Arthur Machen's *The Hill of Dreams* (1907) observed the 'distorting medium of the mist, changing all things'.[191] In Davidson's 'Yuletide' (1905), 'The woven gloom | Of smoke and mist, | The soot-entangled rain | . . . jumbles day and night,' making accurate observation of the type of detail beloved by realists impossible and transforming the city

[183] J. Wolfreys, *Writing London, Volume 2: Materiality, Memory, Spectrality* (Basingstoke: Macmillan, 2004), 43.

[184] R. L. Stevenson, *The Strange Case of Dr Jekyll and Mr Hyde*, ed. E. Letley (1886; Oxford: Oxford University Press, 1987), 32.

[185] 'In a November Fog', *Punch's Almanack* (January 1897).

[186] Claude Monet quoted by René Gimpel, *Diary of an Art Dealer*, trans. J. Rosenberg (London: Hodder and Stoughton, 1966), entries for 1 February 1920 and 28 November 1918, 88, 82.

[187] Gissing to Margaret Gissing, 18 September 1881, *Letters of George Gissing to Members of his Family*, collected and arranged by A. and E. Gissing (London: Constable, 1927), 104.

[188] R. Kipling, *The Light that Failed* (1891; London: Macmillan, 1895), 59, 96.

[189] A. H. Simmons, 'Impressionism', *The Oxford Reader's Companion to Conrad*, ed. O. Knowles and G. M. Moore (Oxford: Oxford University Press, 2000), 188.

[190] James, 'London', *English Hours*, 10–11.

[191] A. Machen, *The Hill of Dreams* (1907; Leyburn: Tartarus Press, 1998), 142.

into a phantasmal and temporally uncertain realm.[192] It was this, as much as the author's nautical associations, that led H. G. Wells to compare Conrad's style to 'river mist' where 'for a space things are seen clearly, and then comes a great grey bank of printed matter, page on page, creeping round the reader, swallowing him up'.[193] Literal and textual fogs converge, as in Beerbohm's drawing of James, with any knowledge gleaned being subjective, provisional, and, in many cases, momentary. Conrad himself recalled 'an autumn day with an opaline atmosphere, a veiled, semi-opaque, lustrous day, with fiery points and flashes of red sunlight . . . while the trees of the square were like tracings of Indian ink on a sheet of tissue paper.'[194] Even though he is not usually associated with impressionism, Eliot's first collection is fascinated by fog. It screens the 'darkened room' in 'Portrait of a Lady', tosses 'up to me | Twisted faces from the bottom of the street' in 'Morning at the Window', and 'rubs its back upon the window panes' in the title poem. *The Waste Land* has the deathly 'brown fog of a winter dawn', and even early poems such as 'First Caprice in North Cambridge' (1909) seem notably aware of the creative role of fog in the literary response to the modern city, helped by Eliot's prolonged exposure to it in St Louis, London, and Paris.[195]

Less ambitious writers simply used fog as a means of dismissing unpleasant realities, as Laurence Binyon does in 'Deptford' (1896), where the speaker 'welcome[s] this dull mist, that drapes | The path of the heavy sky above the street,' since it casts 'a phantom dimness on these shapes | That pass, by toil disfeatured'.[196] At such moments, with London's citizens poisoned, unindividuated, and picturesque, it becomes difficult to reconcile the artistic possibilities of the fog with the thousands of deaths it caused before the passing of the Clean Air Act in 1956.

Late-Victorian realist fiction had often focused on specific areas of London, detaching them from the wider city so that they might be studied and described in detail. Its concern with character, narrative, and the creation of a believable milieu that was accurate in so far as it could be narrowed its geographical focus and led it into competition with sociological and journalistic writing. The type of impressionism influenced by Whistler, Pater, and contemporary French art was freed from many of these obligations, not least because during the *fin de siècle* it tended to be employed in topographical essays and

---

[192] J. Davidson, 'Yuletide', *The Poems of John Davidson* i. 161.

[193] N. Sherry, ed., *Conrad: The Critical Heritage* (London: Routledge and Kegan Paul, 1973), 73.

[194] J. Conrad, *A Personal Record* (1912), in *A Mirror of the Sea and A Personal Record* (London: Dent, 1946), 73.

[195] T . S. Eliot, *The Complete Poems and Plays* (London: Faber, 1969), 22, 13, 18, 27; *Inventions of the March Hare, Poems 1909–1917*, ed. C. Ricks (London: Faber, 1996), 13.

[196] L. Binyon, *London Visions* (1896; London: Elkin Matthews, 1908).

lyric poems rather than novels. Rejecting the 'settled', 'comprehensive', and 'exhaustive', Blanchard Jerrold had designated *London: A Pilgrimage* (1872) 'a touch and go chronicle'.[197] Only later would the revolution in perception that impressionism represented merge with a corresponding revolution in the portrayal of consciousness. Novels such as Woolf's *Mrs Dalloway* (1925) and Dorothy Richardson's *Revolving Lights* (1923), with its fifty-page evocation of Miriam Henderson's walk through London, would combine the revelation of consciousness and the impressionist response to the city in symbiotic union, producing fiction that was both topographically engaged and psychologically adept.

Impressionistic word painting was, in one important respect, as geographically circumscribed as fiction set in the East End, being tied to areas that offered congenial views without the intervention of teeming humanity. There was therefore a recurrent concentration on a depopulated version of the Thames, the fog and darkness that reduced pedestrians to 'insubstantial things' and the 'clouds that dye the city sky'.[198] Areas of the metropolis that offered little visual stimulus were ignored, making the literary impressionist version of London a highly selective one.

'FLEETING AND TRANSITORY THINGS': SPEEDING LONDON

There was, however, another version of literary impressionism less interested in the painting of languid word pictures. Realism had struggled to adapt to the ever-increasing pace of city life, but impressionist painters from Turner onwards had been interested in the depiction of speeding machinery. One need only compare Turner's *Rain, Steam and Speed—The Great Western Railway* (1844) with the misleadingly harmonious arrangement of figures in William Powell Frith's *The Railway Station* (1862) to see a tension between narratives founded in the observation of human beings, and fleeting visions of dynamic energy.[199] Christopher Wood has described Frith's *Derby Day* (1858) as a 'curiously static, immobile picture' in which 'figures seem frozen into an

---

[197] B. Jerrold and G. Doré, *London: A Pilgrimage* (1872; New York: Dover, 1970), 16.

[198] J. Davidson, 'November' (1894), *Poems of John Davidson*, i. 71.

[199] Symons draws a similar parallel between 'the photographed surface' of 'Derby Day' and the 'careful and expressive subtlety' of Degas's racehorse paintings in 'James Thomson', *Studies in Two Literatures*, 232. It should be noted that although Frith's reputation was on the wane by the 1870s, social panorama pictures were still popular during the 1890s. See for example George Earle's *Going North—King's Cross Station* (1893).

immense, life-like tableau' to present a 'sanitized' and 'ordered' panorama.[200] The same point could be made of *The Railway Station*, where locomotives are far less important than their passengers. Might literary impressionist techniques be able to capture Symons' 'automobilisation' of London, the city that had become 'a series of flashes'?[201]

In 1891, D. S. MacColl pronounced that the 'most proper sense' of the term impressionism was 'the effort to catch and render fleeting and transitory things'.[202] For readers of Pater, such a definition applied to all aspects of life, even the moment of apprehending the apparent stasis of mist on the river, and posed a significant artistic challenge. Photography seemed to offer one answer, especially once increased shutter speeds allowed the instantaneous capture of objects. 'It's a pity . . . that [Whistler] didn't live long enough to use a camera, it would have saved him so much time,' Coburn ingenuously remarked.[203] Rebuked for his rapid rate of production, Coburn defended himself by maintaining that his 'apparently unseemly hurry has for its object my burning desire to record, translate, create, if you like, these visions of mine before they fade.'[204] However, for a 'pictorialist' photographer, a photograph was created as much in the studio as it was on location, with prints being cunningly treated to achieve a variety of intensely painterly effects. The resulting picture or 'vision' was in no way an artless snap or unqualified transcription of external reality. The photographer's work in processing and manipulating the image as it moved from film to print exposed not only the picture but also the problem at the heart of the impressionist ethos.

Discussing Symons in *The Sacred Wood* (1920), T. S. Eliot noted that while the impressions he conveys may be authentic in terms of the emotions which they encouraged or which accompanied them, the actual practice of recording impressions in words introduces additional material which alters the experience. '[Y]ou can never rest at the pure feeling,' he argued. 'The moment you try to put the impressions into words, you either begin to analyse and construct, to *ériger en lois*, or you begin to create something else.'[205] Ford Madox Ford identified a similar difficulty, distinguishing between impressionism as 'a thing altogether momentary' and the misleading effect of 'import[ing] into the record of observations of one moment the observations of a moment altogether different'. 'Superimposed emotions' are permissible,

---

[200] C. Wood, *Victorian Painting* (London: Weidenfeld and Nicolson, 1999), 65.

[201] Symons, *London*, 171, 163.

[202] D. S. MacColl, 'The New English Art Club', *The Spectator*, 66 (18 April 1891), 544.

[203] *American Photography* II/1 (January 1908), 19, in M. Weaver, *Alvin Langdon Coburn: Symbolist Photographer: Beyond the Craft* (New York: Aperture Foundation, 1986), 29.

[204] A. L. Coburn, 'The Relation of Time to Art', *Camera Work*, 36 (1911), in J. Green, ed., *Camera Work: A Critical Anthology* (New York: Aperture Foundation, 1973), 215–16.

[205] T. S. Eliot, *The Sacred Wood* (London: Methuen, 1920), 5.

but the impressionist writer should always aim for 'the impression, not the corrected article'.[206] Impressionist writers disdained the scaffolding of detail erected by certain realists, yet their own work was no less artificial. 'England', Monet wrote, 'is not a country where one can finish anything on the spot; the effect can never be found twice, and I should have done nothing but sketches, real impressions.'[207] His aim, he told Gustave Geoffroy in October 1890, was to convey 'instantaneity'.[208] Looking back on his early prose experiments with Conrad, Ford would later claim 'that life did not narrate, but made impressions on our brains.' The consequence of this was that a writer wishing 'to produce . . . an effect of life, must not narrate, but render'.[209]

In visual impressionism, 'rendering' had to be swift, since the transience of the moment made the rapid execution of pictures essential. Each had to be completed before prevailing conditions changed. Acutely aware of minute changes of hue, Monet worked on up to 100 paintings at a time, and noted in 1901 that 'objects change in appearance in a London fog more and quicker than in any other atmosphere, and the difficulty is to get every change down on canvas.'[210] For Alan Robinson, his 'serial paintings of 1899–1904' embodied 'a meditative consciousness of transience'.[211] If successive canvases were viewed in order at an exhibition, they could record changes across several hours in ways that echo the glacial progress of James's successive clauses, or the frames of Eadweard Muybridge's *Animal Locomotion* (1887), albeit from the subjective viewpoint of the painter rather than the scientific neutrality of Muybridge's cameras. John Rewald suggests that this would lead to 'a true impression of a certain aspect of nature' rather than 'a composite picture', but Monet's paintings of the Thames and Parliament were in fact both, with each picture complete in itself and informing a wider conception of the scene.[212] 'Impressionist pictures are thoroughly on the brink of *a*–rather than *the*—next moment,' notes Clive Scott, adding, 'do not all Impressionist paintings imply that they are one of a series?'[213]

[206] F. M. Ford, 'On Impressionism', *Poetry and Drama*, 2 (June, December 1914) in *idem*, *Critical Writings*, ed. F. MacShane (Lincoln: University of Nebraska Press, 1964), 40–1.

[207] Monet to Alice Monet, London, 10 March 1901, in Spate, *Claude Monet: The Colour of Time*, 243.

[208] J. Rewald, *The History of Impressionism* (New York: Museum of Modern Art, 1973), 589.

[209] F. M. Ford, 'Techniques', *Southern Review*, 1 (July 1935), 31.

[210] House, 'The Impressionist Vision of London', in *Victorian Artists and the City*, 88, quoting E. Bullet, 'Macmonnies, the Sculptor, Working Hard as a Painter', *The Eagle* (Brooklyn) (8 September 1901).

[211] A. Robinson, *Imagining London, 1770–1900* (Basingstoke: Palgrave, 2004), 158.

[212] Rewald, *The History of Impressionism*, 589.

[213] C. Scott, 'Symbolism, Decadence and Impressionism', in M. Bradbury and J. McFarlane, eds., *Modernism: A Guide to European Literature 1890–1930* (London: Penguin, 1991), 222.

Literary impressionists faced an analogous dilemma, in that they had to convey impressions before they either faded or were overtly transfigured by the act of recollection. In his notes for 'London Town' in August 1907, Henry James noted the 'charm' of 'vague dim pretty sunshine' as he sought to capture the effect of '*silvery*, watery, misty light—or say misty, watery, silvery—*that* order'.[214] This quest for adjectival exactitude made Coburn, his collaborator, wonder if he had 'sensitive plates in his brain on which to record his impressions', failing to appreciate that it was less the taking of the picture than its subsequent development that was the essence of James's literary art, just as it was his own.[215]

When describing the misty Thames or a historic church, impressionist writers could make a virtue of lapidary expression, since poetic effects were part of their self-fashioning as artists removed from the common herd. The communication of more dynamic experience and sensation was, however, far more difficult. Rather than revisiting debates about the delineation of consciousness in impressionist writing, I consider two accounts of London life that focus on the problem of conveying the experiences of rapid travel and immersion in the feverish activity of the streets. Impressionism was associated with speed throughout the late nineteenth century, but British commentators tended to see this in negative terms. Conservative critics were suspicious of the 'unfinished' nature of Impressionist canvases; Whistler's swift composition having been another bone of contention at the Ruskin trial. George Meredith rebuked the 'hurried habit of mind that comes of addiction to Impressionist effects', while in 1886, the *Spectator* commented that 'Impressionists are effecting very injuriously the literature of the day,' since their presumed hastiness encouraged 'a loss of distinct standards of thought and judgement'.[216] Impressionism was by no means the only response to what Arnold had termed the 'sick hurry' of modern life, but its sheer newness encouraged its advocacy by young writers. This was why, in 'Impressionistic Writing', Symons took such pains to differentiate between brevity and concision.

There are many late-Victorian and modernist representations of the sensation of speeding travel, from the insistent rhythms of R. L. Stevenson's 'From a Railway Carriage' in *A Child's Garden of Verses* (1885) to the narrator of Woolf's 'The Mark on the Wall' (1917) 'torn from the old lady about to pour out tea . . . as one rushes past in the train' and claiming that life

[214] 22 August 1907 in *The Notebooks of Henry James*, ed. F. O. Matthiessen and K. B. Murdock (New York: Oxford University Press, 1961), 325.

[215] A. L. Coburn, *Photographer: An Autobiography*, ed. H. & A. Gernsheim (London: Faber & Faber, 1966), 58.

[216] G. Meredith, 5 July 1894, *Letters*, ed. C. L. Cline (Oxford: Clarendon Press, 1970), iii. 1163; 'Literary Impressionists', *The Spectator* 59 (1886), 811, in Matz, *Literary Impressionism*, 82–3.

is like 'being blown through the Tube at fifty miles an hour', and Auden's 'Night Mail' (1936).[217] Arthur Symons described the 'Lights, red, yellow, and brown, | From curtain and window-pane' seen from a train window in 'City Nights' (1892), a poem which excludes both 'finite verbs, as these would impose a temporal sequence' and 'narrative progression' in conjuring the poet's feelings of 'excitement and adventure'.[218] Davidson's 'Song of a Train' (1894) suggested the rushing express through its attenuated lines and brutal verbs. The distinct challenges of recording detail and conveying experience occupied alike the avant-garde and the pragmatic journalist. E. V. Lucas's essay 'Seen from the Line' suggested that railway companies subsidize guide-books that would 'enlarge upon the towns, villages, cathedrals, mansions, parks, and other objects of interest, glimpses of which could be obtained from carriage windows'.[219] For Ford, approaching London in a train, an electric tram, or even a motor car was an astonishing experience, offering a rebuttal of traditional ideas of narrative in its 'happenings' that 'one never sees completed,' and an adrenaline-enhanced reconfiguration of landscape:

There are hedgerows, church towers moving rapidly as if drawn along among clumps of trees, on the horizon; then come brickfields, inn signs, more signboards, a roadside house, bits of paper on the footpath, then a bus, dust whitening hedges, whitening them more, a villa, half a dozen villas, then new shops set one into another without a break, a swift glimpse of a great plain of roofs, gray and without visible limits, a long way below; a swift drop down a slope—a drop that one feels more internally than through the eyes—and one is dodging the close traffic, slowing down, slipping past a dray, boring a hansom in towards the pavement, and it is all over.[220]

The description of the passing scenery initially seems a largely unmediated commentary on Ford's surroundings, the type Symons would describe as 'a shorthand note, which the reporter has not even troubled to copy out', instead of 'the exquisite record of an instant' that was the true aim of impressionist art.[221] The effects of the dust and the multiplication of the villas provide a sense of directness, artfully concealing the fact that the journey has long since concluded, and that Ford knew its outcome before beginning to write about it. 'More' and 'then' act as regulating devices, but risk being overwhelmed throughout by the speed and diversity of onrushing material, the disconcerting images of the church towers 'drawn along clumps of trees' and

---

[217] V. Woolf, *The Mark on the Wall and Other Short Fiction*, ed. D. Bradshaw (Oxford: Oxford University Press, 2001), 3, 4.
[218] A. Symons, 'City Nights I: In the Train', in *Collected Works*, i: *Poems*, 152; Gibbons, *Rooms in the Darwin Hotel*, 77.
[219] Lucas, 'Seen from the Line', in *Loiterer's Harvest*, 1.
[220] Ford, *The Soul of London*, 43, 28.
[221] Symons, 'The Painting of the Nineteenth Century', 25–6.

the shops merging into each other 'without a break'. This effect is reinforced by the use of the phrase and the comma, which allows Ford to avoid a too obviously assembled list of sights, and the passage's irregular rhythmic pulse, which offers an almost subliminal evocation of movement, something felt 'internally than through the eyes'. The final 'slowing down' that signifies a return to the largely horse-drawn transport of the city is accompanied by verbs suggesting a growing sense of human agency, rather than the passive exposure to the world beyond the train window.

In this passage, as in the descriptions of car and tram journeys that occupy succeeding pages, Ford shows himself aware of the need to convey physical sensation alongside what he terms 'psychological effects'.[222] He also succeeds in disguising the description's carefully deployed technical elements, carrying the reader with him rather than encouraging pauses for reflection or analysis. Unfortunately, however, because description of such experiences is only one facet of a book of reflections on different aspects of the city, the passage's radical impetus is quickly lost, with Ford assuming once again the mask of the affable clubman. *The Soul of London* was originally planned as a series of essays for newspaper serialization, and although Ford was unsuccessful in securing its publication in this form, its influence lingers in that its author does not fully develop his ideas for fear of alienating less radical readers.

Alienating the average reader rarely troubled Arthur Symons, though it is perhaps surprising to find his account of a walk down the Edgware Road in the *Anglo-American Magazine* of February 1902. 'Edgware Road: A Study in Living', later included in *London: A Book of Aspects*, depicts a scene of hectic activity:

On Saturday night the Road is lined with stalls; naphtha flames burn over every stall, flaring away from the wind, and lighting up the faces that lean towards them from the crowd on the pavement. There are stalls with plants, cheap jewellery, paper books, scarves and braces, sweets, bananas, ice-cream barrows, weighing-machines; long rows of rabbits hang by their trussed hind legs, and a boy skins them rapidly with a pen-knife for the buyers; raw lumps of meat redden and whiten as the night drifts over and away from them; the salesmen cry their wares. The shops blaze with light. [223]

For Symons, as for Ford, the long sentence is crucial in capturing the bewildering juxtapositions of people and objects and the speed at which such encounters occur, but the account also shows how Symons sought to apply ideas from Verlaine to urban commerce as well as to depictions of the Thames. It was characteristic of the French poet, Martin Sorrel remarks, to convey sensation 'with immediacy and without explanatory links'. 'Things are set out

[222] Ford, *The Soul of London*, 29.   [223] Symons, *London*, 217–18.

unexplained,' he adds, 'The effect is to remove objects from expected contexts, and to bring them directly to our senses without the agency of a rationalising intellect.'[224] This approach is reflected in the spontaneity of the scene. '[Y]ou plunge instantly into a dense, parching, and enveloping smell, made up of stale fish, rotting vegetables, and the must of old clothes,' observes Symons. 'The pavement is never clean; bits of torn paper, fragments of cabbage leaves, the rind of fruit, the stalks of flowers, the litter swept away from the front of shops and lingering on its way to the gutter, drift to and fro under one's feet, moist with rain or greased with mud.'[225] When the young Symons pored over Pater's resonant claim, 'While all melts under our feet, we may well catch at any exquisite passion,' he could never have imagined wandering London by night and skidding on refuse while 'a gaudy sheet slung across a window announces a fat woman on show, or a collection of waxworks with the latest murder.' Pater translated the epigraph from Heraclitus that introduces the conclusion of *The Renaissance* as 'All things give way, nothing remaineth,' and the market's rubbish offers a visual and olfactory underlining of this truth. Flowers are stripped to their stalks, fruit becomes mere rind, but Symons resists the temptation to attribute symbolic significance to these objects, or the natural cycles that have been accelerated and by implication perverted by the city. Instead, he dwells on the immediacy of the scene, its vivid smells and lights, the mingling of excitement and disgust that accompany its exploration.

The account of the Edgware Road shows how such writing could communicate 'impreshuns and sensashuns' in memorable form, but it also exposes again the limitations of the impressionistic method. Impressionism made for vivid description, but unless it was hitched to narrative or the revelation of consciousness, it struggled to extend beyond the finely honed setpiece of *The Ten O' Clock Lecture*. When Symons describes the experience of walking through the myriad stalls of the street market, he succeeds in 'flash[ing] the impression of the moment' and 'preser[ving] the very heat and motion of life' in line with the ambitions set out in 'The Decadent Movement in Literature' in 1893. This had also been accomplished by Henley in his account of nocturnal Edinburgh, 'In the Dials':

> The music reels and hurtles, and the night
> Is full of stinks and cries; a naphtha-light
> Flares from a barrow . . . [226]

Unfortunately, when the 'rationalising intellect' reviews the scene in this poem, or in the latter half of the essay, the results reveal elitist politics rather than

[224] Verlaine, *Selected Poems*, xxiii.   [225] Symons, *London*, 214–15.
[226] Henley, 'Bric-À-Brac' (1877–88), *Poems*, 73.

remarkable perception. Henley offered a conventionally judgmental portrait of 'two loitering hags...each with her inch of clay', while Symons went further, asking 'why these people exist, why they take the trouble to go on existing'. The passage is disconcerting for liberal readers a century later—Rick Allen calls it 'the unacceptable face of aestheticism'—but it also demonstrates all too clearly the consequences of 'importing' reflections from one moment into those of another.[227]

Symons allied himself with radical new art during the 1890s, but for all that *London: A Book of Aspects* vaunts its allegiances to the complementary innovations of impressionism and symbolism, his description of the Edgware Road market is often reminiscent of accounts of the city from earlier in the century. The filthy contents of Krook's shop in *Bleak House* or Ruskin's listing of 'indescribable' horrors of Croxted Lane, the 'mixed dust of every unclean thing that can crumble in drought' in *Fiction, Fair and Foul* (1880–1), springs to mind, as do the urban inventories of G. A. Sala's *Twice Round the Clock* (1859), and, earlier still, Wordsworth's struggle to represent Bartholomew Fair in *The Prelude*.[228] In a discussion of Sala, Carol Bernstein notes how 'a fixation upon objects...opposes the possibilities of narrative', and suggests that '[t]o represent the city in all its objectness could become an exercize in description, a survey of urban objects whose only meaning lies in their plenitude'. Writing truthfully about the city, she continues, 'seems to entail a commitment to the visible, at whatever cost to narrative relevance', leaving writers 'as much threatened by, as supported with, an endless progression of observed details, whether they appear as catalogues or as more sophisticated descriptions'.[229] Symons does not confine himself entirely to the visual, but he seems torn between an evocation of the scene and a reaction to it, which, even if felt at the time, inevitably seems a later rationalization of his confusion and disgust. Repelled, fearful, and yet fascinated, Symons attempts to insist that he is not a journalist exposing life in the poorer quarters of the city to the gaze of middle class readers but a Baudelairean *flâneur* enjoying what the French poet called 'a bath of multitude'.[230] To call the piece 'a study in living' is to combine the Paterian 'imaginary portrait' with the pseudo-scientific objectivity of Zola, but for all Symons's insistence on his intellectual

---

[227] R. Allen, ed., *The Moving Pageant* (London: Routledge, 1998), 211.

[228] Dickens, *Bleak House*, 67–8; Ruskin, *Fiction, Fair and Foul, The Works of John Ruskin*, xxxiv. 265.

[229] C. L. Bernstein, *The Celebration of Scandal: Toward the Sublime in Victorian Urban Fiction* (University Park: Pennsylvania State UP, 1991), 29.

[230] Symons, *London*, 178. 'It is not given to every man to take a bath of multitude: to play upon crowds is an art...The solitary and thoughtful walker derives a singular intoxication from this universal communion' ('Crowds' ['Les Foules'], *Poems in Prose from Baudelaire*, trans. A. Symons (London: Elkin Mathews, 1905), 28–9).

credentials, and the evocative nature of the overall description, he fails to solve the problems that had confronted his Victorian forebears. Adrian Poole even notes perhaps surprising parallels between Symons's impressionism and the realism of Gissing:

[T]he created style is concerned with revealing certain limited aesthetic impressions with extreme absorption, and with resisting any more challenging connections with the actual human beings who live in the city . . . The fellow-creatures who pass us in the street are not unknown-but-knowable; they are absolute and permanent aliens. The cultivation of surface and spectacle becomes therefore the virtue of necessity. London becomes transmuted by Symons (as the Cockney by the slum-realist) into a finished and stylized art-object. Yet beneath it all, it is the helpless scepticism of the detached cosmopolitan observer that we feel, as he tours London, Paris, Rome, Warsaw, the connoisseur of their sights and sounds, but not their people.[231]

Symons may not be able to solve problems of representation, but he does have several means of evading them. One is to focus entirely on his response to his surroundings, his feelings and attitudes. He makes virtually no effort to record speech, partly because he considers the denizens of the Edgware Road rather bestial, partly because their presence is visual rather than derived from character. The only speaker is a man who offers the 'contemptuous comment', 'Twelve o'clock! we may all be dead by twelve o'clock!' 'Hurry up please, it's time,' one might say, as this wanderer picks his way through cackles, whinnies, and 'two opposing currents of evil smells', partly Gissing's Mad Jack, partly an overhead remark given additional meaning by the hearer's political preconceptions.[232] Symons's description of stalls and flaring light is echoed in the illustration to 'Saturday Night in the Edgware Road', a comic vignette that appeared in *Punch* in 1895. The piece emphasizes the raucous vigour of 'promenaders' and tradesmen, in being a series of dialogues, but Symons shuts his ears to the 'lugubrious vendor' and 'sanctimonious young man'.[233] The writer moves through the metropolis 'as with his head in a cloud of humming presences', and constantly risks groaning 'under the weight of one's accumulations', wrote Henry James, and although Symons occasionally struggles with this burden, his refusal to engage with the human element of the scene in any capacity beyond that of observer means that he is not drawn into narrative or, until the end of the episode, analysis.[234] The 'humming presences', so fascinating for Gissing or Morrison, exist only to provide Symons with sensations. Unlike these novelists, Symons does not have to

---

[231] A. Poole, *Gissing in Context* (London: Macmillan, 1975), 55–6.

[232] Symons, *London*, 221. The passage also anticipates in some respects Eliot's 'Rhapsody on a Windy Night', from *Prufrock and Other Observations* (1917).

[233] 'Saturday Night in the Edgware Road', *Punch or the London Charivari* (13 April 1895), 172.

[234] James, Preface to *The Princess Casamassima*, 13, 30.

place the account in any wider context. Exploiting his pose as a cosmopolitan Celt, he makes a clean break from the unsavoury world he describes, without becoming involved in the painful separations of self and subject matter so evident in Gissing's early fiction. Poet, traveller, and ballet connoisseur, Symons seems free from material want and domestic responsibility, and uses Jerrold's 'touch and go chronicle' to demonstrate his refined taste and modish artistic associations.

Finally, 'The Decadent Movement in Literature' had hailed impressionism's ability to escape the constraints of 'traditional form'. As a magazine article, 'A Study in Living' had simply been one feature among many: limited by pressures of space, it did not have to suggest that it was anything other than complete, whatever loose ends may have dangled from it. The informal organization of the 'book of aspects' also helps Symons to escape becoming swamped by his material. Impressionism did not compel a fixed viewpoint of any kind, and Symons seizes on this to move swiftly from description of the scene to reflection, and then to a comparison with life in a Cornish village without having to integrate the account into a wider narrative scheme.

TOWARDS THE WITHIN

Realist versions of London approached the city with an optimistic belief in empiricism that gradually ebbed away in the face of oppressive realities and the competing discourses of late-nineteenth-century culture. Impressionist responses to the city were built on more pragmatic foundations in accepting that if London could be known, any knowledge was subjective and ephemeral. Such views offered, as John House remarks, a new 'framework of expectation and classification', and encouraged a recognition of the city's aesthetic potential. For some at least, there were marked compensations for London's industrialization and pollution, and ways of perceiving the environment that rendered it exotic, even fantastical.

Holbrook Jackson classed impressionism as another aspect of the 'search for reality' which was prevalent in the final decade of the nineteenth century.[235] As we have seen, 'realists' and 'impressionists' asked many of the same questions of reality and representation, and in some respects an opposition between the two groups is a false one. Alan Robinson notes how Monet and Whistler frequently compromise between 'naturalistic detail' and 'abstracted simplification of form and spatial relationships', while there are notable similarities between

---

[235] Jackson, *The Eighteen Nineties*, 276.

Symons's evocation of a busy street and descriptions of such places by Gissing and others.[236] Similarly, while Arthur Morrison's sketches of East End life owed something to contemporary newspaper reporting, Symons was inspired by J.-K. Huysmans's *Croquis parisiens* (1880), which, though it was in turn inspired by Baudelaire and Degas, offered vivid, journalistic accounts of the city.[237] In a discussion of Conradian impressionism, Bruce Johnson points out how any notion of 'objective' artistic representation is conditioned by cultural and aesthetic traditions. Conrad was able to evoke his subject matter 'with all the emotional and visual peculiarities of the individual point of view' while at the same time reminding his readers how apparently 'objective' portrayals are the result of 'complex cultural prejudices'.[238] The consequence is, he says, that realism can never represent an 'easy' alternative to impressionism, since the impressionist continually makes manifest the compromises of the apparently objective realist method.

Impressionism was, in essence, a fragmentary realism with none of 'traditional' realism's claims of objectivity or totality. Its vision was both fleeting and partial. Like Pater's criticism, impressionism tended to steer clear of uncongenial subject matter, avoiding in the process large areas of the capital and the overwhelming majority of its inhabitants. While the delineation of consciousness became the dominant feature of the impressionist novel, topographic writing preferred homage to Whistler and Monet. Also, because impressionism of this type was especially suited to fugitive descriptions, it tended to be most popular in brief lyric poems, such as those of *London Nights*, essays, and short stories that evoked mood and atmosphere rather than relying on plot. Elements from impressionist writing of this type passed into imagism, much as Pound liked to disguise the fact. 'Pseudo impressionism' excelled in memorable description, but when such writing appeared in novels, it often signalled an abrupt change of register in the manner of Rook's description of the moonlit Thames. Indeed, Jackson devoted a chapter of *The Eighteen Nineties* to what he termed 'purple patches and fine phrases'. Writing of this type was much dictated by fashion, and its popularity was short-lived, extending only slightly beyond the first decade of the twentieth century. The art of the transient became transient in itself, supplanted by later movements.

[236] Robinson, *Imagining London, 1770–1900*, 159.

[237] Symons, 'Impressionistic Writing'; J.-K. Huysmans, *Parisian Sketches*, trans. B. King (Sawtry: Dedalus, 2004), 15–23; J. Birkett, *The Sins of the Fathers: Decadence in France 1870–1914* (London: Quartet, 1986), 63–8.

[238] B. Johnson, 'Conrad's Impressionism and Watt's "Delayed Decoding"', in R. C. Murfin, ed., *Conrad Revisited: Essays for the Eighties* (Tuscaloosa, AL: University of Alabama Press, 1985), 51.

By 1926, Rose Macaulay's *Crewe Train* could depict the *Times Literary Supplement* sneering at the 'rather hackneyed impressionist manner'.[239] Few prose impressionists are now regarded as 'important' writers, but they certainly exercised considerable influence on the representation and perception of the English capital between the late 1870s and the First World War.

The London of realist fiction seldom moved more quickly than a cab horse, but impressionist writing proved more willing to address the sensation of speed. Its accounts of train and car travel now seem somewhat quaint, overtaken by faster transport and by more aggressively 'modern' art, such as Futurism and Vorticism, that seemed more suited to the machine age. It is notable that while some writers, Ford for example, or Henley, whose final poem describes an exhilarating ride in a Mercedes, savoured the possibilities of new technology, others could only be considered modern in their aesthetic allegiances. 'London was once habitable,' wrote Symons, 'The machines have killed it,' driving out 'everything old and human [with] wheels and hammers and the fluids of noise and speed'.[240]

By abandoning any pretensions to represent London beyond how it appeared to the individual, impressionist writers were able to reconfigure the city in ways that celebrated its surprising beauty, and, on occasion, its reckless dynamism. However, the suspicion lingered that by replacing tangible realities with luxurious perceptions, and ignoring so much of metropolitan life, impressionism risked superficiality. Joséphin Péladan was prepared to denounce impressionist painting as materialistic because of its reliance on direct sensory, rather than spiritual perception, and Gauguin complained that it 'neglected the mysterious centres of thought'.[241] Wilde's Lady Bracknell regretted living in 'an age of surfaces', and it is another indication of Mark Ambient's limitations in 'The Author of *Beltraffio*' that he should devote such attention to the cultivation of 'the surface I dream of' rather than venturing beneath a 'firm and bright' 'shell'.[242] He envies those who think a surface unnecessary, a comment that applies both to 'realist' writers trading on an authenticity that occasionally disregards stylistic solecism, and perhaps, those more mystically inclined figures who pondered what lay underneath. James himself had explored the political intrigues that rumbled below the surface of London in *The Princess Casamassima*, but other writers went further in imagining a mysterious and occult realm, a strange shadow—London that lay

---

239 R. Macaulay, *Crewe Train* (1926; London: Virago, 1998), 37.

240 Symons, *London*, 171.

241 Péladan attacked impressionism, along with realist and naturalist literature, in his 'L'art Ochloratique', first published in *Le Foyer Illustré* (1883) and reprinted in book form in the first volume of his *La Décadence Esthétique* (1888).

242 James, *Complete Stories 1874–1884*, 891.

within or alongside the everyday city yet was but dimly apprehended. 'We see nothing real, we can no more see anything real than we can take our afternoon tea in the white, central heat of a blast furnace,' wrote Arthur Machen. 'We see the shadows cast by reality . . . though poets catch strange glimpses of reality, now and then, out of the corners of their eyes.' It is these 'strange glimpses' that will be the focus of the next chapter.[243]

---

[243] A. Machen, *The London Adventure or The Art of Wandering* (1924; London: Village Press, 1974), 70–1.

3

'That Untravell'd World': Symbolist London

Yet all experience is an arch wherethrough
Gleams that untravell'd world, whose margin fades
For ever and for ever when I move.

Alfred Tennyson, 'Ulysses' (1842)

But, naturally, there is a very great difficulty in expressing these unprecedented visions in the language of everyday experience.

H. G. Wells, 'The Stolen Body' (1898)

Mysteries are always mysteries, so long as they are not conveyed to profane ears.

Celio Calcagnini, *Opera Aliquot* (1544)

DOORS IN THE WALL

In H. G. Wells's story, 'The Door in the Wall' (1906), an ambitious MP, Lionel Wallace, tells his friend Redmond how he is troubled by a recurring vision of a green door in a white wall. As a small child he had opened the door and entered a garden of surpassing loveliness where he played with gentle panthers and met a 'sombre dark woman, with a grave, pale face and dreamy eyes' who might have stepped from a Burne-Jones painting. When he returns to 'a long grey street in West Kensington, in that chill hour of afternoon before the lamps are lit', he is overpowered by a Wordsworthian sense of loss that he carries with him into adult life.[1] Although the door appears before him on several subsequent occasions, worldly pressures prevent him from going through it, further intensifying the distance between his earthly life and his ideals. As Wallace nears 40, he sees the door with increasing regularity and is stricken with a terrible emptiness regarding his achievements and career. Soon afterwards, he is found dead at the bottom of an excavation shaft at East Kensington Station.

---

[1] H. G. Wells, *Complete Short Stories* (London: Ernest Benn, 1927), 150–1.

This fate, akin to that of another Wellsian visionary, the psychic experimenter Mr Bessel in 'The Stolen Body', is puzzling. Has Wallace simply stumbled into the shaft by accident, or has his death resulted from another sighting of the green door? Is it an accident, suicide, or an (attempted) act of transcendence? Wells often explores the desire to escape the quotidian, but 'The Door in the Wall' is very different from other stories of altered or alternative realities such as 'The Stolen Body' or 'Under the Knife' (1896). It is also notably distinct from his various ideal worlds from *A Modern Utopia* (1905) to Alfred Polly's blissful life at the Potwell Inn. Wallace is not a time traveller, nor is he an obvious dreamer in the manner of Morris's *News From Nowhere* (1890). One could certainly read the story as his fantasy of escaping a world of adult responsibility, or even, since he was 40 in 1906, as a reflection by Wells on his own achievements, but its meaning is less clearly demarcated than such literal interpretations will allow. Wallace is obsessed by the door, but Redmond is never convinced that it exists, and the reader, whose own perceptions are refracted through layers of evasion and equivocation, is unable to reach a definitive version of events. The final paragraph of the story leaves the reasons behind Wallace's death unresolved, raising questions of perception, epistemology, and metaphysics:

> Was there, after all, ever any green door in the wall at all?
> I do not know . . . There are times when I believe that Wallace was no more than the victim of the coincidence between a rare but not unprecedented type of hallucination and a careless trap, but that indeed is not my profoundest belief. You may think me superstitious, if you will, and foolish; but, indeed, I am more than half convinced that he had, in truth, an abnormal gift, and a sense . . . that in the guise of wall and door offered him an outlet, a secret and peculiar passage of escape into another and altogether more beautiful world. At any rate, you will say, it betrayed him in the end. But did it betray him? There you touch the inmost mystery of these dreamers, these men of vision and the imagination. We see our world fair and common, the hoarding and the pit. By our daylight standard he walked out of security into darkness, danger, and death.
> But did he see it like that?[2]

Redmond might be bewildered, but Wallace is far from being the only man of 'vision and the imagination' wandering London's streets during the *fin de siècle*. In Wells, such characters are usually scientists, inventors, or even businessmen, figures of grand schemes and heroic vitality such as Edward Pondorevo in *Tono-Bungay* (1909) or Cavor in *The First Men in the Moon* (1901). Wallace, however, is characterized in curiously Yeatsian terms as ultimately a man with no ambitions beyond his private fulfilment. As Joseph

---

[2] H. G. Wells, *Complete Short Stories* (London: Ernest Benn, 1927), 161.

Conrad suggested, while 'the thinker or the scientist . . . speak authoritatively
to our common sense', the artist 'descends within himself'.[3] Wallace's vision
can be expressed but not shared: Redmond is sympathetic but uncertain, and
his childhood account of the magical garden led only to beatings from his
school fellows and the withdrawal of his books of fairy tales on the grounds
that he was 'too imaginative'. '[M]y story was driven back upon myself,'
Wallace confesses, and its secret goes with him to his grave.[4]

Twenty years later, another man of 'vision and the imagination', Arthur
Machen, would maintain that 'The unknown world is, in truth, about us
everywhere, everywhere near to our feet; the thinnest veil separates us from it;
the door in the wall of the next street communicates with it.'[5] This chapter will
examine how such apprehension of another London, hidden within or beyond
both the quotidian city and the self, emerged as an alternative to the materialist
preoccupations of realism and impressionism. 'If the doors of perception were
cleansed, everything would appear to man as it is: infinite,' wrote Blake in
The Marriage of Heaven and Hell (1790). By viewing the metropolis with 'the
eyes of the spirit', symbolist writers, a variety of Peter Ackroyd's 'Cockney
visionaries', uncovered a secret realm, conceiving the city as 'a sacred place
with its own joyful and sorrowful mysteries'.[6]

MYSTERIES AND INITIATIONS

Wallace's barely credible story emerges from a realm of temporal and linguistic
indeterminacy, a 'shadowy room' lit by a 'shaded table light . . . quite cut off
from everyday realities'. The morning after he hears it, Redmond finds himself
trying 'to account for the flavour of reality that perplexed me in his impossible
reminiscences, by supposing they did in some way suggest, present, convey—I
hardly know which word to use—experiences it was otherwise impossible
to tell.'[7] This world of shadows and uncertainty is often the setting for
symbolist-inflected London fictions. Without co-opting Dickens into their
ranks, one might note how, at the beginning of Book Three of *Our Mutual
Friend* (1864–5), the intrigues of 'Fascination' Fledgeby are enacted within a

---

[3] J. Conrad, Preface to *The Nigger of the 'Narcissus'* (1897; Harmondsworth: Penguin,
1977), 11.
[4] Wells, *Complete Short Stories*, 152.
[5] A. Machen, *The London Adventure or The Art of Wandering* (1924; London: Village Press,
1974), 100.
[6] Ibid. 75; V. Lee, *Genius Loci* (London: Grant Richards, 1899), 61; P. Ackroyd, *London: The
Biography* (London: Vintage, 2001), 15–16.
[7] Wells, *Complete Short Stories*, 144.

London that fog transforms into 'a sooty spectre, divided in purpose between being visible and invisible, and so being wholly neither'.[8] In *The Time Machine* (1895), Wells's time traveller finds the London of the future set within a 'misty and vague' landscape where hills rise 'grey and dim' and 'huge buildings rise up faint and fair, and pass like dreams'.[9] In Algernon Blackwood's 'The Old Man of Visions' (1907), the sage teaches his mystical lessons in 'a dim room' that is 'always shadowy in a kind of gentle dusk'. '[T]he whole universe lies in this room, or just beyond that window-pane,' he says, prompting visions that 'floated in silence, unencumbered, unlimited, unrestrained by words'.[10] Joseph Conrad's *Heart of Darkness* (1899/1902) exploits similar ambiguities, inhabiting a realm of what Peter Brooks terms 'suspended temporality'. The men who listen to Marlow await the turn of the tide while poised midway between the 'luminous estuary' and the 'gloom' of London as day turns slowly to night. 'Marlow's tale inserts itself,' Brooks notes, 'in a moment of indefinable suspension between the flood and the ebb of the tide, at a decisive turning point that passes undiscerned to those who depend upon it.'[11] Such a setting is entirely appropriate for an account of 'one of Marlow's inconclusive experiences', since these are recounted not with the 'direct simplicity' of typical yarns but with extraordinary subtlety. For Marlow, 'the meaning of an episode was not inside like a kernel but outside, enveloping the tale which brought it out only as a glow brings out a haze.'[12] Haze and shadow are not, as they might be in Impressionist painting, the means of transfiguring the banal into the momentarily beautiful, but something more elusive and difficult to classify, suggesting the imperceptible boundary that, in a rather different context, Conrad later termed the 'shadow-line'.[13] Paul Wheelwright suggests that this 'soft focus' effect is a characteristic of symbolist discourses, arguing, in words that seem reminiscent of Conrad:

Sometimes there is doubt as to what a symbol means, even though one feels that it does mean something, that it is not meaningless. Or, what is more often and more characteristically the case, there might be a bright focussed center of meaning together with a penumbra of vagueness that is intrinsically ineradicable; which is to say, the vagueness could not be dispelled without distorting the original meaning.[14]

---

8 C. Dickens, *Our Mutual Friend*, ed. A. Poole (1865; London: Penguin, 1997), 417.

9 H. G. Wells, *The Time Machine*, ed. J. Lawton (1895; London: Dent, 1995), 17.

10 A. Blackwood, *The Insanity of Jones and Other Tales* (Harmondsworth: Penguin, 1966), 162–4.

11 P. Brooks, *Reading for the Plot: Design and Intention in Narrative* (Oxford: Clarendon Press, 1984), 256.

12 J. Conrad, *Heart of Darkness*, ed. R. Hampson (1902; London: Penguin, 1995), 15–19.

13 J. Conrad, *The Shadow-Line*, ed. J. Berthoud (1917; London: Penguin, 1986), 3.

14 P. Wheelwright, 'The Archetypal Symbol', in *Perspectives in Literary Symbolism*, ed. J. Strelka (University Park, PA: Pennsylvania State University Press, 1968), 220.

In *Heart of Darkness*, nothing is as it seems, least of all Marlow, who is at once 'seaman', 'wanderer', company man, mysterious 'idol', and 'meditating Buddha'.[15] Even the text itself is shadowed by its rejected alternatives, for, as Ian Watt records, the manuscript originally suggested that 'the meaning of an episode was . . . outside in the unseen', the invisible realm of visionary experience as well as un-narrated detail.[16]

Marlow begins his tale with a comparison of contemporary and classical imperialism, in which he imagines a hapless young Roman thrust into the savagery of ancient Britain. 'There's no initiation into such mysteries,' he remarks. 'He has to live in the midst of the incomprehensible . . . And it has a fascination, too, that goes to work upon him. The fascination of the abomination.'[17] Nineteen centuries later, London was as incomprehensible and yet as fascinating as Britain had been to the Romans, but with the important difference that its immigrants and colonizers often did undergo the initiations that Marlow denies. '[T]here are London mysteries (dense categories of dark arcana) for every spectator,' noted Henry James noted in 1909.[18]

Richard Maxwell sagely remarks that 'one can learn from an initiation . . . only if one survives it.'[19] Initiation into London's mysteries was rarely recognized as such immediately, and was usually articulated by those who had come to the city in adult life. Such writers had thus to consciously adapt to the capital's often brutal demands and the 'unbetrayed ingenuities' sensed by James as they underwent the transformative processes he termed 'Londonization', or becoming 'cockneyfied'.[20] James was not the first writer to notice this—'I was new here once,' the 'Londonized' Wemmick tells Pip in *Great Expectations* (1860–1), 'Rum to think of it now!'—but he pondered it in a very different cultural context, and in some ways, a very different London, from those who had gone before.[21] The Scottish poet James Thomson did his best to seem 'cockneyfied' in poems of exuberant celebration such as 'Sunday up the River' (1869), an account of boating on the Thames that he subtitled, 'An Idyll of Cockaigne'. However, it would be the unremitting pessimism of works such as 'In the Room' (1872), 'Insomnia' (1882), and, most famously, *The City of Dreadful Night* (1874/1880) that would establish his reputation. A world

---

[15] Conrad, *Heart of Darkness*, 18, 16, 123.
[16] I. Watt, *Conrad in the Nineteenth Century* (Berkeley and Los Angeles: University of California Press, 1979), 180.
[17] Conrad, *Heart of Darkness*, 19–20.
[18] H. James, Preface (1909) to *The Princess Casamassima*, ed. D. Brewer (1886; London: Penguin, 1987), 35.
[19] R. Maxwell, *The Mysteries of Paris and London* (Charlottesville: University of Virginia Press, 1992), 16.
[20] H. James, 'London', in *English Hours* (London: Heinemann, 1905), 10, 12.
[21] C. Dickens, *Great Expectations*, ed. M. Cardwell (1861; Oxford: Clarendon Press, 1993), 170.

away from the high spirits of the earlier poem, they conjured cities of isolation and misery, charting their course with sonorous language and flashes of bleak humour. *The City of Dreadful Night* does not mention London by name, but was widely regarded as being inspired by Thomson's residence there: the cover of Bertram Dobell's edition of 1899 shows an obvious silhouette of London seen from the Thames, complete with the dome of St Paul's in the background. The introduction to an American printing of 1892 even went so far as to call *The City* 'a *fata morgana* of London projected upon a cloud'.[22]

Thomson's magnum opus suggested that urban 'mysteries' were labyrinthine and esoteric:

> O sad Fraternity, do I unfold
> Your dolorous mysteries shrouded from of yore?
> Nay, be assured; no secret can be told
> To any who divined it not before:
> None uninitiate by many a presage
> Will comprehend the language of the message,
> Although proclaimed aloud for evermore.[23]

This sense of an occluded metropolis that revealed its secrets only to enlightened (or cursed) souls transformed the idle urban connoisseurship of a writer such as E. V. Lucas into something far richer and stranger. Even here, revelation is not always synonymous with understanding. In Marie Corelli's *The Sorrows of Satan* (1895), Geoffrey Tempest insists that 'the world *is* real,' only for the suave Prince Lucio to call his certainties into question. 'Is it?' he asks. 'You accept it as such, I daresay, and things are as they appear to each separate individual. . . . there may be conflicting opinions as to the reality or non-reality of this present world.'[24] Another tale of satanic visitation, George R. Sims's *The Devil in London* (1908), posits an unknown London within the familiar city in referring to a newspaper article that asks:

How many of London's ordinary citizens can realise or can hope to realise what London really means? The mother of cities lays her whole heart bare to none. There is no man living who has fathomed her depths. There is no man living who has mastered her mysteries.[25]

Alluding to James's 'The Figure in the Carpet' (1896), Machen, a Welshman who moved to London in the early 1880s, commented that 'the pattern in

---

[22] R. Crawford, 'James Thomson and T. S. Eliot', *Victorian Poetry*, 23 (1) (1985), 29.

[23] J. Thomson, *The City of Dreadful Night*, in D. Karlin, ed., *The Penguin Book of Victorian Verse* (London: Penguin, 1997), 552.

[24] M. Corelli, *The Sorrows of Satan*, ed. P. Keating (1895; Oxford: Oxford University Press, 1998), 97.

[25] G. R. Sims, *The Devil in London* (London: Stanley Paul, 1908), 11.

my carpet' was 'the sense of the eternal mysteries, the eternal beauty hidden beneath the crust of common and commonplace things'.[26] Such beauty that could only be seen with 'purged eyes', and Machen trod a variety of spiritual paths from occultism to Celtic Christian mysticism in his quest for revelation. In his short story, 'The Inmost Light' (1894), Mr Dyson describes his study of what he calls 'the great science', 'the science of the great city; the physiology of London; literally and metaphysically the greatest subject that the mind of man can conceive'. He laments that no contemporary author has managed to engage with 'the mystery of London', that is, its 'vastness and complexity'.[27] Machen would later term the search for the secret city the '*Ars Magna* of London . . . an adventure into the unknown', employing the alchemical terminology Ruth Temple has seen as typical of symbolism to convey a suggestion of hermeticism and obsession.[28] His notion of a perhaps impossible quest, one that has 'nothing to do with any map or guide-book or antiquarian knowledge' is paralleled in James's story, where the precise nature of the figure is never revealed, and the act of interpretation is pursued more in hope than in expectation. Both writers employ the language of pagan religion: James's George Corvick has 'no wish to approach the altar before he had prepared the sacrifice'.[29] A crucial difference between the two remains, however, in that Machen at least knows what he is looking for, whereas readers of Hugh Vereker do not. Corvick claims that he knows Vereker's secret, but he does not pass on his knowledge, and his death, like Wallace's in 'The Door in the Wall', means that the visionary spark is lost. Exegesis becomes impossible, and the quest for meaning must be sustained by faith alone. As Pierre Brunel comments in a discussion of the Symbolist aesthetic, '[t]he mystery, therefore, is not only that of the unknown, it is in the actual indecision of the search, and in the expression of the Ideal or the Idea.'[30]

Raymond Williams notes the enduring symbolic dimension of the 'religious image of the Holy City, the City of God' in writing about the Victorian metropolis.[31] Similarly, Robert Stange reminds us of 'the custom of building the ancient metropolis according to a mythical model of the celestial city'. As

[26] For Machen's initial encounters with the metropolis, see N. Goodrick-Clarke, 'The Enchanted City: Arthur Machen and Locality: Scenes from his Early London Years (1880–85)', *Durham University Journal*, 56 (2) (1995), 301–13.

[27] A. Machen, 'The Inmost Light', in *The House of Souls* (1906; London: Martin Secker, 1923), 241.

[28] A. Machen, *Things Near and Far* (London: Martin Secker, 1923), 62–3; R. Z. Temple, *The Critic's Alchemy: A Study of the Introduction of French Symbolism into England* (New Haven: College and University Press, 1953), 14.

[29] H. James, *Embarrassments* (London: Macmillan, 1896), 32.

[30] P. Brunel, 'An Incomplete Translation', in J. Cassou, ed., *The Concise Encyclopedia of Symbolism*, trans. S. Saunders (London: Omega, 1984), 156.

[31] R. Williams, *The Country and the City* (1973; London: Paladin, 1975), 283.

he points out, the lingering power of 'St Augustine's distinction between the heavenly city of *caritas* and the earthly city of *cupiditas*' implies that 'the most positivistic urban planners have a conception of the City of God which they pose against the Babylon of our everyday life.'[32] The tradition was powerfully expressed in the poetry of Francis Thompson. In 'The Kingdom of God' (*c*.1902), Thompson posed a sequence of paradoxes that only belief can resolve:

> O world invisible, we view thee,
> world intangible, we touch thee,
> world unknowable, we know thee,
> Inapprehensible, we clutch thee!

The poem concludes with visions of Christ walking on the Thames and Jacob's Ladder, a symbolic device which Ruskin had memorably termed the 'narrowed and imperfect intimation' of a truth the human mind was unable to accommodate, 'Pitched betwixt Heaven and Charing Cross'.[33] 'The Kingdom of God' derives from Thompson's reading of the Bible, Christian mystics, and the essays of Thomas Carlyle, whose *Sartor Resartus* (1838) had declared that 'In the Symbol proper... there is ever, more or less distinctly and directly, some embodiment and revelation of the Infinite.' Man, Carlyle continued, 'everywhere finds himself encompassed with Symbols, recognised as such or not recognised: the Universe is but one vast Symbol of God.'[34] Symbol was, the *OED* reminds us, once used to mean 'a creed or a confession of faith'.

Such beliefs manifest themselves in the religious poetry of Ernest Dowson, where the poet's search for 'virginal ecstasy' was expressed in a fascination with ritual and worldly renunciation.[35] 'Benedictio Domini' (1896), for instance, dwells on the 'Strange silence' of a retreat from 'the sounding street' that 'Heralds the world's swift passage to the fire'.[36] Both 'Benedictio' and 'The Kingdom of God' celebrate revelations that transcend the 'sullen noises' of Dowson's 'inarticulate' London, employing the discourse of Christian mysticism, 'the still-living language of symbolism shared by religion and poetry', to articulate suggestions of, or longings for, London as the heavenly kingdom.[37]

---

[32] G. R. Stange, 'The Frightened Poets', in H. J. Dyos and M. Wolff, eds., *The Victorian City: Images and Realities*, 2 vols. (London: Routledge and Kegan Paul, 1973), ii. 475.

[33] F. Thompson, *The Poems of Francis Thompson* (Oxford: Oxford University Press, 1937), 349–50; J. Ruskin, 'Grotesque Renaissance', in *The Stones of Venice, The Complete Works of John Ruskin*, ed. E. T. Cook and A. Wedderburn (London: George Allen, 1903–12), iii. 181.

[34] T. Carlyle, *Sartor Resartus* (1838; London: Dent, 1908), 225–6.

[35] W. B. Yeats, *Autobiographies* (London: Macmillan, 1955), 311.

[36] E. Dowson, 'Benedictio Domini', in *The Poetical Works of Ernest Dowson*, ed. D. Flower (London: Cassell, 1967), 48.

[37] B. M. Boardman, *Between Heaven and Charing Cross: The Life of Francis Thompson* (New Haven: Yale University Press, 1988), 355.

Similar ideas surface in Machen's work. His short story, 'The Holy Things', written in 1897, imbues Holborn with resonant Christian associations, 'the long aisle of the street' leading to houses that 'seemed to meet and join' in union to suggest 'a rich tabernacle, mysterious, the carven house of holy things'.[38] In the same year, Thompson proclaimed 'I yet have sight beyond the smoke,' insisting upon the power of Christian vision to transcend and transfigure quotidian surroundings.[39]

Allusion to Carlyle was not purely the preserve of Christian poets. Neither was the Catholic element of Thompson and Dowson universal. Arthur Symons, the son of a Wesleyan minister, claimed in a thinly fictionalized version of his early life that his childhood had been spent 'in continual communication with the other world'. Christian images of this world 'for the most part . . . meant nothing to me', he added, though by 1905 his exposure to varieties of mystical thought through his reading of Carlyle and Huysmans and his friendship with Yeats had meant that he was more sympathetic to visionary experience.[40] He took Carlyle's remark 'In a Symbol, there is concealment and yet revelation: hence therefore, by Silence and by Speech acting together, comes a double significance,' as the epigraph to *The Symbolist Movement in Literature* (1900).[41] Algernon Blackwood belonged at various times to both the Theosophical Society and the Hermetic Order of the Golden Dawn, yet his Old Man of Visions is likened to Teufelsdröckh, 'alone among the stars'. The story's reverence for the Invisibles is surely a response to the claim in 'Signs of the Times' (1829) that 'men have lost their belief in the Invisible, and believe, and hope, and work only in the Visible'.[42] The Old Man 'ponder[s] the mysteries' in a Bloomsbury attic that the narrator calls a 'temple . . . a little holy place out of the world', though the sage does not claim any denominational allegiance.[43] Lionel Johnson invoked classicism and Christianity in works such as 'Plato in London' and 'Mystic and Cavalier' from his *Poems* (1895). James Elroy Flecker's 'Ballad of the Londoner' (1908)

---

[38] A. Machen, *Ornaments in Jade* (1924; Horam: Tartarus Press, 1997), 50.

[39] F. Thompson, 'From the Night of Foreboding' (1897), in *The Poems of Francis Thompson*, 215.

[40] For Symons's problematic relationship with his father's teachings, see K. Beckson, *Arthur Symons: A Life* (Oxford: Clarendon Press, 1987), 6–10; A. Symons, 'A Prelude to Life', in *Spiritual Adventures* (London: Archibald Constable, 1905), 17–18.

[41] A. Symons, *The Symbolist Movement in Literature* (1900; London: Constable, 1908). The idea was widespread in Renaissance occultism. 'By a judicious use of enigmatic words and images it was possible, [Celio Calcagnini] thought, to combine speech with silence: and that was the language of the mysteries.' E. Wind, *Pagan Mysteries in the Renaissance* (Harmondsworth: Peregrine, 1967), 12.

[42] Blackwood, *The Insanity of Jones and Other Tales*, 156; T. Carlyle, 'Signs of the Times', in P. Keating, ed., *The Victorian Prophets* (Glasgow: Fontana, 1981), 60.

[43] Blackwood, *The Insanity of Jones and Other Tales*, 159–60.

combined the love lyric with the type of secret realities sought by Lionel Wallace:

> I know a garden in a street
> Which no one ever knew;
> I know a rose beyond the Thames,
> Where flowers are pale and few.[44]

The poem's derivative language—its obvious borrowings from Yeats and Dowson—and its antique central pun on flowers and the beloved's name cannot disguise its intimation of another London existing beyond ordinary metropolitan experience. T. S. Eliot was another writer who gestured towards the religious and ineffable in recounting his London explorations, telling Eleanor Hinkley that he had 'made a pilgrimage to Cricklewood' in April 1911. 'Cricklewood is mine,' he joked, 'I discovered it.' He continues, in language reminiscent of Machen, 'No one will go there again. It is like the sunken town in the fairy story, that rose just every May-day eve, and lived for an hour, and only one man saw it.'[45] For Edwin Pugh, it was only by becoming 'a pilgrim and a wanderer for her sake' that one could discover London and 'ponder on its mysteries'.[46] Henry James meanwhile used the language of the neophyte to describe one of his early encounters with the city, recognizing that although his coach ride from Euston to Trafalgar Square was 'not lovely—it was in fact rather horrible,' it remained 'the first step in an initiation'.[47] The voyage from Westminster Bridge to Greenwich offered the same mixture of distaste and mystery, since 'It initiates you into the duskiness, the blackness, the crowdedness, the intensely commercial character of London.' The book was addressed to James's 'less initiated countrymen'.[48]

Reading symbolist representations of London, it often seems as though the apocalypse is imminent or that the city has become a hellish underworld. The visions of Conrad, Chesterton, and M. P. Shiel suggest the epic vistas of early Victorian painters such as John Martin, in whose work humans were dwarfed and rendered insignificant beside the forces of nature and the divine. As in certain formulations of sublimity, the moment of vision reveals darkness and terror. '[W]ho can explain Westminster Bridge Road or Liverpool Street in the morning,' asks E. M. Forster's *Howards End* (1910). 'We reach in desperation

---

[44] J. E. Flecker, *The Collected Poems of James Elroy Flecker*, ed. J. Squire (1916; London: Secker and Warburg, 1942), 79.

[45] T. S. Eliot to Eleanor Hinkley, 26 April 1911, *The Letters of T. S. Eliot*, i: *1898–1922*, ed. V. Eliot (London: Faber, 1988), 18–19.

[46] E. Pugh, *The City of the World* (London: Thomas Nelson, 1912), 15.

[47] James, 'London', in *English Hours*, 3.

[48] H. James, 'London at Midsummer' (1877), in *Portraits of Places* (London: Macmillan, 1883), pp. 219, v.

beyond the fog, beyond the very stars, the voids of the universe are ransacked to justify the monster, and stamped with a human face.'[49] The horrors of James's journey paled beside these darker visions. On the eve of his release from a Parisian asylum in late 1854, Gérard de Nerval had signed himself 'initiate and vestal': less than three months later, he had hanged himself in the rue de la Vieille Lanterne.[50] London's chroniclers did not descend into quite the same depths, but many late-nineteenth- and early-twentieth-century writers record their fears of destruction at the hands of the metropolis. Eliot's 'The Little Passion From "An Agony in the Garret" ' (*c.*1914–15) imagined a city in which a nameless figure follows 'the lines of lights' to 'one inevitable cross | Whereon our souls are pinned, and bleed.'[51] It was, of course, very easy to suffer and die through material want in late-Victorian London: a number of the writers discussed in this study experienced dismal privations at some time or other. The type of suffering that Eliot dwells upon, however, is psychological and depressive, and it is often induced by recognizing one's insignificance within the great city, or by the failure of creative projects, as James Thomson and John Davidson, both significant influences on Eliot, understood only too well. As Eliot complained in February 1922, 'One bleeds to death very slowly here'.[52]

There was, however, another version of metropolitan suffering that emerged from the contemplation of the city itself. In her study of *fin de siècle* Gothic, Kelly Hurley notes how:

anxious perception of London as a *chaosmos*—a space of meaningless noise, activity, sensation in which narratives indiscriminately crowd one another and no one narrative has any more significance than the next—has its inverse in the paranoid fantasy of a London whose *seeming* indifferentiation masks a network of deeply-laid and infernal designs.[53]

In *Tono-Bungay*, Edward Ponderevo eventually arrives at 'a kind of theory of London' which seems much like that described by Hurley. 'I do think I see lines of an ordered structure,' he maintains, detecting 'a process that is something more than a confusion of casual accidents'. However, he goes on to suggest that it 'may be no more than a process of disease'.[54] Glimpses of this 'network', or 'line of lights', were vouchsafed only to the few, but the

[49] E. M. Forster, *Howards End*, ed. O. Stallybrass (1910; London: Penguin, 1983), 116.

[50] G. de Nerval, *Selected Writings*, trans. R. Sieburth (London: Penguin, 1999), xxx.

[51] T. S. Eliot, *Inventions of the March Hare: Poems 1909–1917*, ed. C. Ricks (London: Faber, 1996), 57.

[52] Eliot to Lytton Strachey, 17 February 1922. *The Letters of T. S. Eliot*, i. 367.

[53] K. Hurley, *The Gothic Body: Sexuality, Materialism, and Degeneration at the Fin de Siècle* (Cambridge: Cambridge University Press, 1996), 185.

[54] H. G. Wells, *Tono-Bungay*, ed. J. Hammond (1909; London: Dent, 1994), 85.

consequences of such apprehension were invariably ruinous. John Davidson's Earl Lavender found himself baffled by the seemingly cryptic meaning of a pub's sign. 'There is not a vein upon a leaf, not a scratch upon a pebble, not a name above a shop, not a torn word on a scrap of paper, without a message for me,' he complains, 'and I am in despair because I cannot read the meaning here.'[55] Davidson's novel was comic, but its anxieties often recurred in more serious texts, where the hidden meaning of the streets seemed to appal both its literate interpreters and those whom it only bewildered.[56] As we have seen, part of the reason for Sherlock Holmes's popularity was precisely his ability to read the signs Earl Lavender can only see: Holmes interrogates them in order to reveal clues and narratives in miniature that restore the reader's faith in rationality. Such faith certainly needed to be restored when every aspect of London seemed to hint at frightening secrets. Thomson's friend Philip Bourke Marston depicted it as a realm of louring prophecy in which church bells, stripped of any semblance of Christian compassion, 'forecast' the sorrows of the speaker's life and taunt him with their hidden knowledge as he lies 'between veiled future and disastrous past'.[57] According to Aleister Crowley, London should have been painted by Goya rather than by Whistler, since 'the city is monstrous and misshapen' and 'its mystery is not a brooding but a conspiracy'.[58] Recalling the city of the 1890s, he confessed that 'there were excellent reasons for a poet to feel unhappy' in London, since its 'spiritual atmosphere weighs upon the soul'.[59] Edwin Pugh saw nocturnal suburbia as in some way 'mystical . . . a dead, deserted city in which move a few infrequent shadowy figures, as if they had been the last survivors of the human race', and its shops as 'vague and nebulous, pricked out with ghostly cabalistics'.[60] In Machen's *The Three Impostors* (1895), Joseph Walters is initiated into a sinister magical fraternity, and finds himself enmeshed in a deadly conspiracy from which there is no escape. Machen's later novel, *The Hill of Dreams* (1907), sees the young Welsh novelist Lucian Taylor unconsciously following

---

[55] J. Davidson, *A Full and True Account of the Wonderful Mission of Earl Lavender* (London: Ward and Downey, 1895), 250.

[56] I distinguish here between the ability to 'read' the streets and the possession of basic literacy, though the two certainly intersect. In *Bleak House*, for example, Jo is 'unfamiliar with the shapes, and in utter darkness as to the meaning, of those mysterious symbols, so abundant over the shops, and at the corners of streets . . . what does it all mean, and if it means anything to anybody, how comes it that it means nothing to me?' (C. Dickens, *Bleak House*, ed. N. Bradbury (1853; London: Penguin, 1996), 257).

[57] P. B. Marston, 'Bells of London,' *A Last Harvest* (London: Elkin Matthews, 1891), 113.

[58] A. Crowley, *Moonchild: A Prologue* (London: Mandrake Press, 1929), 9. The novel was written in 1917.

[59] A. Crowley, *The Confessions of Aleister Crowley: An Autohagiography*, ed. J. Symonds and K. Grant (London: Arkana, 1978), 116.

[60] Pugh, *The City of the World*, 42–3.

Rimbaud's advice concerning the 'systematic derangement of the senses' through drugs, lust, and semi-starvation, peering into London's mysterious heart.[61] He fears he has 'deluded himself with imagination', but the city he perceives is that of 'unknowable . . . unplumbed depth' found elsewhere in Machen's autobiographical writings:

He could not look out and see a common suburban street foggy and dull . . . he saw a vision of a grey road vanishing, of dim houses all empty and deserted, and the silence seemed eternal. And when he went out and passed through street after street, all void, by the vague shapes of houses that appeared for a moment and were then instantly swallowed up, it seemed to him that he had strayed into a city that had suffered some inconceivable doom, that he alone wandered where myriads had once dwelt. It was a town great as Babylon, terrible as Rome, marvellous as Lost Atlantis, set in the middle of a white wilderness surrounded by waste places. It was impossible to escape from it. . . . All London was one grey temple of an awful rite, ring within ring of wizard stones circled about some central place, every circle was an initiation, every initiation eternal loss. Or perhaps he was astray for ever in a land of grey rocks.[62]

This passage, suggests Alexandra Warwick, emerges from a London which lacks 'plan and design', a city that 'confirm[s] the isolation of the single walker while simultaneously reminding him of his inescapable part in a pattern of which he cannot make sense'. For Warwick, both Machen and his characters are 'aware of loss and incompletion', perceiving patterns that are 'oppressive and threatening rather than liberating and empowering'.[63]

In October 1859, the *Daily Telegraph* suggested that London was 'an amalgam of worlds within worlds', each of which 'has its special mysteries and its generic crimes'. Commenting on this editorial, Thomas Boyle observes how it 'reinforces the sense of mystery in familiar places', rendering the city 'a kind of puzzle, a mystery story of its own, without an ending, certainly without a *happy* ending—which cries out to be interpreted (or, more precisely reinterpreted)'. This reading, while illuminating in some respects, offers a straightforward linking of the mystery and the crime, rather than examining the pairing's metaphysical implications, the 'inexplicable mysteries of conscious existence' pondered by Inspector Heat in *The Secret Agent*.[64] As

[61] Rimbaud suggested that 'le poète se fait voyant'—the poet makes himself a seer—through 'le long, immense, et raisonné dérèglement de tous les sens'. C. Chadwick, *Symbolism* (London: Methuen, 1971), 30.

[62] Machen, *The London Adventure*, 100; *idem, The Hill of Dreams* (1907; Leyburn: Tartarus Press, 1998), 141–3.

[63] A. Warwick, 'Lost Cities: London's Apocalypse', in G. Byron and D. Punter, eds., *Spectral Readings: Towards a Gothic Geography* (Basingstoke: Macmillan, 1999), 82.

[64] J. Conrad, *The Secret Agent: A Simple Tale*, ed. J. Lyon (Oxford: Oxford University Press, 2004), 65.

his discussion progresses, the *Telegraph*'s writer moves away from 'accurate topographical knowledge' and towards mysticism, pointing out that anyone who lays claim to exactitude is 'but picking up shells on the shore, while all before him lies a vast and undiscovered ocean'.[65] 'Mysteries' has a very different meaning in this context from the 'kind of puzzle' found in Conan Doyle or before him, in Ann Radcliffe or Eugène Sue, since its origins lie not in crime or initially unexplained circumstances, but in mysticism's 'obscure words about the ineffable' and their anagogical understanding.[66] In George Sims's words, they are to be 'mastered' rather than 'solved'. Their connections are not those of Sherlock Holmes's chain of reasoning, but 'an establishment of the links which hold the world together, the affirmation of an eternal, minute, intricate, almost invisible life, which runs through the whole universe'.[67] It is worth remembering that Machen's favourite Latin tag, carved on his gravestone, was 'Omnia Exeunt in Mysterium': 'Mystery ends all things.'

Richard Maxwell has argued that what he terms the 'mysteries' novel was at heart an allegory by which nineteenth-century writers made sense of the city, or rather, recognized the limits of its coherence and their understanding of it. For him, its recurrent 'individual figures', the labyrinth, for example, could be 'interpreted by a formalized, almost a ritualized means', and 'enigmas . . . *gradually* unravelled'. Allegory was, he claims, a means by which writers such as Dickens and Hugo were able to 'reveal' the city, providing 'rhetorical claims to historical, as opposed to timeless or transcendent, understanding'. The consequence is the demarcation of 'a probable and provisional order rather than an eternal one', a realm in which 'divination' is replaced by what he calls 'urbanation'.[68] Knowledge lies in the recognition of metropolitan incoherence and is 'useless or even maddening unless it is treated as autonomous', that is, 'existing fundamentally apart from human consciousness and human experience'.[69] Although Maxwell goes further than Boyle in noting the differing applications of 'mystery' to the city, and concedes that 'The novel of urban mysteries never died—not in the nineteenth century anyway,' his focus on Dickens and Hugo means that his study does not extend much beyond the 1860s.[70] By the 1890s, the urban mysteries of London were perceived

---

[65] *Daily Telegraph* (10 October 1859), in T. Boyle, *Black Swine in the Sewers of Hampstead: Beneath the Surface of Victorian Sensationalism* (New York: Viking, 1989), 205–6.

[66] Maxwell, *The Mysteries of Paris and London*, 4.

[67] Symons, *The Symbolist Movement in Literature*, 145.

[68] Maxwell, *The Mysteries of Paris and London*, 15.   [69] Ibid. 292.

[70] R. Mighall's 'From Udolpho to Spitalfields: Mapping Gothic London', in his *A Geography of Victorian Gothic Fiction: Mapping History's Nightmares* (Oxford: Oxford University Press, 1999), 27–77, pursues similar ideas to those of Maxwell, but similarly confines itself to the Dickensian city.

quite differently, at least in some quarters. Gothic's increasing fondness for metropolitan settings during the late-Victorian period, allied to a revival of interest in Catholicism and the occult, and the evolution of the symbolist movement throughout Europe had encouraged an altogether more mystical response to London's 'labyrinth'. The city was bewildering in itself, and was also viewed through a prism of spiritual affiliations that encouraged belief in the transcendent and the eternal which Dickens's pragmatic Anglican theology and political commitments had tended to ignore.

Of course, a substantial sector of the British reading public still wished to endorse earlier certainties, one reason for the continued popularity of Dickens and the commercial success of Sherlock Holmes. London might seem a labyrinth to his clients or the police, but the great detective is its Theseus, following a golden thread of logical deduction to the heart of the maze and apprehending its Minotaur. The linking of Conan Doyle and Dickens is a little misleading, since Holmes never encounters panoramic intrigue on the scale of *Bleak House*, and is bound by the constrictive parameters of the evolving genre of detective fiction. Nevertheless, both writers insist that riddles can be solved, even if their answers, or Dickens's at any rate, sometimes stress only the arbitrary or provisional nature of urban insight.

Carlyle had envisaged the universe as 'a mighty Sphinx-riddle, which I knew so little of, yet must rede, or be devoured', and the mystically inclined writers, Machen for instance, or Chesterton, who shared such views, saw the metropolis very differently from those of more empiricist sensibilities.[71] In *The Law and the Lady* (1875), Wilkie Collins used the image of the maze as a blunt instrument of social criticism, 'a dingy brick labyrinth of streets, growing smaller and smaller, and dirtier and dirtier' from which his heroine emerges at last into the wastes of a new northern suburb.[72] For the mystically inclined, however, such symbols could not be deployed so carelessly. The city as symbol could not be 'decoded' since it was, in itself, an emblem of a higher, unreadable reality rather than an ultimately transparent earthly metaphor. There was a unbridgeable gulf between a decorative extended conceit such as Alfred Douglas's 'Impression de Nuit: London' (1899), with its image of the nocturnal city as a bejewelled woman, and the 'mysteries' of *The Hill of Dreams* or *The Man Who Was Thursday* (1908). Following on from Hegel's rejection of allegory as a 'chilled symbol' that encapsulated only a single meaning, Machen and Chesterton embraced the symbol's multiplicity, the 'semantic plenitude' of 'plurisignation'.[73] When Dickens depicts London as a labyrinth, it is one

---

[71] Carlyle, *Sartor Resartus*, 132.
[72] W. Collins, *The Law and the Lady*, ed. D. Skilton (1875; London: Penguin, 1998), 188.
[73] Brunel, 'An Incomplete Translation', 156; Wheelwright, 'The Archetypal Symbol', 219.

where 'secrecy . . . often signifies crime', and where connections are 'hidden but real'.[74] The labyrinth encapsulates the bewildering confusion of proliferating and dangerously similar streets, engendering frightening claustrophobia or even deadening ennui, but alternatives to it frequently present themselves, the idealized countryside of *Oliver Twist* (1837–9), for instance, welcoming coaching inns, even colonial emigration. When James Thomson employs the same image, however, it is to suggest the quintessentially irresolvable nature of the metaphysical concerns that the maze embodies, as well as its more immediate application to urban reality.

As Marlow maintains, London is 'incomprehensible'. The city is a labyrinth, but the labyrinth itself suggests meanings beyond a straightforward parallel. Dickens insists that the city is a realm of tangled passages and monstrous artifice in which lurk such threatening apparitions as Bill Sikes and Bradley Headstone. Symbolism, however, adds another quantity to the equation: London is a labyrinth, which is not only unknowable in itself but a suggestion of all that cannot be known. When Thomson writes, 'Our vast poor petty life is one dark maze of dreams,' it is to insist that existence lacks the Theseus who can track its complexities to their source, and that men 'thread mere puppets all their marvellous maze'.[75] Peter Brooks likens the mysterious knitting women of *Heart of Darkness* to Ariadne, whose thread runs into what he terms a 'dark labyrinth'.[76] It is a revealing allusion, for by 1899, London was increasingly associated with mazes and, in W. T. Stead's eyes at least, the Minotaur. Conrad's thread leads ever deeper into structures of bewilderment and illusion, without allowing escape or answers to the questions they might raise.

For the commonplace writer, such as the travel journalist H. V. Morton, the labyrinth is a dead metaphor, as he demonstrates in the assemblage of cliché that is *In Search of England* (1927). 'Of course,' he writes blithely, 'no living man has seen London. London has ceased to be visible since Stuart days . . . Today, even if you climb to the dome of St. Paul's you see not London the City State but London the labyrinth.'[77] For others, however, the symbol of the labyrinth was unfathomable, though this is not to say that such revelations are inevitably pessimistic, paranoid, or, as Warwick says, 'oppressive and threatening', since the image is used to very different ends elsewhere in Machen's work. In *The London Adventure* (1924), he revisits his notebooks of the early twentieth century, including a passage in which he argues that 'the maze was not only

[74] Maxwell, *The Mysteries of Paris and London*, 16.

[75] J. Thomson, 'Insomnia' (1882), *The City of Dreadful Night and Other Poems* (London: P. J. and A. E. Dobell, 1919), 161; *The Penguin Book of Victorian Verse*, 578.

[76] Brooks, *Reading for the Plot*, 240.

[77] H. V. Morton, *In Search of England* (London: Methuen, 1927), 5.

the instrument, but the symbol of ecstasy... a pictured "inebriation," the sign of some age-old "process" that gave the secret bliss to men.'[78]

Such ideas received fuller expression several years later in his story 'A Fragment of Life' (1906), which concerns the mystical awakening of a London clerk, Darnell, who gradually realizes that the 'whole world is but a great ceremony or sacrament, which teaches under visible forms a hidden and transcendent doctrine'. Maxwell's 'fomalized' or 'ritualized' processes here become those of the Celtic Church. Darnell's initial view of London is of 'a fatal labyrinth of grey desolation', but as his mystical sense flowers, his vision changes and his environment is transformed until London's 'labyrinths of streets' become 'an enchanted maze' and 'its long avenues of lighted lamps were as starry systems.' To Darnell, the 'immensity' of the metropolis is 'an image of the endless universe', a revelation similar to that which overcomes Frank Burton in *The Three Impostors*, imbuing him with 'the glamour of the infinite... an immensity as in the outer void of the universe' as he passes 'from unknown to unknown', 'street leading into street, as it seemed, to the world's end'.[79] Darnell cannot change his environment, but he can perceive it differently, by remembering 'the mysteries and far-shining glories of the kingdom which was his', the world Carlyle would term his 'celestial birthright'.[80] In the process, Machen transforms a semi-comic realist story of lower middle class into a more profound meditation on spiritual enlightenment. By realizing the vastness of the heavens, Darnell begins a long process of reconstituting the capital as the city of gratified desire and eventually 'aw[akes] from a dream of a London suburb'.[81] The labyrinth and the mystery cease to be images of confusion and pass into the wider vocabulary of visionary experience.

The popular understanding of 'mystery' in the late nineteenth century was very much the secular meaning of the term articulated by Thomas Boyle as the unsolved puzzle. Concealed within it, however, were very different meanings sensed only by the mystically inclined, as Lionel Johnson suggested in comparing Walter Pater to 'the awed rejoicing priest' who knows 'how deep within the liturgies | Lie hid the mysteries'.[82] Edgar Wind has noted how the origins of these meanings lay in classical pagan religions and their influence on Renaissance occultism, where they intertwined with Christian visionary

---

[78] Machen, *The London Adventure*, 89.

[79] A. Machen, 'A Fragment of Life', in *The Collected Arthur Machen*, ed. C. Palmer (London: Duckworth, 1988), 78–82; *idem*, *The Three Impostors or The Transmutations*, ed. D. Trotter (1895; London: Dent, 1995), 100.

[80] Machen, *The Collected Arthur Machen*, 44; Carlyle, 'Signs of the Times', 58.

[81] Machen, *The Collected Arthur Machen*, 88.

[82] L. Johnson, 'To Walter Pater' (1902), in D. Stanford, ed., *Three Poets of the Rhymers' Club* (Cheadle Hulme: Carcanet, 1974), 129.

writing in complex ways. Subsequent occult traditions influenced such diverse *fin de siècle* writers as Joséphin Péladan, Huysmans, Yeats, and Yeats's fellow initiate of the Hermetic Order of the Golden Dawn, Machen, with Emond Bailly's Paris bookshop, 'La Librairie de l'Art Indépendent' at the centre of many cultural exchanges.[83]

Wind traces mystery's ritual, figurative, and magical applications, the first of which is 'a popular ritual of initiation' such as the Eleusinian Mysteries. Machen claimed that London's 'rawest, reddest modern suburb' witnessed the celebration of such mysteries, 'even as in Eleusis', and Chesterton's *The Man Who Was Thursday*, which opens in the 'red and ragged' suburb of Saffron Park, offers similar glimpses of curious ceremonies.[84] In the 'figurative', terms and images from popular rites were 'transferred to the intellectual disciplines of philosophical debate and meditation'. These recurred in the nineteenth century in the writings of those such as James and Conrad who, though uninterested in occultism in itself, were prepared to exploit the suggestiveness of its vocabulary. Peter Rawlings has noted how James developed a tendency for 'recruiting Shakespeare in the proximity of the unutterable' with the 'unassailable enigma of Shakespeare's life and work . . . a necessary constituent of the grammar of obscurity and secrecy that generated his fiction'.[85] To this one could add James's recruitment of the language of religious or magical ritual, the latter of which was being enthusiastically publicized by the Theosophist Helena Blavatsky from the late 1870s. According to the historian of British occultism, R. A. Gilbert, Blavatsky had introduced 'occultism' and 'occultist' to the English lexicon in *Isis Unveiled* (1877), though the *OED* cites no reference earlier than 1881.[86] The 'mysteries abysmal' and 'occult affiliations' glimpsed by James in composing *The Princess Casamassima* are those of politics rather than magic, but as Crowley and *The Three Impostors* suggest, the line between conspiracy and mystery was a very fine one.[87] Hyacinth Robinson's initiation into revolutionary circles has notably mystical overtones, from his partly ironic view of the 'temple . . . the innermost sanctuary . . . the holy of holies' to his sense of an 'immense underworld' and

---

[83] Bailly's contribution to cross-Channel esotericism is discussed by R. Pincus-Witton in *Occult Symbolism in France: Joséphin Péladin and the Salons de la Rose + Croix* (New York: Garland, 1976), 58–9.

[84] Machen, *The London Adventure*, 43–4; G. K. Chesterton, *The Man Who Was Thursday: A Nightmare* (1908; Bristol: Arrowsmith, 1946), 5.

[85] P. Rawlings, *Henry James and the Abuse of the Past* (Basingstoke: Palgrave Macmillan, 2005), 69.

[86] R. A. Gilbert, 'Seeking That Which was Lost: More Light on the Origins and Development of the Golden Dawn', in W. Gould, ed., *Yeats Annual 14: Yeats and the Nineties* (Basingstoke: Palgrave, 2001), 36.

[87] James, Preface to *The Princess Casamassima*, 48.

the secret societies that work 'In silence, in darkness' at their revolutionary ends. It is no surprise that the Princess responds by telling Hyacinth, 'You have had a vision.'[88]

Wind's final usage of 'mystery' is what he sceptically labels 'bewitching hocus-pocus', a range of magical practices for communicating with 'the Beyond'.[89] As Lothar Hönnighausen observes, a generation of English writers, artists, and musicians was fascinated by the idea of 'transcending the tangible', an aim typically pursued through commitments to Catholicism and, in some cases, ritual magic or other occult practices.[90] Chesterton's Father Brown makes his Catholic sense of humility in the faith of the marvellous a touchstone of his criminal investigations: 'The most incredible thing about miracles is that they happen,' says the narrator of 'The Blue Cross' (1911).[91] Wilde eventually converted to Catholicism, but during the 1880s and 1890s he regularly consulted palmists and soothsayers, a superstition he used as the basis of 'Lord Arthur Saville's Crime' (1887). The story features a young aristocrat who is haunted by the prophecy of the 'chiromantist' Mr Podger, and who flees, like the soul from God in St Augustine or Francis Thompson's 'The Hound of Heaven' (1890), through the 'incoherence' and dissonance of 'a labyrinth of sordid houses' before accepting his criminal destiny.[92] If one extends 'magical practices' to encompass superstitions or habits that have particular significance for those who practise them, such as Symons's belief that 'it is never wise to enter a city except by night', then even 'hocus-pocus' played its part when pondering the metropolis.[93] Wilde's Mr Podger and Eliot's Madame Sosostris may be ludicrous figures in some respects, but their ironic treatment does not wholly undermine their insights, even if the latter's vision is less fulsome as that of Tiresias.

Visionary conceptions of London implied an unknown, often threatening world at every turn. Chesterton's Gabriel Syme senses 'an unnatural symbolism' in the members of the Anarchist Committee, who '[seem] to be, somehow, on the borderland of things'.[94] John Davidson's 'London' (1894) imagines St Paul's as 'shadowy, | Of some occult magician's rearing'

[88] James, *The Princess Casamassima*, 330.

[89] Wind, *Pagan Mysteries in the Renaissance*, 1–6.

[90] L. Hönnighausen, *The Symbolist Tradition in English Literature: A Study of Pre-Raphaelitism and the Fin-de-Siècle* (Cambridge: Cambridge University Press, 1988), 213.

[91] G. K. Chesterton, *The Father Brown Stories* (London: Cassell, 1929), 11.

[92] O. Wilde, 'Lord Arthur Saville's Crime' (1887), in *Complete Works* (London: HarperCollins, 1994), 167–8.

[93] A. Symons, *London: A Book of Aspects*, in *Cities and Sea-Coasts and Islands* (London: W. Collins, 1918), 162. Afterwards *London*.

[94] Chesterton, *The Man Who Was Thursday*, 59.

or else 'swung in space of heaven's grace | Dissolving, dimly reappearing'.[95] In Kipling's *The Light That Failed* (1891), Dick Heldar stares out of his window into 'the greater darkness of London' in which lurk the 'uncouth brick and zinc mysteries' that James Thomson had portrayed as 'more dubious than the things of vision'.[96] The 'dull roar of the streets' and 'crooked [chimney] cowls that looked like sitting cats' offer a powerful glimpse of London existing as an untamed animal that lurks in wait for the unwary.[97] Such imagery is echoed in A. L. Coburn's photogravures of the stone lions in Trafalgar Square in *London* (1909) and James's fears of the 'tiger-pounce of homesickness' that lay in wait for him in the city streets.[98] This is not the straightforward evocation of the 'urban jungle' but a belief that London's true nature is both untameable and only properly understood by an artistic elect. Moreover, as in Thomson's city, the acknowledgement of such perception rarely consoles, and frequently leads instead to the 'undefined existential torment' Donald Friedmann identifies as characteristic of Belgian symbolist art.[99]

Wilde's use of the language of mystery was more light-hearted in 'The Sphinx without a Secret' (1887), but his story emphasized nonetheless the inexplicable rituals of the city, into which Gerald Murchison so helplessly blunders. The cryptic Lady Alroy delights in encouraging ceremonial observance without revelation, and has 'a mania for mystery' and 'incessant secrecy'. The narrator offers a neat explanation for her behaviour, but the tale finishes with the unanswered question, 'I wonder?' Staring at a photograph of Lady Alroy, Murchison is drawn into pondering an ultimately indecipherable image, the face of a '*clairvoyante*', 'moulded out of many mysteries' and possessing a secret that resists moral attribution.[100] His 'wonder' is therefore ambiguous, being a feeling of curiosity and of astonished awe: Lady Alroy is a wonder in herself. Her true identity remains undiscovered, and it seems that Murchison's love for her will be replaced by 'undefined existential torment' if he broods on her fate, assuming that the two are not already synonymous.

Howard Finn perhaps overstates the case when he claims that the 'interaction between materialism and mysticism' was 'characteristic of the 1890–1914 period', but there was undoubtedly some tension between rationalist and

---

[95] J. Davidson, *The Poems of John Davidson*, ed. A. Turnbull, 2 vols. (Edinburgh: Scottish Academic Press, 1973), i. 57.

[96] R. Kipling, *The Light That Failed* (1891; London: Macmillan, 1895), 156; *The Penguin Book of Victorian Verse*, 557.

[97] Kipling, *The Light That Failed*, 156.

[98] James, 'London', *English Hours*, 8.

[99] D. Friedman, 'Belgian Symbolism and a Poetics of Place', in S. Goddard, ed., *Les XX and the Belgian Avant-Garde* (Kansas: Spencer Museum of Art, 1992), 130.

[100] O. Wilde, 'The Sphinx without a Secret', in *Complete Works*, 205–8.

positivist worldviews and those that sought the enduring or transcendent.[101] Symbolism offered the most likely route to enlightenment for those such as the music historian and mystic Edouard Schuré, who beheld 'eternal horizons', and pursued, in words that recall Blavatsky, 'the secret doctrine and the occult influence of the great initiates' that placed the spiritual before the material.[102] As Blackwood's story demonstrates, symbolism promised a glimpse of the sacred, and allowed the use of religious discourses, without the necessity of surrendering to religious discipline or dogma. In *The Symbolist Movement in Literature*, Arthur Symons argued that literature has become 'a kind of religion, with all the duties and the responsibilities of the sacred ritual'. Symbolism sought 'to spiritualise literature, to evade the old bondage of rhetoric, the old bondage to exteriority' which he saw as a defining characteristic of realist fiction.[103] It transformed its practitioners into priests and savants, Wells's 'men of vision and the imagination', whose intense imaginative powers set them apart from the common herd. Their art was rare, arcane, and defiantly uncommercial, drawing on 'that "inner light" by which most mystics have symbolised that which at once guides us in time and attaches us to eternity'.[104] 'The whole visible world itself, we are told, is but a symbol,' he wrote elsewhere, 'made visible in order that we may apprehend ourselves, and not be blown hither and thither like a flame in the night.'[105] Machen implicitly agreed. Great literature, he remarked, in language that suggests both Symons and his master, Pater, should give 'an overpowering impression of "strangeness," of remoteness, of withdrawal from the common ways of life.' 'There are', he continued, 'two solutions of existence; one is the materialistic or rationalistic, the other, the spiritual or mystic.'[106]

However, by dismissing the material, or at least the realist aesthetic that had dominated its perception during the nineteenth century, Symons and Machen raised a question that has important consequences for city writing. In 1900, London was overcrowded, dirty, and noisy, with its lack of spiritual or aesthetic sophistication a recurrent cause for concern. If symbolism required a dedication to beauty above all else, how could an artist hope to 'revolt against . . . a materialistic tradition' when his subject matter, the modern

[101] H. Finn, ' "In the Quicksands of Disintegrating Faiths": Dorothy Richardson and the Quakers', *Literature and Theology*, 19 (1) (March 2005), 34.

[102] E. Schuré, *Les Grands initiés* (1889), in P. Jullian, *Dreamers of Decadence*, trans. R. Baldick (London: Phaidon, 1974), 33. Blavatsky's most influential work was *The Secret Doctrine: The Synthesis of Science, Religion and Philosophy* (1888).

[103] Symons, *The Symbolist Movement in Literature*, 8–9.

[104] Ibid. 164.

[105] A. Symons, *London Nights* (London: Leonard Smithers, 1897), xiv.

[106] A. Machen, *Hieroglyphics: A Note upon Ecstasy in Literature* (1902; London: Unicorn Press, 1960), 57, 71.

metropolis, was itself quintessentially materialistic?[107] D. G. Rossetti had spent years attempting to graft Pre-Raphaelite ideals onto an urban setting in his unfinished *Found* (1854–81), discovering only that the two were irreconcilable. As Andrew Wilton points out, Rossetti's version of Pre-Raphaelitism was quite different from that of Millais and Holman Hunt, painters who did succeed in imbuing scenes from modern life with a symbolic dimension.[108] His 'style deliberately evoked a blurred, almost dream-like world of the spirit, where profounder and more exalted passions played than were to be found in the practical, if foggy, air of modern London.'[109] Much critical interest in symbolism has tended to accept this, concentrating on ways in which symbolist painters retreated from the material world into realms of the imagination. The symbolist city, such as it is, seems confined to the stricken Bruges of Fernand Khnopff and Georges Rodenbach, the satanic conspiracies of Huysmans's *Là-bas* (1891), or the forlorn, seemingly abandoned Paris of the photographer Eugène Atget.

And yet, in the late nineteenth and early twentieth centuries, London's 'practical, if foggy' streets were regularly perceived through eyes that 'reverence[d] the signs, omens, messages that are delivered in queer ways and queer places, not in the least according to the plans laid down either by the theologians or the men of science'.[110] Robert Stange confesses his disappointment that the sonnet 'Found', 'which serves as a program note for the painting' should fall back on 'the underlying moral patterns' of Cowper and Rousseau.[111] Nonetheless, Rossetti had managed in 'Jenny' (1870) to imbue aspects of London with a visionary strangeness. Street lamps 'Wind on together and apart | A fiery serpent for your heart', while Jenny herself becomes a 'sphinx', revealed by 'veils withdrawn'.[112] It is not my intention to label writers as 'symbolist' or to posit a coherent grouping around a mythically normative philosophy: as Ian Watt remarked in 1979, there is little to be gained from such categorizations, especially as their definition is seemingly 'insuperable'. 'If Conrad belongs to the symbolist tradition it is only in a limited, eclectic, and highly idiosyncratic way,' he insists.[113] However, a number of late-nineteenth-century writers

---

[107] Symons, *The Symbolist Movement in Literature*, 8–9.

[108] Symons was strongly critical of Hunt's *The Awakening Conscience* (1853), denouncing it as 'futile and repulsive' and saying that its realism 'tortures the eyes'. 'The Pre-Raphaelites at Whitechapel', *Outlook*, 15 (1 April 1905), 451, quoted by S. A. Porterfield, 'Arthur Symons as Critic of the Visual Arts', *English Literature in Transition*, 44 (3) (2001), 274.

[109] A. Wilton, 'Symbolism in Britain', in A. Wilton and R. Upstone, eds., *The Age of Rossetti, Burne-Jones and Watts: Symbolism in Britain, 1860–1910* (London: Tate Gallery, 1997), 18.

[110] Machen, *The London Adventure*, 14.   [111] Stange, 'The Frightened Poets', 486.

[112] D. G. Rossetti, *Collected Poetry and Prose*, ed. J. McGann (New Haven: Yale University Press, 2003), 64, 67, 68.

[113] Watt, *Conrad in the Nineteenth Century*, 198.

display affinities with symbolist aesthetics at certain points in their careers, especially when writing about London, and their symbolist city deserves to take its place alongside those of empiricism and impressionism.

Arthur Symons hailed impressionism and symbolism as the 'two main branches' of the decadent movement in 'The Decadent Movement in Literature' (1893), and throughout the following decade he explored the possibilities of both for radical urban representation. Impressionism, he suggested, sought 'the truth of appearances to the senses, of the visible world to the eyes that see it', whereas symbolism revealed 'the finer sense of things unseen, the deeper meaning of things evident' and the essence of that which 'can be apprehended only by the soul'.[114] Eliot turned a Laforgue-tinged eye to the implications of this statement in 'Afternoon' (*c.*1914), where women visitors to the British Museum 'fade beyond the Roman statuary . . . | Towards the unconscious, the ineffable, the absolute'.[115] The two aesthetic ideologies were less competitive than complementary innovations that represented new ways of seeing in *fin de siècle* culture. For Symons, as for other writers and artists of the time, adjudicating between the claims of two radical movements in contemporary art implied not a contest but an expression of preference, and one that was rarely consistent or binding. Such negotiations were the source of lengthy debate in the French press, as Pamela Genova has shown.[116] In some respects, Whistler's mysterious nocturnes were as much proto-symbolist visions of the city as they were influential on impressionism: Mallarmé was the first to translate the *Ten O' Clock Lecture* into French. When confronting the 'problematic of the imaginary', Symons, like Verlaine, was selecting whichever techniques best suited his purposes, rather than endorsing the claims of one above another, and throughout his career he proved willing to blend impressionist and symbolist modes.[117]

Unfortunately, his ability to amalgamate differing aesthetic strategies has not always received its due, largely because of Eliot's characterization of him in *The Sacred Wood* (1920) as essentially impressionistic. This has meant that his symbolist credentials, outside his specialist study of the movement, tend to be overlooked and that his symbolist vision of London remains largely unappreciated. Admittedly, some writers and artists did see impressionism

[114] A. Symons, 'The Decadent Movement in Literature', in D. Stanford, *Critics of the 'Nineties* (London: John Baker, 1970), 111.

[115] T. S. Eliot, *Inventions of the March Hare*, 53. See too Ricks's discussion of the poem's influences, 203–7.

[116] P. A. Genova, *Symbolist Journals: A Culture of Correspondence* (Aldershot: Ashgate, 2002), 129–90.

[117] P. Florence, *Mallarmé, Manet, and Redon: Visual and Aural Signs and the Generation of Meaning* (Cambridge: Cambridge University Press, 1986), 10. Her phrase derives from Pierre Francastel's *La Réalité Figurative: éléments structurels de l'art* (1965).

and symbolism as mutually incompatible, endorsing one at the expense of the other, but many were more pragmatic. What later became 'modernism' had yet to receive elaborate codification, and many of the leading French *symbolistes*, Mallarmé for example, never used the term of themselves. With the obvious exception of Yeats, symbolism was, and in some respects still is, a largely concealed presence in English writing that was often unacknowledged or even unrecognized. It was instead what Yeats termed a 'mood' that 'wanders the world, enlarging its power as it goes, awaiting the time when it shall be, perhaps alone, or with other moods, master over a great new religion'.[118]

FASHIONING THE SYMBOL

Writing in the *Century Guild Hobby Horse* in April 1891, Lionel Johnson considered the present state of symbolism in England:

In English, *symbolisme*, and its literature, mean this: a recognition, in things, of a double existence: their existence in nature, and their existence in mind. The *sun sets*: what is the impression upon your mind, as you say the words? Clearly, that is the 'true truth' of the thing; its real and eternal significance: not the mere natural fact, but the thing, as it is in thought. So, literature is the evocation of truth from the passing show of things.[119]

A number of discourses are drawn upon here; a semi-submerged Platonism, the writing of Pater, surely the inspiration for the final phrase, French *symbolisme*, impressionism, perhaps there is even an anticipation of structuralist theories of signification. However, it is the recognition of what Johnson calls 'a double existence' of things that is crucial for English writers grappling with the representation of the city since it allowed the formulation of distinctions between 'their' London and 'the' London that were convincing beyond the commonsensical. The 'London *cognita*' and the 'London *incognita*' were, as Machen recognized, very different cities that coexisted uneasily in the same physical space.[120]

It is from this world of 'double existence,' or as Carlyle might term it, 'double revelation', that 'The Door in the Wall' and even *Heart of Darkness* in part emerge. Indeed, John Lucas has called the latter 'a symbolist tale' that 'uses language as a way of evoking terrible and final truths that lie somewhere

---

[118] Yeats, *The Secret Rose, Stories by W. B. Yeats: A Variorum Edition*, ed. W. Gould, P. L. Marcus, and M. J. Sidnell (London: Macmillan, 1992), 143–4.

[119] J. D. Hunt, *The Pre-Raphaelite Imagination 1848–1900* (London: Routledge and Kegan Paul, 1968), 147–8.

[120] Machen, *The London Adventure*, 49.

beneath the surface of things'.[121] Whereas impressionism focused on these surfaces, symbolism pondered unplumbed depths, the complex workings of the unconscious, dreams, magic, mysticism, and death, drawing upon centuries of religious and occult thought as well as more recent developments in Western art. Yet, despite or because of its lofty heritage, it remains difficult to qualify or to categorize, and Michael Gibson has remarked that it was 'less an artistic movement than a state of mind'.[122] Late-nineteenth-century attempts to elucidate or define the movement were similarly imprecise. Jean Moreas's *Le symbolisme*, a literary manifesto, which appeared in *Le Figaro* on 18 September 1886, was little more than a belated rounding up of artistic developments that had been underway for over a decade under the loose rubric of decadence, maintaining as it did that 'the idea should not make its appearance deprived of the sumptuous trappings of external analogies', since symbolist art's 'essential character . . . consists in never going straight to the conception of the idea itself'.[123] Albert Aurier's 'Paul Gauguin ou le Symbolisme en peinture' (1892) specified subjectivity and idealism as key requirements of Symbolist painting, but such qualities could hardly be monopolized by any single artistic movement. In the confusion, *symbolisme* acquired a variety of new names as well as being absorbed into subsequent artistic developments.[124]

In view of his diagnosis of symbolists as 'degenerate and imbecile', it is perhaps ironic that Max Nordau was able to offer such an effective definition of the movement. Symbolists, he wrote, 'can only think in a mystical, i.e., in a confused way':

The unknown is to them more powerful than the known; the activity of the organic nerves preponderates over that of the cerebral cortex; their emotions overrule their ideas. When persons of this kind have poetic and artistic instincts, they naturally want to give expression to their own mental state. They cannot make use of definite words of clear import, for their consciousness holds no clearly-defined univocal ideas which could be embodied in such words. They choose, therefore, vague equivocal words, because these best conform to their ambiguous and equivocal ideas. . . . Clear speech serves the purpose of communication of the actual. It has, therefore, no value in the eyes of a degenerate subject.[125]

---

[121] J. Lucas, 'From Naturalism to Symbolism', in I. Fletcher, ed., *Decadence and the 1890s* (London: Edward Arnold, 1979), 146.

[122] M. Gibson, *Symbolism* (Köln: Taschen, 1999), 7.

[123] J. Milner, *Symbolists and Decadents* (London: Studio Vista, 1971), 51.

[124] The consequences of this are explored in H. Dorra, ed., *Symbolist Art Theories: A Critical Anthology* (Berkeley and Los Angeles: University of California Press, 1994), and R. C. Smith's *Mallarmé's Children: Symbolism and the Renewal of Experience* (Berkeley and Los Angeles: University of California Press, 1999).

[125] M. Nordau, *Degeneration* (New York: D. Appleton, 1895), 118. Originally *Entartung* (Berlin: C. Duncker, 1892–3).

One would not normally look to Mallarmé for elucidation of an issue, but in the course of a discussion of symbolist painting, Edward Lucie-Smith uses his poetry as the basis for a tabulation of recurrent traits of symbolist writing, one which underlines the essential accuracy of Nordau's 'diagnosis'. In Mallarmé, he notes, ambiguity, and, one might add, indeterminacy, is omnipresent and deliberate. His work also displays a 'feeling for the symbol as catalyst', that is, 'something which, while itself remaining unchanged, generates a reaction in the psyche'.[126] The selection of such an object by the artist allows interiority to be mirrored by the external world, giving a mystical twist to notions of the objective correlative. However, as Charles Chadwick points out, because another of Mallarmé's recurrent preoccupations was the art of revealing moods through the gradual revelation of objects, or extracting from an object a 'mood' by means of 'a series of decipherings', neither the objective correlative nor its 'associated mood' were to be made explicit, merely 'hinted at'. These 'decipherings' were not those of a rationalist investigator, but a more subjective search for 'the suggestiveness of things'.[127] To return to Maxwell, the symbolist meditates on the labyrinth rather than attempting to decode it or render it accessible to a wider audience. The image and the symbol were brought together to present 'a psychological state independent of any narrative element'.[128] Imagism is often regarded as an offshoot from impressionist writing, but one can also see how it is informed by a symbolist aesthetic. When F. S. Flint insists that the symbol, like the image, 'attempts to give you an intuition of the reality itself, and of the forces, vague to us, behind it, by a series of images which the imagination seizes and brings together in an effort to insert into and express that reality', one senses again that neat distinctions between avant-garde movements are not always easily maintained.[129]

Mallarmé's work drew upon hermeticism, a term that implies the esoteric or recondite nature of symbolist thought, as well as its affinities with ancient magical arts and Neoplatonism, and its separation from the exterior concerns. Art therefore 'exists alongside the real world rather than in the midst of it', with synthesis preferred to analysis in attempting 'to combine elements found in the real world, or even borrowed from other works of art, to produce a separate, different, and certainly self-sufficient reality'.[130] Frank Kermode's

---

126 E. Lucie-Smith, *Symbolist Art* (London: Thames and Hudson, 1972), 51.
127 Chadwick, *Symbolism*, 1–2; S. Mallarmé, 'Crisis in Verse', from *Divagations* (1897) in *Symbolism: An Anthology*, ed. and trans. T. G. West (London: Methuen, 1980), 7.
128 Wilton, *The Age of Rossetti, Burne-Jones and Watts*, 108.
129 Quoted by J. T. Gage, *In the Arresting Eye: The Rhetoric of Imagism* (Baton Rouge: Louisiana State University Press, 1981), 26.
130 Lucie-Smith, *Symbolist Art*, 51.

'*rapprochement* between poet and occultist' saw 'Magic c[o]me, in an age of science, to the defence of poetry.'[131] In establishing this connection, symbolism was much inspired by the ancient doctrine of correspondence, memorably expressed in Baudelaire's influential sonnet 'Correspondances' in *Les Fleurs du Mal* (1857). Here, 'L'homme y passe à travers des fôrets de symboles' in order to gain a new perception and understanding of the world. The poem, Wallace Fowlie comments, 'reassigns to the poet his ancient role of *vates*, of soothsayer, who by his intuition of the concrete, of immediately perceived things, is led to the *idea* of these things'.[132] In the hands of Baudelaire, the symbol becomes a transferable icon, no longer bound to straightforward coherence of signifier and signified and open instead to personal readings rather than schematic deciphering. The rejection of 'clear-cut interpretations', argues Shearer West, would hopefully 'answer the ill-defined needs of the spirit which were increasingly the subject of public scrutiny in newspapers and books' in Machen's age of 'bestial materialism' and 'sham marvels'.[133]

Symbols' polysemic nature allowed them to be employed in often cryptic and esoteric ways, which encouraged in turn a synthesis between the quotidian environment, the individual perception of it, and the deeper truths that ran beneath both. Mallarmé, like Pater, sought to represent, 'not things, not facts, but the sensation produced by things and facts', seeking in the process 'new verbal structures that go beyond meaning and describing'.[134] Opponents of symbolism charged its practitioners with laziness and imprecision, but, in the course of a discussion of Maeterlinck, Symons differentiated between 'the vague' and the 'mysterious', 'two opposites very commonly confused, as the secret with the obscure, the infinite with the indefinite'. '[T]he artist who is a mystic', he concluded, 'hates the vague with a more profound hatred than any other artist.'[135] For such men, the urban world became a place of self-absorption, where only those who have the facility to see beyond its surface can hope to address its complex meaning.

Even they may face disappointment. Machen remarked that though men see 'appearances and outward shows of things, symbols of all sorts', 'essences' remain forever beyond them.[136] In *The Great God Pan* (1894), he maintained that 'those who are wise know that all symbols are symbols of something,

---

[131] F. Kermode, *Romantic Image* (London: Routledge and Kegan Paul, 1957), 110.

[132] W. Fowlie, *Poem and Symbol: A Brief History of French Symbolism* (University Park: Pennsylvania State University Press, 1990), 29.

[133] S. West, *Fin-de-Siècle: Art and Society in an Age of Uncertainty* (London: Bloomsbury, 1993), 105; Machen, *The London Adventure*, 13.

[134] L. M. Johnson, *The Metaphor of Painting: Essays on Baudelaire, Ruskin, Proust and Pater* (Ann Arbor: University of Michigan Press, 1980), 200.

[135] Symons, *The Symbolist Movement in Literature*, 307.

[136] Machen, *The London Adventure*, 70.

not nothing. It was, indeed, an exquisite symbol beneath which men long ago veiled their knowledge of the most awful, most secret forces which lie at the heart of all things.'[137] 'One must never explain symbols. One must never penetrate them,' wrote Pierre Louÿs. 'Have confidence—oh! Do not doubt. He who has drawn the symbol has hidden a truth inside it, but he must not show it—or else why symbolise it in the first place?'[138] Oscar Wilde reached a similar conclusion in the Preface to *The Picture of Dorian Gray* (1891):

> All art is at once surface and symbol.
> Those who go beneath the surface do so at their peril.
> Those who read the symbol do so at their peril.[139]

When these attitudes were applied to the metropolis, they encouraged a kind of Gnosticism in which truths could only be recognized by those readers who were able to enter into an imaginative communion or companionship with the writer. Baudelaire had made this explicit in his startling conclusion to *Les Fleurs du Mal*'s dedicatory poem 'Hypocrite lecteur,—mon semblable, mon frère'. Thomson's 'Proem' to *The City of Dreadful Night* also addressed itself to 'a brother' who 'Travels the same wild paths though out of sight'.[140] Those who used symbolist techniques in the representation of London relied upon readers who shared the belief that, as Chesterton wrote, '[C]rowded and noisy as it is, there is something about London: it is full of secrets and anomalies; and it does not like to be asked what it is.'[141] Not all of them were as direct as Thomson was in addressing a fraternity of initiates, but each in his own way implied a reader less concerned with materialist depiction than with evocation, mood, and the unanswerable. Such interpreters sensed that the 'real', 'ideal', or 'true' city lurked within, beneath or beyond the London of surfaces, but its discovery was difficult, even perilous and its literary representation all but impossible.

During the 1890s, Machen repeatedly pondered 'symbolizing the story of a soul by the picture of exterior things', though the London of *The Hill of Dreams* eventually descends into nightmares and madness.[142] Margaret Schlegel sees London as 'a caricature of infinity' in *Howards End*.[143] In Symons's 'The Journal of Henry Luxulyan' (1905), the diarist is overcome by a revelation that threatens his sanity:

a strange and terrifying sensation takes hold of me as the cab turns suddenly out of a tangle of streets, into a broad road between trees and houses: one enters into it as into

---

[137] A. Machen, *The Great God Pan* (1894; London: Creation, 1993), 107.
[138] P. Louÿs, in Cassou, ed., *The Concise Encyclopedia of Symbolism*, 156.
[139] O. Wilde, Preface to *The Picture of Dorian Gray, Complete Works*, 17.
[140] Thomson, *The City of Dreadful Night*, 552.
[141] G. K. Chesterton, *London* (Minneapolis: Edmund D. Brookes [privately printed], 1914), 13.
[142] Machen, *The London Adventure*, 137.   [143] Forster, *Howards End*, 275.

a long dimly lighted alley, and at the end of the road is the sky, with one star hung like a lantern upon the darkness; and it seems as if the sky is at the end of the road, that if one drove right on one would plunge over the edge of the world. All that is solid on the earth seems to melt about one; it is as if one's eyes had been suddenly opened, and one saw for the first time. And the great dread comes over me: the dread of what may be on the other side of reality.[144]

The sense of the 'melting' here is perhaps an indication that Luxulyan's existential anxieties are an aspect of Matthew Arnold's 'strange disease of modern life', the world in which, as Karl Marx had maintained, 'all that is solid melts into air'.[145] However, although modernity may be partially responsible for Luxulyan's plight, his visions themselves are the 'fatal initiation of madness' Symons identified elsewhere as a mystical revelation at the heart of the Symbolist ethos, the 'central secret of the mystics . . . "As things are below, so are they above".'[146] This mystical insight allows Luxulyan, like Lucian Taylor, Lionel Wallace, and indeed, Symons himself, to realize that 'the visible world is no longer a reality and the unseen world no longer a dream,' but such knowledge has a terrible price.[147]

The symbolist version of London, like its impressionist counterpart, derived considerable imaginative impetus from contemporary French aesthetics, but it also drew upon the British artistic tradition explored by John Dixon Hunt which ran from Blake to the Pre-Raphaelites. The urban writer who felt the weight of this tradition most forcefully was James Thomson, whose *The City of Dreadful Night* is one of the important symbolist responses to London. Thomson's doomed necropolis, with its River of the Suicides, 'shadowy streets', and 'street-lamps burn[ing] amid the baleful glooms' may have obvious affinities with the capital, but it refused unproblematic equivalence.[148] The poem was widely known during the 1890s, with the 1894 collected edition of Thomson's work widely reviewed, notably by Symons, who reprinted his essay in *Studies in Two Literatures* (1897), and John Davidson, who praised his fellow Scot's evocation of 'the offal of the world' in 1899.[149] The young Rudyard Kipling found his early Christian faith shattered by the poem, borrowing its title for his evocation of a fever epidemic in Lahore (1885/1891) and granting Thomson's 'Melencolia' a key role in *The Light that Failed.*

---

[144] A. Symons, 'The Journal of Henry Luxulyan', *Spiritual Adventures*, 254–5.
[145] M. Arnold, 'The Scholar Gypsy' (1853); K. Marx and F. Engels, *The Communist Manifesto*, trans. D. McLellan (1848; Oxford: Oxford University Press, 1992), 6.
[146] Symons, *The Symbolist Movement in Literature*, 32.
[147] Ibid. 4.
[148] Thomson, *The City of Dreadful Night*, 563, 553.
[149] J. Davidson, 'Pre-Shakespearianism', *The Speaker*, 19 (28 January 1899), 107.

The poem's memorable title quickly became detached from the work itself, and like Booth's 'Darkest England' and Morrison's 'mean streets', passed into the rhetoric of metropolitan crisis, where it signalled a general moral and spiritual blindness rather than the complexities of poetic vision. Such a fate was doubly ironic for a visionary atheist to endure.[150] Thomson's phrase was tailor-made for harassed subeditors, social commentators, or, ironically given the poet's lack of religious conviction, apocalyptically minded preachers. Ford Madox Ford employed it in the memorable conclusion to *The Soul of London* (1905), imagining an 'immense Town . . . black, walled in, peopled by gibbering neurasthenics . . . this image of a City of dreadful Night'.[151] In M. P. Shiel's *The Purple Cloud* (1901), London is wiped out by a deadly gas from a volcanic explosion and becomes a 'city of dreadful night . . . lugubrious as Babylons long grass grown' crammed with twenty million corpses.[152] *Punch*'s commentators denounced 'Our dreary, weary City of Dreadful Dirt' in 1897.[153] As late as 1922, the punning 'City of Dreadful Knights' was used by English newspapers to refer to Cardiff, home of several Welshmen ennobled in dubious circumstances by Lloyd George's post-war administration.

The title of Thomson's poem was undeniably resonant for an increasingly urbanized late-nineteenth-century readership, but those who appropriated it for journalistic crusades misrepresented and localized its symbolic language. As Isobel Armstrong demonstrates, Thomson did not offer an account of the city's 'physical horror' or 'psychological estrangement as an end in itself'. He aimed instead to deploy the city as a 'symptomatic' symbol of 'the representations which despair, imprisoned in theological fallacies, makes for itself'. By combining the dismal realities of 'outcast' London with the *Inferno* and the Bible, Thomson's city becomes both 'an incarcerating material environment' and 'a universal metaphysical condition' that is 'far more coercive than the mere unreality of nightmare'.[154] 'We gaze into the living world and mark | Infinite mysteries for ever dark,' Thomson wrote in 1881, twisting the arguments of medieval theologians of the *via negativa* to secularist purposes. Since God could never be encompassed by human thought, Thomson argues, 'He will not blame the eyes he made so dim | That

---

[150] Thomson seems to have anticipated Lewis Mumford's theory, summarized by Emrys Jones, that the metropolis belongs to 'a cycle of growth and decay, from polis to metropolis to megalopolis and finally to necropolis'. The poet composed *The City* in a London passing into its final stage. L. Mumford, *The Culture of Cities* (1940), in E. Jones, *Metropolis: The World's Great Cities* (Oxford: Oxford University Press, 1990), 15.

[151] F. M. Ford, *The Soul of London: A Survey of a Modern City*, ed. A. G. Hill (1905; London: Dent, 1995), 106.

[152] M. P. Shiel, *The Purple Cloud* (1901; London: Allison and Busby, 1983), 107.

[153] 'Unclean! Unclean! (A Cry from St. Pancras)', *Punch* (13 February 1897), 75.

[154] I. Armstrong, *Victorian Poetry: Poetry, Poetics, Politics* (London: Routledge, 1993), 462.

they cannot discern a trace of him.'[155] Few of those who came after him made war upon Christianity with such doleful enthusiasm, but the combination of Dante and the modern city proved powerfully influential.

Whether Thomson initiated the vogue for reading London in Dantean terms is difficult to know, but the practice was a significant one from the 1870s, growing out of a more general revival of interest in Dante pioneered chiefly by D. G. Rossetti.[156] Evangelists and social reformers were particularly fond of equating London with hell. Mrs Humphry Ward's best-selling *Robert Elsmere* (1888) depicted a London of 'rainy fog' and 'indescribable gloom', where a reference to the *Inferno* made further scene-setting unnecessary.[157] In Margaret Oliphant's Christian allegory 'The Land of Darkness' (1887), the Little Pilgrim experiences 'the whirling and sickening sensation of passing downward through the air, like the description Dante gives of his descent upon Geryon', arriving in a brutal city where Christianity is regarded as a 'modern pretence'.[158] Dante became another element of W. T. Stead's sensationalist city, which, combining as it did Babylon, Crete, and 'those whose lives are passed in the London *Inferno*', showed long before Eliot how a phantasmagoria of urban references could create an 'unreal city'.

Evangelical writing did not, however, have a monopoly on seeing London as hell. Edward Lear told Lord Derby that 'London life is of all punishments the most shocking.'[159] *Punch* enlisted Dante for the purposes of fatalistic comedy when mourning the annual arrival of London's winter weather, 'Grey Malebolges of cold clinging muck'.[160] Hume Nisbet's horror tale, 'The Phantom Model' (1894), openly appropriated Dante in its 'search for the Spiritual, through the Inferno of the East [End]', and located a modern Beatrice in the slums of Wapping.[161] Symons remarked that reading Dante prepared London's visitors for the ordeal of the fog.[162] 'P. R.', who wrote the introduction to the colonial edition of Gissing's *The Nether World* in

---

[155] J. Thomson, 'Address on the Opening of the New Hall of Leicester Secular Society', privately printed, 1881. T. Leonard, *Places of the Mind: The Life and Work of James Thomson ('B.V.')* (London: Jonathan Cape, 1993), 246.

[156] R. Zweig, ' "Death-in-Love": Rossetti and the Victorian Journey Back to Dante', in R. Barreca, ed., *Sex and Death in Victorian Literature* (Basingstoke: Macmillan, 1990), 178–93.

[157] Mrs H. Ward, *Robert Elsmere* (1888; London: John Murray, 1911), ii. 167.

[158] M. Oliphant, *A Beleaguered City and Other Tales of the Seen and Unseen*, ed. J. Calder (Edinburgh: Canongate, 2000), 313, 321.

[159] Lear to Lord Derby, 23 July 1880, in V. Noakes, *Edward Lear* (1968; London: Ariel Books, 1985), 237.

[160] 'The Snow Fiend's Song', *Punch* (16 January 1886), 26.

[161] H. Nisbet, 'The Phantom Model', in H. Lamb, ed., *Gaslit Nightmares* (London: Futura, 1988), 40.

[162] Symons, *London*, 211. Symons later saw his own madness in Dantean terms, imagining that a fellow inmate of the asylum 'who always walked round and round in a circle regulated the course of the sun' (*Confessions: A Study in Pathology* (New York: Fountain Press, 1930), 87).

1890, referred to 'the unlovely and monotonous regions of Clerkenwell' as 'the Inferno of grinding poverty'. A reviewer of Gissing's novel wrote of how readers 'seem to have been transported, not to another postal district of the metropolis, but to some horrible region of damned souls, such as Dante might imagine as the final punishment of the most degraded types of humanity'.[163]

Other writers were more oblique. Chesterton's vision of the Thames, 'a stream of literal fire winding under vast caverns of a subterranean country', suggests the flaming river that pours upon those damned souls in the seventh circle of Hell.[164] In *The Secret Agent*, nocturnal footsteps die away 'as if the passer-by had started to pace out all eternity, from gas-lamp to gas-lamp in a night without end', implying a connection between the endless if futile exertion of the prison yard and hell itself.[165] Fifteen years later, in the winter of 1921–2, Conrad Aiken rarely saw T. S. Eliot without his copy of the *Inferno*. It had, Robert Crawford concludes, 'replaced Baedeker' as his guide to the capital.[166]

It was from Dante that Thomson derived the motif of the circle, with its intimations of infinity and connotations of hellish imprisonment and repetitive, pointless endeavour. As we have seen, Gustave Doré's 'Newgate—Exercise Yard' in *London: A Pilgrimage* (1872), and the researches of Beatrice Webb offered various Dantean analogues to late-Victorian London. Doré had illustrated the *Divine Comedy* in 1861, and there are perhaps echoes of these drawings in the illustrations for *London: A Pilgrimage*. Such a suggestion recurs in Machen's 'The Shining Pyramid' (1895), where Dyson announces that 'Doré could not have designed anything more wonderful and mystic than Oxford Street as I saw it the other evening, the sunset flaming, the blue haze transmuting the plain street into a road "far in the spiritual city".'[167] Thomson made explicit the connection between London and the *Inferno*, using a quotation from Dante as one of his poem's epigraphs. David Seed notes the apparent paradox of a poet so sceptical towards Christianity 'even contemplating imitating an allegory based on medieval Catholicism', but the perversion of Christian texts was a common feature of secularist writing of the period.[168] Thomson's use of Dante allowed him to rework an image with

[163] 'P. R.', Introduction to *The Nether World* (London: E. A. Petherick, 1890); unsigned review, *Court Journal* (27 April 1889), quoted in P. Coustillas and J. Spiers, eds., *Gissing: The Critical Heritage* (London: Routledge and Kegan Paul, 1972), 135, 137.

[164] Chesterton, *The Man Who Was Thursday*, 40.

[165] Conrad, *The Secret Agent*, 42–3.

[166] R. Crawford, *The Savage and the City in the Work of T. S. Eliot* (Oxford: Clarendon, 1987), 44.

[167] A. Machen, *Tales of Horror and the Supernatural* (London: Panther, 1963), 7–8.

[168] D. Seed, 'Hell Is a City: Symbolic Systems and Epistemological Scepticism in *The City of Dreadful Night*', in Byron and Punter, eds., *Spectral Readings*, 95.

which an educated audience was already familiar in order to critique a belief system he regarded as discredited by centuries of human suffering.

Within the Dantean hell, the circle was a means of organization and punishment. It served similar purposes in London, at least for Henry James. In the aftermath of the *Guy Domville* fiasco of 1895, he considered London 'the nethermost circle of the Inferno' and fled to Torquay for several months.[169] His 'London Town' would, in theory, 'circle out concentrically to the City and the suburbs' but the impossible project caused him only frustration and disappointment.[170] John Davidson employed Dantean imagery with wry humour during his own explorations of London and its environs:

The raw and glaring station, the white railway track with the grey shining lines, would vanish shortly as the train had done, and he would be left to wander about in this doleful, dying region for ever and ever. He thought he had taken a train from Baker Street to Amersham, but it was all a snare of the Evil One; he was dead and in a circle of Hades unexplored by Dante, being unknown in his day, the leprous land appointed for the punishment of descriptive writers.[171]

The Man Who Was Thursday's Gabriel Syme, 'a poet who had become a detective' and who is peculiarly sensitive to the atmosphere and analysis of the city, finds himself extending the conceit of the endless circle to the orbit of the Earth. As in Wells and Conrad, a key moment of initiation is ambiguously illumined, with the moon 'so strong and full . . . that it seemed like a weaker sun' giving 'not the sense of bright moonshine, but rather of a dead daylight'. The Embankment becomes a phantasmal realm where Syme feels himself to be 'on some sadder and emptier planet, which circled round some sadder star'.[172] Syme's intuitions link his London with the distant realms of *The City of Dreadful Night* that are but 'worlds as sad as this' as well as prefiguring the interminable circularity of *The Waste Land*.[173] Later in the novel, Syme beholds the 'innumerable roofs of slate' comprising the London skyline, and finds himself 'daunted and bewildered by their infinite series'. Their infinity is 'like the empty infinity of arithmetic, something unthinkable, yet necessary to thought'.[174] The intensity of the experience robs him of the flippancy that allowed the more pragmatic G. S. Street to quip, 'Bayswater suggests eternity, and that, as we all know, depresses even the most buoyant of us,' leaving him humble and afraid.[175]

[169] H. M. Hyde, *Henry James at Home* (London: Methuen, 1969), 70.
[170] E. Gosse, *Aspects and Impressions* (London: Cassell, 1922), 60.
[171] J. Davidson, *A Random Itinerary* (London: Elkin Matthews and John Lane, 1894), 40.
[172] Chesterton, *The Man Who Was Thursday*, 38, 48.
[173] Thomson, *The City of Dreadful Night*, 578.
[174] Chesterton, *The Man Who Was Thursday*, 98.
[175] G. S. Street, 'Bayswater and St. John's Wood', in *A Book of Essays* (London: Archibald Constable, 1902), 38.

These worlds of aimless and bleak repetition did not simply equate London with the monotonous punishments of the afterlife. Instead they demonstrate the city's encouragement of nihilistic circularity, creating a space in which inhabitants or characters are doomed to exhaust and destroy themselves through repetition without progress. Lucian Taylor's hopeless wanderings in *The Hill of Dreams* are inevitably circular, and lead him back again and again to the same 'site of degraded fascination'.[176] Ian Watt suggests that the turn of the tide in *Heart of Darkness* is 'a reminder of the endless and apparently meaningless circularity of the physical and the human world', circularity 'finally enacted in the fictional setting and the larger meaning of the tale itself'.[177] Stevie's obsessively drawn 'innumerable' circles in *The Secret Agent*, which suggest 'a rendering of cosmic chaos, the symbolism of a mad art attempting the inconceivable', are a potent diagram of such hopelessness.[178] 'Thus Stevie's art. Thus London,' Joseph McLaughlin concludes.[179]

The City of Dreadful Night's 'self-sufficient reality' and pessimistic mood undoubtedly helped to shape certain writers' perceptions of London, but its technical influence was far more limited. Its highly artificial verse, with laboured polysyllabic rhymes underscoring the weary inevitability of its conditions of existence, and its antagonistic engagement with Christian allegory were both far more elaborate and systematic than the preferred techniques of a subsequent generation.[180] Consequently, its inspiration was emotional as much as formal, though it was one of the poems, alongside *Maud* and Rochester's 'Upon Nothing', from which Stephen Phillips derived his 'The New "De Profundis"' (1898):

> I am discouraged by the street,
> The pacing of monotonous feet;
> Faces of all emotion purged;
> From nothing unto nothing urged;
> The living men that shadows go,
> A vain procession to and fro.
> The earth an unreal course doth run,
> Haunted by a phantasmal sun [181]

---

[176] Warwick, 'Lost Cities: London's Apocalypse', 83.

[177] Watt, *Conrad in the Nineteenth Century*, 253.   [178] Conrad, *The Secret Agent*, 34.

[179] J. McLaughlin, *Writing the Urban Jungle: Reading Empire in London from Doyle to Eliot* (Charlottesville: University Press of Virginia, 2000), 160.

[180] The poem's complex composition is documented by William Schaefer, 'The Two Cities of Dreadful Night', *PMLA*, 77 (1962), 609–16.

[181] S. Phillips, *Poems* (London: John Lane/The Bodley Head, 1898), 68.

Thomson placed his experience of London at the service of a wider symbolic design, but later writers would emphasize the poem's realist elements in creating substantially different versions of the symbolist city.

REALIST VEILS

'Realism', Yeats declared in 1916, 'is created for the common people and was always their peculiar delight, and it is the delight today of all those whose minds, educated alone by schoolmasters and newspapers, are without the memory of beauty and emotional subtlety.'[182] At the fifth exhibition of the Salon de la Rose + Croix in 1896, the painters Armand Point and Léonard Saluis 'depicted an ideal creature half Perseus and half Saint George dangling at arm's length the severed head of Zola'.[183] However, while realism could be dismissed, it was not easily replaced, especially when one apparent alternative to it, impressionism, which is perhaps what Yeats had in mind when he rebuked 'picturesque writing, . . . word-painting', retained its concern with what Symons called 'exteriority'.[184] Besides, 'realism' was an increasingly imprecise term by 1916, and often used merely as a convenient catch-all for novels and plays deemed unimaginative and unambitious by more self-consciously 'innovative' writers. To stereotype it in this way was unfair, since realists were by no means insensitive to their limitations. Gissing satirized theosophy and spiritualism in *Among the Prophets*, a novel that he composed between November 1899 and late January 1900 but destroyed as unsatisfactory, and his *The Private Papers of Henry Ryecroft* (1903) ridiculed 'superficial forms of reaction against scientific positivism' such as 'esoteric Buddhism'. Nonetheless, Henry Ryecroft is prepared to consider 'the unknowable', the 'appalling Mystery' of existence and the 'pathos' of humanity's limited eschatological awareness, and to lament that 'One symbol, indeed, has obscured all others—the minted round of metal.'[185] Some 'realists' at least were far from the complacent materialists Yeats castigated.

Realist techniques were in fact crucial to English Symbolist writing. What might be termed 'esoteric realism' adopted and subverted them in ingenious

[182] W. B. Yeats, 'Certain Noble Plays of Japan' (1916), in *Essays and Introductions* (London: Macmillan, 1961), 227.

[183] Pincus-Witton, *Occult Symbolism in France*, 47.

[184] W. B. Yeats, 'The Symbolism of Poetry' (1900), in *The Major Works*, ed. E. Larrissy (Oxford: Oxford University Press, 1997), 359.

[185] G. Gissing, *The Private Papers of Henry Ryecroft*, ed. M. Storey (1903; Oxford: Oxford University Press, 1987), 109–11, 159.

ways similar to those in which symbolist painting used largely figurative techniques but transplanted them to worlds of myth and the imagination, or stressed, as in Khnopff's pastels of female faces, the existence of inscrutable inner currents. Without a title to guide the interpreter, Khnopff's use of Christina Rossetti's poetry in '*I lock my door upon myself*' (1891), for instance, the meaning of symbolist pictures is often occluded or simply obscure. Painters regularly employ a dense and private symbolic language, sometimes at odds with artistic convention, or offer scenes that invite allegorical interpretation without admitting any allegorical design. Some symbolist art, G. F. Watts's *Hope* (1876), for example, continued to employ traditional allegorical techniques, but more ambitious productions resisted such temptation, seeking to induce instead a reflective state of mind through an altogether wider frame of reference, rather than matching an image to a set of historically accepted rules.[186] Gustave Moreau was particularly associated with such procedures. His unfinished painting of the slaughtered suitors of Penelope, *Les Prétendants* (begun 1852) was, Philippe Jullian suggests, seen by some poets as an allegory of their likely fate within a rationalist universe personified by Athene, though Moreau gives no clue that this is his aim.[187] A portrait or a scene from myth or literature was imbued with secret meanings discerned only by those of sympathetic temperament. At the end of *The Secret Agent* even a newspaper, the emblem of modern mundanity, is able to assume mystic properties. In labelling Mrs Verloc's death 'an impenetrable mystery', the newspaper report acquires a totemic significance for Ossipon, who fears insanity lurks within its lines as he derides 'the beauties of its journalistic style'.[188]

A generation of French writers, from Gautier to Flaubert, had witnessed the rise of realism as the preferred art form of the post-1830 middle class, with the latter's *Madame Bovary* (1857) pioneering the use of apparently realist art to critique both the form and its bourgeois associations. The novel had subverted realism by concealing savage critique within seemingly neutral detail. The lazy reader, inclined to skip passages of no immediate narrative import, missed its satirical barbs and saw only a seemingly 'accessible' melodrama. Arguing that realism was a 'disgusting insult . . . not a new method of creation, but a minute description of what is superfluous', Baudelaire's 1857 review of *Madame Bovary* had concluded by terming the novel the 'secret recess of

---

[186] The relationship between conventional allegory and symbolist 'development of a new kind of subject matter that lay somewhere between allegory and expressionism' is discussed further by Robert Goldwater, *Symbolism* (London: W. H. Allen, 1979), 5–8. For Yeats's discussion of the difference between symbolism and allegory, see 'Symbolism in Painting' (1898).

[187] Jullian, *Dreamers of Decadence*, 35. Symons saw Watts' use of symbolism as 'false' because 'it is obvious, and because its meaning can be detached entirely from the manner of its expression' ('Watts', *Studies in Seven Arts* (London: Constable, 1906), 97).

[188] Conrad, *The Secret Agent*, 224–7.

his mind' and praising Flaubert's ability to 'deliberately veil' his flair for irony and lyricism.[189] *Madame Bovary* offered a seemingly detached narration that revealed its attitudinal subtleties only to the like-minded, enriching an apparently 'realist' text with an esoteric substance. Flaubert therefore concealed the 'true' novel beneath a vulgar surface.

Consciously or otherwise, such an approach was in line with the Neoplatonic teachings that insisted that 'All those who are wise in divine matters and are interpreters of the mystical revelations prefer incongruous symbols for holy things, so that divine things may not be easily accessible.'[190] Symbolism shared Flaubert's ferocious contempt for the bourgeoisie, with Symons calling him 'the one impeccable novelist who has ever lived'.[191] Huysmans's *À rebours* (1884), a novel that began as a naturalist case history yet metamorphosed into something glittering and exotic, went still further in defying middle-class expectations. As Huysmans realized, the everyday details of contemporary reality could be recorded relatively faithfully, at least up to a point, but the mimetic representation of life and objects was only the beginning of the symbolist endeavour. Ideally, suggests his anti-hero, Des Esseintes, 'the novel would become a communion of thought between a magical writer and an ideal reader, a spiritual collaboration of a handful of superior beings scattered throughout the universe, a treat for literary epicures, accessible to them alone.'[192] It is only this reader, one assumes, who can properly appreciate the ironies of Conrad terming *The Secret Agent* 'a simple tale'.

One might expect symbolist Londons to be found in personal reactions to the city rather than in narratives set within it, for the simple reason that symbolism lent itself so well to enraptured oneiric contemplation, or, to put it less charitably, solipsistic and enervated mysticism. Its adherents sometimes resembled the 'visionary' of Oliphant's 'The Land of Darkness', 'who could not speak plainly, who broke off into mysterious inferences, and appeared to know more than he would say'.[193] However, as Symons discovered in blending his amalgam of impressionism, symbolism, and decadence, a purely symbolist voice, which transforms language from 'the vehicle of everyday communication' into 'opaque . . . incantation' was difficult to maintain in discussing quotidian surroundings at length, assuming that it existed at all.[194] One could defamiliarize or make strange the urban landscape in painting,

[189] C. Baudelaire, '*Madame Bovary* by Gustave Flaubert', in his *Selected Writings on Art and Literature*, trans. P. E. Charvet (Harmondsworth: Penguin, 1972), 248, 255.

[190] 'Dionysus Areopagita', *De Coelesti hierarchia*, in Wind, *Pagan Mysteries in the Renaissance*, 12–13.

[191] Symons, *The Symbolist Movement in Literature*, 5.

[192] J.-K. Huysmans, *Against Nature*, trans. M. Mauldon (1884; Oxford: Oxford University Press, 1998), 162.

[193] Oliphant, *A Beleaguered City*, 324.   [194] Temple, *The Critic's Alchemy*, 14.

photography, poetry, or brief essays, but more substantial prose works, even those such as Rodenbach's *Bruges-la-Morte* (1892), needed a skeleton narrative for their solitary musing. Besides, symbolists may have been deaf to the siren songs of commerce, but their publishers were not.

What resulted from the collision of the personal and the commercial, at least in philistine Albion, was a compromise. In it, the avant-garde elements of symbolist perception were concealed, or at least diluted, through their being mixed with less visionary forms, such as belle-lettres evocations of the spirit of place. 'A Fragment of Life' even oscillates between mystical elevation and Pooteresque comedy. Peter Brooks has noted how *Heart of Darkness* 'suggests affinities to that pre-eminently nineteenth-century genre, the detective story, but a detective story gone modernist: a tale of inconclusive solutions to crimes of problematic status'.[195] *The Man Who Was Thursday* also undermines the form and expectations of the early-twentieth-century detective story, culminating in Sunday's miraculous revelations that, as 'the peace of God', pass all understanding.[196] Part of prose symbolism's invisibility today is that it is rarely recognized as such, so well is it disguised by its generic obligations.[197] Even when it is considered, it is usually subordinated to overarching master narratives that grudgingly afford it legitimacy, 'modernism' perhaps, or 'the Gothic'. The avowedly secular nature of much recent critical writing on London has tended to ignore symbolism, finding its spiritual or occult dimension uncongenial, even embarrassing. However, as Ackroyd has maintained in discussing Blake's blending of spiritual and material concerns, 'I believe I am describing London in almost a religious sense, although I cannot be sure what particular religion it is.'[198] Clearly, for Ackroyd at least, the numinous has a crucial role to play in the perception, and consequently the discussion of the metropolis, but his view remains a marginal one in contemporary urban theory.

Symbolists concealed their vision of the city, and, sometimes the cosmos, behind generic veils that few have been willing to lift. Hence, for David Trotter, *The Three Impostors* is a 'a mystery story with a sting in the tale' and, awkwardly, 'a stylish novel about the pleasures of stylishness which is in the end sickened by style' rather than a meditation on mystery in its older sense.[199] *The Secret Agent*

[195] Brooks, *Reading for the Plot*, 238.   [196] Chesterton, *The Man Who Was Thursday*, 187.

[197] Jean Pierrot points out that deaths and illnesses of French Symbolist writers and artists during the late 1890s, and the closure of the key Symbolist theatre, the Théâtre de l'Oeuvre in 1898, had a deleterious effect on the development of symbolism. *The Decadent Imagination*, trans. D. Coltman (Chicago: Chicago University Press, 1981), 214–42.

[198] P. Ackroyd, 'Cockney Visionaries', *The Independent* (18 December 1993).

[199] D. Trotter, introduction to *The Three Impostors*, xvii, xxx. Trotter does touch on Machen's explorations of the 'mysteriousness' of the London streets, but connects it with a questionable claim that 'Authors were supposed to be connoisseurs of street-life' rather than a recognition of Machen's mystical sensibilities (*The Three Impostors*, xx).

cannot be linked to symbolism—there is no entry for the movement in the *Oxford Reader's Companion to Conrad* (2000)—because to do so would be to jeopardize Conrad's 'modernist' credentials. *Heart of Darkness* has sometimes been considered a symbolist, rather than a symbolic, novel, but it is usually associated with impressionism since that movement is seen as part of 'modern' art, just as impressionists themselves had proclaimed in the 1870s. By contrast, symbolism, which preferred the 'defeat of Athens to the triumph of the violent Macedonian', is still often regarded as a frowzy hangover from the *fin de siècle*, a Janus-faced movement caught between 'the end of Naturalism and the start of our own era of modernity'.[200] Symbolist art certainly suffered from changes in fashion: Burne-Jones's *Love Leading the Pilgrim* (1896–7), which had fetched £5,775 in 1898, sold for just £94.10s in 1943. Andrew Lloyd Webber has recalled how even illustrous late-Victorian pictures could still be bought for very little money as recently as the mid-1960s.[201] A marked revival of interest in symbolism began in the late 1960s, when Philippe Jullian noted the affinities between the decadents of the 1890s and their counter-cultural successors.[202] However, while symbolist art was the subject of several major exhibitions during the 1990s, notably at Montreal's Museum of Fine Arts (1995) and London's Tate Gallery (1997), studies of symbolist writing in English invariably conclude with the early Yeats. Later Symbolist visions of the city, such as Machen's enigmatic 'N' from *The Cosy Room* (1936), have tended to be ignored, left behind by more obviously 'modernist' innovations.

Roger Luckhurst terms the material amassed by the Society for Psychical Research 'a set of *doxai*, a shadow-record of beliefs and semi-legitimate knowledges which failed to find sanction in orthodox channels of information'.[203] Influenced by Foucault's 'subjugated knowledges', those which have 'been disqualified as inadequate to their task or insufficiently elaborated' and which as so-called 'naïve knowledges' exist 'beneath the required level of cognition or scientificity', Luckhurst suggests that belief in telepathy and its 'allied notions'

[200] Paul Bourget in *La Nouvelle Presse* (1881), in Milner, *Symbolists and Decadents*, 1; J. Clair, 'Lost Paradise', in *Lost Paradise: Symbolist Europe* (Montreal: Montreal Museum of Fine Arts, 1995), 17. For recent discussions of the relationship between occult and symbolist thought and the construction of modernity, see R. Luckhurst's *The Invention of Telepathy 1870–1901* (Oxford: Oxford University Press, 2002) and A. Owen's *The Place of Enchantment: British Occultism and the Culture of the Modern* (Chicago: University of Chicago Press, 2004).

[201] *Burne-Jones: The Paintings, Graphic and Decorative Work of Sir Edward Burne-Jones 1833–1898* (London: Arts Council of Great Britain, 1975), 65; *Pre-Raphaelites and Other Masters: The Andrew Lloyd Webber Collection* (London: Royal Academy of Arts, 2003).

[202] Jullian, *Dreamers of Decadence*, 11–15.

[203] Luckhurst, *The Invention of Telepathy*, 151. 'I will use *doxa* throughout in the senses of 'opinion,' 'conjecture,' or belief,' he adds, rather than as the 'popular opinion' rejected by Barthes in *Roland Barthes* (1977). M. Foucault, 'Two Lectures', in *Power/Knowledge: Selected Interviews and Other Writings*, trans. C. Gordon et al. (New York: Pantheon, 1980), 82.

ran the risk of 'disqualification' from 'knowledges of erudition'. Symbolist
literary responses to London constitute a similar 'shadow-record', and indeed,
a record of shadows that has gone largely unacknowledged beyond those such
as Robert Crawford and Ronald Schuchard, who have considered the complex
nature of Eliot's debts to Thomson and the 1890s.[204] However, even these
have tended to concentrate on poetry at the expense of prose, except where
Eliot himself admitted or signalled debts such as the epigraph from *Heart of
Darkness* deleted at Pound's behest in the drafts of *The Waste Land*.

It is somehow appropriate that London's incarnation as a symbolist city
should be hidden or veiled, since the veil was a recurrent reference point in
symbolist writing. Conrad, for instance, described *The Mirror of the Sea* (1906)
as 'an unreserved attempt to unveil for a moment the profounder intimacies of
the sea and the formative influences of nearly half my lifetime', and described
the death of Kurtz in *Heart of Darkness* as being 'as though a veil had been
rent'.[205] As we have seen, Whistler had described the London mist in *The Ten
O' Clock Lecture* as a 'kindly veil' which transfigured the unpleasant industrial
and commercial realities of the Thames waterfront. Here the veil was a poetic
flourish that served pictorial rather than symbolic purposes, but its use by
Machen was rather different. Machen's familiarity with classical philosophy
and occult learning encouraged him to perceive the world either in Platonic
terms, whereby humanity saw only the flickering shadows of deeper realities,
or else to posit that such truths exist behind a veil that it is dangerous to lift.
Tennyson and George Eliot had both deployed the image of the lifted veil,
but Machen's use of it is more likely to derive from older sources.[206] Shelley
had argued that 'Poetry lifts the veil from the hidden beauty of the world,
and makes familiar objects be as if they were not familiar,' fusing Platonism
with more general ideas of ineffability.[207] Machen embraced such notions,

---

[204] James Thomson did not merit a mention in Herbert Howarth's *Notes on Some Figures
behind T. S. Eliot* (1965), but our understanding of the relationship between Eliot and late-
Victorian poetry has since been thoroughly chronicled by studies such as Crawford's *The Savage
and the City in the Work of T. S. Eliot*, Schuchard's *Eliot's Dark Angel: Intersections of Life and Art*
(Oxford: Oxford University Press, 1999), and Ricks's editorial work on Eliot's *Inventions of the
March Hare*.

[205] Conrad, 'Author's Note' (1920), to *The Secret Agent*, 229; *Heart of Darkness*, 111–12.

[206] Notable examples include Shelley's sonnet 'Lift Not the Painted Veil' (1824), Eliot's short
story 'The Lifted Veil' (1859), and Tennyson's forlorn question in *In Memoriam* (1850), 'What
hope of answer or redress? | Behind the veil, behind the veil' (LVI). Machen disliked George
Eliot's works, and memorably dismissed them as the productions of 'a superior insect' in
Hieroglyphics, 71. Yeats prefaced his memoirs of the 1890s, *The Trembling of the Veil* (1922) with
a recollection of 'a saying from Stéphane Mallarmé, that his epoch was troubled by the trembling
of the veil of the Temple' (*Autobiographies*, 109).

[207] P. B. Shelley, *A Defence of Poetry*, ed. J. E. Jordan (1821; New York: Bobbs-Merrill,
1965), 41.

along with the Gospels' account of rending of the veil in the temple at the moment of Jesus's death. As an occultist and erstwhile book cataloguer, he may also have known of the veil's importance in the Kabbalah, or in the mystery religions of the ancient Mediterranean world, dramatized by Flaubert in *Salammbô* (1862).[208] He makes particularly insistent use of the conceit in *The Three Impostors*, a novel that delights in both epistemological uncertainty and hideous revelation. 'The divine ray cannot reach us unless it is covered with poetic veils,' wrote 'Dionysus Areopagita', and when the lifting of such veils places the protagonists of *The Three Impostors* in the terrifying position of Semele beholding Zeus, the reader is grateful that they are raised but rarely.[209]

Machen maps metaphysical anxieties of life and death on to the London cityscape as Dyson and Phillips become embroiled in Dr Lipsius's murderous plot. Early in the novel, Dyson finds himself 'slowly overpower[ed]' by 'the lust of the marvellous':

a man is sauntering along a quiet, sober, everyday London street, a street of grey houses and blank walls, and there, for a moment, a veil seems drawn aside, and the very fume of the pit steams up through the flagstones, the ground glows, red-hot, beneath his feet, and he seems to hear the hiss of the infernal cauldron.[210]

The collision of mystical traditions suggested by the lifted veil transforms London into a site of pagan amorality, as represented by Lipsius and his hedonistic associates, and the Christian hell, embodied in the fiery death that awaits 'the young man with spectacles' at the end of the novel. Here Symbolism and the occult combine to destabilize pressing temporal realities, and make 'a quiet, sober, everyday London street' the venue for startling revelation.

James Thomson's pessimistic atheism led him to conclude 'none can pierce the vast black veil uncertain | Because there is no light beyond the curtain,' only 'vanity and nothingness', but later writers use the veil trope more ambiguously to provide glimpses of the 'true' reality rather than to impose limits on perception.[211] Wells's George Ponderevo realizes that London, 'the whole illimitable place', teems with 'suggestions of indefinite and sometimes outrageous possibility, of hidden but magnificent meanings'. Exploring the city first by poring over a map and then by wandering its streets, Ponderevo receives both 'a vast impression of space and multitude and opportunity' and a sense that 'intimate things were also dragged from neglected, veiled and darkened corners into acute vividness of perception.'[212] Ponderevo is a scientist, a materialist, yet even he is susceptible to mystical interpretation

---

[208] Machen's work as a cataloguer for George Redway and other London booksellers is discussed by R. B. Russell, 'Sub Rosa', *Faunus*, 1 (Spring 1998), 7–11.

[209] Wind, *Pagan Mysteries in the Renaissance*, 14.   [210] Machen, *The Three Impostors*, 13.

[211] Thomson, *The City of Dreadful Night*, 586.   [212] Wells, *Tono-Bungay*, 92.

of the city, and dwells on the extraordinary 'unveiling' of its life, a process which, at twilight, reveals 'a great mysterious movement of unaccountable beings'.[213] In *The Secret Agent*, another 'unaccountable being', the murderess, Winnie Verloc, veiled 'as if masked' and 'all in black from head to foot except for some flowers in her hat', wanders the London streets as she contemplates suicide in the Thames. Conrad blurs the Thames's familiar reputation with Thomson's River of the Suicides, and links the stricken woman with doom-laden Symbolist art such as Thomas Gotch's *Death the Bride* (1895).[214] Veils and masks here suggest secretive initiations into conspiracies and the human cost of such, but allude also to the 'mysteries' pondered by Inspector Heat earlier in the novel. *London: A Book of Aspects* meanwhile puts the smoke and steam of Whistler's 'kindly veil' at the service of an experience strikingly similar to Dyson's encounter with the 'fumes of the pit', or perhaps even the final moments of the doomed Lionel Wallace:

There are in London certain gaps or holes in the earth, which are like vent-holes, and out of these openings its inner ferment comes for a moment to the surface. One of them is at Chalk Farm Station. There is a gaunt cavernous doorway leading underground, and this doorway faces three roads from the edge of a bridge. The bridge crosses an abyss of steam, which rises out of the depths like the depths of a boiling pot, only it is a witches' pot of noise and fire; and pillars and pyramids of smoke rise continually out of it, and there are hoarse cries, screams, a clashing and rattling, the sound as of a movement which struggles and cannot escape like the coiling of serpents twisting together in a pit. Their breath rises in clouds, and drifts voluminously over the gap of the abyss; catching at times a ghastly colour from the lamplight. Sometimes one of the snakes seems to rise and sway out of the tangle, a column of yellow blackness. Multitudes of red and yellow eyes speckle the vague and smoky darkness.[215]

These subterranean fires are very different from the sterile, monotonous wastes of writers who drew upon the *Inferno*. They reflect instead the seemingly hellish dynamism of Shelley's 'populous and smoky city', and suggest that it is only the imaginative or spiritually elevated connoisseur of his surroundings who can see things such as the ventilation shaft at Chalk Farm as they are rather than as they appear to be.[216] At such moments, London is again a realm that refuses to divulge its secrets, though it will allow glimpses of them to poets, mystics, and visionaries.

Wilde's mysterious 'Sphinx' had wandered the city 'with her veil down, . . . imagining she was a heroine', and concealed her secrets to the last.[217] In his essay on Constantinople in *Cities* (1903), Symons depicted the East as 'one

---

213 Wells, 92.   214 Conrad, *The Secret Agent*, 196–7.
215 Symons, *London*, 212–13.   216 P. B. Shelley, 'Peter Bell the Third' (1819).
217 Wilde, 'The Sphinx without a Secret', *Complete Works*, 208.

great enigma, presented to us almost on the terrifying terms of the Sphinx'. 'We are on the threshold of a mystery,' he wrote, 'a curtain trembles over some veiled image, perhaps the image of wisdom.'[218] The two sphinxes, oriental and metropolitan, met in Coburn's photograph, 'On the Embankment' from *London*, re-titled 'The Sphinx' in his privately printed illustrated version of *London: A Book of Aspects* (1914). In working with James and Symons, Coburn had shown himself able to pursue the two recommended paths from 'The Decadent Movement in Literature', leading him to be termed both an impressionist and a symbolist photographer. However, having a marked interest in Freemasonry, though he did not become an initiate until 1919, Coburn was drawn increasingly to ways by which images could serve as the vessels for esoteric meaning.

Mike Weaver suggests that while Coburn's earlier pictures are not explicitly Masonic, they can be approached through a related symbolic system, demonstrating such interpretations in a discussion of 'St Paul's from the River', another view from the *London* folio. The photograph operates, Weaver explains, on three levels. It is 'literally' a picture of St Paul's Cathedral, Waterloo Bridge, and a river. On an allegorical level, it becomes 'a dome of knowledge, supported on pillars of Wisdom, over the Great Flood'. 'Anagogically', however, it reveals eternity triumphing over time. 'That Coburn could publish the picture in the *Daily Graphic* shows that such an image could be safely displayed before the public while concealing its true meaning for the initiated,' he concludes.[219]

'On the Embankment' is a similarly complex image, though it resists the interpretative stratification Weaver applies to the photograph of St Paul's. In *London: A Book of Aspects*, Symons had mentioned Cleopatra's Needle rather than the Sphinx, merely noting how that 'corner' of the Embankment has 'a mysterious air'.[220] Responding to this suggestion, what Coburn later called 'the opened eye of the artist' transformed even ordinary scenes into striking formal compositions imbued with cryptic association: how many Londoners who passed the statue each day even noticed it, let alone pondered its meaning?[221]The photogravure of the monument, taken in daylight, at first seems merely matter-of-fact, yet, as Weaver reminds us, the Sphinx was the image placed before a temple by the Egyptians 'to warn the priests against

---

[218] A. Symons, *Cities* (London: Dent, 1903), 259.

[219] M. Weaver, *Alvin Langdon Coburn, Symbolist Photographer 1882–1966: Beyond the Craft* (London: Aperture, 1986), 57. The picture was Plate VI in *London,* and appeared in the *Daily Graphic* on 23 October 1909, though it was probably taken during his metropolitan explorations with Symons and James in 1906.

[220] Symons, *London*, 164.

[221] A. L. Coburn, 'Photography and the Quest for Beauty', *The Photographic Journal* (April 1924), 159–60.

Figure 3.1. Alvin Langdon Coburn, 'On the Embankment', from *London* (1909).

revealing divine secrets to the profane'.[222] *The Man Who Was Thursday* draws comparisons between the 'great stones of the Embankment' and 'the colossal steps of some Egyptian palace', and one wonders whether Coburn had had a similar revelation.[223] He pictures the statue from below, seemingly inviting the viewer to climb the stairs before it in an act of worship or abasement and ponder whether the Sphinx is an idol in itself or the guardian of a greater mystery. Everyday London fades into the background as the Sphinx's face gazes serenely, inscrutably, and unavoidably, from the top of the photograph.

The picture insinuates an oblique connection between London and the Sphinx, which is in it but not of it, yet it is difficult to articulate what the connection might be beyond the unreadability of each. Is this the symbol Wilde warned against interrogating in the Preface to *Dorian Gray*, the 'loathsome mystery' apostrophized in 'The Sphinx' (1894)? An allusion to the sphinx of 'cold majestic face | Whose vision seemed of infinite void space' in *The City of Dreadful Night*, or the 'White Sphinx' of Wells's *The Time Machine*, with its 'sightless eyes' and 'faint shadow of a smile'?[224] Could it even be

---

[222] Weaver, *Alvin Langdon Coburn: Symbolist Photographer*, 57.
[223] Chesterton, *The Man Who Was Thursday*, 49.
[224] Thomson, *The City of Dreadful Night*, 584; Wells, *The Time Machine*, 19.

a self-referential caprice on the part of a photographer who values beauty and wonder above interpretation?[225] By photographing the Sphinx, is Coburn claiming secret knowledge or admitting his ignorance?

Coburn's photogravures of the city, many of which were taken for Henry James's New York edition, reveal a fascination with walls, doors and windows, barriers, and lines of demarcation.[226] They repeatedly return to the symbolic portals between the literal and the metaphoric—he illustrated a privately printed edition of 'The Door in the Wall' in 1911—in search of what James called in his preface to *The Golden Bowl* (1907) the recognition of the 'last fineness'.[227] Just as James's fiction tended to throw the burden of interpretation onto the reader, creating scenarios in which meaning became ever more negotiable, so Coburn's photographs offered further levels of teasing ambiguity. Symbolist portraiture, Coburn's *Men of Mark* (1913) for example, frequently employed the motif of eyes as windows or mirrors of the soul. Coburn extended such concerns to everyday architectural features that were transmuted, to borrow from the subtitle of *The Three Impostors*, into interfaces between interior and exterior worlds. The photogravures of *London* raised similar ontological questions to James's fiction. Each image invites symbolic reading yet refuses definitive explanation, offering at last a beautiful surface and irresolvable deeper meaning that alludes to the city, or to some unspoken aspect or meaning of the city, as much as depicting it. The viewer may recognize the object, but not what Coburn may intend by it, and, as so often in Symbolist art, the effect is one of indefinitely delayed resolution and suggestiveness rather than explicit confirmation. Coburn understood this perfectly in images that suggest to the many but reveal only to the few.

By concealing the 'true' meaning of an image or text within an apparently unexceptional, even familiar, surface, Symbolism invested art objects, and by extension, London itself, with Lionel Johnson's 'double significance'. However, symbolist writers were not simply the ultra-observant Holmes to the reading public's Watson. Their 'last fineness' was not the crucial clue in a criminal investigation but a mystical recognition of London's innate unfathomability. Surface perceptions offer only partial revelation. In Machen's mystically entitled story 'The Inmost Light', Dyson tells Salisbury, 'You may point out a street, correctly enough, as the abode of washerwomen; but in that second

[225] O. Wilde, 'The Sphinx', *Complete Works*, 882.
[226] For a detailed consideration of the illustrations for the New York edition, see R. F. Bogardus, *Pictures and Texts: Henry James, Alvin Langdon Coburn and New Ways of Seeing in Literary Culture* (Ann Arbor: UMI Research Press, 1984) and J. Hillis Miller's essay, 'The Grafted Image: James on Illustration', in D. McWhirter, ed., *Henry James's New York Edition: The Construction of Authorship* (Stanford: Stanford University Press, 1995).
[227] H. James, Preface to *The Golden Bowl* (1907; London: The Bodley Head, 1972), 12.

floor, a man may be studying Chaldee roots, and in the garret over the way a forgotten artist is dying by inches.'[228] One building, or as is often the case in Machen's work, narrative, conceals another, offering not the solvable puzzle of detection fiction but a recognition of the London cityscape as containing an infinitude of possible meanings, each buried beneath or within the others. Even in this example, the familiar image of London as Babylon becomes the more intriguing man 'studying Chaldee roots': evocative associations of ancient languages, astrology, and history jostle for space with prosaic domestic service and the cliché of the misunderstood genius starving in his attic. The 'real' London lies behind the curtains of its houses, but while this phrasing suggests the populist language of a newspaper's exposé of suburban life, Machen is actually suggesting that conclusive knowledge is ultimately unobtainable, hence Dyson's resorting to repeating his speculative 'may be'. In 'The Yellow Face' (1894), Holmes misinterprets the meaning of a face at a window, but by dynamic action—bursting into the room in question—he is able to solve the case and maintain, 'Any truth is better than indefinite doubt.'[229] In Machen however, the truth *is* indefinite doubt. There is 'no hope of answer or redress' behind the twitching curtains of the city's houses.

Symbolist writing employed elements of the detective story on a number of occasions, at once subverting its claims to revelation and the restoring of order and treating it as a contemporary incarnation of older, more mystically inflected quests that sought the Holy Grail or the Philosopher's Stone. *The Man Who Was Thursday* offers memorable comic incidents, notably the scene when an anarchist meeting is found to be comprised entirely of undercover policemen, alongside provocative theological speculation. Equally striking, however, was Symbolism's engagement with the language and techniques of social investigation. George Sims, who had distinguished himself as a 'social explorer' in the 1880s, showed in *The Devil in London* how such discourses might be combined with more fantastic visions of the city. A strikingly packaged paperback retailing at 1/-, the novel used the unambitious narrative techniques of popular fiction to agitate for social change, but it showed too how a wily and experienced writer was sensitive to the fashions of the day, even if he did not necessarily appreciate the seriousness with which they were taken by others. Sims's hero, Alan Fairfax, reads a newspaper article that leads him to ponder the existence of another London within the city he felt he knew, just as Sims's revelations of London poverty might have done forty years earlier. By 1908, though, these revelations had acquired a mystical air.

---

[228] Machen, 'The Inmost Light', 250.
[229] A. Conan Doyle, 'The Yellow Face', in *The Penguin Complete Sherlock Holmes* (London: Penguin, 1981), 360.

Sims had published *Mysteries of Modern London* in 1905, and Arthur Machen would shortly begin a series of articles for the *Daily News* that conjured an unearthly city from seemingly everyday surroundings:

until he read those lines he had never recognised that within the four corners of the mighty capital lay a land that a man might travel all his life, gleaning every day some new knowledge of its strange humanity, peering far down into the gloom of its unfathomed depths, and waiting for the moment when favouring chance might reveal to him the mysteries that lie beyond the veil.[230]

Fairfax ends up touring thieves' kitchens, gambling and opium dens in the company of the devil, with Sims combining social exploration and pleas for reform with a sentimental love story.

This intersection of symbolism and social exploration had begun in the early 1890s. 'The Inmost Light', for example, offers a parodic version of Charles Booth's house-by-house classification of the city, a doggedly empiricist project for which Machen had little sympathy. However, when Booth remarked that 'It is not in the country but in the town that "terra incognita" needs to be written on our social map,' he was, like Machen, recognizing how aspects of London had evaded previous cartographers. '[W]e live in darkness,' he announced, a recognition with which symbolist writing typically concurred.[231] Booth responded to unanswered questions with systematic rigour, but symbolists consciously avoided secular interrogation of reality, a legacy of both a mystically inclined worldview and entrenched political conservatism. They were quite willing to adapt the trope of the 'dark' city, the heathen wastes of the so-called 'dark continent that is within easy walking distance of the General Post Office', but they stripped it of its moral or physical connotations.[232] Like Shelley, they believed that 'A poet participates in the eternal, the infinite, and the one; as far as relates to his conceptions, time, place, and number are not.'[233] Darkness became therefore a potent symbol of the limits of human knowledge rather than prompting social research. In this respect, the 'universal darkness' of Pope's *Dunciad* (1743) anticipated the apocalyptic tone of some *fin de siècle* fictions, as did the 'darkness visible' of *Paradise Lost* (1667).

However, while Pope, like Dickens, had definite satiric targets in view, and Milton a deliberate Christian message, the symbolist uses of darkness were, appropriately enough, less clear. In *Heart of Darkness*, for example, Conrad makes sophisticated and ironic reference to the 'darkest London' motif in

---

[230] Sims, *The Devil in London*, 11.
[231] Quoted by R. Porter, *London: A Social History* (1994; London: Penguin, 2000), 335.
[232] G. Sims, *How the Poor Live* (1883), in P. Keating, ed., *Into Unknown England, 1866–1913: Selections from the Social Explorers* (Glasgow: Fontana, 1976), 85. For a useful discussion of Booth's use of the 'darkest Africa' trope, see McLaughlin, *Writing the Urban Jungle*, 79–103.
[233] Shelley, *A Defence of Poetry*, 32.

Marlow's claim, 'this too has been one of the dark places of the earth,' and in the closing comment about the Thames seeming 'to lead into the heart of an immense darkness'.[234] London is equated with the jungles of the Congo not only because the latter form a convenient index of unenlightened savagery to the late-Victorian mind, a notion that Conrad bends to his own purposes, but also because a mystically charged pessimism insists on the metaphysically imponderable as a central condition of human life. The heart of darkness itself refuses to be localized, in that it is both within and without humanity. Hence whatever Kurtz saw inside himself, and the dark air and 'mournful gloom, brooding motionless over the biggest, and the greatest, town on earth', are one.[235] Africa becomes another of James Thomson's 'worlds as sad as this', as it is in *The Secret Agent* when the Assistant Commissioner feels 'as though he had been ambushed all alone in a jungle many thousands of miles away from departmental desks and official inkstands'.[236]

Crucially, neither Thomson nor Conrad offers answers to the metaphysical questions that their narratives raise. Indeed, for Thomson, drawing on Milton's *Samson Agonistes* (1671), the city is 'dark, dark, dark, withdrawn from joy and light', equally resistant to perception and interpretation.[237] For politically committed readers, this may seem an evasion, even a betrayal, of a writer's responsibilities, especially where the sordid realities of imperialism are concerned, but it is precisely this concern with 'sordid realities' from which Symbolism seeks to escape. It is scarcely a surprise to see vague but menacing darkness, a 'brooding and enigmatic glow', concluding *The Soul of London* by Conrad's friend and collaborator, Ford Madox Ford.[238] Margaret Oliphant had imagined 'a lowering canopy of cloud, dark, threatening, with a faint reddish tint diffused upon the vaporous darkness' over her hellish metropolis, but her Christian intentions were relatively explicit.[239] Somerset Maugham's notebook for 1900 saw him applying similar techniques, in imagining the 'western clouds of the sunset' as being 'like the vast wing of an archangel, flying through the void on an errand of vengeance; and the fiery shadow cast a lurid light upon the city'.[240] Ford and Conrad surely seek to allude to writing of this type, but while they wish to deploy some of its associations, they resist a fixing of meaning, preferring suggestiveness and ambiguity to Oliphant's 'It was, however, quite sufficiently clear to see everything.' '[T]he prevailing feeling of London is one of darkness,' wrote Ford in the 'Author's Note' to *England and the English* (1907). 'The Londoner never sees very far; his vistas

---

[234] Conrad, *Heart of Darkness*, 18, 124.   [235] Ibid. 15.
[236] Conrad, *The Secret Agent*, 110.   [237] Thomson, *The City of Dreadful Night*, 573.
[238] Ford, *The Soul of London*, 112.   [239] Oliphant, *A Beleaguered City*, 313.
[240] W. S. Maugham, *A Writer's Notebook* (London: Heinemann, 1949), 39.

are cloudy, tenebrous, opacitic.'[241] Where symbolist writing is concerned, clarity and totality of vision are rare gifts, and not always to be welcomed.

In Conrad's case, the deployment of symbolist strategies allows provocative ambiguity that resists transforming complex fable into more schematic political allegory. One reason for this is that they destabilize the image of London, disavowing a polarized opposition between a safely unified capital and a similarly unified 'other' space such as the African wilderness. Conrad and Charles Booth were both drawn to unmapped terrain, but while one would create maps that appeared to compartmentalize and explain, the other found that exploring the city in no way prevented it from being the 'exciting spaces of white paper' later discussed in 'The Romance of Travel' (1924).[242] Apparently separate realms overlap and coexist within the same space, and the effects are often bewildering: if they are 'exciting', then it is an excitement tinged with fear. Joseph McLaughlin points out that in *The Secret Agent*, sites such as the vile Italian restaurant frequented by the Assistant Commissioner constitute 'a monstrous series of undifferentiated or "unstamped" dishes and sites that, because they are not authentic "places," render their inhabitants placeless and the social landscape an unreadable map'.[243] However, even if the 'social map' were readable, it would constitute only superficial knowledge rather than genuine understanding of the metropolitan realm. The disorienting foreignness of Conrad's London lies not only in its international residents but also in the sense that city itself is 'other' or alien, representing what McLaughlin, in homage to Michel de Certeau, terms a 'fraudulent . . . symbolic order' and 'a cityscape of endlessly repeated forms devoid of any landmarks'.[244] In it, characters lose both their moral values and a wider sense of meaning, becoming, in the end, the doomed wanderers of Dante or Thomson. Indeed, there are telling parallels between Conrad's 'Professor', who stalks the streets with a detonator in his pocket, threatening death and destruction to society, and Thomson's creature 'that had been a man' menacing the narrator of *The City of Dreadful Night* with a deadly poison. 'I fling this phial if you seek to pass,' he hisses, 'And you are forthwith shrivelled up like grass.'[245] Both are forced into desperate acts of self-assertion in the face of a universe that is either beyond their understanding or else utterly inexplicable.

---

[241] F. M. Ford, 'Author's Note' to *England and the English: An Interpretation*, ed. S. Haslam (1907; Manchester, 2003), 331. Ford's words were intended for an American audience—this is surely why he sweetened the pill with the unconvincing claim that this darkness was a 'comfortable' one.

[242] The essay was retitled 'Geography and Some Explorers' in Conrad's *Last Essays* (London: Dent, 1926), 19.

[243] McLaughlin, *Writing the Urban Jungle*, 161.   [244] Ibid. 161, 166.

[245] Thomson, *The City of Dreadful Night*, 579–80. As so often in this poem, Thomson is making an ironic biblical allusion, in this case to Isaiah 40: 6.

The London of *The Secret Agent* is more obviously akin to that of William Booth in its spiritual associations and Charles Booth in its insistent mapping of urban space than was *Heart of Darkness*, but again, Conrad imbues the language of social exploration with metaphysical overtones. In his 'Author's Note' (1920), Conrad differentiates between his approach and one of his novel's inspirations, Sir Robert Anderson's *Sidelights on the Home Rule Movement* (1906). The policeman's memoirs contained, Conrad says, 'no revelations' but 'ran over the surface agreeably'.[246] Recalling an argument between Anderson and Sir William Harcourt, Conrad claims to have been 'struck' by the latter's 'angry sally', namely, 'your idea of secrecy is keeping the Home Secretary in the dark'. Darkness becomes, for Conrad, symptomatic of espionage and intrigue, but while these associations are conventional enough, they gain much when set within a city he describes as 'a cruel devourer of the world's light' possessing 'darkness enough to bury five millions of lives'.[247] As the Assistant Commissioner watches from the shadows, people, including a police constable, disappear into the darkness of Brett Street, never to be heard of again. In this world, light itself becomes 'suspect', though it also drives 'the obscurity of the street back upon itself, making it more sullen, brooding, and sinister'.[248] The capital becomes the setting for 'impenetrable mystery' and an unreadable symbol, with the novel offering at once the precisely mapped London of realist fiction and a realization that beyond this lies 'a totalising, apparently unqualified, negativity'.[249] The doomed Winnie Verloc finds herself at last in 'a maze of streets', 'sunk in a hopeless night', and imprisoned in 'a black abyss' from which no woman could escape unaided.[250] London is now a world where the material environment and the psychological states of those within it have become one, as in the drowned city of *Bruges-la-Morte* or the memorable pastel portrait of its author by Lucien Lévy-Dhurmer (1896).

PHANTASMAGORIA: THE STREET BEYOND THE STREET

Machen's *The Hill of Dreams* appeared in the same year as *The Secret Agent*, though it had been composed a decade earlier. London publishers, wary of Machen's reputation as a purveyor of stories of sex and horror, and reconsidering the presumed 'proper' content and social mission of the novel

---

[246] Conrad, 'Author's Note', *The Secret Agent*, 230.   [247] Ibid. 231.
[248] Conrad, *The Secret Agent*, 110–11.
[249] C. Watts, 'Conrad and the Myth of the Monstrous Town', in G. M. Moore, ed., *Conrad's Cities: Essays for Hans van Marle* (Amsterdam: Rodopi, 1992), 18.
[250] Conrad, *The Secret Agent*, 198.

in the wake of Wilde's downfall, rejected the book on its initial submission in 1897. When it finally appeared the critical response was generally negative. Despite the attempts by Arthur Symons to reclassify decadence as symbolism, reviewers agreed that the book was profoundly unwholesome, with Lucian Taylor's visionary sensibility dismissed as madness, morbidity, or disease.

The Hill of Dreams is a remarkable example of how symbolism could subvert realist fiction while maintaining its outward appearance. In many ways, Lucian could be a character from *New Grub Street*, a struggling provincial writer drawn into the metropolis by literary ambition, only to be destroyed by material want and his inability to live up to his exacting creative standards. When Gissing's Reardon and Biffen discuss the 'huge misfortune, this will-o'-the-wisp attraction exercised by London on young men of brains', their conclusions are prophetic:

'They come here to be degraded or to perish, when their true sphere of life is a peaceful remoteness. The type of man capable of success in London is more or less callous and cynical. If I had the training of boys, I would teach them to think of London as the last place where life can be lived worthily.'

'And the place where you are most likely to die in squalid wretchedness.'[251]

While this discussion is horribly applicable to Lucian, it does not convey the feverishness of his visions of the London streets. These, lurid and overwritten as Machen's detractors alleged, clearly demonstrate the differences between realist, impressionist, and symbolist accounts of the capital. Indeed, as Linda Dowling recognizes, the final revelation that Lucian's much-prized manuscript is entirely illegible shows how he has succeeded in producing 'a language so perfected in its private symbolism that it will no longer yield its meaning even to the select few, but only to the unique reader, Lucian himself'.[252]

Descriptions of street life by Gissing and other problematically 'realist' writers often use identifiable landmarks and make a virtue of the accuracy of their observations. Detail is multisensory, with attention given to the sights, sounds, and smells of the metropolis. There is often an attempt to relate character to environment, or vice versa, and, in Gissing at least, a distinction between the voices of individual characters and that of an omniscient narrator whose educated allusions and polysyllabic vocabulary encourage him to be identified with the author himself.

An 'impressionist' description, such as that of the Edgware Road by Arthur Symons, is similar in many respects. However, it is less likely to occur in a

---

[251] G. Gissing, *New Grub Street*, ed. J. Goode (1891; Oxford: Oxford University Press, 1993), 438.

[252] L. Dowling, *Language and Decadence in the Victorian Fin de Siècle* (New Haven: Yale University Press, 1986), 160.

fictional context, in that its interest in the workings of consciousness, and heightened sensitivity to external stimuli, can prove difficult to integrate into a traditional plot. The dominant element of the description becomes visual, and often centres on the perceptions of a single character, typically purporting to be a faithful record of individual experiences. The omniscient narrator is generally replaced by more subjective or partial comment.

'Realism' and 'impressionism' overlap in several respects, but neither shows noticeable interest in anything beyond the immediate, perceivable realities of the scene described. Both are essentially materialist in character, though they treat the notion of the factual with varying degrees of scepticism. Symbolism, however, uses 'realist' detail as the basis of a spiritual or mystical engagement with its material. John Christian notes that a Symbolist picture is 'neither an arrangement of lines and colours, nor a transcript from nature' but an admission that 'behind' it 'lies another order of meaning'.[253] Lucian Taylor has already discovered this in his wandering among the Roman ruins of his home town, but while this vision had a luxuriant sensuousness, those of London which torment him in the novel's closing chapters are terrifying.

At first, Lucian makes 'vigorous efforts toward sanity', fearing that 'he had lost the sense of humanity' and become alienated from his fellow creatures through excessive preoccupation with artistic matters.[254] By now a user of laudanum, Lucian is beginning to echo other London visionaries—De Quincey, for example, or James Thomson, who, according to Bertram Dobell, had the 'peculiarity—perhaps in some degree his misfortune' of being 'continually engaged in dissecting his own emotions, sensations and impulses'. Brooding in his lodgings, the poet 'thought rather of the universe as it related to himself than of himself as related to the universe. He did not sufficiently realise that self-forgetfulness is better than self-absorption.'[255] Thomson and Lucian also share the affliction of insomnia, which leads them to walk the city streets for hours in a futile attempt to exhaust themselves.

As he lies dying in his seedy lodging house, Lucian has a final vision of the streets of Notting Hill where, a few months before, he has witnessed what he terms 'the Bacchic fury unveiled and unashamed'. Saturday night sees an 'orgy' of drinking and wantonness where 'To his eyes it seemed as if these revellers recognised him as a fellow, and smiled up in his face, aware that he was in the secret.'[256] He rejects the advances of a prostitute, but this act of

---

[253] J. Christian, *Symbolists and Decadents* (London: Thames and Hudson, 1977), 1.
[254] Machen, *The Hill of Dreams*, 143.
[255] J. Thomson, *The City of Dreadful Night and Other Poems* (London: Bertram Dobell, 1899), x–xi.
[256] Machen, *The Hill of Dreams*, 151.

self-denial brings him no peace. The woman's image haunts him in his final moments:

Then suddenly a flaring street shone before him. There was darkness round about him, but it flamed with hissing jets of light and naphtha fires, and great glittering lamps swayed very slowly in a violent blast of air. A horrible music, and the exultation of discordant voices, swelled in his ears, and he saw an uncertain tossing crowd of dusky figures that circled and leapt before him. There was a noise like the chant of the lost, and then there appeared in the midst of the orgy, beneath a red flame, the figure of a woman. Her bronze hair and flushed cheeks were illuminate, and an argent light shone from her eyes, and with a smile that froze his heart her lips opened to speak to him. The tossing crowd faded away, and then she drew out from her hair pins of curious gold and glowing brooches of enamel, and poured out jewels before him from a silver box, and then she stripped from her body her precious robes, and stood in the glowing mist of her hair, and held out her arms to him. But he raised his eyes and saw the mould and decay gaining on the walls of a dismal room, and a gloomy paper was dropping to the rotting floor . . . .

And presently the woman fled away from him, and he pursued her. She fled before him through the midnight country, and he followed her, chasing her from thicket to thicket, from valley to valley. And at last he captured her and won her with horrible caresses, and they went up to celebrate and make the marriage of the Sabbath. They were within the matted thicket, and they writhed in the flames, insatiable, for ever. They were tortured, and tortured one another, in the sight of thousands who gathered thick about them; and their desire rose up like a black smoke.[257]

One can see why Machen's reviewers found the novel so 'unwholesome,' yet to read it as lurid masturbatory fantasy does it a considerable disservice. Lucian's bohemianism has not succeeded in throwing off the internalized strictures of bourgeois convention, and his fantasies, like those of Symons after his breakdown, are dominated by ungovernable, and to his mind damnable, sexual desire.

Lucian's visionary consciousness transfigures London, imbuing the mundane amusements of its nocturnal streets with bewildering associations. The London streets merge with recollections of the Welsh border country of his childhood, creating the destabilizing effects found in Conrad and, indeed, Yeats, whose *John Sherman* (1891) sees its homesick hero imaginatively transported to Ireland when he hears 'a faint trickling of water' while '[d]elayed by a crush in the Strand'.[258] Like the narrator of de Nerval's *October Nights* (1852), Lucian 'parodies the sight-seeing tours of night-time Paris (or London) offered to armchair slummers by contemporary magazines', presenting 'a

---

[257] Ibid. 194–5.
[258] W. B. Yeats, *John Sherman*, in *idem*, *Short Fiction*, ed. G. J. Watson (London: Penguin, 1995), 46.

private phantasmagoria of recollection and desire' instead of the neatly ordered world of Robert Machray.[259] Machen's prose, with its stylized rhythms and consciously 'decadent' vocabulary, 'curious', 'precious', is quite unlike that of contemporaneous 'realist' texts. Lucian is exactly the type of reader from whom Pater wished to keep the conclusion of *The Renaissance*, but he is not simply a poseur. In the final pages of the book, the stricken novelist is himself transformed from a struggling writer into a Kurtz-like figure, who, like Conrad's colonizer, embodies an 'impenetrable darkness' and witnesses the wild revelry of a savage people.[260] London is no longer the civilized opposing pole of barbarism but a place in which the two are inextricable just as at the end of *Heart of Darkness*, when Marlow, traumatized by his experiences in the Congo, finds that the 'vision' of Kurtz's final moments 'seemed to enter the house with me— . . . the wild crowd of obedient worshippers, the gloom of the forests, . . . the beat of the drum'.[261] Machen had finished *The Hill of Dreams* long before the original version of Conrad's novella appeared in *Blackwood's Magazine* between February and April 1899, so the similarities between the two are partly coincidental. In other respects, however, their phantasmal city shows how symbolist or mystical conceptions of London were more widespread than is generally realized.

The ornate cataloguing of the woman's jewels, and her transformation from common prostitute to symbolist femme fatale suggest affinities between Machen and Moreau's many paintings of Salome, and between *The Hill of Dreams* and the inventories of *À rebours* and *The Picture of Dorian Gray*. Lucian, who shares his creator's distaste for George Eliot, privileges the exuberantly imaginative over the dourly realist, but he does not forsake the everyday detail of naphtha flames. The effect is to make indivisible the quotidian and the exotic, the homely and the foreign, the mundane and the magical. London becomes at once a brutal and, to use a favourite term of Lucian's, 'philistine', realm of noise and aggressive ignorance, and a bewildering, dangerous, and strangely beautiful world to which only the visionary can gain access, and only then at great cost. The eroticism of Lucian's ecstasies is far removed from the gentle Pre-Raphaelite beauties of Lionel Wallace's secret garden, yet ultimately both men seek doors in the wall of the city, hoping to pass beyond it into another, perhaps higher, reality. '[W]ant of imagination is always equated with sanity,' wrote Machen in 'A Fragment of Life':

So, day after day, he lived in the grey phantasmal world, akin to death, that has, somehow, with most of us, made good its claim to be called life. To Darnell the true life would have seemed madness, and when, now and again, the shadows and vague

[259] Richard Sieburth in de Nerval's *Selected Writings*, 185.
[260] Conrad, *Heart of Darkness*, 111.   [261] Ibid. 117.

images reflected from its splendours fell across his path, he was afraid, and took refuge in what he would have called the sane 'reality' of common and usual incidents and interests.[262]

For such men, it is the everyday world of 'tin-tacks and gas-plugs and matters that no man needed' that constitutes the 'strange unreal city'.[263]

AN IMMENSE DARKNESS

The speaker of A. Mary F. Robinson's sonnet 'Neurasthenia' (1888) watches 'the happier people of the house . . . glide, like skaters on a stream | Across the brilliant surface of the world,' while she remains 'underneath', mired in darkness and separation.[264] The poem's title suggests the limited understanding of mental illness in the *fin de siècle*, but at the same time conveys something of the symbolist response to London. The neurasthenic, like the visionary—and the two categories, as Nordau suggests, are often synonymous—sees beyond surfaces into the often threatening world beneath them. Such knowledge leads to the 'darkness, danger and death' of 'The Door in the Wall', the final delirium of Lucian Taylor, or Henry Luxulyan's agonized speculation about the other side of reality. This is not to say that symbolism was a delusion, but to suggest instead that its insistence on transcending the immediate material realities of the city pushed it into a marginal position from which it has yet to properly emerge.

Symbolist London was composed of a small set of recurring images or associations: the sphinx, the labyrinth, the veil, dimness, darkness, and the persistent suggestion that surfaces were merely the outward show of far more significant realities. That this vocabulary was shared by writers rarely connected either by the late-Victorian reading public or by subsequent literary history is suggestive less of some concealed sodality than of a more general influence of occult ideas on the literature of the period. The imaginative potential or connotations of such ideas is ultimately more significant than the religious or occult practices from which they were derived. They functioned instead as a means by which the unknown or ineffable could be articulated. Once, it was the peace of God that passed all understanding. By 1900, the city had become similarly inscrutable and resistant to linguistic representation,

---

[262] Machen, 'A Fragment of Life', in *The Collected Arthur Machen*, 75, 44.
[263] Kipling, *The Light That Failed*, 329.
[264] A. Mary F. Robinson, 'Neurasthenia', in Karlin, ed., *The Penguin Book of Victorian Verse*, 713.

but such were its negative connotations that it was likened not to the Christian God but to some barbarous deity of ancient times, one seemingly incapable of propitiation by human beings. 'It is mainly when you fall on your face before her that she gobbles you up,' wrote Henry James.[265] London's persistent association with Babylon and the heathen idols of Moloch and Baal employed Christian rhetoric in demonizing the metropolis, admitting both the city's spiritual failings and the continuing totemic power of religious language in describing its realities. John D. Rosenberg has suggested that 'The Victorians never felt more cut off from the transcendent than in their cities,' but such a generalization is, inevitably, only partially true.[266] The transcendent signals other orders of reality beyond the quotidian, and the idea that these might be malign or simply indifferent to human wishes was yet more terrifying than being abandoned by God. '[T]he literary imagination has among its tasks that of domesticating our apprehension of the terrifying or the unknown,' argues Robert Stange. 'Literature can transform into myth, and thus make manageable to our consciousness experience we must live with, but which may appal or derange our immediate understanding.'[267] He may not be discussing the specifically symbolist response to the city, but his words are nonetheless an encapsulation of both its aims and its effects.

By adopting symbolist approaches, writers made a number of declarations about themselves. They exalted the world of the imagination beyond that of everyday realities. They allied themselves with both native tradition and aspects of the contemporary European avant-garde, insisting on an unashamed elitism that proclaimed the superiority of the artist's perceptions and ways of living over those of 'ordinary' people. Symbolism's contempt for materialism made it an appealing philosophy for high-minded aesthetes with little ready capital, while its spiritual leanings offered a glimpse of the sacred without having to surrender to unsympathetic, or simply demanding, belief systems. Finally, it was very much a male-dominated artistic credo that offered a haven and reassurance during an era of increasingly high levels of female emancipation and cultural visibility.

Although some of Machen's stories employed symbolist techniques to present a more positive, even joyous, vision of London, most symbolist writing, including Machen's early work, emphasized the threat represented by a city that, like the sphinx, posed riddles none could answer. Indeed, the sphinx and the labyrinth, the seemingly unfathomable enigmas of classical myth, recur regularly in works as far removed from one another as Stead's

---

[265] James, 'London', *English Hours*, 24.
[266] J. D. Rosenberg, *Elegy for an Age: The Presence of the Past in Victorian Literature* (London: Anthem, 2005), 239.
[267] Stange, 'The Frightened Poets', 479.

hysterical journalism and Coburn's meditative photogravures. Perhaps it was not surprising to see a generation of classically educated writers employing allusions of this kind, but it nonetheless suggests a persistent anxiety about the city and the language in which it is to be represented. By choosing to portray it through these ancient symbols, or indeed, allusions to the medieval hell of Dante, writers publicly rejected the practical, empirically focused views of the world typified by sociology and the increasingly bureaucratic systems of London County Council. 'Every visionary knows that the mind's eye soon comes to see a capricious and variable world, which the will cannot shape or change,' Yeats argued. The solution was to 'call it up and banish it again'.[268]

It would be easy to pronounce Symbolism 'escapist', with all the negative, irresponsible connotations the word carries. It would, however, be fairer to see the symbolist response to London as an attempt to transcend ordinary reality, and to retain or rediscover elements of human imagination that existed before urbanism. A reverence for mystery, a recognition of humanity's ultimate insignificance in the face of cosmic forces far greater than itself, and a concern with what Machen termed 'the holy things', the eternal realities that exist beyond the demands of everyday life, were all central to the symbolist worldview. James Joyce's Stephen Hero used the term 'epiphany' for 'a sudden spiritual manifestation, whether in the vulgarity of speech or of gesture or in a memorable phase of the mind itself', believing that 'it was for the man of letters to record these epiphanies with extreme care, seeing that they themselves are the most delicate and evanescent of moments'.[269] Writers such as Machen stripped this formula of its vulgar content where possible, concentrating instead on the ways in which the seer or savant recorded intimations of hitherto unapprehended worlds. Nonetheless, they believed strongly in the perceiving and transcription of such moments, attempting to embody the revelation in language.

Impressionism made 'delicate and evanescent moments' the basis of its art, accepting that sight and sensation were, of necessity, fleeting and ephemeral, but symbolism was frustrated by the inability to sustain its visions and to capture the spiritual in words. The most important consequence of this was that, where London was concerned, a wholly symbolist literary text was all but impossible to produce. Coburn's photographs could offer images of teasing complexity without the necessity for narrative, personal interjection, or the demands of genre, but prose and poetry were forced to combine symbolism with other techniques or risk producing Lucian Taylor's indecipherable manuscript. Novelists concealed symbolism within other forms of writing,

---

[268] Yeats, 'Symbolism in Painting', in *The Major Works*, 357.
[269] J. Joyce, *Stephen Hero*, ed. T. Spencer (London: Jonathan Cape, 1944), 216.

often exploiting the dual meaning of mystery in detective stories, or else focusing on psychological portraiture that allows visionary glimpses without entirely abandoning plot, an obligation that, in the years before the First World War, they were unable to avoid except in very short stories and mood pieces. Elsewhere, Arthur Symons used symbolist techniques in his brief travel essays, since here he could describe visions and dwell on the workings of consciousness without the need for narrative beyond a given itinerary.

Poetry was probably the literary art form that promised most for the symbolist depiction of London. As was the case with impressionism, the brief lyric seemed especially suited to the recording and dramatizing of intense experience, but results were mixed, and no British writer could match the formal innovations that characterized the writing of Mallarmé and Rimbaud. Short poems such as Francis Thompson's 'The Kingdom of God' or Dowson's 'Benedictio Domini' showed how Christian imagery could be applied to the modern city, but with English religious poetry in decline by the turn of the twentieth century, their impact was limited. Symons had used the lyric to great effect in detailing his impressions of London in *Silhouettes* (1892) and *London Nights* (1895), but his most successful symbolist writing was found in his travel essays and the short stories of *Spiritual Adventures*. As his work as a critic and literary journalist became increasingly time-consuming, the quality of his poetry declined. Symons was strongly influenced by Yeats in his post *London Nights* poems, but the latter did not share his urban enthusiasms. Thus it is that the most notable practitioner of symbolist writing in *fin de siècle* Britain rarely accorded the city significant attention in his early work. The 'roadway' and 'pavements grey' of 'The Lake Isle of Innisfree' (1893) are unwelcome reminders of the poet's distance from an idealized, rural Ireland, and a long way, in all senses, from his later visions of Byzantium.

Despite Symbolism's rejection of schematic allegory, *The City of Dreadful Night* was undeniably influential on the portrayal of the metropolis. In other ways, however, its necropolitan gloom marked an appropriately dead end. Its stylistic solecisms, morbid atmosphere, and anti-Christian motivations limited its impact. One can see how Thomson affected Eliot, or individual poems such as Ford's 'Antwerp' (1914), with its vision of Charing Cross filled with dead women awaiting the return of doomed soldiers, but the reading of his work was highly selective.[270] Eliot dispensed with sonorously 'Victorian' diction in favour of a more 'modern' poetic idiom. *The Waste Land* certainly contained elements of Thomson, and Eliot showed himself as guardedly sympathetic to symbolist engagement with the city, but this, and indeed, his earlier poems

---

[270] P. Jones, ed., *Imagist Poetry* (Harmondsworth: Penguin, 1972), 81.

of city life, were frequently graced by a flair for sardonic irony at odds with Thomson's laborious doom-mongering.

Of the philosophies discussed in this book, symbolism was certainly the one most at odds with the material conditions of its age. Realism struggled to adapt to the challenges of metropolitan life, but its practitioners, much as they may have disliked the term 'realism', showed themselves to be resourceful and willing to adapt from the richly detailed triple-decker of *Workers in the Dawn* to the sketchier evocations of *Liza of Lambeth*. At the same time, impressionism recognized as no previous art had done the speed of modern life, seizing the opportunities it presented for technical experiment and fresh subject matter. It reconfigured the canon of beauty in visual art, finding beguiling vistas in the polluted streets, skies, and watercourses of the capital. Symbolism, however, rejected the new and the modern. Metaphysical rather than material in its inclinations, it attempted to stabilize London by linking it to enduring transcendent realities. However, as many of these realities seemed threatening rather than benign, and as symbolists were more willing to explore darkness than light, the city they created was generally one in which individuals lived frightened and lonely lives, alienated both from the metropolis and from their fellows. The symbolist claim that a spiritual or imaginative elect was capable of perceiving London's rejection of meaning brought no comfort. Indeed, it is perhaps the central irony of this study that those writers who looked into 'the heart of an immense darkness' were those who most accurately predicted what the great cities of the twentieth century would become.

Afterword

Reflecting on his London pictures of the late 1880s, William Logsdail wrote:

I had always thought that London of all places in the world, ought to be painted but it appeared too formidable, too unassailable . . . I do not wonder that so few have even dared to touch it. However, I did take courage to try and leave a few records of it, only after a very few years to acknowledge myself beaten.[1]

The painter was not alone in feeling defeated. The artistic representation of London was eagerly debated, even contested, from the death of Dickens to the outbreak of the First World War, and most were prepared to acknowledge the importance of London as a subject. However, there was never a consensus as to how it might be written about, painted, or photographed. There was widespread disagreement about London's dimensions, location, and meaning. The literature and art of the past jostled for precedence with new innovations. John Davidson even argued that such an elusive theatre of contradiction could only be properly chronicled by what he termed the 'unmethodical man':

There are doubtless many ways of seeing, but for the Londoner or the visitor who has some time at his disposal, perhaps the best method is the least methodical. Want of method, when rightly considered, is really a kind of faculty, and not the absence of one. . . . The unmethodical method of seeing London is doubtless the best; but then it requires the unmethodical man, and he is rare.[2]

   The 'unmethodical man' is the perfect observer of urban life because he does not attempt to classify or create hierarchies. He instead records what he sees without attempting to order it. Ford Madox Ford, who certainly approached this ideal, was a little more precise than Davidson in formulating his own preferred observer. '[T]o to see London steadily and see it whole,' he wrote:

a man must have certain qualities of temperament so exhaustive as to preclude, on the face of it, the faculties which go to the making or the marring of great fortunes . . . But before all things he must have an impressionability and an impersonality, a single-mindedness to see, and a power of arranging his illustrations cold-bloodedly, an

---

[1] L. Lambourne, *Victorian Painting* (London: Phaidon, 1999), 497–8.
[2] J. Davidson, *Sentences and Paragraphs* (London: Lawrence and Bullen, 1893), 85–8.

unemotional mind and a great sympathy, a life-long engrossment in his 'subject,' and an immediate knowledge, for purposes of comparison, of other cities. He must have an avidity and a sobriety of intellect, an untirable physique and a deliberately tempered mind. These things are antitheses.[3]

An impossible city requires, it seems, an impossible chronicler, words which bring little cheer to the modern students of the urban. Even if a book on London can be written, it may prove too like its subject to be entirely satisfying to the analytical intelligence. 'The readers of this book must wander and wonder,' writes Peter Ackroyd in *London: The Biography* (2000):

They may become lost upon the way; they may experience moments of uncertainty, and on occasions strange fantasies or theories may bewilder them. On certain streets various eccentric or vulnerable people will pause beside them, pleading for attention. There will be anomalies and contradictions—London is so large and so wild that it contains no less than everything—just as there will be irresolutions and ambiguities. But there will also be moments of revelation, when the city will be seen to harbour the secrets of the human world.[4]

My inclusion of these comments may seem a plea for critical clemency, or an admission of defeat in the task this book sets for itself. I would prefer to regard them as suggestions of the difficulty of writing about London, and how the self-conscious recognition of the city's imaginative challenge is a recurrent note in works from either end of the last century. '[I]t isn't a constructed tale I have to tell, but unmanageable realities,' says George Ponderevo in *Tono-Bungay* (1909).[5] The questions that faced chroniclers as diverse as Gissing, Monet, and Conrad remain as provocative and irresolvable as they were a hundred or so years earlier, and 'the problem of London' is as baffling as ever.[6]

The search for a metropolitan language pursued by the writers and artists of the *fin de siècle* did not, of course, produce some sort of cockney Esperanto that subsequent figures could employ in the belief that their use of it would be understood by all. Neither was it, in many cases, a deliberate search, being often a by-product of attempts to convey what Symons called 'my own feeling for London, my own point of view there'. He was, he recalled, 'only trying to render what I saw before me, what I felt, and to make my art out of living material'.[7]

---

[3] F. M. Ford, *The Soul of London: A Survey of a Modern City*, ed. A. G. Hill (1905; London: Dent, 1995), 18–19.

[4] P. Ackroyd, *London: The Biography* (London: Vintage, 2000), 2–3.

[5] H. G. Wells, *Tono-Bungay*, ed. J. Hammond (1909; London: Dent, 1994), 6.

[6] *London* (w/d. Patrick Keillor, BFI/FilmFour, 1994).

[7] A. Symons, *London: A Book of Aspects* in *Cities and Sea-Coasts and Islands* (London: W. Collins, 1918), 199.

Nonetheless, such attempts led to the recognition that any 'language' of London needed to be derived from many different sources and blended to best suit the purposes of each individual user. The three modes of writing and seeing discussed in this book, the empiricist, the impressionist, and the symbolist, are in some ways akin to colours mixed or disregarded as required, producing both bold primaries and subtle shadings. Writers rarely confined themselves to one category. For all that Ford later identified himself with literary impressionism, *The Soul of London* shows him equally willing to employ techniques drawn from social exploration, Dickensian fiction, the sentencious editorials of the newspapers he affects to despise, mysticism, popular history, memoir, and allusion. Davidson evolved a hybrid of poetry and prose that bewildered Edwardian reviewers termed 'Davidsonese'. One could note too how Logsdail's *St Martin-in-the-Fields* (1888) combined social comment and sentimental genre painting in its portrayal of a flower-seller, yet was produced with altogether more radical *plein-air* techniques associated with certain modes of Impressionism. According to Lionel Lambourne, the artist 'hired a removal van with a tarpaulin roof, parked it outside Morley's Hotel, and for several cold winter months worked on the composition, his feet kept warm by bales of straw'.[8]

In *A Study in Scarlet* (1887), Dr Watson describes London as 'that great cesspool into which all the loungers and idlers of the Empire are irresistibly drained'.[9] I would argue instead that London was a great palette, on which all the literary and artistic innovations of the day could be mixed to provide the precise tints needed to capture, or at least suggest with a measure of conviction, the nuances of city life. The parallel is admittedly a contrived one, yet it does suggest how writers in particular rejected the conveniences of 'schools' or 'movements' in favour of personal stances less easy to classify. Some, Symons is an obvious example, were well informed about the contemporary avant-garde and actively engaged in the dissemination of its ideas; others, Edwin Pugh for instance, were less ambitious. Both, however, asked similar questions of the city that they sought to answer by customizing the artistic tools of the day, predominantly versions of realism, for their particular purposes. One might even argue that these tools were those that the next generation of 'modernists' altered to their own specifications. Eliot, for instance, blends the closely observed low-life chatter of slum fiction, the visionary glimpses of symbolists, the foggy vistas of impressionists, and the importance of London's history found in Walter Besant, in *The Waste Land* and other early poems.

[8] Lambourne, *Victorian Painting*, 497.
[9] A. Conan Doyle, *The Penguin Complete Sherlock Holmes* (London: Penguin, 1981), 15.

I need hardly add that modernist versions of London were not merely a schematic plundering of late-Victorian and Edwardian artistic languages. Neither am I suggesting that we should regard the literature of the *fin de siècle* as no more than a precursor of developments now regarded as being of greater significance. However, one should recognize how different ways of representing London emerged throughout the period, and that these have had a major impact on the way it has been conceived of ever since in literature, visual art, cinema, and critical theory. The intense creative debates of the final decades of the nineteenth century continue into the present, and, in so far as one can ever make a prediction about London, will most likely continue into the future.

Bibliography

ACKROYD, PETER, *T. S. Eliot* (1984; London: Abacus, 1985).
—— *Dickens* (London: Sinclair Stevenson, 1990).
—— 'Cockney Visionaries', *The Independent* (18 December 1993).
—— *London: The Biography* (London: Vintage, 2000).
ADAM, HANS CHRISTIAN, ed., *Atget's Paris* (Köln: Taschen, 2001).
AINSWORTH, WILLIAM HARRISON, *The Tower of London* (1840; London: John Dicks, 1894).
ALFORD, NORMAN, *The Rhymers' Club: Poets of the Tragic Generation* (1974; New York: St Martin's Press, 1994).
ALLEN, GRANT, 'Beautiful London', *Fortnightly Review* (July 1893), 42–54.
—— *The British Barbarians: A Hill-Top Novel* (London: John Lane, 1895).
ANON., 'The Snow Fiend's Song', *Punch or the London Charivari* (16 January 1886), 26.
—— 'A Rondel of the Fog', *Punch or the London Charivari* (4 December 1886), 273.
—— 'Horrible Murder in Whitechapel', *Lloyd's Weekly News* (8 April 1888), 1.
—— *Enquire within upon Everything 1890* (1890; Moretonhampstead: Old House Books, 2003).
—— 'Saturday Night in the Edgware Road', *Punch or the London Charivari* (13 April 1895), 172.
—— 'Fathers of Literary Impressionism in England', *Quarterly Review*, 369 (January 1897), 173–94.
—— 'Modern French Art', *Quarterly Review*, 370 (April 1897), 360–89.
—— 'Nocturne in Black-and-Blue', *Punch or the London Charivari* (13 November 1897), 221.
—— 'Recent Verse', *The Athenaeum* (21 December 1901), 838.
—— 'Arthur Symons' Cities', *The Athenaeum* (14 November 1903), 642.
—— 'Henry James, English Hours', *The Athenaeum* (28 October 1905), 578.
ARMSTRONG, ISOBEL, *Victorian Poetry: Poetry, Poetics, Politics* (London: Routledge, 1993).
ARMSTRONG, NANCY, *Fiction in the Age of Photography: The Legacy of British Realism* (Cambridge, MA: Harvard University Press, 1999).
Arts Council of Great Britain, *Burne-Jones: The Paintings, Graphic and Decorative Work of Sir Edward Burne-Jones 1833–1898* (London: Arts Council of Great Britain, 1975).
Baedeker's Handbook for London: London and its Environs (Leipzig: Karl Baedeker, 1911).
BALAKIAN, ANNA, *The Symbolist Movement: A Critical Appraisal* (New York: Random House, 1967).
BANKS, BRIAN, 'J.-K. Huysmans', *Book and Magazine Collector*, 109 (April 1993), 76–87.

BARRETT BROWNING, ELIZABETH, *Aurora Leigh*, ed. Margaret Reynolds ([1856] 1859; New York: W. W. Norton, 1996).

BAUDELAIRE, CHARLES, 'Madame Bovary by Gustave Flaubert' [1857], *Selected Writings on Art and Artists*, trans. P. E. Charvet (Harmondsworth: Penguin, 1972), 244–55.

—— *Poems in Prose from Baudelaire*, trans. Arthur Symons (London: Elkin Matthews, 1905).

BECKSON, KARL, *Arthur Symons: A Life* (Oxford: Clarendon, 1987).

—— *London in the 1890s: A Cultural History* (New York: W. W. Norton, 1992).

—— Ian Fletcher, Lawrence W. Markert, and John Stokes, *Arthur Symons: A Bibliography* (Greensboro, NC: ELT Press/University of North Carolina, 1990).

BEERBOHM, MAX, 'Dr Conan Doyle's Latest Case', *Saturday Review* (2 January 1897), 16.

—— *Seven Men and Two Others* (1919; Harmondsworth: Penguin, 1954).

—— *Max in Verse: Parodies and Rhymes by Max Beerbohm*, collected and annotated by J. G. Riewald (London: Heinemann, 1964).

—— *Caricatures*, ed. N. John Hall (New Haven: Yale University Press, 1997).

BENNETT, ARNOLD, *The Man From the North* (London: John Lane/The Bodley Head, 1898).

—— *The Grand Babylon Hotel: A Fantasia on Modern Themes* (1902; London: Penguin, 1972).

BENSON, A. C., *The Diary of Arthur Christopher Benson*, ed. Percy Lubbock (London: Hutchinson, 1926).

BERGSON, HENRI, *Creative Evolution*, trans. Arthur Mitchell (1911; London: Macmillan, 1960).

BERNSTEIN, CAROL L., *The Celebration of Scandal: Toward the Sublime in Victorian Urban Fiction* (University Park: Pennsylvania State University Press, 1991).

BESANT, WALTER, *All Sorts and Conditions of Men*, ed. Helen Small (1882; Oxford: Oxford University Press, 1997).

—— *Children of Gibeon* (London: Chatto and Windus, 1887).

—— *The Autobiography of Sir Walter Besant* (London: Hutchinson, 1902).

BINYON, LAURENCE, *London Visions* (1896; London: Elkin Matthews, 1908).

BIRCH, DINAH, 'A Life in Writing: Ruskin and the Uses of Suburbia', in *Writing and Victorianism*, ed. J. B. Bullen (London: Longman, 1997), 234–49.

BIRKETT, JENNIFER, *The Sins of the Fathers: Decadence in France 1870–1914* (London: Quartet, 1986).

BLACKWOOD, ALGERNON, *The Insanity of Jones and Other Tales* (1964; London: Penguin, 1966).

BLAKE, WILLIAM, *Poems & Prophecies* (London: Dent, 1984).

BLATCHFORD, ROBERT, *A Bohemian Girl and McGinnis* (London: Clarion Newspaper Co., 1899).

BLOOM, CLIVE, *Cult Fiction: Popular Reading and Pulp Theory* (Basingstoke: Macmillan, 1996).

BOARDMAN, BRIGID M., *Between Heaven and Charing Cross: The Life of Francis Thompson* (New Haven: Yale University Press, 1988).

BOGARDUS, RALPH F., *Pictures and Texts: Henry James, Alvin Langdon Coburn and New Ways of Seeing in Literary Culture* (Ann Arbor: UMI Research Press, 1984).

BOOTH, CHARLES, *Charles Booth's London,* ed. Albert Fried and Richard L. Elman (1969; Harmondsworth: Pelican, 1971).

—— *Life and Labour of the People in London, Volume I: East London* (London: Williams and Norgate, 1889).

BOOTH, MICHAEL R., ed., *The Lights O' London and Other Victorian Plays* (Oxford: Oxford University Press, 1995).

BOOTH, WILLIAM, *In Darkest England and the Way Out* (London: International Headquarters of the Salvation Army, 1890).

BOYLE, THOMAS, *Black Swine in the Sewers of Hampstead: Beneath the Surface of Victorian Sensationalism* (New York: Viking, 1989).

BRADBURY, MALCOLM, and JAMES McFARLANE, eds., *Modernism: A Guide to European Literature 1890–1930* (Harmondsworth: Penguin, 1976).

BRIGGS, ASA, *Victorian Cities* (London: Odhams Press, 1963).

BROOKS, PETER, *Reading for the Plot* (Oxford: Clarendon Press, 1984).

BURDETT, OSBERT, *The Beardsley Period: An Essay in Perspective* (London: John Lane, 1925).

CAMPBELL, IAN, 'And I Burn Too': Thomson's *The City of Dreadful Night*', *Victorian Poetry*, 16(2) (1978), 123–33.

CAREY, JOHN, *The Intellectuals and the Masses: Pride and Prejudice among the Literary Intelligentsia, 1880–1939* (London: Faber, 1992).

CARLYLE, THOMAS, 'Signs of the Times' [1829], in Peter Keating, ed., *The Victorian Prophets: A Reader from Carlyle to Wells* (Glasgow: Fontana, 1981).

—— *Sartor Resartus: The Life and Opinions of Herr Teufelsdröckh* (1838; London: Dent, 1908).

CASSOU, JEAN, *The Concise Encyclopedia of Symbolism*, trans. Susie Saunders (London: Omega, 1984).

CHADWICK, CHARLES, *Symbolism* (London: Methuen, 1971).

CHAPPLE, J. A. V., *Documentary and Imaginative Literature 1880–1920* (London: Blandford Press, 1970).

CHESTERTON, G. K., 'A Defence of Detective Stories', *The Defendant* (London: Johnson, 1902), 158–60.

—— *The Napoleon of Notting Hill* (1904; London: Penguin, 1986).

—— *The Club of Queer Trades* (1905; London: Penguin, 1986).

—— *The Man Who Was Thursday: A Nightmare* (1908; Bristol: Arrowsmith, 1946).

—— *London* (Minneapolis: Edmund D. Brookes [privately printed], 1914).

CHILVERS, IAN, HAROLD OSBOURNE, and DENNIS FARR, eds., *The Oxford Dictionary of Art* (Oxford: Oxford University Press, 1988).

CHRISTIAN, JOHN, *Symbolists and Decadents* (London: Thames and Hudson, 1977).

—— ed., *The Romantic Tradition in British Art: Burne Jones to Stanley Spencer* (London: Lund Humphries, 1989).

CHRISTIANSEN, RUPERT, *The Visitors: Culture Shock in Nineteenth-Century Britain* (London: Chatto and Windus, 2000).

CLARK, T. J., *The Painting of Modern Life: Paris in the Art of Manet and his Followers* (London: Thames and Hudson, 1985).

COBURN, ALVIN LANGDON, *London* (London: Duckworth, 1909).

—— *Men of Mark* (London: Duckworth, 1913).

—— 'Photography and the Quest for Beauty', *The Photographic Journal* (April 1924), 159–67.

—— *Photographer: An Autobiography*, ed. Helmut and Alison Gernsheim (London: Faber and Faber, 1966).

COHEN, PHIL, 'Dual Cities, Third Spaces and the Urban Uncanny', in *A Companion to the City*, ed. Gary Bridge and Sophie Watson (Oxford: Blackwell, 2003), 316–30.

COLLINS, PHILIP, ed., *Dickens: The Critical Heritage* (London: Routledge and Kegan Paul, 1971).

—— 'Dickens and London', in H. J. Dyos and Michael Wolff, eds., *The Victorian City: Images and Realities*, 2 vols. (London: Routledge and Kegan Paul, 1973), ii. 537–57.

—— 'Dickens and the City', in William Sharpe and Leonard Wallock, eds., *Visions of the Modern City* (Baltimore: Johns Hopkins University Press, 1987), 101–21.

COLLINS, WILKIE, *Basil*, ed. Dorothy Goldman (1852; Oxford: Oxford University Press, 1990).

—— *The Woman in White*, ed. John Sutherland (1860; Oxford: Oxford University Press, 1996).

—— *The Law and the Lady*, ed. David Skilton (1875; London: Penguin, 1998).

CONRAD, JOSEPH, *The Nigger of the 'Narcissus'* (1897; Harmondsworth: Penguin, 1977).

—— *Heart of Darkness*, ed. Robert Hampson (1899/1902; London: Penguin, 1995).

—— *The Secret Agent: A Simple Tale*, ed. John Lyon (1907; Oxford: Oxford University Press, 2004).

—— *A Personal Record* (1912), in *The Mirror of the Sea and A Personal Record* (London: Dent, 1946).

—— 'Poland Revisited' (1915), in *Notes on Life and Letters* (London: Dent, 1921).

—— *The Shadow Line*, ed. Jacques Berthoud (1917; London: Penguin, 1986).

—— *Last Essays* (London: Dent, 1926).

CORBETT, DAVID PETERS, 'Seeing into Modernity: Walter Sickert's Music-Hall Scenes, c.1887–1907', in David Peters and Lara Perry, eds., *English Art 1860–1914: Modern Artists and Identity* (2000; New Brunswick: Rutgers University Press, 2001), 150–67.

CORELLI, MARIE, *The Sorrows of Satan*, ed. Peter Keating (1895; Oxford: Oxford University Press, 1998).

COUSTILLAS, PIERRE, and JOHN SPIERS, eds., *Gissing: The Critical Heritage* (London: Routledge and Kegan Paul, 1972).

CRACKANTHORPE, DAVID, *Hubert Crackanthorpe and English Realism in the 1890s* (Columbia: University of Missouri Press, 1977).

CRACKANTHORPE, HUBERT, *Wreckage* (London: Heinemann, 1893).

—— 'Reticence in Literature', *Yellow Book*, 2 (1894), 259–69.

CRANE, STEPHEN, 'London Impressions', *Saturday Review* (14 August 1897), 158.

CRAWFORD, ROBERT, 'James Thomson and T. S. Eliot', *Victorian Poetry*, 23(1) (1985), 23–41.

CRAWFORD, ROBERT, *The Savage and the City in the Work of T. S. Eliot* (Oxford: Clarendon, 1987).

CROSS, NIGEL, *The Common Writer: Life in Nineteenth Century Grub Street* (Cambridge: Cambridge University Press, 1985).

CROWLEY, ALEISTER, *Moonchild* (London: Mandrake Press, 1929).

—— *The Confessions of Aleister Crowley: An Autohagiography*, ed. John Symonds and Kenneth Grant (London: Arkana, 1978).

CUDDON, J. A., *The Penguin Dictionary of Literary Terms and Literary Theory* (London: Penguin, 1998).

CURTIS, ANTHONY, and JOHN WHITEHEAD, eds., *W. Somerset Maugham: The Critical Heritage* (London: Routledge and Kegan Paul, 1987).

DAVIDSON, JOHN, *Sentences and Paragraphs* (London: Lawrence and Bullen, 1893).

—— *A Random Itinerary* (London: Elkin Matthews and John Lane, 1894).

—— *A Full and True Account of the Wonderful Mission of Earl Lavender* (London: Ward and Downey, 1895).

—— 'Pre-Shakespearianism', *The Speaker*, 19 (28 January 1899), 107.

—— *John Davidson: A Selection of his Poetry*, ed. Maurice Lindsay (London: Hutchinson, 1961).

—— *The Poems of John Davidson*, 2 vols., ed. Andrew Turnbull (Edinburgh: Scottish Academic Press, 1973).

—— *Selected Poems and Prose of John Davidson*, ed. John Sloan (Oxford: Clarendon Press, 1995).

DE CERTEAU, MICHEL, *The Practice of Everyday Life* (Berkeley: University of California Press, 1984).

DE LA MARÉ, ERIC, *The London Doré Saw: A Victorian Evocation* (London: Allen Lane, 1973).

DENNY, NORMAN, ed., *The Yellow Book: A Selection* (London: The Bodley Head, 1949).

DENVIR, BERNARD, ed. *The Impressionists at First Hand* (London: Thames and Hudson, 1987).

DICKENS, CHARLES, *Bleak House*, ed. Nicola Bradbury (1853; London: Penguin, 1996).

—— *Hard Times*, ed. Kate Flint (1854; London: Penguin, 1995).

—— *Great Expectations*, ed. Margaret Cardwell (1861; Oxford: Clarendon Press, 1993).

—— *Our Mutual Friend*, ed. Adrian Poole (1865: London: Penguin, 1997).

DICKENS, CHARLES, Jr., *Dickens's Dictionary of London, 1888: An Unconventional Handbook* (London: Macmillan, 1888).

DISRAELI, BENJAMIN, *Lothair*, ed. Vernon Bogdanor (1870; Oxford: Oxford University Press, 1975).

DIXON HUNT, JOHN, *The Pre-Raphaelite Imagination* (London: Routledge and Kegan Paul, 1968).

DODD, PHILIP, ed., *Walter Pater: An Imaginative Sense of Fact* (London: Frank Cass, 1981).

DORÉ, GUSTAVE, and BLANCHARD JERROLD, *London: A Pilgrimage* (1872; New York: Dover, 1970).

Dorra, Henri, ed., *Symbolist Art Theories: A Critical Anthology* (Berkeley and Los Angeles: University of California Press, 1994).

Dowling, Linda, *Language and Decadence in the Victorian Fin de Siècle* (New Haven: Yale University Press, 1986).

Dowson, Ernest, *Poetical Works*, ed. Desmond Flower (London: Cassell, 1967).

Doyle, Arthur Conan, *The Penguin Complete Sherlock Holmes* (London: Penguin, 1981).

Dreiser, Theodore, *A Traveller at Forty* (1913; New York: Century, 1920).

Dyos, H. J., *Victorian Suburb* (Leicester: Leicester University Press, 1961).

—— and Michael Wolff, eds., *The Victorian City: Images and Realities*, 2 vols. (London: Routledge and Kegan Paul, 1973).

Egerton, George, *Discords* (London: John Lane, 1894).

—— *Symphonies* (London: John Lane, 1897).

Eliot, T. S., *The Sacred Wood* (London: Methuen, 1920).

—— *Complete Poems and Plays* (London: Faber, 1969).

—— *The Waste Land: A Facsimile and Transcript of the Original Drafts*, ed. Valerie Eliot (London: Faber, 1971).

—— *The Letters of T. S. Eliot*, i: *1898–1922*, ed. Valerie Eliot (London: Faber, 1988).

—— *Inventions of the March Hare: Poems 1909–1917*, ed. Christopher Ricks (London: Faber, 1996).

Ellmann, Richard, *Oscar Wilde* (London: Hamish Hamilton, 1987).

Engels, Friedrich, *The Condition of the Working Class in England* (1845; Harmondsworth: Penguin, 1987).

Englander, David, 'Booth's Jews: The Presentations of Jews and Judaism in *Life and Labour of the People in London*', *Victorian Studies*, 32(4) (summer 1989), 551–71.

Feldman, David, and Gareth Stedman Jones, *Metropolis London: Histories and Representations since 1800* (London: Routledge, 1989).

Finn, Howard, ' "In the Quicksands of Disintegrating Faiths": Dorothy Richardson and the Quakers', *Literature and Theology*, 19(1), (March 2005), 34–46.

Fishman, William J., *East End 1888: A Year in a London Borough among the Labouring Poor* (London: Duckworth, 1988).

Flecker, James Elroy, *Collected Poems*, ed. John Squire (1916; London: Secker and Warburg, 1942).

Fletcher, Ian, *Walter Pater* (London: Longman/British Council, 1971).

—— ed., *British Poetry and Prose 1870–1905* (Oxford: Oxford University Press, 1987).

Flint, Kate, ed., *Impressionists in England: The Critical Reception* (London: Routledge, 1984).

Florence, Penny, *Mallarmé, Manet and Redon: Visual and Aural Signs and the Generation of Meaning* (Cambridge: Cambridge University Press, 1986).

Flukinger Roy, Larry Schaaf, and Standish Meacham, *Paul Martin: Victorian Photographer* (Austin: University of Texas Press, 1977).

Ford, Ford Madox (= Hueffer), 'William Hyde: An Illustrator of London', *The Artist* (January 1898), 1–9.

—— *The Cinque Ports* (Edinburgh and London: William Blackwood, 1900).

FORD, FORD MADOX (= HUEFFER), *The Soul of London: A Survey of a Modern City*, ed. Alan G. Hill (1905; London: Dent, 1995).

—— *England and the English: An Interpretation*, ed. Sara Haslam (1907; Manchester: Carcanet, 2003).

—— *The Critical Attitude* (London: Duckworth, 1911).

—— *Ancient Lights and Certain New Reflections* (London: Chapman and Hall, 1911).

—— *Collected Poems* (London: Max Goschen, 1914).

—— 'Techniques', *Southern Review*, 1 (July 1935), 20–35.

—— *Critical Writings*, ed. Frank MacShane (Lincoln: University of Nebraska Press, 1964).

FORSTER, E. M., *Howards End*, ed. Oliver Stallybrass (1910; London: Penguin, 1983).

FOUCAULT, MICHEL, 'Of Other Spaces' ['Des Espaces Autres' 1967], trans. Jay Miskowiec, *Diacritics*, 16(1) (spring 1986), 22–7.

FOWLIE, WALLACE, *Poem and Symbol: A Brief History of French Symbolism* (University Park: Pennsylvania State University Press, 1990).

FREEDMAN, JONATHAN, *Professions of Taste: Henry James, British Aestheticism and Commodity Culture* (Stanford: Stanford University Press, 1990).

FRIEDMANN, DONALD FLANELL, *The Symbolist Dead City: A Landscape of Poesis* (New York: Garland, 1990).

—— 'Belgian Symbolism and a Poetics of Place', in *Les XX and the Belgian Avant-Garde*, ed. Stephen H. Goddard (Kansas: Spencer Museum of Art, 1992), 126–39.

GAGE, JOHN T., *In the Arresting Eye: The Rhetoric of Imagism* (Baton Rouge: Louisiana State University Press, 1981).

GELFANT, BLANCHE, *The American City Novel* (Norman: University of Oklahoma Press, 1954).

GENOVA, PAMELA A., *Symbolist Journals: A Culture of Correspondence* (Aldershot: Ashgate, 2002).

GIBBONS, TOM, *Rooms in the Darwin Hotel: Studies in Literary Criticism and Ideas, 1880–1920* (Nedlands: University of Western Australia Press, 1973).

GIBSON, MICHAEL, *Symbolism* (Köln: Taschen, 1999).

GILBERT, PAMELA K., *Imagined Londons* (New York: State University of New York Press, 2002).

GILBERT, R. A., 'Seeking That Which Was Lost: More Light on the Origins and Development of the Golden Dawn', in Warwick Gould, ed., *Yeats Annual 14: Yeats and the Nineties* (Basingstoke: Palgrave, 2001), 33–49.

GISSING, GEORGE, *Workers in the Dawn* ed. Pierre Coustillas (1880; Hassocks: Harvester, 1985).

—— *Thyrza* (1887; London: Eveleigh Nash & Grayson, 1927).

—— *The Nether World*, ed. Stephen Gill (1889; Oxford: Oxford University Press, 1992).

—— *New Grub Street*, ed. John Goode (1891; Oxford: Oxford University Press, 1993).

—— *The Whirlpool*, ed. William Greenslade (1897; London: Dent, 1997).

—— *Charles Dickens: A Critical Study* (1898; London: Gresham, 1903).

—— *The Private Papers of Henry Ryecroft*, ed. Mark Storey (1903; Oxford: Oxford University Press, 1987).

—— *The Immortal Dickens* (London: Palmer, 1925).

—— *Letters of George Gissing to Members of his Family*, collected and arranged by Algernon and Ellen Gissing (London: Constable, 1927).

—— *London and the Life of Literature in Late Victorian England: The Diary of George Gissing*, ed. Pierre Coustillas (Hassocks: Harvester, 1978).

GLINERT, ED, *A Literary Guide to London* (London: Penguin, 2000).

—— *The London Compendium* (London: Allen Lane, 2003).

GOLDWATER, ROBERT, *Symbolism* (London: Allen Lane, 1979).

GOODE, JOHN, *George Gissing: Ideology and Fiction* (London: Vision Press, 1978).

GOODRICK-CLARKE, NICHOLAS, 'The Enchanted City: Arthur Machen and Locality: Scenes from his Early London Years (1880–85)', *Durham University Journal*, 56 (2) (1995), 301–13.

GORDON, LYNDALL, *Eliot's Early Years* (Oxford: Oxford University Press, 1988).

GOSSE, EDMUND, *Aspects and Impressions* (London: Cassell, 1922).

GRAHAM, KENNETH, *English Criticism of the Novel, 1865–1900* (Oxford: Clarendon Press, 1965).

GRAVES, ROBERT, *Poems 1929* (London: Seizin Press, 1929)

GRAY, DONALD J., 'Views and Sketches of London in the 19th Century', in Ira Bruce Nadal and F. S. Schwarzbach, eds., *Victorian Artists and the City: A Collection of Critical Essays* (New York: Pergamon, 1980), 43–58.

GREEN, JONATHAN, ed., *Camera Work: A Critical Anthology* (New York: Aperture Foundation, 1973).

GREENSLADE, WILLIAM, *Degeneration, Culture and the Novel, 1880–1940* (Cambridge: Cambridge University Press, 1994).

GROSSMITH, WEEDON, and GEORGE, *The Diary of a Nobody*, ed. Kate Flint (Oxford: Oxford University Press, 1995).

GUNSTEREN, JULIA VAN, *Katherine Mansfield and Literary Impressionism* (Amsterdam: Rodopi, 1990).

GUY, JOSEPHINE M., *The British Avant-Garde: The Theory and Politics of Tradition* (Hemel Hempstead: Harvester Wheatsheaf, 1991).

HAMMOND, J. R., *An H. G. Wells Companion* (Basingstoke: Macmillan, 1979).

HAPGOOD, LYNNE, *Margins of Desire: The Suburbs in Fiction and Culture 1880–1925* (Manchester: Manchester University Press, 2005).

HARDY, FLORENCE EMILY, *The Life of Thomas Hardy* (London: Macmillan, 1962).

HARDY, THOMAS, *The Life and Works of Thomas Hardy*, ed. Michael Millgate (London: Macmillan, 1984).

—— *Jude the Obscure*, ed. Patricia Ingham (1895; Oxford: Oxford University Press, 1985).

—— *The Pursuit of the Well-Beloved and The Well Beloved*, ed. Patricia Ingham (Harmondsworth: Penguin, 1997).

—— *Thomas Hardy's 'Facts' Notebook*, ed. William Greenslade (Aldershot: Ashgate, 2004).

HARKER, MARGARET F., *The Linked Ring: The Secession Movement in Photography in Britain, 1892–1910* (London: Heinemann, 1979).

HARKNESS, MARGARET, *In Darkest London* (Cambridge: Black Apollo Press, 2003). Originally published as *Captain Lobe: A Story of the Salvation Army* by John Law (London: Hodder and Stoughton, 1889).

HARRIS, FRANK, 'Why drag in—Pennell?', *Saturday Review* (10 April 1897), 371–3.

HARTMANN, SADAKICHI, *The Whistler Book* (Boston: L. C. Page, 1910).

HARVEY, DAVID DOW, *Ford Madox Ford 1873–1939: A Bibliography of Works and Criticism* (Princeton: Princeton University Press, 1962).

HEMMINGS, F. W. J., ed., *The Age of Realism* (Harmondsworth: Pelican, 1974).

HENLEY, W. E., ed., *A London Garland* (London: Macmillan, 1895).

—— *Poems* (London: Macmillan, 1926).

HENNGAN, ALISON, 'Personalities and Principles: Aspects of Literature and Life in *Fin-de-Siècle* England', in Mikuláš Teich and Roy Porter, eds., *Fin de siècle and its Legacy* (Cambridge: Cambridge University Press, 1990), 170–215.

HERBERT, ROBERT L., *Impressionism: Art, Leisure and Parisian Society* (New Haven: Yale University Press, 1988).

HERRMANN, LUKE, *Nineteenth Century British Painting* (London: Giles de la Mare, 2000).

HICHENS, ROBERT, *The Green Carnation* (1894; London: Robert Clark, 1992).

HIGHMORE, BEN, *Cityscapes: Cultural Readings in the Material and Symbolic City* (Basingstoke: Palgrave, 2005).

HOLDER, ALAN, *Three Voyagers in Search of Europe: A Study of Henry James, Ezra Pound and T. S. Eliot* (University Park: University of Pennsylvania Press, 1966).

HÖNNIGHAUSEN, LOTHAR, *The Symbolist Tradition in English Literature* (Cambridge: Cambridge University Press, 1988). Originally published as *Praraphaeliten und Fin de Siècle: Symbolistiche Tendenzen in der Englischen Spatromantik* (Munich: Wilhelm Fink, 1971).

HOPE MONCRIEFF, A. R., *London*, reprinted as *Victorian and Edwardian London* (1910; London: Brockhampton Press, 1999).

HORNUNG, E. W., *The Collected Raffles* (London: Dent, 1985).

HOUGH, GRAHAM, *The Last Romantics* (1949; London: Duckworth, 1979).

HOUSE, JOHN, 'The Impressionist Vision of London', in Ira Bruce Nadel and F. S. Schwarzbach, eds., *Victorian Artists and the City* (New York: Pergamon Press, 1980), 78–90.

—— 'London in the Art of Monet and Pissarro', in Malcolm Warner et al., eds., *The Image of London* (London: Trefoil/Barbican Art Gallery, 1987), 73–98.

HOWARTH, HERBERT, *Notes on Some Figures Behind T. S. Eliot* (London: Chatto and Windus, 1965).

HUGHES, LINDA K., 'A Woman on the Wilde Side: Masks, Perversity, and Print Culture in Poems by "Graham R. Tomson"/Rosamund Marriott Watson', in Joseph Bristow, ed., *The Fin-de-Siècle Poem: English Literary Culture and the 1890s* (Athens: Ohio University Press, 2005), 101–30.

HULIN, JEAN-PIERRE, and PIERRE COUSTILLAS, *Victorian Writers and the City* (Lille: University of Lille, 1979).

HURLEY, KELLY, *The Gothic Body: Sexuality, Materialism, and Degeneration at the Fin de Siècle* (Cambridge: Cambridge University Press, 1996).

HUYSMANS, J.-K., *Against Nature [À Rebours]*, trans. Margaret Mauldon (1884; Oxford: Oxford University Press, 1998).

—— *Parisian Sketches [Croquis parisiens]*, trans. Brendan King (1880; Sawtry: Dedalus, 2004).

JACKSON, HOLBROOK, *The Eighteen Nineties: A Review of Art and Ideas at the Close of the Nineteenth Century* (1913; Harmondsworth: Pelican, 1950).

JAMES, HENRY, 'Parisian Festivity', *New York Tribune* (13 May 1876), 2.

—— *Portraits of Places* (London: Macmillan, 1883).

—— *The Princess Casamassima*, ed. Derek Brewer (1886; London: Penguin, 1987).

—— *Partial Portraits* (London: Macmillan, 1888).

—— *Embarrassments* (London: Macmillan, 1896).

—— 'In the Cage' (1898; London: Hesperus, 2002).

—— *English Hours* (London: William Heinemann & Co, 1905).

—— *The Golden Bowl* (1907; London: The Bodley Head, 1972).

—— *The Spoils of Poynton* (1908; New York: Augustus M. Kelley, 1976).

—— *The Painter's Eye: Notes and Essays on the Pictorial Arts by Henry James*, ed. John L. Sweeney (Cambridge, MA: Harvard University Press, 1956).

—— *The House of Fiction: Essays on the Novel*, ed. Leon Edel (London: Rupert Hart-Davis, 1957).

—— *The Notebooks of Henry James*, ed. F. O. Matthiessen and Kenneth B. Murdock (New York: Oxford University Press, 1961).

—— *The Letters of Henry James*, i: *1843–1875*, ed. Leon Edel (Cambridge, MA: Harvard University Press, 1974).

—— *The Letters of Henry James*, ii: *1875–1883*, ed. Leon Edel (Cambridge, MA: Harvard University Press, 1978).

—— *The Correspondence of Henry James and the House of Macmillan, 1877–1914*, ed. Rayburn S. Moore (London: Macmillan, 1993).

—— *Essays on Art and Drama*, ed. Peter Rawlings (Aldershot: Scolar Press, 1996).

—— *Complete Stories 1864–1874* (New York: Library of America, 1999).

—— *Complete Stories 1874–1884* (New York: Library of America, 1999).

JAMES, SIMON J., *Unsettled Accounts: Money and Narrative in the Novels of George Gissing* (London: Anthem, 2003).

JARRETT, DEREK, *The Sleep of Reason: Fantasy and Reality from the Victorian Age to the First World War* (London: Weidenfeld and Nicolson, 1988).

JEFFERIES, RICHARD, *After London or Wild England* (1885: Oxford: Oxford University Press, 1980).

JERROLD, BLANCHARD, and GUSTAVE DORÉ, *London: A Pilgrimage* (1872; New York, Dover, 1970).

JOHNSON, BRUCE, 'Conrad's Impressionism and Watt's "Delayed Decoding"' in Ross C. Murfin, ed., *Conrad Revisited: Essays for the Eighties* (Tuscaloosa, AL: University of Alabama Press, 1985), 51–70.

JOHNSON, E. D. H., 'Victorian Artists and the Urban Milieu', in H. J. Dyos and Michael Wolff, eds., *The Victorian City: Images and Realities*, 2 vols. (London: Routledge and Kegan Paul, 1973), ii. 449–75.

—— *Painting of the British Social Scene from Hogarth to Sickert* (London: Weidenfeld and Nicolson, 1986).

JOHNSON, LEE MCKAY, *The Metaphor of Painting: Essays on Baudelaire, Ruskin, Proust and Pater* (Ann Arbor: University of Michigan Press, 1980).

JONES, EMRYS, *Metropolis: The World's Great Cities* (Oxford: Oxford University Press, 1990).

JONES, PETER, ed., *Imagist Poetry* (Harmondsworth: Penguin, 1972).

JOYCE, JAMES, *Stephen Hero*, ed. Theodore Spencer (London: Jonathan Cape, 1946).

JOYCE, SIMON, *Capital Offenses: Geographies of Class and Crime in Victorian London* (Charlottesville: University of Virginia Press, 2003).

JUKES, PHILIP, *A Shout in the Street: The Modern City* (London: Faber, 1990).

JULLIAN, PHILIPPE, *Oscar Wilde* (London: Constable, 1969).

—— *Dreamers of Decadence: Symbolist Painters of the 1890s*, trans. Robert Baldick (London: Phaidon, 1974). Originally published as *Esthètes et Magiciens* (Paris: Librarie académique Perrin, 1969).

KARLIN, DANIEL, ed., *The Penguin Book of Victorian Verse* (London: Penguin, 1997).

KASINITZ, PHILIP, ed., *Metropolis: Centre and Symbol of Our Times* (London: Macmillan, 1995).

KEATING, P. J., *New Grub Street* (London: Edward Arnold, 1968).

—— ed., *Working Class Stories of the 1890s* (London: Routledge and Kegan Paul, 1971).

—— *The Working Classes in Victorian Fiction* (London: Routledge and Kegan Paul, 1971).

—— ed., *Into Unknown England, 1866–1913: Selections from the Social Explorers* (Glasgow: Fontana/Collins, 1976).

—— 'The Metropolis in Literature', in Anthony Sutcliffe, ed., *Metropolis 1890–1940* (London: Mansell, 1984), 129–46.

—— *The Haunted Study: A Social History of the English Novel 1875–1914* (1989; London: Fontana, 1991).

KENDALL, RICHARD, ed., *Degas by Himself* (1987; London: Time Warner, 2004).

KENNER, HUGH, *The Invisible Poet* (London: W. H. Allen, 1960).

KERMODE, FRANK, *Romantic Image* (London: Routledge and Kegan Paul, 1957).

—— *The Sense of an Ending: Studies in the Theory of Fiction* (Oxford: Oxford University Press, 1966).

KERN, STEPHEN, *The Culture of Time and Space, 1880–1918* (Cambridge, MA: Harvard University Press, 1983).

KIJINSKI, JOHN L., 'Ethnography in the East End: Native Customs and Colonial Solutions in A Child of the Jago', *English Literature in Transition 1880–1920*, 37(4) (1994), 490–501.

KIMMEY, JOHN L., 'The "London Book"', *Henry James Review*, 1 (1979), 61–72.

—— *Henry James and London: The City in his Fiction* (New York: Peter Lang, 1991).

KIPLING, RUDYARD, *Life's Handicap: Being Stories of Mine Own People* (London: Macmillan, 1891).

—— *The Light that Failed* (1891; London: Macmillan, 1895).

—— *Many Inventions* (1893; London: Macmillan, 1928).

—— *Collected Poems of Rudyard Kipling*, ed. R. T. Jones (Ware: Wordsworth, 2001).

KNOWLES, OWEN, and GENE M. MOORE, *The Oxford Reader's Companion to Conrad* (Oxford: Oxford University Press, 2000).

KORG, JACOB, and CYNTHIA, *George Gissing on Fiction* (London: Enitharmon, 1978).

KOVAL, ANNE, *Whistler in his Time* (London: Tate Gallery, 1994).

LAFOURCADE, GEORGES, *La Jeunesse de Swinburne, 1837–1867* (Paris: 1928).

LAMBOURNE, LIONEL, *The Aesthetic Movement* (London: Phaidon, 1996).

—— *Victorian Painting* (London: Phaidon, 1999).

LEDGER, SALLY, and SCOTT MCCRACKEN, eds., *Cultural Politics at the Fin de Siècle* (Cambridge: Cambridge University Press, 1995).

—— and ROGER LUCKHURST, eds., *The Fin de Siècle: A Reader in Cultural History c.1880–1900* (Oxford: Oxford University Press, 2000).

LEE, VERNON, *Genius Loci* (London: Grant Richards, 1899).

LE GALLIENNE, RICHARD, *Attitudes and Avowals* (London: John Lane/The Bodley Head, 1910).

—— *The Romantic '90s* (1926; London: Robin Clark, 1993).

LEHAN, RICHARD, *The City in Literature: An Intellectual and Cultural History* (Berkeley and Los Angeles: University of California Press, 1998).

LEONARD, TOM, *Places of the Mind: The Life and Work of James Thomson ('B.V.')* (London: Jonathan Cape, 1993).

LEVY, AMY, *A London Plane-Tree and Other Verse* (London: T. Fisher Unwin, 1889).

—— *The Complete Novels and Selected Writings of Amy Levy 1861–1889*, ed. Melvyn New (Gainesville: University Press of Florida, 1993).

LEWIS, WYNDHAM, ed., *Blast*, 20 June 1914 (London: John Lane).

LHOMBREAUD, ROGER, *Arthur Symons: A Literary Biography* (London: Unicorn Press, 1963).

LIDDLE, DALLAS, 'Anatomy of a "Nine Days" Wonder: Sensational Journalism in the Decade of the Sensation Novel', in Andrew Maunder and Grace Moore, eds., *Victorian Crime, Madness and Sensation* (Aldershot: Ashgate, 2004), 89–104.

LOGUE, CHRISTOPHER, ed., *London in Verse* (London: Penguin, 1984).

LONDON, JACK, *The People of the Abyss* (1903; London: Thomas Nelson, [n.d.]).

LUCAS, E. V., *A Wanderer in London* (1906; London: Methuen, 1913).

—— *Loiterer's Harvest: A Book of Essays* (London: Methuen, 1913).

LUCAS, JOHN, 'From Naturalism to Symbolism', in Ian Fletcher, ed., *Decadence and the 1890s* (London: Edward Arnold, 1979), 131–50.

—— 'Hopkins and Symons: Two Views of the City', in John Stokes, ed., *Fin de Siècle / Fin du Globe* (London: Macmillan, 1992), 52–68.

LUCIE-SMITH, EDWARD, *Symbolist Art* (London: Thames and Hudson, 1972).

LUCKHURST, ROGER, *The Invention of Telepathy 1870–1901* (Oxford: Oxford University Press, 2002).

MACAULAY, ROSE, *Crewe Train* (1926; London: Virago, 1998).

MACCOLL, D. S., 'The New English Art Club', *The Spectator*, 66 (18 April 1891), 544.

McCONKEY, KENNETH, *Memory and Desire: Painting in Britain and Ireland at the Turn of the Twentieth Century* (Aldershot: Ashgate, 2002).

—— *Impressionism in Britain* (London: Barbican Art Gallery, 1995).

McDONALD, PETER D., *British Literary Culture and Publishing Practice 1880–1914* (Cambridge: Cambridge University Press, 1997).

MACHEN, ARTHUR, *The Great God Pan* (1894; London: Creation, 1993).

—— *The Three Impostors or The Transmutations*, ed. David Trotter (1895; London: Dent, 1995).

—— *Hieroglyphics: A Note upon Ecstasy in Literature* (1902; London: Unicorn Press, 1960).

—— *The House of Souls* (1906; London: Martin Secker, 1923).

—— *The Hill of Dreams* (1907; Leyburn: Tartarus Press, 1998).

—— *Things Near and Far* (London: Martin Secker, 1923).

—— *Far Off Things* (London: Martin Secker, 1923).

—— *Precious Balms* (1924; Horam: Tartarus Press, 1999).

—— *The London Adventure or The Art of Wandering* (1924; London: Village Press, 1974).

—— *The Cosy Room* (London: Rich and Cowan, 1936).

—— *Tales of Horror and the Supernatural* (London: Panther, 1963).

—— *The Collected Arthur Machen*, ed. Christopher Palmer (London: Duckworth, 1988).

MACHRAY, ROBERT, *The Night Side of London* (London: John Macqueen, 1902).

MACKWORTH, CECILY, *English Interludes: Mallarmé, Verlaine, Paul Valéry, Valery Larbaud in England, 1860–1912* (London: Routledge and Kegan Paul, 1974).

McLAREN, ANGUS, *A Prescription for Murder: The Victorian Serial Killings of Dr Thomas Neill Cream* (Chicago: University of Chicago Press, 1993).

McMULLEN, ROY, *Victorian Outsider: A Biography of J. A. M. Whistler* (London: Macmillan, 1973).

McWHIRTER, DAVID, ed., *Henry James's New York Edition: The Construction of Authorship* (Stanford: Stanford University Press, 1995).

MARKERT, LAWRENCE W., *Arthur Symons: Critic of the Seven Arts* (Ann Arbor: UMI, 1988).

MARKINO, YOSHIO, *A Japanese Artist in London* (London: Chatto and Windus, 1911).

MARKS, PATRICIA, 'Tipping Mr. Punch "the Haffable Wink": E. J. Milliken's Cockney Verse Letters', in Jennifer A. Wagner-Lawlor, ed., *The Victorian Comic Spirit: New Perspectives* (Aldershot: Ashgate, 1999), 67–90.

MARSH, RICHARD, *The Beetle* (1897), in *The Penguin Book of Victorian Villainies*, sel. Hugh and Graham Greene (London: Penguin, 1984), 441–715.

MARSTON, PHILIP BOURKE, *A Last Harvest* (London: Elkin Matthews, 1891).

MATZ, JESSE, *Literary Impressionism and Modernist Aesthetics* (Cambridge: Cambridge University Press, 2001).

MAUGHAM, W. SOMERSET, *Liza of Lambeth* (1897; London: Pan, 1978).

—— *A Writer's Notebook* (London: Heinemann, 1949).

MAXWELL, RICHARD, *The Mysteries of Paris and London* (Charlottesville: University of Virginia Press, 1992).

MAYHEW, HENRY, *London Labour and the London Poor* (1865 edn), sel. and intro. Victor Neuberg (London: Penguin, 1985).

MEREDITH, GEORGE, *Letters*, Vol. III, ed. C. L. Cline (Oxford: Clarendon Press, 1970).

MIGHALL, ROBERT, *A Geography of Victorian Gothic Fiction* (Oxford: Oxford University Press, 1999).

MILLARD, KENNETH, *Edwardian Poetry* (Oxford: Oxford University Press, 1991).

MILNER, JOHN, *Symbolists and Decadents* (London: Studio Vista, 1971).

Montreal Museum of Fine Arts, *Lost Paradise: Symbolist Europe* (Montreal: Montreal Museum of Fine Arts, 1995).

MOORE, GENE M., ed., *Conrad's Cities: Essays for Hans van Marle* (Rodopi: Amsterdam, 1992).

MOORE, GEORGE, *Confessions of a Young Man* (1888; London: William Heinemann, 1937).

—— *Modern Painting* (London: Walter Scott, 1893).

MORETTI, FRANCO, *Atlas of the European Novel, 1800–1900* (London: Verso, 1998).

MORRISON, ARTHUR, *Tales of Mean Streets* (1894; Woodbridge: Boydell, 1983).

—— *A Child of the Jago*, ed. P. J. Keating (1896; London: Panther, 1971).

—— *A Child of the Jago*, ed. Peter Miles (1896; London: Dent, 1996).

MORTON, H. V., *In Search of England* (London: Methuen, 1927).

MUNRO, JOHN M., *Arthur Symons* (New York: Twayne, 1969).

NADEL, IRA BRUCE, and F. S. SCHWARZBACH, eds., *Victorian Artists and the City* (New York: Pergamon Press, 1980).

NAGEL, JAMES, *Stephen Crane and Literary Impressionism* (University Park: Pennsylvania State University Press, 1980).

NAIPAUL, V. S., *The Enigma of Arrival: A Novel in Five Sections* (London: Penguin, 1987).

NEAD, LYNDA, *Victorian Babylon: People, Streets and Images in 19th Century London* (New Haven: Yale University Press, 2000).

NELSON, JAMES G., *The Early Nineties: A View from the Bodley Head* (Cambridge, MA: Harvard University Press, 1971).

NERVAL, GÉRARD DE, *Selected Writings*, trans. Richard Sieburth (London: Penguin, 1999).

NICHOLLS, PETER, *Modernisms: A Literary Guide* (Basingstoke: Macmillan, 1995).

NISBET, HUME, 'The Phantom Model or A Wapping Romance' from *The Haunted Station* (1894), in *Gaslight Nightmares*, ed. Hugh Lamb (London: Futura, 1988), 35–47.

NOAKES, VIVIEN, *Edward Lear* (1968: London: Ariel Books, 1985).

NORD, DEBORAH EPSTEIN, *Walking the Victorian Streets: Women, Representation and the City* (London: Cornell University Press, 1995).

NORDAU, MAX, *Degeneration* (New York: D. Appleton, 1895).

O'CONNOR, MARY, *John Davidson* (Edinburgh: Scottish Academic Press, 1987).

OLIPHANT, MARGARET, *A Beleaguered City and Other Tales of the Seen and Unseen*, ed. Jenni Calder (Edinburgh: Canongate, 2000).

ONEGA, SUSANA, and JOHN A. STOTESBURY, eds., *London in Literature: Visionary Mappings of the Metropolis* (Heidelburg: C. Winter, 2002).

OWEN, ALEX, *The Place of Enchantment: British Occultism and the Culture of the Modern* (Chicago: Chicago University Press, 2004).

OWEN, DAVID, *The Government of Victorian London, 1855–1889* (Cambridge, MA: Harvard University Press, 1982).

PARSONS, DEBORAH L., *Streetwalking the Metropolis: Women, the City and Modernity* (Oxford: Oxford University Press, 2000).

PATER, WALTER, *Letters of Walter Pater*, ed. Lawrence Evans (Oxford: Clarendon Press, 1970).

—— *Essays on Literature and Art*, ed. Jennifer Uglow (London: Dent, 1973).

—— *The Renaissance: Studies in Art and Poetry*, ed. Adam Philips, 4th edn (1893; Oxford: Oxford University Press, 1986).

PEARSON, GEOFFREY, *Hooligan: A Brief History of Respectable Fears* (Basingstoke: Macmillan, 1983).

PEARSON, JOHN H., *The Prefaces of Henry James: Framing the Modern Reader* (University Park, PA: Pennsylvania University Press, 1997).

PENNELL, ELIZABETH ROBINS, *The Life and Letters of Joseph Pennell*, 2 vols. (London: Ernest Benn, 1930).

PENNELL, JOSEPH, 'Adventures of an Illustrator II: In London with Henry James', *Century Magazine* (February 1922), 543–8.

PETERS, ROBERT L., 'Whistler and the English Poets of the 1890s', *Modern Language Quarterly*, 18 (1957), 251–61.

PETERSON, C. V., *John Davidson* (New York: Twayne, 1972).

PETT RIDGE, W., *A Story Teller: Forty Years in London* (London: Hodder and Stoughton, 1923).

PHILIPS, STEPHEN, *Poems* (London: John Lane/The Bodley Head, 1898).

PHILISTINE, THE (= J. A. Spender), 'The New Art Criticism: A Philistine's Remonstrance', *Westminster Gazette* (9 March 1893), 1–2.

PIKE, BURTON, *The Image of the City in Modern Literature* (Princeton: Princeton University Press, 1981).

PINCUS-WITTON, ROBERT, *Occult Symbolism in France: Joséphin Peladan and the Salons de la Rose + Croix* (New York: Garland, 1976).

POOLE, ADRIAN, *Gissing in Context* (London: Macmillan, 1975).

PORTER, ROY, *London: A Social History* (1994; London: Penguin, 2000).

PORTERFIELD, SUSAN AZAR, 'Arthur Symons as Critic of the Visual Arts', *English Literature in Transition*, 44(3) (2001), 260–74.

PRESTON, HARLEY, *London and the Thames: Paintings of Three Centuries* (London: National Maritime Museum, 1977).

PUGH, E. W., *A Street in Suburbia* (London: Heinemann, 1895).

—— *The City of the World* (London: Thomas Nelson, n.d. [1912]).

PYNCHON, THOMAS, *V* (1963; New York, Vintage, 1985).

RANSOME, ARTHUR, *Bohemia in London* (1907; Oxford: Oxford University Press, 1984).

RAWLINGS, PETER, 'Pater, Wilde, and James: "The Reader's Share of the Task" ', *Studies in English Language and Literature* (Kyushu University), 48 (February 1998), 45–64.

—— *Henry James and the Abuse of the Past* (Basingstoke: Palgrave Macmillan, 2005).

REDGROVE, PETER, *The Black Goddess and the Sixth Sense* (1987; London: Paladin, 1989).

REWALD, JOHN, *The History of Impressionism* (New York: Museum of Modern Art, 1973).

RICHARDSON, ANGELIQUE, ed., *Women Who Did: Stories by Men and Women, 1890–1914* (London: Penguin, 2002).

—— *Love and Eugenics in the Late Nineteenth Century: Rational Reproduction and the New Woman* (Oxford: Oxford University Press, 2003).

RICHARDSON, JOHN, *The Annals of London* (London: Cassell, 2000).

RICKETTS, ARTHUR COMPTON, *The London Life of Yesterday* (London: Constable, 1909).

RICKS, CHRISTOPHER, *The Force of Poetry* (Oxford: Clarendon Press, 1984).

RIGNALL, JOHN, *Realist Fiction and the Strolling Spectator* (London: Routledge, 1992).

ROBINSON, ALAN, *Poetry, Painting and Ideas 1885–1914* (Basingstoke: Macmillan, 1985).

—— *Imagining London, 1770–1900* (Basingstoke: Macmillan, 2004).

RODENBACH, GEORGES, *Bruges-la-Morte*, trans. Thomas Duncan and Terry Hale (1892; London: Atlas, 1993).

RODNER, WILLIAM S., 'The Making of a London Samurai: Yoshio Markino and the illustrated press in Edwardian Britain', *The British Art Journal*, 5(2) (autumn 2004), 43–52.

ROLFE, FREDERICK, *Hadrian VII* (1904; London: Picador, 1987).

ROSE, ANDREW, *Stinie: Murder on the Common* (1985; London: Penguin, 1989).

ROSENBERG, JOHN D., *Elegy for an Age: The Presence of the Past in Victorian Literature* (London: Anthem 2005).

ROSSETTI, DANTE GABRIEL, *Collected Poetry and Prose*, ed. Jerome McGann (New Haven: Yale University Press, 2003).

ROSTON, MURRAY, *Victorian Contexts: Literature and the Visual Arts* (London: Macmillan, 1996).

ROTHENSTEIN, WILLIAM, *Men and Memories 1872–1938*, ed. and abridged by Mary Lago (London: Chatto and Windus, 1978). Originally published in three volumes (1931, 1932, 1939).

Royal Academy, *Pre-Raphaelites and Other Masters: The Andrew Lloyd Webber Collection* (London: Royal Academy of Arts, 2003).

RUSKIN, JOHN, *The Complete Works of John Ruskin*, ed. E. T. Cook and A. Wedderburn, 39 vols. (London: George Allen, 1903).

RUSSELL, R. B., 'Sub Rosa', *Faunus*, 1 (spring 1998), 7–11.

SAKI [H. H. MUNRO], *The Complete Saki* (London: Penguin, 1982).

SAMUEL, RAPHAEL, 'Comers and Goers', in H. J. Dyos and Michael Wolff, eds., *The Victorian City: Images & Realities* 2 vols. (London: Routledge and Kegan Paul, 1973), i. 123–60.

SATO, TOMOKO, and LIONEL LAMBOURNE, *The Wilde Years: Oscar Wilde and the Art of his Time* (London: Barbican Centre, 2000).

SCHAEFER, WILLIAM, 'The Two Cities of Dreadful Night', *PMLA* 77 (1962), 609–16.

SCHOOLFIELD, GEORGE C., *A Baedeker of Decadence: Charting a Literary Fashion, 1884–1927* (New Haven: Yale University Press, 2003).

SCHUCHARD, RONALD, *Eliot's Dark Angel: Intersections of Life and Art* (Oxford: Oxford University Press, 1999).

SCHWARZBACH, F. S., *Dickens and the City* (London: Athlone, 1979).

SEABOURNE, MIKE, *Photographers' London 1839–1994* (London: Museum of London, 1995).

SEAMAN, OWEN, *The Battle of the Bays* (London: John Lane/The Bodley Head, 1896).

—— *Borrowed Plumes* (1902; London: Constable, 1916).

SECKER, MARTIN, ed., *The 1890s: A Period Anthology* (London: The Richards Press, 1948).

SEED, DAVID, 'Hell Is a City: Symbolic Systems and Epistemological Scepticism in *The City of Dreadful Night*', in Glennis Byron and David Punter, eds., *Spectral Readings: Towards a Gothic Geography* (Basingstoke: Macmillan, 1999), 88–107.

SEIBERLING, GRACE, *Monet in London* (Atlanta: High Museum of Art, 1988).

SEILER, R. M., ed., *Walter Pater: The Critical Heritage* (London: Routledge and Kegan Paul, 1980).

SHANES, ERIC, *Impressionist London* (London: Abbeville, 1994).

SHARPE, WILLIAM, 'Learning to Read *The City*', *Victorian Poetry*, 22(1) (1984), 65–84.

—— and LEONARD WALLOCK, eds., *Visions of the Modern City: Essays in History, Art, and Literature* (Baltimore: Johns Hopkins University Press, 1987).

SHAW, GEORGE BERNARD, *Pygmalion: A Romance in Five Acts* (1914; London: Penguin, 1983).

SHELLEY, PERCY BYSSHE, *A Defence of Poetry*, ed. John E. Jordan (1821; New York: Bobbs-Merrill, 1965).

SHERRY, NORMAN, ed., *Conrad: The Critical Heritage* (London: Routledge and Kegan Paul, 1973).

SHIEL, M. P., *The Purple Cloud* (1901; London: Allison and Busby, 1983).

SICKERT, WALTER, *Sickert Paintings*, ed. Wendy Baron and Richard Shone (London: Royal Academy, 1992).

SIMS, GEORGE, *How the Poor Live* (1883), in Peter Keating, ed., *Into Unknown England, 1866–1913: Selections from the Social Explorers* (Glasgow: Fontana/Collins, 1976), 65–90.

—— *The Devil in London* (London: Stanley Paul, 1908).

SMITH, GROVER, *The Waste Land* (London: George Allen, 1983).

SMITH, RICHARD CÁNDIDA, *Mallarmé's Children: Symbolism and the Renewal of Experience* (Berkeley and Los Angeles: University of California Press, 1999).

SMITH, T. HARPER, 'Re-Readings 2: The Jago', *East London Papers*, 2(1) (1959), 39–47.

SPATE, VIRGINIA, *Claude Monet: The Colour of Time* (London: Thames and Hudson, 1992).

SPENCER, ROBIN, 'The Aesthetics of Change: London as seen by James McNeill Whistler', *The Image of London: Views by Travellers and Emigrés 1550–1920* (London: Trefoil/Barbican Art Gallery, 1987), 49–72.

SPIERS, JOHN, ed., *Gissing and the City: Cultural Crisis and the Making of Books in Late Victorian England* (Basingstoke: Palgrave Macmillan, 2006).

STANFORD, DEREK, ed., *Poets of the 'Nineties* (London: John Baker, 1965).

—— ed., *Critics of the 'Nineties* (London: John Baker, 1970).

—— ed., *Writing of the 'Nineties: From Wilde to Beerbohm* (London: Dent, 1971).

—— ed., *Three Poets of the Rhymers' Club* (Cheadle Hulme: Carcanet, 1974).

STANGE, G. ROBERT, 'The Frightened Poets', in H. J. Dyos and Michael Wolff, eds., *The Victorian City: Images and Realities*, 2 vols. (London: Routledge and Kegan Paul, 1973), ii. 475–94.

STARKIE, ENID, *From Gautier to Eliot: The Influence of France on English Literature, 1851–1939* (London: Hutchinson, 1960).

STEDMAN JONES, GARETH, *Outcast London* (Oxford: Oxford University Press, 1971).

STEVENSON, ROBERT LOUIS, *The Strange Case of Dr Jekyll and Mr Hyde*, ed. Emma Letley (1886; Oxford: Oxford University Press, 1987).

—— and LLOYD OSBOURNE, *The Ebb-Tide*, ed. David Daiches (1894; London: Dent, 1993).

STOKES, JOHN, *In the Nineties* (Chicago: University of Chicago Press, 1989).

—— ed., *Fin de Siècle/Fin du Globe* (London: Macmillan, 1992).

STOWELL, PETER, *Literary Impressionism: James and Chekhov* (Athens: University of Georgia Press, 1980).

STREET, G. S., *A Book of Essays* (London: Archibald Constable, 1902).

STRELKA, JOSEPH, ed., *Perspectives in Literary Symbolism* (University Park, PA: Pennsylvania State University Press, 1968).

STURGIS, MATTHEW, *Passionate Attitudes: The English Decadence of the 1890s* (London: Macmillan, 1995).

—— *Walter Sickert: A Life* (London: HarperCollins, 2005).

SUGDEN, PHILIP, *The Complete History of Jack the Ripper* (London: Robinson, 2002).

SWEETMAN, JOHN, *The Artist and the Bridge 1700–1920* (Aldershot: Ashgate, 1999).

SYMONS, ARTHUR, *An Introduction to the Study of Browning* (London: Cassell, 1886).

—— 'Paul Verlaine', *Black and White*, 1 (20 June 1891), 649.

—— 'The Decadent Movement in Literature', *Harper's New Monthly Magazine*, 87 (November 1893), 858–67.

—— *London Nights* (1895; London: Leonard Smithers, 1897).

—— *Studies in Two Literatures* (London: Leonard Smithers, 1897).

—— *The Symbolist Movement in Literature* (1899; London: Constable, 1908).

—— 'Edgware Road: A Study in Living', *Anglo-American Magazine*, 7 (February 1902), 108–12.

—— *Studies in Prose and Verse* (London: Dent, 1904).

—— *Spiritual Adventures* (London: Constable, 1905).

—— *Studies in Seven Arts* (London: Constable, 1906).

—— *London* (Minneapolis: Edmund D. Brooks [privately printed], 1909).

SYMONS, ARTHUR, *London* with twenty photogravures by Alvin Langdon Coburn (Minneapolis: Edmund D. Brooks [privately printed], 1914).

—— *London: A Book of Aspects* in *Cities and Sea-Coasts and Islands* (London: W. Collins and Son, 1918), 159–226.

—— *Collected Works*, 9 vols. (London: Martin Secker, 1924).

—— *Dramatis Personae* (1923; London: Faber and Gwyer, 1925).

—— *Confessions: A Study in Pathology* (New York: Fountain Press, 1930).

—— *Wanderings* (London: J. M. Dent and Temple Press, 1931).

—— *Selected Letters 1880–1935*, ed. Karl Beckson and John M. Munro (Basingstoke: Macmillan, 1989).

TEMPLE, RUTH Z., *The Critic's Alchemy: A Study of the Introduction of French Symbolism into England* (New Haven, CT: College & University Press, 1953).

THACKER, ANDREW, *Moving Through Modernity: Space and Geography in Modernism* (Manchester: Manchester University Press, 2003).

THESING, WILLIAM B., *The London Muse: Victorian Poetic Responses to the City* (Athens: University of Georgia Press, 1982).

THOMAS, EDWARD, *The Complete Poems of Edward Thomas*, ed. R. George Thomas (Oxford: Clarendon Press, 1978).

THOMPSON, FRANCIS, *The Poems of Francis Thompson* (Oxford: Oxford University Press, 1937).

THOMSON, JAMES, *The City of Dreadful Night and Other Poems*, ed. Bertram Dobell (London: Bertram Dobell, 1899).

—— *Poems and Some Letters of James Thomson*, ed. Anne Ridler (Carbondale: Southern Illinois University Press, 1963).

—— *The City of Dreadful Night* (1874/1880), in *The Penguin Book of Victorian Verse*, ed. Daniel Karlin (London: Penguin, 1997), 550–86.

—— *The City of Dreadful Night*, ed. Edwin Morgan (Edinburgh: Canongate, 1998).

THOMSON, JOHN, and ADOLPHE SMITH, *Street Life in London* (London: Sampson Low, Marston, Searle and Rivington, 1877).

THORNTON, R. K. R., *The Decadent Dilemma* (Basingstoke: Macmillan, 1983).

—— ed., *Poetry of the 'Nineties* (London: Penguin, 1970).

—— and MARION THAIN, eds., *Poetry of the 1890s* (London: Penguin, 1997).

TICKNER, LISA, *Modern Life and Modern Subjects: British Art in the Early Twentieth Century* (New Haven: Yale University Press, 2000).

TINTNER, ADELINE R., *The Book World of Henry James: Appropriating the Classics* (Ann Arbor: University of Michigan Press, 1987).

TOWNSEND, J. BENJAMIN, *John Davidson: Poet of Armageddon* (New Haven: Yale University Press, 1961).

TRAILL, H. D., 'Two Modern Poets', *Fortnightly Review* (1 March 1895), 393–407.

TROTTER, DAVID, *Cooking With Mud: The Idea of Mess in Nineteenth Century Art and Fiction* (Oxford: Oxford University Press, 2000).

TURNER, JANE, ed., *From Monet to Cézanne: Late 19th-century French Artists* (London: Macmillan, 2000).

VADILLO, ANA PAREJO, 'Immaterial Poetics: A. Mary F. Robinson and the Fin-de-Siècle Poem', in Joseph Bristow, ed., *The Fin-de-Siècle Poem: English Literary Culture and the 1890s* (Athens: University of Ohio Press, 2005), 231–60.

—— *Women Poets and Urban Aestheticism: Passengers of Modernity* (Basingstoke: Palgrave Macmillan, 2005).

VERLAINE, PAUL, *Selected Poems*, trans. Martin Sorrell (Oxford: Oxford University Press, 1999).

VON ECKARDT, WOLF, SANDER L. GILMAN, and J. EDWARD CHAMBERLIN, *Oscar Wilde's London* (New York: Doubleday, 1987).

VOX, 'Talks by Three, V.—On the Victoria Embankment', *The Artist* (March 1899), 166.

WALKOWITZ, JUDITH R., *City of Dreadful Delight: Narratives of Sexual Danger in Late-Victorian London* (1992; London: Virago, 1998).

WALL, CYNTHIA, *The Literary and Cultural Spaces of Restoration London* (Cambridge: Cambridge University Press, 1998).

WALLACE, EDGAR, *The Four Just Men*, ed. David Glover (1905; Oxford: Oxford University Press, 1995).

WALLER, P. J., *Town, City and Nation: England 1850–1914* (Oxford: Oxford University Press, 1983).

WALSH, JOHN, *Strange Harp, Strange Symphony: The Life of Francis Thompson* (London: W. H. Allen, 1968).

WARD, MRS HUMPHRY, *Robert Elsmere* (1888; London: John Murray, 1911).

WARWICK, ALEXANDRA, 'Lost Cities: London's Apocalypse', in Glennis Byron and David Punter, eds., *Spectral Readings: Towards a Gothic Geography* (Basingstoke: Macmillan, 1999), 73–87.

WATSON, COLIN, *Snobbery with Violence: English Crime Stories and their Audience* (1971; London: Eyre and Spottiswode, 1987).

WATT, IAN, *Conrad in the Nineteenth Century* (Berkeley and Los Angeles: University of California Press, 1979).

WEBB, BEATRICE, *Autobiography* (London: Longmans Green, 1926).

WEINREB, BEN, and CHRISTOPHER HIBBERT, eds., *The London Encyclopaedia* (London: Macmillan, 1995).

WELLS, H. G., *The Time Machine*, ed. John Lawton (1895; London: Dent, 1995).

—— *Tono-Bungay*, ed. John Hammond (1909; London: Dent, 1994).

—— *Complete Short Stories* (London: Ernest Benn, 1927).

WELSH, ALEXANDER, *The City of Dickens* (Oxford: Clarendon Press, 1971).

WEST, SHEARER, *Fin-de-Siècle: Art and Society in an Age of Uncertainty* (London: Bloomsbury, 1993).

WHEATLEY, HENRY B., *Round about Piccadilly and Pall Mall, or A Ramble from the Haymarket to Hyde Park* (London: Smith, Elder, 1870).

WHEELWRIGHT, PAUL, 'The Archetypal Symbol', in Joseph Strelka, ed., *Perspectives in Literary Symbolism* (University Park: Pennsylvania State University Press, 1968), 214–43.

WHISTLER, JAMES McNEIL, *The Gentle Art of Making Enemies* (London: Heinemann, 1890).

WHISTLER, JAMES MCNEIL, *Whistler on Art: Selected Letters and Writings*, ed. Nigel Thorp (Manchester: Carcanet/Centre for Whistler Studies, 1994).

WHITEING, RICHARD, *No.5, John Street* (London: Grant Richards, 1899).

WILDE, OSCAR, *Complete Works* (London: HarperCollins, 1994).

WILLSHER, JAMES, ed., *The Dedalus Book of English Decadence* (Sawtry: Dedalus, 2004).

WILTON, ANDREW and ROBERT UPSTONE, eds., *The Age of Rossetti, Burne-Jones and Watts: Symbolism in Britain 1860–1910* (London: Tate Gallery, 1997).

WIND, EDGAR, *Pagan Mysteries of the Renaissance* (Harmondsworth: Peregrine, 1967).

WINTER, JAMES, *London's Teeming Streets 1830–1914* (London: Routledge, 1993).

WOLFREYS, JULIAN, *Writing London: The Trace of the Urban Text from Blake to Dickens* (Basingstoke: Macmillan, 1998).

—— *Writing London 2: Materiality, Memory, Spectrality* (Basingstoke: Palgrave Macmillan 2004).

WOOD, CHRISTOPHER, *Victorian Painting* (London: Weidenfeld and Nicolson, 1999).

WOOLF, VIRGINIA, 'Mr Bennett and Mrs Brown' (1924), *Collected Essays*, ed. Leonard Woolf (London: Hogarth Press, 1966), i. 319–37.

—— *The Mark on the Wall and Other Short Fiction*, ed. David Bradshaw (Oxford: Oxford University Press, 2001).

—— *Mrs Dalloway* (London: Hogarth Press, 1925).

YEATS, W. B., 'Certain Noble Plays of Japan' (1916), in *Essays and Introductions* (London: Macmillan, 1961).

—— 'Magic' (1904), in *The Major Works*, ed. Edward Larrissy (Oxford: Oxford University Press, 1997).

—— ed., *The Oxford Book of Modern Verse, 1892–1935* (Oxford: Clarendon Press, 1936).

—— *Autobiographies* (London: Macmillan, 1955).

—— *The Secret Rose, Stories by W. B. Yeats: A Variorum Edition*, ed. Warwick Gould, Phillip L. Marcus, and Michael J. Sidnell (London: Macmillan, 1992).

—— *Short Fiction*, ed. G. J. Watson (London: Penguin, 1995).

ZANGWILL, ISRAEL, *The Big Bow Mystery* (1891), in E. F. Bleiler, ed., *Three Victorian Detective Novels* (New York: Dover, 1978).

—— *Children of the Ghetto: A Study of a Peculiar People*, ed. Meri-Jane Rochelson (Detroit: Wayne State University Press, 1998).

ZWEIG, ROBERT, ' "Death-in-Love": Rossetti and the Victorian Journey Back to Dante', in Regina Barreca, ed., *Sex and Death in Victorian Literature* (Basingstoke: Macmillan, 1990), 178–93.

Index